The World Turned Upside-Down

The World Turned Upside-Down

THE STATE OF EIGHTEENTH-CENTURY AMERICAN STUDIES
AT THE BEGINNING OF THE TWENTY–FIRST CENTURY

Edited by Michael V. Kennedy
and William G. Shade

Lehigh
University
Press

Bethlehem: Lehigh University Press
London: Associated University Presses

Associated University Presses
440 Forsgate Drive
Cranbury, NJ 08512

Associated University Presses
16 Barter Street
London WC1A 2AH, England

Associated University Presses
P.O. Box 338, Port Credit
Mississauga, Ontario
Canada L5G 4L8

The paper used in this publication meets the requirements of the American National Standard for Permanence of Paper for Printed Library Materials Z39.48-1984.

Library of Congress Cataloging-in-Publication Data

The world turned upside-down : the state of eighteenth-century American studies at the beginning of the twenty-first century / edited by Michael V. Kennedy and William G. Shade.
     p. cm.
   Includes bibliographical references.
   ISBN 0-934223-62-9 (alk. paper)
   1.   United States—History—Colonial period, ca. 1600-1775—Study and teaching. 2. United States—Civilization—To 1783—Study and teaching. 3. United States—Social conditions—To 1865—Study and teaching. 4. Great Britain—Colonies—North America—Study and teaching. I.Kennedy, Michael V., 1954- II. Shade, William G.

E188.5 .W67 2001
973.2'07'2—dc21

                                                                              00-069161

PRINTED IN THE UNITED STATES OF AMERICA

For Larry Leder
who conceived of the Gipson Institute
and made it work.

Contents

Preface

THE PRESENT VOLUME is a product of a larger project of the council of the Lawrence Henry Gipson Institute for Eighteenth-Century Studies at Lehigh University to make available the papers that have been presented at the Institute's yearly symposia. In the early 1990s, when I was the codirector of the Gipson Institute, we decided to supplement the publication of *Virtue, Corruption, and Self-Interest: Political Values in the Eighteenth Century*, edited by Richard K. Matthews, which was the product of two symposia, with two other books. One of these was designed to bring together the best of the papers that had been presented in the three decades of the Institute's existence, since they were not easily available to scholars and thus represented some of the unknown work of some of the leading historians and literary scholars of the eighteenth century. While the initial plan was altered in the process of collecting, choosing and publishing this group of essays, *Revisioning the British Empire in the Eighteenth Century: Essays from Twenty-five Years of the Lawrence Henry Gipson Institute for Eighteenth-Century Studies* eventually appeared in 1998 and included just essays pertaining to the British empire.

At my urging, the council decided to devote three years' symposia, and several occasional lectures given during these years, to the consideration of the state of the study of early America, with the primary focus being on British North America in the eighteenth century. While the essays in this book do not cover all of the possible subjects in an expanding and vibrant field, they generally fulfill our initial goal, and taken with the other volumes that the Institute and Lehigh University Press have published, give some indication of just how successful the Gipson Institute has become at encouraging the study of the eighteenth century, and achieving the promise that Larry Leder, the first Institute director, envisioned in the early 1970s.

William G. Shade
Bethlehem, Pennsylvania

Prologue

"GROPING TO UNDERSTAND":
RECONSTRUCTING EARLY AMERICAN HISTORY

William G. Shade

> What did it mean to Jefferson, slaveowner and *philosophe*, that he grew up in this far western borderland world of Britain, looking out from Queen Anne rooms of spare elegance onto a wild, uncultivated land? We can only grope to understand.
>
> – Bernard Bailyn

AWRENCE HENRY GIPSON, the grand historian of the British Empire before the American Revolution, whose beneficence made possible the preparation and publication of the following essays, completed his monumental work just two years before his death in 1971. Although his fifteen volumes are filled with insights on nearly every aspect of eighteenth-century life in his "spacious empire," it was clear as the final volumes appeared in the 1950s and 1960s that Gipson's general approach represented the thrust of an earlier generation of scholars who had forged the "imperial school" of historians of eighteenth-century America.[1] At the time, the study of early American history, or as it is often called, colonial history, concentrated on the internal political and social history of the colonies in British North America culminating in the American Revolution. Political history formed the central thread, the focus was for the most part on dead white men, and the theme was American exceptionalism. Although some decried the vitality of the field, it was informed by the work of such major scholars as Perry Miller, Carl Bridenbaugh, Wesley Frank Craven, and Richard B. Morris and it witnessed the emergence of two historians who would continue to dominate the field until the present day, Edmund S. Morgan and Bernard Bailyn.

In the 1960s and 1970s, however, historians in the United States generally, and in particular, those dealing with the history of the eighteenth century turned their energies to social history and shifted their perspective to one that viewed matters "from the bottom up."[2] Scholars began to study more intensively the "meaner sort," the "inarticulate," or the "other"– slaves, women, and native Americans. Francis Jennings shocked traditional sympathies with his book entitled *The Invasion of America: Indians, Colonialism, and the Cant of Conquest* (1975). Yet this book was published under the auspices of the Institute of Early American History and Culture, and the changing fashion in colonial history was reflected in the pages of the institute's journal, *The William and Mary Quarterly*, and at numerous Institute-sponsored symposia.[3] For anyone involved in the field this revisionism was neither surreptitious nor the product of an underground movement; rather, it represented a broadening of interest that was supported in such seminars as those of Morgan at Yale and Bailyn and Oscar Handlin at Harvard, as well as those of Jack P. Greene at Johns Hopkins and Richard S. Dunn at the University of Pennsylvania. Taken together, they trained a good portion of the most active scholars of eighteenth-century America practicing their trade today.[4] This work has made the study of the eighteenth century one of the most vital and interesting areas of American history.

The following essays reflect upon various aspects of eighteenth-century American studies, illustrating the many ways in which the work done in the last quarter of the twentieth century has radically changed the portrait of colonial history painted by Gipson not that long ago. They have turned his empire upside down and no longer view it from the vantage point of Whitehall. It is not that most of the recent historians have revised Gipson. Actually the interest in imperial politics has been of late dominated by British historians often looking to the south and east rather than at the mainland North American colonies.

In the United States, historians have subsumed the work of Gipson and his predecessors of the Imperial School such as Gipson's mentor, Charles M. Andrews, and turned their gaze upon more narrowly defined, if sometimes expansive, subjects, producing such brilliant books as Bernard Bailyn's *The Ideological Origins of the American Revolution* (1966), David Brion Davis's *The Problem of Slavery in Western Culture* (1966), Winthrop D. Jordan's *White Over Black* (1968), Gordon Wood's *The Creation of the Republic* (1969), Peter Wood's *Black Majority* (1974), and Edmund S. Morgan's

American Slavery/American Freedom (1975). In the past decade, half of all
of the Pulitzer prizes in history have gone to students of the eighteenth
century. With the exception of Jack N. Rakove's *Original Meanings: Politics
and Ideas in the Making of the Constitution* (1996), all of the winning books
have been primarily social histories – dealing with immigration, women,
class and social structure.[5]

    This might suggest that colonial history has become a "glamor" field;
in truth, eighteenth-century American studies is thriving as never
before.[6] There is an embarrassment of riches. The central problem has
been to integrate this new and detailed, but fragmented, social history
into the body of institutional and political scholarship handed down by
Gipson to subsequent generations. Because colonialists are part of any
team to write a textbook these days, the general quality of the first part
the most popular survey texts is exceptionally high. The general reputation of historians of the eighteenth century is even greater than it was
when Gipson won his Pulitzer Prize in 1962.

    The essays presented here are by scholars who have emerged during
the past quarter of a century, writing about the current state of the
scholarship on the subjects with which they deal. The marvelous volume
entitled, *Colonial British America: Essays in the New History of the Early
Modern Era*, edited by Jack P. Greene and J. R. Pole and published in
1984, set the standard for subsequent attempts to deal creatively with
the historiography of the field. Inevitably the present volume will be
compared with this formidable predecessor and there is a surface
similarity. In fact, two prominent scholars, Richard Bushman and David
Hall, contributed to both collections. The differences between their
older and current contributions highlight one of the contrasts between
the present volume and that edited by Greene and Pole. The essays in
Colonial British America essentially and often brilliantly summarized the
historiography of the subfields on which they focused. The essays
presented here all deal briefly with the historiography, but then move on
to specific discussions of the authors' current research and indicate the
direction in which new research is moving. They do not summarize the
historiography of the past quarter-century, but rather place their research
within that literature and signal new trends. A second major difference
– a matter of convenience to the contributors rather than important
conceptual disagreement – is that the subfields included are different
and those that are similar are differently defined. Finally, the essays in

this volume concentrate on the eighteenth century, especially the period which most interested Gipson. Consequently, the two books are actually quite different in content and intention.

Since the 1960s, the reconstruction of early American history has prompted historians to examine in greater detail than ever before certain basic elements – the land and the people.[7] Historians have dealt with the interactions of people and the environment and the conflict between groups and their accommodation to each other. The domain of American colonial history has grown and scholars have become specialists in both the seventeenth century and the eighteenth before the Revolution in which the provinces of British North America matured economically, became the home of hundreds of thousands of non-English migrants, and spawned both religious revivalism and radical politics. Economic and social historians particularly have opened up scholarly perspectives on the new American society that was springing up on the frontier of Europe. While often primarily interested in the cultural results, historians have generally begun with economic and social structures and the processes of their development.

From this perspective the eighteenth-century experience appears to be distinctly different from that of the seventeenth when overall economic expansion was tentative and uncertain. Underlying the difference between the two eras was the extensive economic growth and significant increase in living standards which characterized the eighteenth century. This led to a growing complexity of the economy in which planters and merchants often built luxurious lives while a sizable number of successful independent farmers and skilled artisans made up an expanding group termed at the time, "the middling sort." At the same time both slavery and the huge servant class grew. The output of the colonial economy increased tenfold and the distribution of wealth became more skewed.[8]

The provincial economy of British North America had evolved by the eighteenth century into five main regions that had their origins in the production of staples for the export market – New England, the Middle Colonies, the Chesapeake, the Lower South, and the Caribbean. Each of these regions was also taking on a different character because of alternative sources of immigration and contrasting demography (particularly the introduction of African slaves) and the various patterns of conflict

and assimilation between native and immigrant peoples. The eighteenth-century economy was growing and diversifying; a differentiated
and increasingly stratified social structure was appearing; yet, at the end
of the century, the large majority of colonists – between 80 and 90
percent of the workforce – were involved in agriculture. As Richard
Sheridan noted in his contribution to the Greene and Pole volume, "The
production of foodstuffs for personal consumption was the chief source
of real income for southern as well as northern farmers."[9]

In a general overview of American history the consummate "Consensus" historian, Carl Degler, expressed the widespread view in the
1950s and early 1960s that "Capitalism Came in the First Ships."[10]
British North America was settled by joint stock companies, whose basic
intent – which hardly ever worked out – was to make money for the
shareholders. The rise and fall of the Virginia Company could be described in a quite modern phrase –"the bottom line." The original colonists were of the middling class, and the adventurers, merchant capitalists. The social economy that replaced the company in the Chesapeake was driven by the profit motive and wildly individualistic as well.[11]

While no one denied there were capitalist elements from the beginning, Degler's phrase became a lighting rod for historians of the New
Left who wanted to portray a precapitalist period in which the promise
of America and communal democracy had a chance of survival. Unfortunately, like many textbook writers, Degler tended to telescope the
seventeenth century and the eighteenth, giving the impression that
there was no effect of the quantitative and qualitative changes that had
taken place during a period of 170 years from Jamestown to the
Revolution.

At the same time this debate was ironically more about the nineteenth century than the eighteenth. The two groups of historians
involved in this controversy have used slightly different descriptions of
the process. For nineteenth-century social historians, the central revisionist concept has been "the market revolution." Scholars primarily
concerned with the eighteenth century settled upon the more sweeping
idea of a "transition to capitalism."[12]

There are actually two aspects to this debate. One involves the
means and processes of production, forms of labor, and the relationship
between the employers and workers. The other involves what the
French historians call *mentalité* – the consciousness, or ideological and

emotional aspects of people's lives. In his 1978 critique of earlier writers, James Henretta took to task James T. Lemon, whose study of south-eastern Pennsylvania in the eighteenth century had represented a depar-ture from the standard consensus view, but nonetheless emphasized the liberal middle class orientation of the settlers.[13]

Lemon used the term "liberal" in its "classic sense"– that is "placing individual freedom and material gain over that of the public interest." In contrast to this focus on individualism, Henretta emphasized the traditional nature of British American colonial society and the centrality of family and community – a set of precapitalist values that resisted the encroachments of the emerging market society. Gary Nash pointed out that the difference between Lemon and Henretta may have been a prod-uct of the different areas that they studied and most economic historians define different regions with varied relationships to markets.[14]

Clearly, all have agreed that most Americans throughout the eigh-teenth century were farmers, farm laborers (including slaves) or mem-bers of farm families. In "The Place of the Eighteenth Century in American Agricultural History," Richard Bushman reviews the debate and points out problems related to timing, regional differences, and the distribution of farmers who produced for the market. Ultimately he focuses upon the matter of how colonial farms actually worked. Bushman finds that in fact there were few farmers who did not have to go into markets and trade for some things, he develops the concept of the mixed farm in order to transcend the schematic and ultimately unproductive argument. In this essay Bushman also relates the debate to questions concerning debt, tenancy, and the land market which has been ignored by others.

Bushman's historicist tendency to emphasize the particular is echoed in the essay by Judith McGaw, "'So Say It! No Ideas but in Things': Touching the Past through Early American Technology." Historians and philosophers have argued that contemporary society is being overcome by technology. Americans have microwave ovens, VCRs, home com-puters, and incredibly sophisticated automobiles that talk back to their owners. Technologies channel both the means of production and those of reproduction. But as McGaw points out, technology is not a modern monster, but one of those demons that has been always with us.

The history of technology grew out of the "old" economic history as that field fragmented into business history and "cliometrics." Historians who were primarily concerned with how things worked ended up doing the history of technology. In the 1960s under the auspices of the Institute of Early American History and Culture, a historian who had been concerned with eighteenth-century science, Brooke Hindle, raised a call for a social history of technology.[15]

Following Hindle, McGaw argues that technology is about things and the ideas embodied in things. Historians should not only look to literary sources to judge what people thought, but also consider the things themselves, how they must have been built (reverse engineering), and how they would have affected life. These "things" must be seen in their social context, but also in the physical context and how they affected human spacial and kinetic interactions. She notes that students of material culture often have much to teach historians if we actually deal with the artifacts, the things that constitute a technology. But she warns against romanticizing the works of past artisans, as their products were often poorly designed and constructed and very dangerous, providing little margin of error for those who used these "things."

McGaw suggests that historians must go to the museums to see how things really worked. It is important to understand how people actually made the things of their life: Colonial Williamsburg and Sturbridge Village have done a marvelous job at this and allow visitors to participate. Material culture offers a different venue of "hands-on" research that stimulates greater insights among historians who traditionally have been better at studying social relationships through the analysis of written documents.

Christine Daniels argues in favor of extending the use of archaeological data and methodologies in studying the demographics of colonial town development. While the new social history, which grew out of labor history, has revived the focus on agricultural technologies, it has focused primarily on the labor of the one out of ten colonial residents who were artisans.[16] Many of these blacksmiths, shoemakers, and carpenters were rural, but the grist mills and saw mills and iron forges where many others worked served as the seeds of markets and villages across the colonies from Massachusetts to Georgia. In the nascent cities of eighteenth-century North America master artisans and apprentices made up a large segment of the population. Daniels, who has contributed importantly to the recent writing about artisans and various forms of free and slave labor in the eighteenth century focuses her essay, "'No Towns of Any Consequence'?" on the "lost" urban or town history of colonial America.

Taking her title from Thomas Jefferson's *Notes On the State of Virginia*, she challenges several major assumptions of previous historians that seem to rely on this text. The urban economic and social history of the eighteenth century has concentrated either on the five large port cities – Boston, New York, Philadelphia, Newport (Rhode Island) and Charles Town (South Carolina) – or "the New England town."[17] Daniels traces the development of Chestertown, Maryland, relating its growth to the needs created for a complex economy generated by the emergence of the wheat culture on the Eastern Shore and the expansion of the economic role of the town and its population of merchants, artisans, laborers and others who served the surrounding country side. She argues that historians' focus on towns that succeeded and grew into major cities like Baltimore across the bay has obscured the rise and fall of many other Chestertowns throughout the region. Further the existence of these towns along with the villages and stores that grew up around mills and forges signal the existence of a vibrant network of markets that well predate the transition to capitalism that historians have attempted to date after the Revolution if not in the early nineteenth century.

Although there were a sizable number of African American artisans in colonial America, and eighteenth-century cities all had significant black populations, recent debates about farmers and artisans are about white farmers and artisans since most of the African Americans in British North America – who made up 20 percent of the population on the eve of the Revolution – were slaves employed in plantation agriculture in the Chesapeake and the Low Country of the Carolinas. Since the early 1970s, a revolution in the study of slavery has added immensely to our knowledge of the peculiar institution in the United States and colonial British North America. Yet as late as 1984, Gary Nash could write in the Greene and Pole volume that "so much attention has been paid to the kind of slave systems the Europeans fashioned in the New World" that the history of the slaves remained "largely untold."[18] Most of the emphasis in recent studies has been on the development of indigenous slave culture, or what John Blassingame termed, "the slave community." These studies focused upon the antebellum era and taught historians a great deal about the family life, religion, beliefs, and values of nineteenth-century slaves.[19]

Our understanding of the evolution of slave cultures in the eighteenth century has developed more slowly, primarily because of the paucity of sources. Russell R. Menard and Alan Kulikoff, however, have reconstructed the demographic outlines of the African-American population and considered the effects of changes in these conditions on the Chesapeake slave community.[20] From the 1680s to the 1730s when large numbers of Africans were first brought to British North America, most slaves were adult males, who lived on small plantations, and were cut off from African culture. As the population grew in the eighteenth century, sex ratios came into balance and both the density of the black population and the proportion living on large plantations increased. By the end of the century these changes produced settled creole communities with a certain amount of cultural homogeneity, involving distinct patterns of family life, artistic expression, and religious practices.[21]

Discussion of slave culture emerged during the 1930s in a debate between the anthropologist Melville J. Herskovits, who emphasized the numerous elements of West African culture that were retained by slaves in the Americas, and the sociologist E. Franklin Frazier, who focused upon the destructive impact of the middle passage and slavery on the family and religious practices.[22] This argument, stated in extreme claims and contested definitions of central concepts, remained moot although the sociological perspective and its policy implications dominated the important historical works of Kenneth Stampp and Stanley Elkins that appeared in the 1950s.[23]

The most constructive alternative has been the "encounter" model put forth in the 1970s by anthropologists Sidney Mintz and Richard Price in their studies of the Caribbean world. The Africans forced into slavery came from many regions divided by hundreds of tribes and characterized by cultural and linguistic diversity.[24] There had been no single African culture to be transplanted. Communities could only be formed out of fragments of old cultures and adaption to the ways of the dominant Europeans who defined the boundaries of their new status.

In his essay "Looking into the Night," David H. Fischer sketches the outlines of his forthcoming book on the multiple cultures of African Americans, applying the model he used to study the cultures of British Americans in *Albion's Seed: Four British Folkways in America* (1989). Fischer turns away from Mintz and Price and revives elements of Herskovits's argument. Relying on a growing body of literature that has taken advantage of the increasing sophistication of scholars dealing with African history, Fischer posits a larger number of African-American cultures than any previous historian and tries to connect them more specifically to their African roots.[25]

He also pushes forward another part of the argument of his earlier book, *Albion's Seed*, which had portrayed four different ideas of freedom in the United States; each a legacy of one of the four sets of British folkways planted in early America. Here he adds the freedom of thought, feeling, and expression found in the cultural experiences of African Americans. Fischer's focus on cultural studies, innocent of the language or attitude of postmodernism, stands at a point outside much of the recent debate over early American literature.

Yet under the cope of cultural studies, the old American Studies movement of the 1950s is being reborn, revitalizing the analysis of eighteenth-century American literature. The foremost intellectual historian of the colonies of British North America was Perry Miller, an English professor at Harvard, and atheist, as adept with nineteenth-century writers such as Melville and Poe as he was with the Puritans. Miller constructed the Puritan "mind" out of relatively little – the sermons, autobiographies and other jottings of the elite – but his work stands as the foremost imaginative achievement of any American historian in the twentieth century.[26]

Miller began with literature. But he defined the subject much more broadly than published novels, short stories, and poems by including sermons, dairies, letters, autobiographies and biographies, and histories. One of his major contributions was the collection of Puritan writings he edited with Thomas Johnson.[27] Miller's Puritan "mind" was, among other things, a revision of the negative portrayal of both the Puritans and religion generally put forth in Vernon Lewis Parrington's classic study of American thought through literature that epitomized Progressive historiography, but was still widely used in history courses in the 1960s.[28]

Philip Gura is well known as a critic of Miller, portraying in *A Glimpse of Sion's Glory* (1984) a more fragmented "mind" of seventeenth-century New England. In that work he emphasized particularly the dissenting tradition that included not only Puritans like Anne Hutchinson and Roger Williams, but also various millinarians, Quakers, and early Baptists. Here, however, Gura builds on an earlier article, which dealt with the seventeenth century, and surveys recent scholarship on the eighteenth century, arguing that students of literature should take these works on their own merits and not attempt to read them in a Progressive fashion as simply the precursors of the great writers of the "American Renaissance."[29] He emphasizes recent concerns with reading, the book, popular culture, and even the unpublished efforts presented to various literary societies that characterized post Revolutionary America and how this has broadened the relevance of criticism of eighteenth-century literature.

Much of the discussion of literature and intellectual life in the eighteenth-century colonies centers on religion and particularly the set of midcentury revivals that are collectively referred to as the Great Awakening. Richard Hofstadter called the Great Awakening "the first major intercolonial crisis of the mind and spirit," and implied a direct connection between the Great Awakening and the American Revolution.[30] Yet others, most particularly Jon Butler, have challenged the coherence of the Great Awakening and denied any clear relationship between these diverse revivals spread over five decades and the Revolution.[31]

While Miller did not deny the relation of the Great Awakening to the social and economic changes transforming Europe at the time nor the trans-Atlantic prominence of George Whitefield, he insisted upon American distinctiveness. Miller described the Great Awakening, which spread from New England to Pennsylvania, Virginia, and the Carolinas, as a crisis in colonial culture growing out of the attempt of the churches to resist Arminian tendencies and revitalize the spirit of Puritanism. In reshaping the colonists' spiritual needs, the Awakening caused an increasing mistrust of the hierarchical European model of ecclesiastical social and political leadership, and thus, unleashed powerful egalitarian forces. He saw this in a Turnerian fashion as a product of impact of the wilderness upon the New England "mind" and even referred to Jonathan Edwards as a "child of the wilderness." Miller's model sketched in his essays and biography of Jonathan Edwards was most fully developed by his disciple Alan Heimert.[32]

Criticism of Miller has taken two forms. Social historians have insisted that he went too far in dismissing sociological analysis, and have found much closer links between spiritual revolution and social change.[33] On the other hand, historians of religion have challenged Miller's narrative on a number of grounds: creating a monolithic orthodoxy; denying the spiritual element; making the Puritans into twentieth-century neo-orthodox Protestants; etc. Few of Miller's critics have been more implacable and consistently intelligent in their criticisms than David D. Hall, presently a professor at the Harvard Divinity School. In his contribution to *Colonial British America*, Hall praised Miller's achievement and then sketched the outlines of an alternative perspective, which he associated with "the Yale school" of religious historians who "in the place of compromise . . . see ambivalence, in the place of change . . . put continuity."[34] His book, *Worlds of Wonder, Days of Judgment* (1989), reflected this outlook and brilliantly portrayed the role that irrational and folk beliefs played in the spiritual lives of early Americans. Obviously the peasant mentality lived on much longer in the New World than most scholars have acknowledged.

In his essay here, "Between Two Worlds: Popular Religion in Eighteenth-century America," Hall addresses a slightly different problem: the relation between the clergy and the laity. Miller constructed not only an incredibly rational, if exceedingly complex, Puritan "mind," but also one that was widely shared among believers. It was of course the common conceit of intellectual historians of his day. Hall asks his readers to consider "the religious," what it means to be religious, and whom can we describe as religious. For Hall, the Great Awakening can be most easily understood in terms of the split between clergy and laity. He illustrates this with a careful analysis of conflict within Edwards's own Northampton church. But Hall is insistent that there is no necessary conflict between popular religion and culture; rather religion and its practice must be seen as part of culture.

In the context of popular religion in a Protestant culture one must consider the question of literacy – who could read the Bible and think for themselves, thus entering willingly into the covenants, rather than simply parroting the clergy? In our times the correlation has been more material and the questions involve the relationship not between literacy and grace, but between education and economic development. Almost a century ago Max Weber related the Protestant ethic to the rise of capitalism and students of modernization in the 1950s and 1960s secularized the indicators into those involving communication. They struck upon the concept of modernization and looked to literacy and education as crucial variables in "making men modern."[35]

In 1960 a little book – essentially an essay followed by an extensive annotated bibliography – Bernard Bailyn's *Education in the Forming of*

American Society, revised early educational history dramatically by dealing with it within the context of social and economic development.[36] In a way it was like Miller and the Puritans, because Bailyn's social history was revised in relatively short order, forcing a suspension of belief in some of the elements of his argument. Nonetheless, this led to an iconoclastic book, Kenneth A. Lockridge's *Literacy in Colonial New England* (1974), which sported the expansive subtitle highlighting its comparative thrust: "An Enquiry into the Social Context of Literacy in the Early Modern West."

In the two long essays that make up this brief volume, Lockridge argued that mass literacy was a product of intense Protestantism rather than rapid changes in wealth or social position and that in general it seemed to have little correlation with modernization. He set out to measure literacy and connect it to economic growth and the sectional differences in the eighteenth-century colonies of Britain. All in all, *Literacy in Colonial New England* was an impressive piece of historical imagination, infused with the author's immense energy. But it is so circumscribed and its methods so limited that its larger relevance is questionable.[37]

Gerald Moran and Maris Vinovskis show how far the study of literacy and education has come in a relatively short time in their essay, "Literacy and Education in Eighteenth-Century North America." They summarize the literature and provide a convincing analysis of the relevant questions. Refreshingly, Moran and Vinovskis extend their discussion beyond white British colonists to those in New France, and, most interestingly, to the enslaved African Americans whose culture or cultures in the colonial era are just beginning to be understood – as Fischer makes clear in his essay.

Moran and Vinovskis' essay also relates to those of Hall and Gura, which discuss the impact of expanding literacy on the common people and the emergence of the public sphere in relation to both the Great Awakening and the Revolution. Following Michael Warner, they state,

> Contrary to what recent historians of the book have argued, new print technologies ... had little to do with revolution. What mattered most was the rise of a new, "bourgeois public sphere," oriented around reading, that was so distinct from state and private life that it could produce a new printed discourse capable of criticizing both.

Such "print discourse" made possible the concept of the people as distinct from the state that was an essential element of the Revolutionary republican argument. Here Vinovskis and Moran indirectly reflect the almost hegemonic role historians have given to the concept of republicanism in their discussion of the ideology of the Founding Fathers.[38] Perhaps no other single book in the second half of this century has been as important for the historiography of the American Revolution than Bernard Bailyn's, *The Ideological Origins of the American Revolution* (1967). It established the republican paradigm, which has totally reoriented the study of political thought and culture in the eighteenth century and well beyond.

In their revolt against the nineteenth century, patriotic historians of the American Revolution, such as George Bancroft, Progressive historians, exemplified by Carl Becker, had emphasized the importance of John Locke. In fact Merle Curti called him "America's philosopher," dominating American thought well into the nineteenth century.[39] Whatever other differences the Consensus historians, who emerged after World War II, had with their predecessors, they agreed on the prominence of Locke and emphasized the dominance in the American past of a consensus on liberal-capitalism. Louis Hartz's brilliant *Liberal Tradition in America* (1955) echoed Alexis de Tocqueville concerning America's revolutionary birth and insisted upon its ideological distinctiveness as a fragment frozen in a liberal, Lockean moment. Edmund Morgan has detailed the commitment of Revolutionary America to liberal individualism captured in the slogan "no taxation without representation."[40] Finally, the English Americanist, J. R. Pole, traced the rise of political individualism in his exhaustive comparative study, *Political Representation in England & the Origins of the American Republic* (1966), which also gave to Locke primacy among political philosophers.

Much of this body of scholarship emerged in the context of the argument over the extent of "middle class democracy" in the eighteeth century. A number of studies emphasized that because of relatively widespread land ownership in the colonies, the laws quite similar to those that restricted the electorate in England allowed the majority of free adult colonial males to vote and that by the eighteenth century a variety of protoparty competitive systems emerged in British North America.[41] Although deference to the social and economic elites assured their dominance of office holding, local leaders represented the colonies' interests against the representatives of the Crown, providing a fertile ground for the growth of republicanism and the appeal of the "country ideology" of the opposition in the mother country.[42]

In detailing the growth of republicanism during the Revolution, Bernard Bailyn and Gordon Wood demoted Locke from his central role, but it was J. G. A. Pocock who banished him entirely from the stage. Instead of commenting upon the casual correlation of the nearly simultaneous publication of the Declaration of Independence and Adam Smith's *Wealth of Nations*, Pocock insisted that the American Revolution was "the last act of the Renaissance." In this context the concept of civic humanism becomes the key to interpreting the ideology of the American Revolution and the republican persuasion that dominated early American political thought.[43]

In their essay "'Narcissism of the Minor Differences': What is at Issue and What is at Stake in the Civic Humanism Question," Asher Horowitz and Richard K. Matthews rehearse the debate over the role of civic humanism in Revolutionary ideology, insisting that this controversy has, among other things, dislodged the discourse of the times from any connection to elements of the socioeconomic order. Most of the "new" social historians whose work has dominated the historiographical world of the late twentieth century have been neo-Progressives interested in defining the conflict of economic interests or nascent classes and quite critical of what one termed the "'idealist' tradition in which thought is viewed as an autonomous construction."[44]

Horowitz and Matthews, as political theorists, approach the problem in a somewhat different fashion, insistent on bringing thought into line with the nature of the social order as they, following Hartz, see it. Much of the argument over the "transition to capitalism" hinges upon the insistence of Hartz's radical critics that the society in British North America was traditional, communal, and familial, suited to the essentially conservative nature of classical republicanism, which they somewhat oddly equate with a kind of primitive socialism.[45]

While rooted in a Marxist perspective, Horowitz and Matthews demonstrate the numerous ways in which civic humanism was inappropriate for the liberal individualist society that emerged from the American Revolution. They insist upon a closer reading of Hartz than most historians have been willing to attempt. In the light of Matthews's book on James Madison, they might have argued that what Wood called the "Revolutionary achievement" was essentially Madisonian and "heartless" at its core, although the new "American science of politics" legitimized America's "liberal civilization" and lionized Locke.[46] Like Hartz, Horowitz and Matthews are not happy with this situation, but ask the historians of eighteenth-century British America to cast aside romanticism and come to terms with what is at stake in their arguments.

Ironically, Carol Berkin asks a similar set of questions of herself and her sister warriors who in the 1970s invented modern women's history. Her essay "'What an Alarming Crisis is This?': American Women and Their Histories," is a personal statement, because the subject she deals with is so relatively new, or at least the range and sophistication that now characterizes the subject is a product of the last three decades. Berkin was a founder of the movement. One need only go back to the first "reader" of scholarly essays intended for the captive college audience to see how the editors had to search the literature available in 1970 and to stretch the topic to provide a useful book.[47] Today the problem is a wealth of riches. In 1992 Laural Ulrich won the Pulitzer Prize for her book, *The Midwife's Tale*, and it was subsequently made into a fine movie. Four years later Mary Beth Norton's *Founding Mothers & Fathers: Gendered Power and the Forming of American Society* was a Pulitzer Prize finalist.

Before the 1960s there was available a better scholarly base for the neophyte who wished to deal with African-American history than one who would examine the role of women in the American past. Women's history was not, of course, a blank page. The Progressive historians, to their credit, interjected the situation of women into their work – in part because so many of the men had wives who were themselves credentialed historians, or at least college educated. There were significant walk-on roles for women in some of the most famous Progressive histories, such as John Franklin Jameson's *The American Revolution as a Social Movement* (1924) and Arthur M. Schlesinger's *New Viewpoints in American History* (1921), and in most of the volumes of "A History of American Life" series, one of which was written by a woman – the Progressive publicist, Ida Tarbell.

Today historians probably know more about women's history than many of the subfields of eighteenth-century American studies previously discussed or surveyed in the Greene and Pole volume.[48] It can be frustrating when one attempts to examine the majority of the population. Berkin begins with a play on words from an eighteenth-century source to illustrate what she thinks is a crisis in the current scholarship on women in colonial America. She focuses on three things. One is a matter of perspective, a problem only too familiar to most historians. Since women became so specialized in the process of economic development, these historians too easily assumed that they lost something that they might have had. Was "Colonial America a Golden Age" for women before they had to settle down into middle class conformity?

Berkin is also willing to consider that she and her cohort were too easily seduced into emphasizing gender as an essential category. Obviously class and race, but also religion, ethnicity, and education, are all important variables. As an ethnic urbanite on the left wing of the political spectrum, Berkin cautions women's historians to carefully consider such influences, noting that subsequent historians of colonial women have done just that.

Like Mary Beth Norton and Linda Kerber, as well as countless other women of their generation, Berkin began her career with a dissertation on a traditional topic.[49] In this essay she also argues that as her generation turned to the study of women, their desire to establish the legitimacy of their subject warped the product. Fortunately the profession seems to have moved beyond that brief phase. Textbooks being written today not only include women authors in their multi-author format, but also integrate women into the story.

The collection edited by Greene and Pole had little on the Indians; however, one of its contributors, Gary Nash, had previously published a synthesis of colonial history, *Red, White, and Black: The Peoples of Early America* (1974), reflecting the sundry interests of the new social historians.[50] This widely-used book summarized the extant literature and prepared the way for more detailed and sophisticated studies of the interaction between the European invaders and the Native Americans as they contested Richard White's metaphorical "middle ground."[51]

Daniel Richter opens new avenues of investigation. Of course, colonialists had not completely ignored Indians, but scholarship tended to focus on the seventeenth century and treat the Indians as supporting characters, if not part of the scenery in a Eurocentric drama. An exception was the anthropologist Anthony F. C. Wallace who, in such books as *Death and Rebirth of the Seneca* (1970), focused on the Indians.[52] In the 1970s and early 1980s William Cronon and James Axtell set a new standard for the study of Anglo-American and Native-American relations in the eighteenth century.[53] Their perspective, which Richter has adopted, involves both the social construction of race and the concern for the impact of the European invasion on the Indian way of life, but it also returns agency to the native Americans.

In their relations with the Europeans, Indians were both producers and consumers; and both roles changed their own economies and societies. Indians did not become Europeans, but they did evolve into something other than what they had been before the invasion. As Richter points out at the end of his essay, the "tribes" with which historians are familiar were themselves a product of the tremendous devastation introduced by the "Columbian exchange" and the New World epidemics that decimated the native population. Perhaps this is the major fact that has emerged in the recent studies of American colonial history. It has led John M. Murrin to entitle an essay summarizing the recent historiography on British North America, "Beneficiaries of Catastrophe."[54]

Richter also discusses "forest diplomacy" in which the native tribes, for their own security, played off various European powers and even individual British colonies against each other. Colonial historians are now trying to understand the internal politics of the tribal groups and their quest for stability as important elements of American colonial history. Richter's essay, like those of Fischer, and Moran and Vinovskis, makes us aware of the importance of French and Spanish presence in the colonization process.

Most historians of British North America have been conversant with the work of J. H. Parry, J. H. Elliot, and Elizabeth A. H. John and other Latin Americanists, but one of the major recent changes in colonial scholarship has been to take a larger perspective which incorporates their work.[55] Oddly this is somewhat like Gipson's own view of the British Empire which extended from Nova Scotia to the West Indies. However, colonial historians have generally ignored the history of large areas of the United States that began as part of the Spanish empire in the New World. In 1991, Ramón A. Gutiérrez's charming book, *When Jesus Came the Corn Mothers Went Away* (Stanford, Calif.: Stanford University Press), made it clear that the Pueblo Revolt, in what is now New Mexico, occurred at the same time as King Philip's War in New England.[56] David Weber's beautifully written panoramic study, *The Spanish Frontier in North America*, appeared the following year, detailing the history of New

Mexico and Florida during the seventeenth and eighteenth centuries with a special focus on the evolution of Spain's Indian policy.

These books drew upon an older tradition of borderlands history that goes back to Hubert Howe Bancroft and has connections to the Turner-ian wing of Progressive historiography. The emphasis on American ex-ceptionalism, among the Consensus historians and in the American Studies movement in the postwar era, left this area to those trained in Latin American history. Study of native Americans has revived this field in new and vibrant ways and caused students of British North America to see their subject in a broader perspective.

Amy Turner Bushnell has contributed a good deal to this literature as the leading historian of Spanish Florida and the southeastern back country in the seventeenth and eighteenth centuries. Richter shows us how the Indians in this region were forced to deal with both the English and the Spanish invaders. Bushnell reveals, by reaching back in time to survey its origins, how different the policy of the Spanish was from that pursued by the British. There was not one policy during these two hundred years, but several, although all were connected to how the col-onizers might deal with the native populations and hostile Europeans. While the Spanish in the area were in conflict with the French as well as the British, their attempts at pacification through the use of the mission system slowly gave way by the eighteenth century to the burn and destroy approach of the English.

One of the things that is interesting in these essays is that students of Colonial America are returning in part to the imperial view for a framework. As Bushnell's essay, along with the other work on the Spanish borderlands, indicates the scope of Gipson's empire – stretching from Canada to the West Indies in the New World and eastward beyond Africa to India – still has meaning. None of the authors delved into post-modernist play with colonialism, because the formula does not work very well when the colonists had a higher living standard than their oppressor and paid relatively low taxes for the advantages they claimed – as Gipson had believed and now economic historians have documented in detail.[57]

The reorientation of early American history has in fact turned the world presented by Gipson and others of his time upside-down and focused on the particular and the local, the mass rather than the elite. Historians have been concerned with how things worked and the culture of which they were a part. Recent detailed studies have served as the basis for compelling if sharply contrasting syntheses by Jack P. Greene, David Hackett Fischer, and Bernard Bailyn. In "Capitalism and Slavery: A Personal Reflection on the Reorientation of Early American History," which serves as the epilogue to this collection, Russell R. Menard takes Greene, Fischer, and Bailyn to task and defends the often-criticized views of Eric Williams.[58] Although one may disagree with Menard's opinions, it is impossible to deny that capitalism and slavery are large topics that have dominated the study of British North America in the eighteenth century and will no doubt serve as the basis for the most important new historical controversies in the twenty-first century. The eighteenth century was characterized by an intense expansion of slavery and an economic boom closely tied to international trade, which was clearly affected by the beginnings of the Industrial Revolution in England, but as these essays make clear debate over these issues takes up only a corner of the empire of eighteenth-century American studies.

While they move about broadly across the historical landscape, these essays do not have the calculated range and scope of the Greene and Pole volume. Their disorder and diversity reflects the state of the art; as does their excitement. Each author in his or her way tries to grasp on to a part of a more complex history that lacks the central narrative that drove and organized Gipson's magisterial, synthetic work. There are clearly areas unrepresented by these essays most obviously those which most concerned Gipson and others of his generation – imperial relations and internal colonial politics. But to have included them would have meant more "parts" that resist the rationalist desire to reconstruct the subject "whole."[59]

As eighteenth-century Americanists grope to more deeply examine these parts, the field itself seems to be fragmenting if not flying apart. The stories of the abandoned child, the wayward woman, or the unsolved murder that so fascinate present scholars and consume their interest and research must somehow be turned back into elements of larger generalizations that we will pass on to our students and a general audience. These essays represent the way in which historians have tried to look differently at the world that Gipson surveyed and how they have ventured into new areas uncharted by the documentary evidence with which Gipson worked. These writers are looking at history from the bottom up, groping to understand the inarticulate and invading the borderlands marked by eighteenth-century cultural claims and twentieth-century disciplinary boundaries. While we probably never will encompass Jefferson's gaze or understand the DNA evidence of his long and passionate encounter with the "other," as a postmodernist might describe Sally Hemings, we must struggle to tie up these threads. Historians face a complex task of taking the fragmented study of the era before independence and somehow drawing it together. Some of the pieces such as towns and technology were hardly formed, and other basic institutions like slavery would encounter a total reorganization in the nineteenth century that in the scholarship on the subject represents a veil that hides the variety which characterizes the formative *centuries* of the institution's history. Recently, in an article in the *Journal of Economic History*, we were told that most economists do not believe in some of the basic propositions that some unwashed traditional historians present everyday to students. This is healthy. The great changes in history can not be dated; they did not happen one day at 3:37 for all to observe. What we know and what these essays reveal is that the past was a diverse and layered experience involving sharp contrasts between similar phenomenon differently located in time and space. As historians unpack the past, historians too often have become entranced with the different little bundles of goodies they have uncovered.

These essays represent the explosion of the many "new" histories. It started in the 1960s and there is as yet no consensus. The various stories presented here, however, do communicate with each other. Their authors are part of a collective enterprise. They are groping together like settlers in the eighteenth century spreading about in a dense forest, attempting to map early American history carefully studying the trees. It is a project in process.

Notes

1. Lawrence Henry Gipson, "The Imperial Approach to Early American History," in *The Reinterpretation of Early American History: Essays in Honor of John Edwin Pomfret*, ed., Ray Allen Billington (New York: W. W. Norton, 1968), 185–99; Richard B. Morris, "The Spacious Empire of Lawrence Henry Gipson," *William and Mary Quarterly* 24 (1967): 169–89; and William G. Shade, ed., *Revisioning the British Empire on the Eve of the American Revolution: Essays from Twenty-five Years of the Lawrence Henry Gipson Institute for Eighteenth Century Studies* (Bethlehem, Pa.: Lehigh University Press, 1998).

2. Jesse Lemisch, "The American Revolution Seen from the Bottom Up," in *Towards a New Past: Dissenting Essays in American History*, ed. Barton J. Bernstein (New York: Pantheon Books, 1968); Alfred F. Young, ed. *The American Revolution: Explorations in the History of American Radicalism* (Dekalb: Northern Illinois University Press, 1976); Gary Nash, *Race, Class, and Politics: Essays on American Colonial and Revolutionary Society* (Urbana: University of Illinois Press, 1986); and Darrett B. Rutman, *Small Worlds, Large Questions: Explorations in Early American Social History, 1600–1850* (Charlottesville: University Press of Virginia, 1994), provide examples and discussions of this work. The books and articles mentioned in the text and footnoted in this essay are intended to be suggestive rather than inclusive.

3. Stephen G. Kurtz and James H. Hutson, eds., *Essays on The American Revolution* (Chapel Hill: Institute of Early American History and Culture, University of North Carolina Press,1973); Richard Beeman, Stephen Botein, and Edward C. Carter II, eds., *Beyond the Confederation: Origins of the Constitution and American National Identity* (Chapel Hill: University of North Carolina Press, 1987); and Bernard Bailyn and Philip D. Morgan, eds., *Strangers within the Realm: Cultural Margins of the First British Empire* (Chapel Hill: University of North Carolina Press, 1991) are among the finest results of such.

4. Alden T. Vaughan and George Athan Billias, eds., *Perspectives on Early American History: Essays in Honor of Richard B. Morris* (New York: Harper & Row, 1973); David D. Hall, John M. Murrin, and Thad W. Tate, eds., *Saints and Revolutionaries: Essays on Early American History* (New York: W. W. Norton, 1984); James A. Henretta, Michael Kammen, and Stanley N. Katz, eds., *The Transformation of Early American History: Society, Authority, and Ideology* (New York: Alfred A. Knopf, 1991); and Nicholas Canny, Joseph E. Illick, Gary B. Nash, and William Pencak, eds., "Empire, Society and Labor: Essays in Honor of Richard S. Dunn," *Pennsylvania History* 64 (1997): 7–369.

5. Bernard Bailyn, *Voyagers to the West: A Passage in the Peopling of America on the Eve of the Revolution* (New York: Knopf, 1986); Laurel Thatcher Ulrich, *A Midwife's Tale: The Life of Martha Ballard, Based on Her Diary, 1785–1812* (New York: Alfred A. Knopf, 1991); Gordon S. Wood, *The Radicalism of the American Revolution* (New York: Alfred A. Knopf, 1992); and Alan Taylor, *William Cooper's Town: Power and Persuasion on the Frontier of the Early American Republic* (New York: Alfred A. Knopf, 1995).

6. Joyce Appleby, "A Different Kind of Independence: The Post-War Restructuring of the Historical Study of Early America," and "Forum: The Future of Early American History," *William and Mary Quarterly* 50 (1993): 245–67, 298–424.

7. Philip D. Curtin, *The Atlantic Slave Trade: A Census* (Madison: University of Wisconsin Press, 1969); Alfred W. Crosby, Jr., *The Columbian Exchange: Biological and Cultural Consequences of 1492* (Westport, Conn.: Greenwood Publishing, 1972); Robert V. Wells, *The Population of the British Colonies in America Before 1776: A Survey*

of Census Data (Princeton: Princeton University Press, 1975); D. W. Meinig, *The Shaping of America: A Geographical Perspective on 500 Years of History. Volume 1: Atlantic America, 1492–1800* (New Haven: Yale University Press, 1986); William Cronon, *Changes in the Land: Indians, Colonists and the Ecology of New England* (New York: Hill and Wang, 1983); Peter H. Wood, Gregory A. Waselkov, and M. Thomas Harley, eds., *Powhatan's Mantle: Indians in the Colonial Southeast* (Lincoln: University of Nebraska Press, 1989); and John Thornton, *Africa and Africans in the Making of the Atlantic World, 1400–1680* (New York: Cambridge University Press, 1992).

8. Robert Galiman, "The Pace and Pattern of American Economic Growth," in *American Economic Growth*, eds., Lance Davis, Richard Easterlin, and William Parker (New York: Harper & Row, 1972); James A. Henretta, *The Evolution of American Society 1700–1815: An Interdisciplinary Analysis* (Lexington, Mass.: Heath, 1973); Marc Egnal, "The Economic Development of the Thirteen Colonies, 1720–1775," *William and Mary Quarterly* 22 (1975): 191–222.

9. Richard Sheridan, "The Domestic Economy," in *Colonial British America*, eds., Jack P. Greene and J. R. Pole, 43–85. See also Jacob M. Price, "The Transatlantic Economy," in *Colonial British America*, eds., Greenwood and Pole, 18–42; and John J. McCusker and Russell R. Menard, *The Economy of British America, 1607–1789* (Chapel Hill: University of North Carolina Press, 1985).

10. Carl Degler, *Out of Our Past: Forces That Shaped Modern America* (New York: Harper & Row, 1959) was an immensely popular text which synthesized the literature of the period. The phrase, which served as the theme of a section in chapter 1, was repeated in the most recent edition published in 1983 and still available.

11. Jack P. Greene put forth a much more sophisticated version of this view in *Pursuits of Happiness: The Social Development of Early Modern British Colonies and the Formation of American Culture* (Chapel Hill: University of North Carolina Press, 1988) which in contrast to Degler emphasizes the seminal nature of the Chesapeake experience for the future. See also Stuart Bruchey, *The Roots of American Economic Growth, 1607–1861: An Essay in Social Causation* (New York: Harper & Row, 1965); and idem, *Enterprise: The Dynamic Economy of a Free People* (Cambridge: Harvard University Press, 1990).

12. Cf. Charles Sellers, *The Market Revolution: Jacksonian America, 1815–1846* (New York: Oxford University Press, 1991); Sean Wilentz, "Society, Politics, and the Market Revolution," in *The New American History*, ed., Eric Foner (Philadelphia: Temple University Press, 1997), 61–84; Allan Kulikoff, *The Agrarian Origins of American Capitalism* (Charlottesville: University Press of Virginia, 1992); James A. Henretta, *Origins of American Capitalism* (Boston: Northeastern University Press, 1991); Winifred Barr Rothenberg, *From Marketplace to Market Economy: The Transformation of Rural Massachusetts, 1750–1850* (Chicago: University of Chicago Press, 1992); and Melvyn Stokes and Stephen Conway, eds., *The Market Revolution in America: Social, Political, and Religious Expressions, 1800–1880* (Charlottesville: University Press of Virginia, 1996).

13. James T. Lemon, *The Best Poor Man's Country: A Geographical Study of Early Southeastern Pennsylvania* (Baltimore: The Johns Hopkins University Press, 1972); idem, "Comment on James A. Henretta's Family and Farms," *William and Mary Quarterly* 37 (1980): 688–96; James A. Henretta, "Families and Farms: *Mentalité* in Pre-Industrial America," *William and Mary Quarterly* 35 (1978): 3–32; idem, "Response to Lemon," *William and Mary Quarterly* 37 (1980): 696–700. See also Jackson Turner Main, *The Social Structure of Revolutionary America* (Princeton: Princeton University Press, 1965) and Gary Nash, *Race, Class and Politics* (Urbana: University of Illinois Press, 1986).

14. Gary B. Nash, "Social Development," in *Colonial British America*, eds. Greene and Pole, 240–42. Although ignored by the participants in this debate, Timothy H. Breen has contributed importantly in three quite different ways. See T. H. Breen: on farming, "Back to Sweat and Toil: Suggestions for the Study of Agricultural Work in Early America," *Pennsylvania History* 49 (1982): 241–58; on *mentalité*, *Tobacco Culture: The Mentality of the Great Tidewater Planters on the Eve of Revolution* (Princeton: Princeton University Press, 1985); and on the demand, "An Empire of Goods: The Anglicization of Colonial America, 1690–1776," *Journal of British Studies* 25 (1986): 467–99, and "'Baubles of Britain': The American and Consumer Revolutions of the Eighteenth Century," *Past and Present* 119 (1988): 73–104. See also Carole Shammas, "How Self-Sufficient Was Early America?" *Journal of Interdisciplinary History* 13 (1982): 247–72; and Lorena S. Walsh, "Urban Amenities and Rural Sufficiency: Living Standards and Consumer Behavior in the Colonial Chesapeake, 1643–1777," *Journal of Economic History* 43 (1983): 109–17.

15. Brooke Hindle, *Technology in Early America: Needs and Opportunities for Study* (Chapel Hill: University of North Carolina Press, 1966). See also Judith A. McGaw, ed., *Early American Technology: Making & Doing Things from the Colonial Era to 1850* (Chapel Hill: University of North Carolina Press, 1994), which reprints the original introductory essay to the Hindle volume and an extensive bibliography of works written since 1966.

16. Richard B. Morris, *Government and Labor in Early America* (New York: Columbia University Press, 1946); and Carl Bridenbaugh, *The Colonial Craftsman* (Chicago: University of Chicago Press, 1950) represent the classic discussions of these matters.

17. Carl Bridenbaugh, *Cities in the Wilderness* (New York: Ronald Press Co., 1938); idem, *Cities in Revolt* (New York: Ronald Press Co., 1955); and Page Smith, *As a City Upon a Hill* (New York: Alfred A. Knopf, 1966) typified the general approach to urban history before the advent of the New England town studies. The best of the newer studies are Michael Zuckerman, *Peaceable Kingdoms: New England Towns in the Eighteenth Century* (New York: Alfred A. Knopf, 1970); and Gary B. Nash, *The Urban Crucible: Social Change, Political Consciousness, and the Origins of the American Revolution* (Cambridge: Harvard University Press, 1979). A typical study of the Chesapeake, which generalizes from the seventeenth century, is

John A. Rainboit's "The Absence of Towns in the Chesapeake," *Journal of Southern History* 35 (1969): 343–60. An exception as in many things is Darrett B. Rutman and Anita H. Rutman, *A Place in Time: Middlesex County Viriginia, 1650–1750* (New York: Norton, 1984), especially 204–33.

18. Nash, "Social Development," in *Colonial British America*, eds., Greene and Pole, 254. There is also relevant material in Richard S. Dunn, "Servants and Slaves: The Recruitment and Employment of Labor," and T. H. Breen, "Creative Adaptations: Peoples and Cultures," in *Colonial British America*, eds., Greene and Pole, 157–232. See also Philip D. Morgan, "British Encounters with Africans and African-Americans, circa 1600– 1780," in *Strangers within the Realm*, eds. Bailyn and Morgan, 157–219; and Ira Berlin and Ronald Hoffman, eds., *Slavery and Freedom in the Age of the American Revolution* (Charlottesville: University Press of Virginia, 1983).

19. George P. Rawick, *From Sundown to Sunup: The Making of the Black Community* (Westport, Conn.: Greenwood Publishing, 1972); John W. Blassingame, *The Slave Community: Plantation Life in the Antebellum South* (New York: Oxford University Press, 1979); Eugene D. Genovese, *Roll, Jordan, Roll: The World the Slaves Made* (New York: Pantheon Books, 1974); Herbert G. Gutman, *The Black Family in Slavery and Freedom, 1750–1925* (New York: Pantheon Books, 1976); Albert J. Raboteau, *Slave Religion: The "Invisible Institution"* (New York: Oxford University Press, 1978); and Elizabeth Fox-Genovese, *Within the Plantation Household: Black and White Women of the Old South* (Chapel Hill: University of North Carolina Press, 1988). See also the discussions of the historiography of slavery in Peter Parish, *Slavery: History and Historians* (New York: Harper & Row, 1989), and Peter Kolchin, *American Slavery, 1619–1877* (New York: Hill and Wang, 1993).

20. Russell Menard, "The Maryland Slave Population, 1658 to 1730: A Demographic Profile of Blacks in Four Counties," *William and Mary Quarterly* 32 (1975): 29–54; idem, "From Servants to Slaves: The Transformation of the Chesapeake Labor System," *Southern Studies* 16 (1977): 355–90; Allan Kulikoff, "A 'Prolifick' People: Black Population Growth in the Chesapeake Colonies, 1700–1790," *Southern Studies* 16 (1977): 391–428; idem, "The Origins of Afro-American Society in Tidewater Maryland and Virginia, 1700 to 1790," *William and Mary Quarterly* 35 (1978): 226–59; and idem, *Tobacco and Slaves: The Development of Southern Culture in the Chesapeake, 1680–1800* (Chapel Hill: University of North Carolina Press, 1986). See also the rejoinder by Jean Butenhoff Lee, "The Problem of Slave Community in the Eighteenth-Century Chesapeake," *William and Mary Quarterly* 43 (1986): 333–61.

21. Gerald W. Mullin, *Flight and Rebellion: Slave Resistance in Eighteenth-Century Virginia* (New York: Oxford University Press, 1972); Mechal Sobel, *The World They Made Together: Black and White Values in Eighteenth-Century Virginia* (Princeton: Princeton University Press, 1987); Idem, *Trablin' On: The Slave Journey to an Afro-Baptist Faith* (Westport, Conn.: Greenwood Press, 1972); and James Sidbury,

Ploughshares into Swords: Race, Rebellion and Identity in Gabriel's Virginia, 1730–1810 (Cambridge: Cambridge University Press, 1997).

22. Melville J. Herskovits, *The Myth of the Negro Past* (Boston: Beacon Press, 1958), originally published in 1941; E. Franklin Frazier, *The American Negro* (New York, 1948), which summarizes his argument that appeared in *The Negro Family in the United States* (Chicago: University of Chicago Press, 1939), and was repeated in *The Negro Church in America* (New York: Schocken Books, 1964).

23. Kenneth M. Stampp, *The Peculiar Institution: Slavery in the Antebellum South* (New York: Alfred A. Knopf, 1956); Stanley Elkins, *Slavery: A Problem in American Institutional and Intellectual Life* (Chicago: University of Chicago Press, 1959).

24. Sidney W. Mintz and Richard Price, *An Anthropological Approach to the Afro-American Past: A Caribbean Perspective* (Philadelphia: Institute for the Study of Human Issues, 1976).

25. Since this essay was written, two masterful books have appeared emphasizing the varied cultures of slavery in British North America in the eighteenth century: Philip D. Morgan, *Slave Counterpoint: Black Culture in the Eighteenth-Century Chesapeake and Lowcountry* (Chapel Hill: University of North Carolina Press, 1998); and Ira Berlin, *Many Thousands Gone: The First Two Centuries of Slavery in North America* (Cambridge, Mass.: Belknap Press of Harvard University, 1998).

26. Perry Miller, *Orthodoxy in Massachusetts, 1630–1650* (Cambridge, Mass.: Harvard University Press 1933); idem, *The New England Mind: The Seventeenth Century* (New York: Macmillan & Co., 1939); and idem, *The New England Mind: From Colony to Province* (Cambridge, Mass.: Harvard University Press, 1953). The literature on Miller's work is itself immense and growing. See the symposium in *American Quarterly* 34 (1982); and "The Puritans: Bigots or Builders," in *Interpretations of American History Patterns and Perspectives*, eds., Gerald N. Grob and George Athan Billias (New York: Free Press, 1992), 1:2, 8–41.

27. Perry Miller and Thomas H. Johnson, eds., *The Puritans: A Sourcebook of Their Writings*, 2 vols. (New York: American Book Company, 1938).

28. Vernon L. Parrington, *Main Currents in American Thought*, 3 vols. (New York, 1927–1930). See Richard Hofstadter, *The Progressive Historians* (New York: Harcourt, Brace and Co., 1968), 347–434.

29. See F. Matthiessen, *The American Renaissance: Art and Expression in the Age of Emerson and Whitman* (New York: Oxford University Press, 1968).

30. Richard Hofstadter, *America in 1750: A Social Portrait* (New York: Alfred A. Knopf, 1971). See also Cedric B. Cowing, *The Great Awakening and the American Revolution: Colonial Thought in the Eighteenth Century* (Chicago: Rand McNally, 1971); William G. McLoughlin, "The Role of Religion in the American Revolution: Liberty of Conscience and Cultural Cohesion in the New Nation," in Kurtz and Hutson, eds., *Essays on the American Revolution*, 197–255; William G. McLoughlin, "'Enthusiasm for Liberty': The Great Awakening as a Key to the Revolution," in *Preachers and Politicians: Two Essays on the Origin of the American Revolution*, eds., Jack P. Greene and William G. McLoughlin, (Worcester, Mass.:

American Antiquarian Society, 1977); Rhys Isaac, *The Transformation of Virginia, 1740–1790* (Chapel Hill: University of North Carolina Press, 1982); and Patricia U. Bonomi, *Under the Cope of Heaven: Religion, Society, and Politics in Colonial America* (New York: Oxford University Press, 1986).

31. Nathan O. Hatch, "The Origins of Civil Millennialism in America: New England Clergymen, War with France, and the Revolution," *William and Mary Quarterly* 31 (1974): 407–30; Jon Butler, "Enthusiasm Described and Decried: The Great Awakening as Interpretive Fiction," *Journal of American History* 69 (1982): 305–25; and idem, *Awash in a Sea of Faith: Christianizing the American People* (Cambridge, Mass.: Harvard University Press, 1990).

32. Perry Miller, *Jonathan Edwards* (New York: W. Sloane Assoc., 1949); idem, *Errand into the Wilderness* (Cambridge, Mass.: Belknap Press of Harvard University Press, 1956); Alan Heimert, *Religion and the American Mind: From the Great Awakening to the Revolution* (Cambridge, Mass.: Harvard University Press, 1966); and Alan Heimert and Perry Miller, eds., *The Great Awakening: Documents Illustrating the Crisis and Its Consequences* (Indianapolis: Bobbs-Merrill, 1967). See also Edwin Scott Gaustad, *The Great Awakening in New England* (New York: Harper & Row, 1957); and Carl Bridenbaugh, *Mitre and Sceptre: Transatlantic Faiths, Ideas, Personalities, and Politics, 1689–1775* (New York: Oxford University Press, 1962).

33. Richard L. Bushman, *From Puritan to Yankee: Character and the Social Order in Connecticut, 1690–1765* (Cambridge, Mass.: Harvard University Press, 1967); and John M. Bumstead and John E. R. Van de Wetering, *What Must I do to be Saved: The Great Awakening in Colonial America* (Hinsdale, Ill.: Dryden Press, 1976).

34. David D. Hall, "Religion and Society: Problems and Reconsiderations," in *Colonial British America*, eds., Greene and Pole, 325. See also David D. Hall: "Understanding the Puritans," in *The State of American History*, ed., Herbert J. Bass (Chicago Quadrangle Books, 1970): 330–49; The Faithful Shepherd (Chapel Hill: University of North Carolina Press, 1972); and David D. Hall, "On Common Ground: The Coherence of American Puritan Studies," *William and Mary Quarterly* 3rd ser., no. 2, 44 (April 1987): 193–229

35. Alex Inkeles, "Modernization of Man," in *Modernization: Dynamics of Growth*, ed., M. Weiner (New York: Basic Books, 1966): 138–50; C. E. Black, *The Dynamics of Modernization: A Study in Comparative History* (New York: Harper & Row, 1966); S. N. Eisenstadt, *Modernization: Protest and Change* (Englewood Cliffs, N.J.: Prentice Hall, 1966); Alex Inkeles, "Making Men Modern," *American Journal of Sociology* 75, no. 2 (1969) 208–25; and Richard D. Brown, Modernization: *The Transformation of American Life, 1600–1865* (New York: Hill and Wang, 1976).

36. See also Lawrence Cremin, *American Education: The Colonial Experience* (New York: Harper & Row, 1970); William J. Gilmore, *Reading Becomes a Necessity of Life: Material and Cultural Life in Rural New England, 1780–1835* (Knoxville: University of Tennessee Press, 1989); Richard D. Brown, *Knowledge is Power: The Diffusion of Information in Early America, 1700–1865* (New York: Oxford University Press,

1989); and idem, *The Strength of a People: The Idea of an Informed Citizenry in America, 1650–1870* (Chapel Hill: University of North Carolina Press, 1996).

37. Cf. Gloria L. Main, "An Inquiry into When and Why Women Learned to Write in Colonial New England," *Journal of Social History* 24 (1991): 579–89.

38. See Robert Shalhope, "Toward a Republican Synthesis: The Emergence of an Understanding of Republicanism in American Historiography," *William and Mary Quarterly* 29 (1972): 49–80; idem, "Republicanism and Early American Historiography," *William and Mary Quarterly* 39, no. 2 (Apr. 1982): 334–56; and Daniel T. Rogers, "Republicanism: The Career of a Concept," *Journal of American History* 79 (1992): 11–38.

39. Carl Becker, *The Declaration of Independence: A Study in the History of Political Ideas* (New York: Harcourt Brace, 1958); and Merle Curti, "The Great Mr. Locke: America's Philosopher, 1783–1861," *The Huntington Library Bulletin* No. 11 (April 1937): 107–51.

40. Edmund S. Morgan (with Helen M. Morgan) *The Stamp Act Crisis: Prologue to Revolution* (Chapel Hill: University of North Carolina Press, 1953); *The Birth of the Republic, 1763–1789* (Chicago: University of Chicago Press, 1956); *The Challenge of the American Revolution* (New York: W. W. Norton Co., 1976); and *Inventing the People: The Rise of Popular Sovereignty in England and America* (New York: W. W. Norton Co., 1988). See also Clinton Rossiter, *The Seedtime of the Republic* (New York: Harcourt Brace, 1953).

41. Charles S. Sydnor, *Gentlemen Freeholders: Political Practices in Washington's Virginia* (Chapel Hill: University of North Carolina Press, 1952); Richard P. McCormick, *The History of Voting in New Jersey: A Study of the Development of Election Machinery, 1664–1911* (New Brunswick, N.J.: Rutgers University Press, 1953); Robert E. Brown, *Middle Class Democracy and the Revolution in Massachusetts, 1691–1780* (Ithaca, N.Y.: Cornell University Press, 1955); Charles S. Grant, *Democracy in the Connecticut Frontier Town of Kent* (New York: W. W. Norton Co., 1961); J. R. Pole, "Historians and the Problem of Early American Democracy," *American Historical Review* 67 (1961): 626–46; Robert E. Brown and B. Katherine Brown, *Virginia, 1705–1786: Democracy or Aristocracy?* (East Lansing: University of Michigan Press, 1964); and Jack P. Greene, "Changing Interpretations of Early American Politics," in *The Reinterpretation of Early American History*, ed., Billington, 151–85. Cf. Michael Zuckerman, *Peaceable Kingdoms*.

42. Jack P. Greene, *The Quest for Power: The Lower House of Assembly in the Southern Royal Colonies, 1689–1776* (Chapel Hill: University of North Carolina Press, 1963); Bernard Bailyn, *The Origins of American Politics* (New York: Alfred A. Knopt, 1969); and John M. Murrin, "Political Development," in *Colonial British America*, eds., Greene and Pole, 408–56.

43. J. G. A. Pocock, *The Machiavellian Moment: Florentine Republican Thought and the Atlantic Republican Tradition* (Princeton, N.J.: Princeton University Press, 1975); Lance Banning, *The Jeffersonian Persuasion: Evolution of a Party Ideology* (Ithaca, N.Y.: Cornell University Press, 1978); Drew R. McCoy, *The Elusive*

Republic: Political Economy in Jeffersonian America (Chapel Hill: University of North Carolina Press, 1980); and Linda Kerber, "The Revolutionary Generation: Ideology, Politics and Culture in the Early Republic," in *The New American History*, ed., Eric Foner, (Philadelphia, 1997), 31–59.

44. Joseph Ernst, "'Ideology' and an Economic Interpretation of the Revolution," in Young, *The American Revolution*, 161. The Republican synthesis has also been criticized by liberal political theorists: Issac Kramnick, *Republicanism and Bourgeois Radicalism: Political Ideology in Late Eighteenth Century England and America* (Ithaca, N.Y.: Cornell University Press, 1990); Joyce Appleby, *Capitalism and a New Social Order: The Republican Vision of the 1790s* (New York: New York University Press, 1984); and idem, *Liberalism and Republicanism in the Historical Imagination* (Cambridge, Mass.: Harvard University Press, 1992).

45. See also Richard K. Matthews, *The Radical Politics of Thomas Jefferson: A Revisionist View* (Lawrence: University of Kansas Press, 1986).

46. Richard K. Matthews, *If Men Were Angels: James Madison and the Heartless Empire of Reason* (Lawrence: University of Kansas Press, 1995). See also Richard K. Matthews, "Liberalism, Civic Humanism, and the American Political Tradition: Understanding Genesis," *The Journal of Politics* 49 (1987): 1127–53; Asher Horowitz and Gad Horowitz, *"Everywhere They Are in Chains": Political Theory from Rousseau to Marx* (Scarborough, Ontario: Nelson, 1988); and Steven M. Dworetz, *The Unvarnished Doctrine: Locke, Liberalism, and the American Revolution* (Durham, N.C.: Duke University Press, 1990).

47. Jean E. Friedman and William G. Shade, eds., *Our American Sisters* (Boston: Allyn and Bacon, 1973). The changes taking place in the field can be seen in the articles and bibliographies in the subsequent editions of 1976, 1982, and 1987.

48. Although there was no essay devoted solely to women in *Colonial British America*, Mary Beth Norton published at the same time, "The Evolution of White Women's Experience in Early America," *American Historical Review* 89 (1974): 593–619, which provided an excellent survey of the new literature.

49. Linda Kerber, *Federalists in Dissent: Imagery and Ideology in Jeffersonian America* (Ithaca, N.Y.: Cornell University Press, 1970); Mary Beth Norton, *The British Americans: Loyalists Exiles in England, 1774–1789* (New York: Little Brown and Co., 1972); and Carol Berkin, *Jonathan Sewall: Odyssey of an American* (New York: Columbia University Press, 1974). See also Joan Hoff, *Law, Gender and Injustice: A Legal History of U.S. Women* (New York: New York University Press, 1991); and Linda K. Kerber, *Toward an Intellectual History of Women* (Chapel Hill: University of North Carolina Press, 1997).

50. See also the excellent set of essays by Nash's mentor Wesley Frank Craven, *White, Red and Black: The Seventeenth Century Virginian* (Charlottesville: University Press of Virginia, 1971). Craven's best known works – *The Southern Colonies in the Seventeenth Century, 1607–1689* (Baton Rouge: Louisiana State University Press, 1949) and *The Colonies in Transition, 1660–1713* (New York: Harper

& Row, 1968) – are notable for their treatment of Indians, although their focus is eurocentric.

51. Richard White, *The Middle Ground: Indians, Empires, and Republics in the Great Lakes Region, 1650–1815* (New York: Cambridge University Press, 1991).

52. The state of scholarship in the 1970s can be seen in two books by historians heavily influenced by the work of anthropologists: Wilcomb E. Washburn, *The Indian in America* (New York: Harper & Row, 1975) and Robert F. Berkhofer, Jr., *The White Man's Indian* (New York: Alfred A. Knopf, 1978).

53. Cronon, *Changes in the Land* and three books by James Axtell: *The European and the Indian: Essays in the Ethnohistory of Colonial North America* (New York: Oxford University Press, 1981); *The Invasion Within: The Contest of Cultures in Colonial North America* (New York: Oxford University Press, 1985); and *Beyond 1492: Encounters in Colonial North America* (New York: Oxford University Press, 1992). James H. Merrell surveys the recent literature in "'Customes of Our Country': Indians and Colonists in Early America," in *Strangers Within the Realm*, eds., Ballyn and Morgan, 117–56.

54. In Foner, ed., *The New American History*, 3–30.

55. J. H. Parry, *The Spanish Seaborne Empire* (London: Hutchinson, 1966); J. H. Elliott, *The Discovery of America and the Discovery of Man* (New York: Oxford University Press, 1972); and Elizabeth A. H. John, *Storms Brewed in Other Men's Worlds: The Confrontation of Indians, Spanish and French in the Southwest, 1540–1795* (College Station: Texas A & M University Press, 1981).

56. See Andrew L. Knaut, *The Pueblo Revolt: Conquest and Resistance in Seventeenth-Century New Mexico* (Norman: University of Oklahoma Press, 1995); and Jill Laporte's brilliant book, *The Name of War: King Phillip's War and the Origins of American Identity* (New York: Alfred A. Knopf, 1997).

57. Aside from McCusker and Menard, *Economy of British America*, see also James F. Shepherd and Gary M. Walton, *Shipping, Maritime Trade, and the Economic Development of Colonial America* (New York: Cambridge University Press, 1973); Gary M. Walton and James F. Shepard, *The Economic Rise of Early America* (New York: Cambridge University Press, 1979); Alice Hanson Jones, *Wealth of a Nation to Be: The American Colonies on the Eve of the Revolution* (New York: Columbia University Press, 1980); and Stanley L. Engerman and Robert E. Gallman, eds., *The Cambridge Economic History of the United States: Volume 1, The Colonial Era* (Cambridge: Cambridge University Press, 1996).

58. See particularly Seymour Drescher, "The Decline Thesis of British Slavery since *Econocide*," *Slavery and Abolition* 7 (1986): 3–23.

59. Thomas Bender discussed this problem for American history generally in "Wholes and Parts: The Need for Synthesis in American History," *Journal of American History* 73 (1986): 120–36; and it is extensively discussed in Part IV of Peter Novick, *That Noble Dream: The "Objectivity Question" and the American Historical Profession* (Cambridge: Cambridge University Press, 1988).

1

THE PLACE OF THE EIGHTEENTH CENTURY
IN AMERICAN AGRICULTURAL HISTORY

Richard L. Bushman

ON THE EVE of the Revolution about 80 percent of the labor force of British North America worked in agriculture.[1] Most colonists spent the majority of their waking hours doing farm work. People of all classes and ethnic origins (men, women, and many children) devoted their days to planting tobacco, husking corn, building fences, milking cows, slaughtering pigs, clearing brush, weeding vegetables, churning butter, killing chickens, salting meat, and hoeing, hoeing, hoeing. Native Americans hunted more than Europeans and Africans, but Indians, too, worked the soil. The vast bulk of the population spent its energies from dawn to dusk, day after day, from childhood to the grave toiling on the land and dealing with the fruits of their labors.

Over the past two decades, the literature on colonial North America has grown to reflect this reality. Agricultural history, once a specialty with its own journal and small band of specialized scholars, has blended with economic and social history. Scholars from a variety of disciplinary perspectives have joined forces to create a complex picture of rural culture. One branch of this scholarship has focused on agricultural *society* and analyzed community formation, gender, class, and migration. Another branch has concentrated on the agricultural *economy*, on the production and marketing of farm products, the organization of labor, and the transmission of farm property down through the generations. Studies of farm society and of the farm economy intermingle, of course, and are conceptually interrelated. In this essay, however, I want to focus on the farm economy literature.

What can we now say about North American agriculture in the eighteenth-century? What part did this century play in the longer history of agriculture in the United States? What were the distinctive develop-

40

ments, and how do they relate to what came before and after?[2] In the most recent writings on agriculture, the eighteenth century, on the whole, is overshadowed by the changes that came after 1800. In the broad sweep of agricultural history, the eighteenth century is usually depicted as a time of expectation and preparation, a proto- or pre-capitalist period, when the market hovered about the edges of farm society, waiting to make its entrance in the first half of the nineteenth century. Eighteenth-century farming is associated more with the *longue duree* of traditional agriculture than with the dynamic transformations of modern capitalism. Although not all agree on the time of the transition to capitalism, most commonly it is located in the first half of the nineteenth century.[3] For some modern social historians, the most interesting eighteenth-century events were the skirmishes between traditional agriculture and the oncoming new order, as the older agricultural world resisted the incursions of the capitalist economy.[4]

The backward condition of eighteenth-century farming has been a staple of the literature for a long time. In summaries of agricultural history for the period up to the Civil War, the single most persistent idea for over three-quarters of a century has been the change from subsistence to commercial agriculture. Percy Wells Bidwell made this transformation the center piece of his essay on *Rural Economy in New England at the Beginning of the Nineteenth Century* in 1916, and in a far more sophisticated form it underlies the best recent work, such as Christopher Clark's *The Roots of Rural Capitalism: Western Massachusetts, 1780–1860*. It is stated more bluntly in Charles Sellers's synthetic survey of the first half of the nineteenth century, *The Market Revolution*.[5] In all of these works, the eighteenth century is a time of preparation. By its very structure, the subsistence-commercial interpretive apparatus demands that the changeover from subsistence to commercial be given star billing. Everything else pales by comparison, and since that moment occurs after 1800 for Clark and at the very end of the eighteenth century for others, the larger part of the century becomes a prelude to the main event.

Commercialization as an idea has been greatly elaborated in twentieth-century historiography; in fact, the basic evaluation of its effect has been reversed. Bidwell's work came out of the agricultural college tradition and the ethos of the Department of Agriculture. His generation of social scientists idealized efficient production for the market; the best and most advanced farmers maximized production and profits. Under the influence of Frederick Jackson Turner's stages of civilization, Bidwell and John I. Falconer, his coworker in writing *History of Agriculture in the Northern United States, 1620–1860*, believed that as one journeyed from urban centers outward to the frontier, the influence of the market declined and so did the quality of agriculture. Frontier subsistence farmers mercilessly depleted the soil to reap the greatest fruits with minimum effort, while commercial farmers adopted the best fertilizing techniques in the interest of profit. "Farming appeared at its worst on the frontier, where the scarcity of labor and capital favored predatory methods, and at its best in the neighborhood of the commercial towns, where ready markets stimulated intensive use of the soil."[6]

Bidwell and Falconer worked in a tradition going back to eighteenth-century agricultural reformers who scorned the backward ways of traditional farmers and lauded the achievements of improving husbandman. The eighteenth- and nineteenth-century agricultural writers drew their inspiration from Arthur Young who thought that the simple farmer scratching a living from the land was hopelessly inert and retrograde.[7] The great agricultural achievements were the work of rational experimenters who kept careful records and practiced business principles. The nineteenth-century reformers' ideas of good farming, drawing scientific support from the burgeoning field of soil chemistry, culminated in the agricultural college and the Department of Agriculture. This agricultural establishment, the handiwork of the reformers, catered to improving farmers. Bidwell and Falconer wrote in the cultural environment that these educators and researchers created. Their agricultural history naturally put improving farmers at the forward edge of development.[8]

Contemporary agricultural history is written from a different viewpoint, in the main by historians without farm backgrounds and no associations with the agricultural establishment. Most were trained as social historians, and many have absorbed the faintly or distinctly Marxist outlook that suffuses contemporary social history. Those with a Marxist orientation rarely depict commercial agriculture as progress; in fact much of the current work is tinged with regret for the loss of the old order. Borrowing from Marx, these historians locate eighteenth-century subsistence farming along the evolutionary line from feudalism to capitalism. The onset of commercial farming marks the great transformation of modern life. For historians with Marxist leanings, feudalism in the remote past has little to recommend it, but neither does capitalism. For them the transition to market farming is riddled with ambiguity. Some farmers prospered to be sure, but many suffered. The communalism and family values of the old order were swept away by competitive individualism and the pursuit of profit, the bane of modern life. In the writings of contemporary social historians, businesslike, rational production for the market appears harsh and selfish instead of progressive and efficient. The market invades the calm of precapitalist villages and destroys the yeoman's communal existence.[9] While fighting off the temptation to seem nostalgic, the social historians cannot help pointing up the praiseworthy values of the old order, a far cry from the ignorance and lethargy of Bidwell's backward husbandman.[10]

The Marxist orientation has provided modern social historians with new terms for describing the subsistence-commercial distinction; subsistence farmers produced for their own "use." not for "exchange" or sale as commercial farmers did. Current historiography makes much of the word "surplus" in the colonial farmers' description of market crops. "Surplus," seems to sum up the attitude toward commercial agriculture in the old era. Farmers grew crops and raised animals first and foremost to sustain their families; only the leftovers went to market. In the writings of contemporary social historians, that attitude set colonial farmers apart from nineteenth-century farmers who managed their farms with markets uppermost in mind.[11]

While the older subsistence-commercial polarity has given way in much modern writing to the larger and more complicated transition from feudalism to capitalism, the emphasis on commercialization has not been displaced. Focusing on capitalism adds new elements to the analysis, notably the appearance of wage labor – an agricultural economy is not fully capitalist, in Marxist theory, until labor becomes a commodity, purchased in a labor market, paid for with wages, and exploited for the benefit of the employer. But market farming is the sole reason for hiring wage labor and so remains central in the analysis of capitalist agriculture.[12]

Elaborated and refined, the subsistence-commercial categories live on in writings about agriculture. Meanwhile new information about farm operations has taken us far beyond the work of Bidwell and Falconer and substantially revised our understanding of the farm economy. We now have a view of the inner workings of farm communities that was invisible to the older writers. In many respects, the new evidence does not fit comfortably into the old framework, leading to various tentative reformulations, but tinkering has not been entirely successful. The new work raises the possibility that a more fundamental revision is needed. The polarity of subsistence and commercial farming in whatever guise may no longer work. If it is abandoned, the eighteenth century will be assigned a new place in agricultural history.

Already the word subsistence has been discarded as an adequate description of eighteenth-century farmers. The word suggests that the sole purpose of farm operations was to provide food, clothing, fuel, and shelter for the farm family. A subsistence farm family would make everything it needed and purchase nothing. Perhaps along the outer rim of European settlement farmers had survival solely in mind, but everywhere else no family could live long without a marketable crop. Payment of taxes, among other demands, required production of marketable grain, meat, or cheese. Even in the unusual times when commodity payments were accepted, the product had to be sold eventually in order for the government to pay its bills. Any farmer who dwelt under the umbrella of civil government could not escape the obligation of presenting money or a marketable equivalent to the authorities each year.[13]

In addition, the existence of a store in the town was evidence of production beyond subsistence. By 1771 in the more settled parts of Massachusetts – in the Connecticut Valley and in all towns east of Worcester – 80 percent of the towns had stores; in the more mountainous area east and west of the Valley, 42 percent of the towns did.[14] The stock of these little shops was modest – rum, cloth, salt, iron, buttons, hats – but they provided goods that every farmer wanted and needed. Payment could be made in goods and sometimes labor, but ultimately the payments had to be transmuted into cash through sale at a market. Carole Shammas's research on colonial imports revealed that a substantial amount of trade was going on, even in the inland towns. On the average, colonists spent more than one quarter of their total incomes on imported goods, and every gallon of rum and yard of cloth in the country stores represented production for exchange beyond subsistence.[15] The term subsistence leaves out these basic parts of the farm economy, critically distorting the reality.

A related term that has come under scrutiny is self-sufficiency. A successful subsistence farmer (if such existed) would be self-sufficient, but a highly successful commercial farmer, producing large amounts for the market, might also be self-sufficient if his farm produced everything consumed by his family. He would sell a substantial portion of his production and buy nothing. Did any eighteenth-century farmers achieve self-sufficiency? The evidence now suggests that none or very few did. In the Chesapeake the great planters were able to accumulate the equipment and the skilled hands to make most of their basic needs, such as shoes, butter, clothing, and simple tools. In a famous boast William Byrd told an English correspondent that a coin remained in his pocket for many months because he bought nothing. But he was thinking only of the bare essentials for his slaves and families. His own artisans did not make the elegant wrought-iron gates for Westover or weave the cloth for Byrd's fine wool suits. Byrd was self-sufficient only in the rudiments, and was constantly purchasing goods in England with the proceeds from his tobacco crop.[16]

The simple-living New Englanders were no more self-sufficient. Bettye Pruitt's close study of the 1771 Massachusetts tax assessment lists revealed that virtually no farm had adequate resources to produce all that the family needed. A self-sufficient farm would require the right quantities of tillage, pasture, meadow, and woodlots with the proper stock and equipment. Farms rarely were in perfect balance. They had too much tillage and not enough pasture, or no woodlots and too many cows. Pruitt calculated that Massachusetts farmers could survive only by exchanging their surpluses for the surpluses of others. The exchanges included labor, the use of land, crops, animals, tools – everything of value that the farm family could bring to the exchanges. Money rarely figured into the transactions, though frequently money values were assigned for purposes of determining a just exchange. But every farmer was enmeshed in a complex network of mutual exchange and obligations, mainly within the village, in order to accumulate the necessities of life.[17]

This new research has undercut subsistence and self-sufficiency as words to describe eighteenth-century farm operations. Neither term tells the whole story. No farm family worked solely to produce for home consumption, and probably no farm was self-sufficient. Moreover, farmers were engaged in far more exchanges than had been realized before. The little stores that dotted the landscape were not the only sites of exchange; it was going on everywhere among neighbors who relied on each other's production to supplement their own. Village exchanges have to be distinguished from production sent to distant markets, but the old words, subsistence and self-sufficiency, do not describe the state of eighteenth-century agriculture.[18]

The effect of this research is to blur the outlines of the old conceptions. No one now believes that farmers produced only for themselves, or that they did not engage in trade and exchange. And yet the old polarity has not dissolved. There is still a tendency to argue that a crucial divide was crossed going from the eighteenth to the nineteenth centuries. The term most commonly used for the old order in current historiography is household production, implying a labor force drawn primarily from the family with production intended primarily for family use. But that becomes one pole of a polarity, the baseline for a major transformation around 1800. The agricultural world did not simply change as it had been doing before and continued to do afterward; it passed through a uniquely significant change – the "transition to capitalism"– in which increased market production played a key role. The polar construction of the subsistence/commercial view can still be discerned in its new garb, with commercial farming a key element.

In current writing, it is frequently said that the spirit of early farming was fundamentally different. Profit-oriented market farmers were more risk-taking and calculating.[19] The implication is that older farmers took few risks and did not carefully plan how to deploy their resources. The belief that calculation entered only with capitalist farming is again reminiscent of the nineteenth-century reformers' scorn for the simple, backward farmer who refused to improve, and Bidwell's and Falconer's belief that frontier husbandry was careless. Modern historians have reversed the spin on the calculating capitalist farmer; he is more of a self-ish schemer than a prudent husbandman, but the results are the same.

Thus the main outline of the old framework persists in altered form. Historians are striving to absorb the new findings on village exchanges and eighteenth-century store purchases without abandoning the older theoretical structure. Current models still posit a major farming transition around 1800 into a fundamentally different form of agriculture with increased market farming as the engine of change. If anything, the feudal-capitalism polarity projects a vaster transformation than subsistence and commercial farming, separating the eighteenth century all the more sharply from the nineteenth.

The research problem emerging from this scheme is to identify empirical data worthy of the portentous theoretical change and to clearly demarcate the eighteenth century from what followed. Locating that data has not been easily accomplished. The contrasting inner spirit of commercial farming and household production, for example, is a distinction that cannot easily be verified. How can the purpose of farmers be identified when most of them left no records, and the remaining account books are factual summaries of exchanges not disquisitions on motives? Can we really discern the spirit that distinguished the eighteenth-century farmer producing for use from the nineteenth-century farmer producing for sale? Are household producers by nature more simple and innocent than market farmers? Is there any objective measure of the contrasting spirits of household production and capitalist farming?[20]

The effort to answer the question of commercial involvement objectively has led to calculations of the amount of production that went into exchanges. If only 5 percent of the farm's yield was traded or exchanged, the farmer presumably was less market oriented than if 25 percent had been directed to market. And 25 percent is less than 40 percent or 60 percent, and so on. But the imprecision of this form of measurement begins to erode the value of the idea of use and exchange. There is no exact point at which the transition to profit occurs. At the extreme edges, the distinction may be clear: a modern wheat farmer who buys Wonder Bread at the supermarket is a commercial farmer, and an eighteenth-century husbandman who trades for an occasional gallon of rum was doubtless more concerned with use. But the dividing line between the two can never be identified. Christopher Clark, one of the most sophisticated and sensitive of the modern social historians, calculated that on average 25 percent of the grain production in one of his Connecticut Valley towns in 1790 was not required to sustain the local population and presumably was available for trade. And yet, in his estimation, farming in the region at that point had not entered the commercial era.[21] On what basis can that judgment be made?[22]

Determining the proportion of production that went to market is itself difficult. The standard method has been to calculate family food consumption and compare it to total farm production. Presumably the surplus was available to trade. But food consumption is notoriously difficult to determine.[23] Consumption calculated for the meridian of

Pennsylvania was generally applied everywhere until Pruitt's close examination of Massachusetts demonstrated that consumption there was much lower.[24] Southern historians have shown that slaves were allotted much less food than whites allowed themselves.[25] Is it not possible that the poor of every color ate less than the rich, and that a family struggling for survival would cut back on its own food if conditions required greater market production? Food consumption is never a fixed quantity and can hardly form a secure basis for determining a farm's actual surplus. The softness of the data on consumption and market surplus added to the newly found prevalence of exchange and trade makes the old description of eighteenth-century agriculture less and less satisfactory.

The failings of the old terms are even more evident when eighteenth-century agriculture is viewed continentally. The literature on the market transformation tends to place the change at one point in time for the entire nation, as if the whole society became commercial or capitalist all at once.[26] That requires that all of eighteenth-century agriculture be in the household mode of production when commercial agriculture is known to have flourished widely in North America. The primary locus of the old subsistence farmer was the small, inland New England village. Historians have enlarged that population to stand for the whole of eighteenth-century agriculture, characterizing farming generally as non-commercial. But if we step back and consider all eighteenth-century farmers, many were energetically producing for the market. Even in the first years of settlement in Massachusetts Bay, farmers at Plymouth found a market for their animals among the new migrants. William Bradford lamented the scattering of his little flock as people sought more land to pasture their herds. By 1650, one-fifth of the Massachusetts Bay population was concentrated in Boston where they could produce only a small part of their own food.[27] The town was dependent on nearby farmers for wood, meat, and grain. Throughout the remainder of the colonial period, cities and towns contained a population that had to be fed and warmed. If between 10 and 20 percent of the population were not laboring on the land, the 80 to 90 percent who were farming had to produce for the rest; a tenth to a quarter of production had to go to cities to keep the population alive, and in the North with its larger urban populations, the proportion would be greater.[28] In addition to the townsmen themselves, the ships that were so essential to New England's balance of trade had to be provisioned, as well as the fishing vessels, and the visiting British fleets. Like every English town, American cities called into existence substantial farm networks in the surrounding countryside producing for the urban market.[29]

After the development of sugar plantations in the British West Indies in the 1650s, New England also had a vigorous external market for its farm products in addition to provisioning its towns and shipping. The primary leg of those complex Atlantic trading voyages was Boston or New London to Barbados or St. Kitts. Cargoes for these voyages were assembled by merchants all over New England from the produce and meat flowing in from the countryside.[30] Around the Narragansett, the mild climate enabled large horse farms to spring up, manned in part by slave labor and aiming at sales in the sugar islands. All the farmers who supplied these markets added a commercial component to their production for family use.[31]

In the literature on regions south of New England the distinction between commercial and noncommercial farming has never figured very prominently. The large markets for wheat in New York and Philadelphia assumed the existence of energetic production to supply those markets. Tenant farming, in the cases where rents were actually collected, required production of marketable crops.[32] Along the Hudson, the owners of the huge patents not only collected rent but sent their agents through the countryside to buy grain for the New York market.[33] Farther south in the Shenandoah Valley farmers were producing for the international market within one generation after settlement.[34] The steep rise in wheat prices after 1745 stimulated a vast increase in production. Before that time, market involvement was probably less, but certainly after midcentury the wheat belt that stretched from middle Virginia to upstate New York was heavily engaged in market farming. Historians who write on these areas have not pretended otherwise.

The seventeenth-century Chesapeake, once tobacco took hold, was as purely devoted to market production as any farming region in American history before the end of the nineteenth century. Lois Carr, Lorena Walsh, and Gloria Main have found very few woolcards, flax hackles, or looms in Maryland inventories before 1680, suggesting that cloth was all imported.[35] In 1705 Robert Beverly complained that Virginians were too lazy to make their own clothing, but the fact was that they concentrated on their market crop and bought fabric.[36] The plantations along the Carolina coast were deeply involved in rice production by the middle of the eighteenth century, and the upcountry settlers raised hemp and indigo for export.[37] The increase in the proportion of farmers owning slaves was one measure of market production. The only reason for purchasing a slave was to produce market crops. In the genial southern environment the farm family could easily produce their own subsistence without the trouble and expense of slave labor. By 1782, 57 percent of the households in Orange County, Virginia, an upland county adjacent to the Blue Ridge, owned slaves, indicating that farmers had market production in mind. The figures for Lunenburg County on Virginia's Southside were the same.[38]

Along the frontier and in the Southern upcountry in the eighteenth century, distance from markets and adverse growing conditions hindered production of the standard southern staples. Farms in these regions more nearly resembled those in New England and New York.[39] But even in these more remote areas slave owners moved in, and the percentage of slaveowning farmers constantly increased through the century, indicating that market production was feasible and being practiced. While not to be classed with the tidewater production of tobacco and rice, these upcountry regions were no more subsistence farms than those in New England. Farmers in both the upland South and New England mixed production for use and production for exchange in that confusing pattern that currently has thrown eighteenth-century agriculture out of focus.[40]

It would be an error, of course, to think that commercial agriculture did not vastly increase after 1800 and work mighty changes in the farm economy. The upcountry and backcountry farmers in South and North in 1750 paled in comparison to the vigorous market farmers in the same regions a century later. The stupendous growth in urban population in the first half of the nineteenth century created an unprecedented market for farm production, and farmers energetically organized their operations to benefit from the opportunities. They opened up land that had long been unimproved, and developed specialty crops to fulfill particular niches – like broom corn to help housewives raise housekeeping standards. They contracted for additional labor and purchased new stock and equipment. There is no doubt that farms changed in the nineteenth century under the stimulus of the market.[41]

The question is what did they change from? How do we characterize eighteenth-century farms where the stimulus of the market was less pronounced and yet present – strongly in many regions, weakly in others?

As Alan Kulikoff notes in a useful essay on "the Transition to Capitalism in Rural America," the European debate "is conceptually clear, dealing with the transition *from* feudalism *to* capitalism," but that clarity fails in America. "Although all agree that feudalism did not reach these shores," Kulikoff writes, "the social order, economic system, or mode of production that preceded capitalism in America is rarely specified." The conceptual language taken from Marxism fails to describe the reality. Feudalism and capitalism are terms too gross to be useful. They are stretched over too many centuries to encompass the multiplicity of changes that occurred during that time. The feudalism-capitalism polarity offers no middle term for American farms through most of our history. "It is evident," Kulikoff concludes, "that the American economy survived for several centuries in a transitional state – clearly not feudal and not yet fully capitalistic."[42] Can we be satisfied with a conceptual scheme that offers no useful description of economic conditions for several centuries? To call this time transitional is excessively teleological, imputing the significance of one period to changes many decades in the future.

The problem with the subsistence-commercial (or feudal-capitalistic) polarity is its structure as much as its content. The polarity forces an either-or decision. Is any given farm subsistence or is it commercial, the structure compels us to ask, when in reality most farms were a bit of both. The idea appeals in the abstract because we can imagine pure subsistence and commercial types, but in the concrete, actual farms do not fit either mold. Moreover, polar historical interpretations think that they describe the flow of time. We are prompted to believe that history moves from subsistence to commercial and from feudal to capitalistic, when in actuality the movement, in the case of subsistence and commercial, is known to go both ways. Polar schemes induce teleological thinking, leading us to believe that the future created the past. For certain purposes teleology illuminates events, but understanding an actual farm in a moment in time is not one of them. We end up with terms like "transitional," which implies that a farm was not what it was, but the embryo of something that it was going to be.

I propose the term "mixed farming" to describe the farm type that persisted in America for at least two centuries, crossing from the eighteenth to the nineteenth centuries and in many places continuing into the twentieth.[43] The subsistence-commercial polarity, along with feudalism-capitalism, should be reserved for the special instances where the broad scope of history is our subject. For close analysis, both conceptions either confuse or fail to illuminate specific eighteenth-century realities. Mixed farming represents the obvious fact that most farmers were involved simultaneously in production for the farm family's subsistence and for the market, and eliminates the need to find the invisible line where a farm became commercial. The term applies to the bulk of the farm families who owned their own land and to the tenants whose numbers increased markedly in the middle of the eighteenth century.[44]

Although mixed farms produced some products for the market, the first priority was the family's welfare. One of the advances in recent scholarship is an understanding of household production and the preeminence of family values. The farm family provided for its own needs and for the descent of property down through the generations before taking chances on risky commercial undertakings. Household producers were cautious about any marketing venture that jeopardized the main enterprise of family support. The eighteenth century's own term for this attitude and the related agricultural practices was "competency."[45] Historians' recognition of family values came in reaction to scholarly work in the post-World War II period when farmers were depicted as aggressive entrepreneurs, profit-seeking businessmen with their eyes on the main chance, grasping at every opportunity to make money whether through land speculation or adoption of the latest agricultural craze.[46] James Henretta is one of those responsible for seeing the error in this caricature, a consequence of one of the historiographical enthusiasms of the 1950s. Partly because farming was so precarious and markets so remote, Henretta recognized, farmers had to see to their own basic needs first and send to market only what could be spared as surplus.[47]

The devotion to family sustenance, however, did not imply an aversion to market production. Many lacked the land, the animals, the labor, or the implements to produce much for the market, but some of the fruits of the farm family's labor had to enter into exchanges with their neighbors, the storekeeper, and the tax collector. They could not survive otherwise. Moreover, there is every indication that farmers developed market products when they could. Farmers near to the Pennsylvania and Maryland iron furnaces cut and hauled wood for the collieries.

Connecticut and Long Island farmers turned to flax growing when the Irish linen industry wanted to buy American-grown seed. Between 1736 and 1756, the exports of flaxseed from American farms increased sevenfold, becoming Connecticut's second most important commercial activity. Massachusetts hill towns hauled sand to the Connecticut Valley towns when housewives started to sand their floors. They produced broom handles when broom corn production boomed. Whenever market opportunities arose, farmers were quick to seize them.[48]

Market production did not imply an abandonment of family values, but the reverse. The purpose of market production was to sustain and advance the family.[49] There is no reason to believe that farmers reluctantly produced for the market, sensing a contradiction with their traditional commitments to family. They produced for the market precisely because of family needs. Farmers doubtless wanted to raise the level of family comfort, but more fundamentally they wanted to provide for the coming generations. One family farm was not enough for even the average American family. If every son were to receive a farm and every daughter an adequate dowry to attract a respectable husband, the farm parents had to accumulate property beyond the requirements of day to day living. The tabulations of farm property by age of owner shows the acreage swelling through a farmer's forties and fifties and then shrinking in his sixties, as land was distributed to offspring.[50] The accumulation of property required a strenuous effort, even with all members striving together. The effort went beyond food for the table and cordwood for the fire. It had to include the accumulation of cash to purchase land. That many families only partially succeeded, or failed altogether, does not diminish the significance of land purchases in the overall family economy. The family had to maximize market production at certain points, not to relish the pleasures of profit or even to enjoy more comforts and conveniences, but to provide land for the rising generation.[51] Debt increased dramatically after 1720 as older systems of dispensing land at minimal cost gave way to auctions and sales by large speculators. Farmers had to incur debt to buy land for the rising generation; if fathers did not go into debt, the sons had to in order to get started.[52]

Mixed farming went on in America under the double mandate to provide for daily living and for the children's future welfare. That double purpose resulted in mixed farming in the more conventional sense of mixed crops. In some respects farms of all sizes up and down the coast from Maine to Georgia resembled one another. Virtually all grew corn and perhaps some other grain crop. They all grazed cows and let swine roam in the woods. Parts of the farm were left in woodlots for fuel and simple construction. Orchards were more common in the North than in the South, but not unknown there. Closer to the house were kitchen gardens and probably chickens, though these creatures left few traces in eighteenth-century records. This complex of varied crops and animals distributed across land was the base of virtually all farms. It was the family provision component.[53]

What distinguished farms in North and South and within the regions was the part of the farm that produced for the market. In the North, the market component was frequently a "surplus" beyond family production: pork or beef beyond what the family consumed, or one of the grains, or butter and cheese. But it could also be potash taken from the ashes of burned trees, or flax seed, or maple syrup, or tanned hides, or coffins and mirror frames made in the off-season. Northern farmers ingeniously devised diverse marketable items from which they could gain a return, and were always alert for new opportunities when they arose. The returns may have been small and only a fraction of their entire productive effort, but within the family economy they played a crucial role.[54]

In the South the market component of farm production was more evident because tobacco, indigo, and hemp were so obviously not consumed at home. Rice production along the steamy Carolina coastal rivers was so vast that it too had to be designated for the market. But the obvious market orientation of Southern planters should not be allowed to obscure the powerful subsistence component of their agriculture. Vast amounts of labor on tobacco farms went to the production of food, the preparation of cloth, and the practice of crafts to keep the large household in operation.[55]

One common mistake is to think of family farming as intrinsically hostile to the market.[56] We assume that commercial farming drove out subsistence production. As one increased, the other decreased. In actual fact, commerce seems to have fostered mixed farming. Commercial farms are known to have increased subsistence production at the same time as they were heavily involved in world markets. One clear instance is the creation of mixed farms in the most commercial section of the colonies in the seventeenth century, the Chesapeake tobacco region. Until the end of the nineteenth century, no area exceeded the seventeenth-century Chesapeake in its whole-souled devotion to a single commercial crop. Planters raised their food and cut their own wood, but leather, cloth, pottery, and iron goods were all imported, while the planters concentrated on the improvement of tobacco production. Not until tobacco prices fell near the end of the century, did planters divert resources to the once-neglected aspects of subsistence.[57] Carville Earle's tabulation of implements from estate inventories measures the increasing incidence of spinning wheels, churns, and other tools for family production in the first half of the eighteenth century.[58] These highly commercial farms edged toward self-sufficiency over the course of the eighteenth century.

The reasons for this change in strategy are not hard to discern. When the returns on a market crop fell, the natural reaction was to reduce costs. If expenditures could be reduced to a minimum, declining prices for the staple would be less painful. If prices fell too far, the planter might be driven to rely entirely on his own production for survival. Not the smallest but the largest planters followed this strategy, the ones who were most heavily involved in the market. Their very dependence on market production made them more eager to buffer the ill effects of falling prices.[59]

The mixed farm, therefore, did not disappear as commercial farming increased. Instead it flourished even in later periods of intense commercialization. The mixed farm was the best defense against the price oscillations that were the terror of market production. Prices could vary by 10 or 20 percent from year to year, and in addition to market ups and downs, the farmer's own yields could vary by as least as much. Sometimes lower yields meant higher prices for farmers as a whole, but an individual farmer, struck by pests or a local drought, could suffer from a down in both yield and price. How could he survive these stomach-wrenching oscillations that were almost entirely out of his control? For the simple survival of his family, he required a subsistence foundation that would guarantee food and warmth whatever the fluctuations in the market.[60]

The utility of a subsistence base was as important in the nineteenth century as it was earlier. Southern cotton farmers concentrated almost wholly on their immensely profitable staple until the 1840s when declining prices brought them to their senses. After the sufferings of that decade, they learned to produce the basics for themselves. Purely commercial farms transmuted into mixed farms, prompted by the market itself.[61] In the same years in tidewater Virginia in the region that had turned from tobacco to wheat, John Walker, a planter with fifteen slaves and nearly five hundred acres, not only grew corn and pork to feed his "family" but raised cotton for fabric. He had it spun and woven and cut for clothing, some of it going into suits for himself. As the years went by, he brought the spinning and weaving, and eventually the tailoring, onto his own farm. He also raised wool and tanned leather for shoes. The strategy, clearly evident from his account books, was to minimize household consumption expenditures at the same time that he was selling wheat in Norfolk and Baltimore, investing in railroad stock, and renting out a skilled slave in Richmond. Every inch a commercial farmer, Walker worked as hard at producing for family consumption as for the market.[62]

Mixed farming was a basic American type from the seventeenth through the nineteenth centuries. Many changes occurred in farm operations over those years, but the fundamental strategy of producing for self and for sale persisted.[63] When the mixed farm strategy finally did fail, it was not because farmers were newly inducted into market production; that had been going on for centuries. The reasons for the failure differed, but the most destructive force was not market sales but market purchases. The time was coming when John Walker could not make what his family needed; crucial items could only be purchased. As rural culture came to feel the shame of its rusticity, farm families required finer clothing and furniture, more genteel flourishes in houses and gardens, and costly educations for the young.[64] These could not be produced on the farm. At that point, sometime in the late nineteenth century, the family provision component of the mixed farm failed in its designated purpose. When homegrown and homemade would not suffice, farmers had to maximize their cash returns in order to purchase the desired goods. As refined tastes and preferences penetrated the farm household, the doom of the mixed farm was sealed. Full blown commercial farming as we understand it came into existence. The mixed farm fell a victim of consumer culture.[65]

The mixed farm was a marvelously supple invention for weathering the storms of commercial expansion. No matter how rapidly the urban population grew, American farmers supplied the cities' agricultural needs. There were no famines, grain shortages, or subsistence crises. Nor did food prices skyrocket as the urban population soared; at worst prices were mildly inflationary. At the same time, farmers who entered into the turbulence of market economics benefitted from commercial sales when they could, and battened down the hatches and lived off the land during the bad years. Hunger was never mentioned as a problem among the rural population.

The mixed farm was the "transitional" type that carried American farm families through two centuries of social change. No fundamental departure from mixed farming was necessary to embrace the heightened commercial opportunities of the nineteenth century. Many farmers combined exchange and use production well into the twentieth century, including sharecroppers in the cotton belt who in 1880 devoted well over half of their land to production of foodstuffs.[66]

From this perspective, the eighteenth century assumes a new place in agricultural history. The century's role was to bring the mixed farm to full flower. Doubtless the combination of self-sufficiency and modest market production existed from the first years of settlement in both North and South. But not until the drop in tobacco prices in the 1680s did Chesapeake planters enlarge their efforts to provide for themselves. The mixed farm in the Chesapeake came into its own after 1700 as subsistence production increased. In the North the sequence was reversed. After 1700 the market for New England farm products expanded greatly when the French sugar islands opened up in the eighteenth century and market production rose.[67] The steep rise in grain prices after 1750, caused by population growth in Europe, further improved the market for farmers in both North and South, making it possible to form the blend of commercial and subsistence farming that was necessary to achieve the ideal of competency. This combination of factors made the eighteenth century the time when the characteristic "mixed farm" came into its own in all sections of the British colonies in North America.[68]

All in all, the century should not be conceived as merely the eve of commercialization, a period that looked forward to great changes but experienced few itself. The eighteenth century laid the foundation for the subsequent commercial transformation. During the significant changes that took place after the Revolution, the mixed farm, an eighteenth-century creation, fed the growing nation while stabilizing the subsistence of millions of farm families as they entered more fully into the turbulence of market production.

I have dealt at length with the issue of subsistence and commercial farming because that idea is so deeply entrenched in thinking about American agricultural history. Even after sharp modification by all active parties to the debate, the subsistence-commercial polarity has resurfaced in recent efforts to summarize the condition of eighteenth-century farming.[69] I hope to replace that misleading idea with one that emphasizes the continuities in the midst of the change going from the eighteenth to the nineteenth century.

But the emergence of the mixed farm was not the sole contribution of the eighteenth century. At least one other development requires comment (albeit more abbreviated) because its importance has been neglected. It is the opening of another market, of equal significance to the market for produce: the market for land. With the land market came a threat to farm life which troubled the farmer more than any other: debt. Debt was the most consuming and ultimately the most dangerous of the farmer's worries, a problem that could cast a pall for decades and in the end wipe out a farm. The words the farmers used in their petitions concerning debt and currency were "ruin" and "destruction."[70]

The eighteenth century was the period when debt emerged as a forbidding presence in the lives of many farmers, and when the mortgaged farm became a standard feature on the agricultural landscape. With the land bank controversies and the court closings which preceded Shays' Rebellion, one of the major causes of political contention in the countryside for the next two centuries began to arouse farmers. Debt may have loomed larger in New England than elsewhere because constraints on agriculture in that cold region limited the alternatives, but debt troubled farmers everywhere beginning in the eighteenth century as the land market became the only way to obtain land.

The growth of debt and the land market were related to the growth of population, the most startling social change in eighteenth-century America, noted by observers at the time and abundantly evident in population records. Between 1690 and 1770 the population of the British North American colonies increased tenfold.[71] The growth came from the high birth and survival rate of the indigenous population and a swelling flood of migration, mainly from England, Scotland, Ireland, the Rhine Valley, and Africa.[72] Benjamin Franklin is the best known contemporary observer of American growth, and at the end of the century Thomas Malthus used American figures to sustain his speculations. By the eve of the Revolution, the British government was worried enough to mount an investigation of emigration to the New World.[73] Population growth affected virtually every aspect of society, the economy, and politics, and farmers no more than anyone could escape the consequences.

Urban areas absorbed their share of the enlarging population, but not a disproportionate number. Most emigrants and native born ended up in rural areas. Land had to be found for these people, and they pushed against every limit that impeded settlement. In the South they left the tidewater with its easy river transportation to the sea and took up lands in the Piedmont and in the valleys beyond the mountains. In the middle colonies they began to fill in the interstices in central Delaware and New Jersey where sandy soils and swamps had rebuffed earlier settlers. In New England they opened farms in the hill country away from the more inviting lowlands. In Pennsylvania and along the eastern borders of New York, New England farmers moved on to lands with questionable titles where the conflicting claims of adjoining colonies were almost certain to lead to controversy. Indeed, virtually every colonial boundary was subject to dispute in the eighteenth century as the rising tide of population pushed into contested areas and for the first time required precise definitions of dividing lines. At the western and northern edges of settlement, native American claims to the soil felt the same pressure. The army of native-born and immigrant settlers, desperate for land, put irresistible pressures on every attempt to regulate expansion, involving the colonial governments and frontier settlers in endless tortured negotiations with the native Americans, marked by dastardly land grabs and punctuated by war. Along this outer edge, government entirely broke down from time to time, as colonial leaders in the provincial capitals could not even provide the rudiments of satisfactory civil authority along the frontier. Like a great ship under full sail in hurricane winds, all the systems of social and political order felt the strain. Breakdown and conflict could not be avoided.[74]

One fortuitous conjunction of circumstances moderated the ill effects of explosive expansion. World grain prices went up sharply at midcentury, giving immediate high returns to migrating farmers who opened new lands, in effect financing the costs of their move. One might predict the impoverishment of large segments of the expanding population as the growing numbers placed too many demands on the continent's economic resources. Such an influx in a European nation would certainly have lowered the wealth per capita. In the eighteenth-century colonies, per capita wealth rose at a low rate, but it did not decline.[75] The rise in grain prices enabled the economic system to absorb the new people and quickly put them to work.

Migration to America and the rise in prices were actually interrelated. The exodus from Britain and the continent was the result of an upward turn in the population, especially on the continent, in the middle of the eighteenth century. Jobs and land could not be found there for the growing numbers of people. They were driven to America to provide for themselves. But those very expulsive forces led to a food shortage in Europe. By the middle of the eighteenth century, Europe could not feed itself. European nations had to import foodstuffs, notably grain, and prices rose.[76] As a result, newly emigrated Europeans in America were put to work immediately, growing the food for their countrymen who remained at home. A double pump action was set up between the two continents, drawing out people from overpopulated Europe into relatively underpopulated America, and at the same time pulling back the surplus foodstuffs grown in America to compensate for production shortfalls in Europe. Improving prices after midcentury, which made grain more profitable than tobacco in many regions of the South, in effect subsidized the costs of migration and gave new American farmers a comfortable return after only a few years in production.[77]

The rise in grain prices could not entirely meliorate the tensions in colonial society as population ballooned. Relationships of farmers to the land began to alter fundamentally. Tenantry, for example, became more common. Until the eighteenth century, large grants had profited their owners largely through land sales. As settlement pressed deeper and deeper inland, away from the port cities and into tribal lands, the benefits of renting from landlords in possession of fertile lands near convenient transportation grew more attractive. The great manors along the Hudson began to fill up. In Maryland the proprietor's lands drew increasing numbers of tenants. The Penns began to make a conscientious effort to collect quit rents on their vast domains as did crown authorities in royal colonies. On the fabulously rich limestone plain west of Philadelphia, individual investors found tenants willing to work the land.[78] Tenant farming grew increasingly common in virtually every colony, especially on the best lands with ready access to markets.[79]

While sometimes beneficial, tenant farming created a class of rural people who lacked the independence of freeholders. A portion of all they produced went to the landlord before the farm family itself received benefits. They were in many cases subject to the owner's caprice, his wish to sell the farm, his criticism of the farm's management, his preference for certain crops, his desire to raise the rent. Tenants were subject to numerous irritations from which freeholders were exempt. From time to time these discontents erupted into concerted violence, notably along the Hudson where tenants rose in protest in the 1760s and again in the 1840s over seeming injustices in their treatment.[80] If not an anomaly, tenants were not completely at ease in America either. Far more than in England, American tenants hoped to earn enough to purchase land of their own and escape their tenantry. For most, tenantry was not a satisfactory ending point for an American farm family. Eighteenth-century population pressures created a class of farmers who were reminders of European lordships and who fell short of the American ideal of independence that emerged in the Revolution.

Tenantry, however, affected many fewer farmers than did the change in the methods of land distribution in the eighteenth century and the emergence of the land market as the sole source of new farms. In the early years of European settlement, the need for people moved colonial governments to distribute land at very low cost. In many of the Southern colonies, 50 acres was awarded for every person whose passage was paid to America as part of the headright system. The claimant had only to pay the cost of surveying the land and small fees for entering the title. Until 1670, the South Carolina proprietors granted 150 acres for each freeman and woman over age sixteen and for each manservant including slaves.[81] William Penn initially charged one bushel of wheat for 100 acres. In New Netherland after 1640, 200 acres was granted to anyone who brought over five adult immigrants.[82] In New England, much land was granted outright to groups who proposed to organize towns. A recent study has shown that even under a policy intended to distribute land at minimal cost to settlers, there was room for profit-making; but on the whole these land speculators raised few barriers to immigrants and much land was granted directly to prospective townsmen.[83] There was plenty of land available to any family that chose to settle in one of the towns. Within the town, the proprietors divided the town lands among themselves at regular intervals as family growth required it.

Both of these systems fell into disuse as the seventeenth century came to an end. In New England the town proprietors became an exclusive land company that refused to admit newcomers as in the early days. The proprietors distributed town lands among themselves, and the remaining inhabitants had to purchase land from the favored few.[84] In unsettled colony lands, Massachusetts and Connecticut began to auction lots in newly opened towns, as the demand for land rose and the need for revenues increased. Instead of making an outright grant to groups of prospective settlers, the provincial governments laid out the new towns into lots and sold them to the highest bidders.[85] In the South and New York, the colonial governments granted thousands of acres to insiders on the assumption that these magnates would bring in settlers. In Maryland, the third Lord Baltimore abolished headrights in 1683 and began raising prices until in 1738 he was charging £5 sterling for each 10 acres.[86] In Pennsylvania the Penn family followed suit, halting the earlier practice of granting tracts to any and all petitioners for small fees and instead selling land at the highest price the market would bear.[87] With the best lands taken up, settlers who wanted to open farms had to buy them from these great landlords. Where headrights were not actually abolished, they lost practical value when the most desirable lands were already patented to large planters.

The amount of land available from these various sources was so immense that through the first half of the century prices rose only slightly. Land was no longer available for the asking as in the seventeenth century, but the costs were low. William Beverly who received 118,491 acres along the headwaters of the Shenandoah, by 1736 had sold land to sixty-seven families for a half shilling or less an acre.[88] But these favorable terms did not last forever. Near the middle of the century, the situation changed in virtually all of the colonies. In Maryland, Connecticut, and Pennsylvania, roughly between 1750 and 1775, the price of land tripled. In Marple township, Chester County, Pennsylvania, land averaged £ .875 per acre between 1700 and 1750; by 1765, it had jumped to £ 2.33 per acre and by 1775 to £ 3.33, a fourfold increase in twenty-five years.[89] Rising prices for wheat do not totally account for the increased land values; land rose at a much faster rate than grain. The available land between the Appalachian Mountains and the ocean may have been effectually absorbed by midcentury. After that time, the unremitting influx of immigrants and the expanding native-born population faced the dangers and cost of going beyond the mountains into regions controlled by Native Americans. Those barriers made people willing to pay higher prices for land east of the Appalachians.[90]

The necessity of paying for land when no more was available for the asking, plus the jump in prices after 1750, introduced new difficulties into the farmer's life planning. No farmer could be content solely with the land the family owned; everyone needed to buy more. Farmers worked on an annual cycle of planting and harvesting to provide for their families' immediate needs. But over a lifetime, their plans had to include provision for establishing their children in independent households. Ideally they would accumulate dowries for their daughters and a farm for each son. Since families averaged five or six children who grew to adulthood, this was a gargantuan task that probably only a few of the wealthiest farmers could accomplish. More commonly, one or two children received farms and then were obligated to repay the others from the farms' proceeds over the years. The parents' farm usually could not be broken up and still function efficiently. The best solution was to give each child (and the widow if one survived) a right to some of the returns. This meant that even the successful heirs were badly encumbered by debts to their siblings.[91] In some instances, fathers sold their farms and used the proceeds to buy much larger tracts in a new area. With the children's help, several farms could be opened up and passed down to the next generation.[92]

Whatever the expedient method, farmers were in the market for land at certain points in the course of their lives. The fathers had to buy land for their children, or the children had to buy land for themselves. Not only immigrants, but every farm family was on the lookout for the right moment to purchase additional property. A few, defeated by the difficulties, left rural areas for the cities, but the large proportion of the work force in the countryside as late as 1800 meant that most remained on the land, waiting for an opportunity to purchase farm property. As mentioned before, studies of estate inventories and tax lists show the average amount of land owned by farmers increasing as they grew older, and then decreasing after the middle fifties. That curve reflects the life plan of farm families in the process of perpetuating themselves on the land.

The price of land obviously made a big difference to farmers who were buying land for their children. Farmers could not barter for new land, exchanging a few bales of hay or the use of an ox. They had to pay for the land at a cost often far beyond their accumulated savings. Inevitably many went into debt. In most cases there was no other way to acquire land after the older systems of distribution gave way to a land market. Not only did the land have to be purchased, there were expenses in stocking the land, buying seed and tools, constructing a house, furnishing it. Some items could be accumulated by a young person while growing up, but at the moment of actual beginning added costs inevitably appeared. Moreover, if the young farmer, or the whole family moved, additional costs were involved. When new land was opening, the desire to purchase as much as possible moved the migrants to borrow all they could. The cost was low, the land would be needed for growing children, and the urge to profit from rising prices was strong. Families were tempted to stretch to the uttermost to buy the maximum amount. And after the family was settled in a new region, there were opportunities to build a mill or open a store or start a tannery.[93] All of these chances for future gain required immediate capital. The entire situation tempted a farmer to extend his credit to the limit.

Some of this indebtedness eventually ended up in court as creditors sued for delinquent payments. The court records provide a rough measure of the amount of indebtedness in the society as a whole. Some court dockets list the names of the debtor and creditor, the type of debt, whether book or bond, and the amount. Book debts were the kind run up with the storekeeper or neighbor in return for purchased goods or services rendered. They represented breakdowns in the local barter system when one party was unable to make returns for services or goods rendered. After 1720 (at least in Connecticut), most debt cases involved bonds or promissory notes which were for agreements to pay a certain amount, usually with interest.[94] Bonds represented cash lent for the purpose of profiting from the interest. Bonded debts usually were not part of the village exchange system, but an effort to raise cash – capital – for whatever the farmer needed.

Although the uses of the money cannot be determined from the court records, they do reveal an immense increase in the amount of bonded indebtedness over the century. The total amount of debt rose much faster than the population. Both the number of debts and the value of the debts per capita rose sharply from 1700 on. In Hartford County, Connecticut, the number of debt cases increased fifteenfold in the first three decades of the eighteenth century.[95] The court records give evidence of a society increasingly involved in a credit system. We can hypothesize that much of this borrowing went toward the purchase or development of land; that need seems to be required by the structure of farm society and the end of the older distribution system.[96] The development of farms, the organization of craft operation and small stores, and pursuit of hundreds of other miscellaneous ventures doubtless played a part too.[97] The important point is that a growing proportion of the farm population carried a debt burden as the century went on.

The eighteenth century brought into existence the indebted farmer and the mortgaged farm. That debt fundamentally altered British American farmers' relationship to the larger society and to government.[98] The barter system was largely isolated from the larger world. Although the local value of farm goods may have oscillated with farm prices in city markets, farmers' fortunes were little affected by market ups and downs. So long as he could find a neighbor with needs to match his resources, a farmer could effect the transactions that supplied his family wants, trading hay for corn, or the use of a pasture for the use of an ox at spring planting. Life went on in the village cocoon unaffected by events in the wider world.

Bonded debts had to be paid in cash, just like taxes. The farmer had to sell his grain or his pork for cash whenever possible. When money was unavailable, as often happened in the currency-short eighteenth-century economy, the farmer's plight could become desperate. How could he pay his debts when money was not to be had? The policies of the government in issuing currency became matters of life and death. Not just his standard of living was at stake, but his very livelihood because debt was ultimately secured by his land. Failure to repay bonded debt could lead to foreclosure and the farmer's "ruin."

Debt made farmers self-conscious political actors. While they doubtless left the intricacies of many governmental policies to the town leaders who represented them in the legislatures, currency questions like the organization of land banks or Massachusetts' disposal of Britain's reimbursement for the Louisburg expedition of 1745, deeply concerned farmers. They wanted stable money, but they required an adequate supply. The unavailability of money made debt repayment impossible.[99] They were angered and terrified when the government failed to supply the economy with money or when the legislature was unsympathetic to the farmers' plight. The New England land bank controversies and the contention leading to Shays' Rebellion marked the entry of the rural rank and file into politics. The prevalence of debt required farmers to turn to politics. Their political engagement, growing out of rural debt, began in the eighteenth century and went on unabated at least until the beginning of the twentieth century.[100]

Our preoccupation with market expansion in the early nineteenth century has blinded us to major changes in the rural economy in the eighteenth century. It is true that vastly enlarged urban markets did alter conditions of life in rural areas between 1790 and 1850, especially in the North; the work of Clark, Rothenberg, and others has illuminated the nature of those changes. But the persistence of the subsistence-commercial model of agricultural change has obscured fundamental change in the eighteenth century and significant continuities from eighteenth to nineteenth centuries. The simple polarity of subsistence and commercial (or feudal and capital) has led researchers to search for a single turning point when the great transformation took place. But Christopher Clark has shown how the process of change was drawn out over a long period, how it consisted of many small steps, and how much of the older era was carried over into the new time. Family values were not abandoned in the nineteenth century, he has argued; they were the very compulsions that involved farmers more and more deeply in market relationships. Local exchange did not end in the nineteenth century; it went on even while farmers were producing more for market and putting their families to work in small manufacturing plants.[101]

In the same spirit, we must now question the sharp division between subsistence and commercial farmers. We are far better off to recognize that the two aspects of the rural economy blended, and in fact were essential to one another. Farmers needed a subsistence component in order to ride out the ups and downs of market prices, and some market sales were necessary to provide for the family, not just for comforts of the moment but to aid in acquiring new farms for the next generation. Subsistence and commercial farming were inextricably interwoven in the eighteenth and nineteenth centuries, and the conception of a mixed farm reflects that fact.

We should also recognize that the market for farm goods was no more important to farmers than the market for land. Farmers needed to sell their products, but they also needed to buy and sell land. Provision for their children required it. Often they wished to sell land in hopes that the profits would enable them to buy more land elsewhere. If they stayed home, they had to raise the money to purchase more expensive land nearby. Either way, they were driven into the land market to give their children a start.

There was a land market in the colonies from the beginning, but when the open-handed seventeenth-century methods of disposing of land came to an end at the beginning of the eighteenth century, the market became virtually the only source of land. In time, as the population grew prodigiously, prices went up sharply. That new fact of life drove farmers into debt. They needed capital to acquire and develop new farms. Some could save for that purpose; many had to borrow. The precipitous rise in court cases reveals the growing presence of debt in many farmers' lives. That ominous reality altered their relationship to government. People may have been concerned about government actions before, but from this time on, farmers participated in politics as farmers. Men and women needed to defend their lands against the ravages of currency fluctuations, debt prosecutions, and foreclosures. The eighteenth century, therefore, saw the politicization of farm life.

I have written as if compelled to defend the eighteenth century against the unjust claims of the nineteenth century to a superior place in American agricultural history. That, of course, is not my intent. It is necessary, however, to displace conventions that have obscured our vision and to reconceive agricultural history so as to reflect the known realities of farm life.

Notes

1. John J. McCusker and Russell R. Menard, *The Economy of British America, 1607–1789* (Chapel Hill: University of North Carolina Press, 1985), 248; Stanley Lebergott, "Labor Force and Employment, 1800–1960," in *Output, Employment, and Productivity in the United States After 1800* (New York: Columbia University Press, 1966).

2. For an answer to these questions from another perspective, see Alan Kulikoff, "The Transition to Capitalism in Rural America," *William and Mary Quarterly* 46 (1989): 120–44.

3. Winifred Barr Rothenberg, *From Market-Places to a Market Economy: The Transformation of Rural Massachusetts, 1750–1850* (Chicago: University of Chicago Press, 1992), moves the transition back to the quarter century after the Revolution, as does James Henretta in "The Transition to Capitalism in America," in *The Transformation of Early America: Society, Authority, and Ideology,* eds., James Henretta, Michael Kammen, and Stanley Katz (New York: Alfred A. Knopf, 1991), 218–38. For the most conventional view, see Daniel P. Jones, *The Economic and Social Transformation of Rhode Island, 1780–1850* (Boston: Northeastern University Press, 1992).

4. David P. Szatmary, *Shays' Rebellion: The Making of an Agrarian Insurrection* (Amherst: University of Massachusetts Press, 1980), 16–17; Paul Boyer and Stephen Nissenbaum, *Salem Possessed: the Social Origins of Witchcraft* (Cambridge, Mass.: Harvard University Press, 1974), 86–109.

5. Percy Wells Bidwell, "Rural Economy in New England at the Beginning of the Nineteenth Century," Connecticut Academy of Arts and Sciences, *Transactions* 20 (1916); Christopher Clark, *The Roots of Rural Capitalism: Western Massachusetts, 1780–1860* (Ithaca, N.Y.: Cornell University Press, 1990); Charles Sellers, *The Market Revolution: Jacksonian America, 1815–1846* (New York: Oxford University Press, 1991), 4–6, 9–17.

6. Percy Wells Bidwell and John I. Falconer, *History of Agriculture in the Northern United States, 1620–1860* (Washington, D. C.: Carnegie Institution of Washington, 1925), 84 (quote), 115, 164–65 198.

7. Christopher Grasso, "The Experimental Philosophy of Farming: Jared Eliot and the Cultivation of Connecticut," *William and Mary Quarterly* 50 (July 1993): 516–18; G. E. Fussell, "The Farming Writers of Eighteenth-Century England," *Agricultural History* 21 (1947): 1–8.

8. Rothenberg notes the contrast of Bidwell and the later historians, *From Market-Places,* 32.

9. Szatmary, *Shays' Rebellion* is an extreme example.

10. This evaluation is implicit in James A. Henretta, "Families and Farms: Mentalite in Pre-Industrial America," *William and Mary Quarterly* 35 (1978): 3–32. Charles Sellers writes that subsistence culture "fostered family obligation, communal cooperation, and reproduction over generations of a modest comfort," *Market Revolution,* 5. Christopher Clark avoids the lament for deserted villages, and insists that farming in all its forms has always been a struggle, *Roots of Rural Capitalism,* 326. The older generation of scholars, with an opposite attitude, were more preoccupied with the question posed by Warren C. Scoville, "Did Colonial Farmers 'Waste' Our Land?" *Southern Economic Journal* 20 (1953): 178–81.

11. Clark, *Roots of Rural Capitalism,* 28–9; Michael Merrill, "Cash Is Good to Eat: Self-Sufficiency and Exchange in the Rural Economy of the United States," *Radical History Review* 4 (1977): 42–72; Jean-Christophe Agnew, "The Threshold of Exchange: Speculations on the Market," *Radical History Review* 21 (1979):

99–118. For a summary of the literature on the complicated question of use and exchange, see Kulikoff, " Transition to Capitalism," 124–26.

12. Clark, *Roots of Rural Capitalism*, 252–61, 304–9. For an analysis of wage labor in the final quarter of the eighteenth century, see James Henretta, "Transition to Capitalism in America," 218–38. For wage labor in Pennsylvania in the eighteenth century, see Paul G. E. Clemens and Lucy Simler, "Rural Labor and the Farm Household in Chester County, Pennsylvania, 1750–1820," in *Work and Labor in Early America*, ed., Stephen Innes, (Chapel Hill: University of North Carolina Press, 1988), 106–43; and Mary M. Schweitzer, *Custom and Contract: Household, Government, and the Economy in Colonial Pennsylvania* (New York: Columbia University Press, 1987), 34–56. The important question of farm labor in the eighteenth century is too large for the limited confines of this essay.

13. The pioneering work of Jackson T. Main, *The Social Structure of Revolutionary America* (Princeton, N.J.: Princeton University Press, 1965) attempted to put an evidential base under the idea of subsistence farmers, but many of Main's conclusions were based on the absence of large farms in a given region rather than any direct evidence of subsistence production. Main concludes that most of Delaware and New Jersey was made up of subsistence farms, a judgment that would be questioned today.

14. Richard L. Bushman, "Shopping and Advertising in Colonial America," in *Of Consuming Interests: the Style of Life in the Eighteenth Century*, eds. Cary Carson, Ronald Hoffman, and Peter J. Albert (Charlottesville: University Press of Virginia, 1994).

15. Carole Shammas, "How Self-Sufficient Was Early America," *Journal of Interdisciplinary History* 13 (1982–83): 247–72.

16. Carville V. Earle, *The Evolution of a Tidewater Settlement System: All Hallow's Parish, Maryland, 1650–1783* (Chicago: University of Chicago Press, 1975), 122–23; Thomas Tileston Waterman, *The Mansions of Virginia, 1706–1776* (Chapel Hill: University of North Carolina Press, 1946), 146.

17. Bettye Hobbs Pruitt, "Self-Sufficiency and the Agricultural Economy of Eighteenth-Century Massachusetts," *William and Mary Quarterly* 41 (1984): 333–64.

18. Rothenberg makes this distinction the heart of her argument in *From Market-Places*.

19. In "Transition to Capitalism," Henretta says that landowners became "aggressive entrepreneurs," who used their resources in a "calculating and risk-taking manner," 20–21, 229.

20. Henretta presents individual cases of risk-taking profit-seeking in "Transition to Capitalism," perhaps the best evidence we can hope for, but it would require many more, drawn from periods before and after the transition, to be wholly persuasive. Rothenberg critically assesses the evidence for a "moral economy" in New England in the eighteenth century and remains skeptical. Rothenberg, *From Market-Places*, 32–55.

21. Clark, *Roots of Rural Capitalism*, 76.

22. Daniel Vickers, one of the closest students of New England agriculture, has commented that "the distinction between production for use and production for sales was sometimes recognizable and sometimes not, but it was never a matter of significance." "Competency and Competition: Economic Culture in Early America," *William and Mary Quarterly* 47 (1990): 7.

23. For a discussion of subsistence requirements in New England, see Carolyn Merchant, *Ecological Revolution: Nature, Gender, and Science in New England* (Chapel Hill: University of North Carolina, 1989), 175–85.

24. Pruitt, "Self-Sufficiency and the Agricultural Economy,"340–48; and James T. Lemon, "Household Consumption in Eighteenth-Century America and Its Relationship to Production and Trade: The Situation among Farmers in Southeastern Pennsylvania," *Agricultural History 41* (1967): 59–70.

25. John T. Schlotterbeck, "Plantation and Farm: Social and Economic Change in Orange and Greene Counties, Virginia, 1716 to 1860" (Ph.D. diss., Johns Hopkins University, 1980), 381; Richard Sutch, "The Breeding of Slaves for Sale and the Westward Expansion of Slavery, 1850–1860," in *Race and Slavery in the Western Hemisphere: Quantitative Studies*, eds., Stanley Engerman and Eugene Genovese (Princeton, N.J.: Princeton University Press, 1975), 261–62.

26. Sellers, *Market Revolution*; Henretta, "Transition to Capitalism in America." For the South, where commercial agriculture was well established before the "transition" occurred, Henretta emphasizes the increase of wage hiring.

27. Darrett B. Rutman, *Winthrop's Boston: A Portrait of a Puritan Town, 1630–1649* (Chapel Hill: University of North Carolina Press, 1965), 179.

28. Karen J. Friedmann, "Victualling Colonial Boston," *Agricultural History* 47 (1973): 189–205.

29. On home markets, see Max George Schumacher, *The Northern Farmer and His Markets During the Late Colonial Period* (New York: Arno Press, 1975): 105–21.

30. Rutman, *Winthrop's Boston*, 184–87; Richard Pares, *Yankees and Creoles: The Trade between North America and the West Indies before the American Revolution* (Cambridge, Mass.: Harvard University Press, 1956).

31. Terry Lee Anderson, *The Economic Growth of Seventeenth-Century New England: A Measurement of Regional Income* (New York: Arno Press, 1975); William D. Miller, "The Narragansett Planters," *Proceedings of the American Antiauarian Society* (1934): 49115; Christian McBurney, "The South Kingstown Planters: Country Gentry in Colonial Rhode Island," *Rhode Island History* 45 (1986): 81–93; Bruce C. Daniels, "Economic Development in Colonial and Revolutionary Connecticut: An Overview," *William and Mary Quarterly* 37 (1980): 429–43.

32. Lucy Simler, "Tenancy in Colonial Pennsylvania: The Case of Chester County," *William and Mary Quarterly* 43 (1986): 558–59; Stephen Innes, *Labor in a New Land: Economy and Society in Seventeenth-Century Springfield* (Princeton, N.J.: Princeton University Press, 1983), xvi–xvii, 6–9.

33. James T. Lemon, *The Best Poor Man's Country: a Geographical Study of Early Southeastern Pennsylvania* (Baltimore: Johns Hopkins University Press, 1972), chap. 6; Sung Bok Kim, *Landlord and Tenant in Colonial New York: Manorial Society, 1664–1775* (Chapel Hill: North Carolina University Press, 1978), 158.

34. Robert D. Mitchell, *Commercialism and Frontier: Perspectives on the Early Shenandoah Valley* (Charlottesville: University Press of Virginia, 1977).

35. Lois Carr and Lorena S. Walsh, "The Planter's Wife: The Experience of White Women in Seventeenth-Century Maryland," *William and Mary Quarterly* 34 (1977): 562; Gloria L. Main, *Tobacco Colony: Life in Early Maryland, 1650–1720* (Princeton, N.J.: Princeton University Press, 1983), 73.

36. Robert Beverly, *The History and Present State of Virginia*, ed. David Freeman Hawke (1705; reprint, Indianapolis, Ind.: Bobbs-Merrill), 155.

37. Peter A. Coclanis, *The Shadow of a Dream: Economic Life and Death in the South Carolina Low Country, 1670–1920* (New York: Oxford University Press, 1989), 48–110; Rachel N. Klein, *The Unification of a Slave State: The Rise of the Planter Class in the South Carolina Backcountry, 1760–1808* (Chapel Hill: University of North Carolina Press, 1990), chap. 1; Richard R. Beeman, *The Evolution of the Southern Backcountry: A Case Study of Lunenburg County, Virginia, 1746–1832* (Philadelphia: University of Pennsylvania Press, 1984), 60–80; A. Roger Ekirch, *"Poor Carolina": Politics and Society in Colonial North Carolina, 1729–1776* (Chapel Hill: University of North Carolina Press, 1981), 30–33. Joyce Chapin argues that besides practicing market agriculture, planters in the lower South absorbed a capitalist and modernist ethic in *An Anxious Pursuit: Agricultural Innovation and Modernity in the Lower South, 1730–1815* (Chapel Hill: University of North Carolina Press, 1993).

38. Schlotterbeck, "Plantation and Farm," 30; Philip D. Morgan and Michael L. Nicholls, "Slaves in Piedmont Virginia," *William and Mary Quaterly* 46 (1989): 215, 217; Beeman, *Evolution of the Southern Backcountry*, 165.

39. Klein, *Unification of a Slave State*, chap. 1; Steven Hahn, *The Roots of Southern Populism and the Transformation of the Georgia Upcountry, 1850–1890* (New York: Oxford University Press, 1983), chap. 1.

40. Daniel Scott Smith has calculated that 20–30 percent of agricultural production was exported in 1710. "Malthusian-Frontier Interpretation of United States Demographic History before c. 1815" in *Urbanization in the Americas: The Background in Comparative Perspective*, eds., Woodrow Borah, Jorge Hardoy, and Gilbert A. Stelter (Ottawa: History Division, National History of Man, 1980), 15–24. Smith also argues that this proportion declined through the eighteenth century, but this was part of a trend continuing into the nineteenth century as the local market absorbed more and more of farm production. T. H. Breen argues that the sense of commercial exchange was strong enough to sustain an imagined community of buyers and sellers who acted politically in the nonimportation agreements. "Narrative of Commercial Life: Consumption, Ideology, and Community on the Eve of the American Revolution," *William and Mary Quarterly* 50 (1993): 471–501.

41. Clark, *Roots of Rural Capitalism*, and Rothenberg, *From Market-Places*, though coming to the problem from different perspectives, document the concrete changes.

42. Kulikoff, "Transition to Capitalism," 133, 140.

43. "Mixed farming," as an interpretive conception, derives from and depends on the subsistence and commercial polarity. "Mixed farming" implies a mixture of two distinct elements. But if we use a derivative term for interpretive purposes, we should not assume that in the farmers' minds the two elements separated. Farm records show them blending into a single operation.

44. Other historians have arrived at something near this same commonsense conclusion. Among them, McCusker and Menard, *Economy of British America*, 297–301; and Vickers, "Competency and Competition," 3–29.

45. The best explication is Vickers' "Competency and Competition." For the nineteenth-century South, see Gavin Wright, *The Political Economy of the Cotton South: Households, Markets, and Wealth in the Nineteenth Century* (New York: W. W. Norton, 1978), 62–74.

46. Charles Grant called the settlers of eighteenth-century Kent, Connecticut, "aggressive opportunists," and entitled one of his chapters "The Drive for Profits." Charles S. Grant, *Democracy in the Connecticut Frontier Town of Kent* (New York: W. W. Norton, 1961), 53–54, chap. 3.

47. Henretta, "Families and Farms." For the literature on the debate that ensued following Henretta'a article, see Kulikoff, "Transition to Capitalism," 124.

48. Bernard Bailyn, *Voyagers to the West: A Passage in the Peopling of America on the Eve of Revolution* (New York, Alfred A. Knopf, 1986), 246–48; Gregory Nobles, "Shays's Neighbors: The Context of Rebellion in Pelham, Massachusetts," in *In Debt to Shays: the Bicentennial of an Agrarian Rebellion*, ed., Robert A. Gross (Charlottesville: University Press of Virginia, 1993), 370, n. 20; J. Ritchie Garrison, *Landscape and Material Life in Franklin County, Massachusetts, 1770-1860* (Knoxville: University of Tennessee Press, 1991), 79–89; Thomas M. Truxes, *Irish-American Trade, 1660-1783* (New York: Cambridge University Press, 1988), 48, 109–13.

49. For family strategy on the frontier, see Gregory H. Nobles, "Breaking into the Backcountry: New Approaches to the Early American Frontier, 1750–1800," *William and Mary Quarterly* 46 (1989): 655–56; Alan Taylor, *Liberty Men and Great Proprietors: The Revolutionary Settlement on the Maine Frontier, 1760–1820* (Chapel Hill: University of North Carolina Press, 1990), chap. 3.

50. Jackson Turner Main, *Society and Economy in Colonial Connecticut* (Princeton, N.J.: Princeton University Press, 1985), 117; Lee Soltow, *Patterns of Wealthholding in Wisconsin Since 1850* (Madison: University of Wisconsin Press, 1971), 42, 46.

51. For the relationship between family values, debt, and market production in a later period, see Sue Headlee, *The Political Economy of the Family Farm: The Agrarian Roots of American Capitalism* (New York: Praeger, 1991); for eighteenth-

and nineteenth-century New England, see Merchant, *Ecological Revolutions*, 185–90, and Christopher Clark, "Economy and Culture: Opening Up the Rural History of the Early American Northeast," *American Quarterly* 43 (1991): 279–301. See also, David F. Weiman, "Families, Farms, and Rural Society in Pre-Industrial America," *Research in Economic History* 10 (1988): supplement.

52. William Cooper went to great effort to find markets for his purchasers, knowing they could never meet the annual 7 percent interest payment, much less repayment of the principle without a commercial crop. See Alan Taylor, *William Cooper's Town: Power and Persuasion on the Frontier of the Early Republic* (New York: Alfred A. Knopf, 1996): 102–10.

53. This fact is well documented in Lewis Cecil Gray, *History of Agriculture in the Southern United States to 1860* (Washington, D.C.: Carnegie Institution of Washington, 1933), and Bidwell and Falconer, *History of Agriculture in the Northern United States*. See also, Paul G. E. Clemens, *The Atlantic Economy and Colonial Maryland's Eastern Shore: From Tobacco to Grain* (Ithaca, N.Y.: Cornell University Press, 1980), 172–74; David C. Kingaman, "The Significance of Grain in the Development of the Tobacco Colonies," *Journal of Economic History* 29 (1969): 268–78.

54. For an illuminating explication of diversification in Pennsylvania, see Schweitzer, *Custom and Contract*, 57–79.

55. The rice plantations may have partially emulated the sugar islands in concentrating on their staple and purchasing food from inland planters. They were the exception on the North American continent. McCusker and Menard, *Economy of British America*, 183–84. For a summary of the literature on South Carolina self-sufficiency, see Coclanis, *Shadows of a Dream*, 147; and Philip D. Morgan, "The Development of Slave Culture in Eighteenth-Century Plantation America" (Ph.D. diss., University College London, 1977), 20–47.

56. For comments on the blend of use and exchange values, and for the best analysis of eighteenth-century rural cultural values see Vickers, "Competency and Competition."

57. Lois Green Carr, "Diversification in the Colonial Chesapeake: Somerset County, Maryland, in Comparative Perspective," in *Colonial Chesapeake Society*, eds., Lois Green Carr, Philip D. Morgan, and Jean B. Russo (Chapel Hill: University of North Carolina Press, 1988), 342–88; Clemens, *Atlantic Economy*, Chap. 6; Alan Kulikoff, *Tobacco and Slaves: The Development of Southern Cultures in the Chesapeake, 1680–1800* (Chapel Hill: University of North Carolina Press, 1986), 99–104.

58. Earle, *Evolution of a Tidewater Settlement System*, 122–23.

59. Lois Green Carr and Lorena S. Walsh, "Economic Diversification and Labor Organization in The Chesapeake, 1650–1820," in *Work and Labor in Early America*, ed., Innes, 181–82; Christine Daniels, "Gresham's Laws: Labor Management on an Early Eighteenth-Century Chesapeake Plantation," *Journal of Southern History* 54 (1997): 205–38.

74 RICHARD L. BUSHMAN

60. For a discussion of the relationship of markets and self-sufficiency, see Rothenberg, *From Market-Places,* 33, 46–48.

61. John Hebron Moore, *The Emergence of the Cotton Kingdom in the Old Southwest: Mississippi, 1770–1860* (Baton Rouge: Louisiana State University Press, 1988), 21–27; Alfred G. Smith, Jr., *Economic Readjustment of an Old Cotton State: South Carolina, 1820–1860* (Columbia: University of South Carolina Press, 1958), 53–111.

62. John Walker, "Diary," Virginia Historical Society, Richmond, and Southern Historical Collection, University of North Carolina, Chapel Hill: 27 Oct., 15 Nov., 7 Dec. 1825 ;15 Jan., 13 June,1827; 8 May 1829; 1 April, 9 Nov. 1833; 6 June, 2 Nov, 29 Nov 1834; 5 Nov. 1836. For an example of another farmer like Walker, see Philip N. Racine, ed., *Piedmont Farmer: The Journals of David Golightly Harris, 1855–1870* (Knoxville: University of Tennessee Press, 1990); and Vickers, *Farmers and Fishermen,* 207.

63. J. Ritchie Garrison finds this to be true for Franklin County, Massachusetts, in 1855 when commercial production was common. *Landscape and Material Life,* 45, 56, 60, 160.

64. Richard L. Bushman, "Opening the American Countryside," in *The Transformation of Early American History: Society, Authority and Ideology,* eds., James A. Henretta. Michael Kammen, and Stanley N. Katz (New York: Alfred A. Knopf, 1991), 239–56.

65. Bushman, "Opening the American Countryside," 239–56. For a different explanation of the end of self-sufficiency in the South, see Wright, *Political Economy of the Cotton South,* 164–76.

66. Hahn, *Roots of Southern Populism,* 150–51.

67. Joyce Appleby, "Commercial Farming and the 'Agrarian Myth' in the Early Republic," *Journal of American History* 68(1982): 833–49.

68. Jack Greene makes a similar argument in *Pursuits of Happiness: The Social Development of Early Modern British Colonies and the Formation of American Culture* (Chapel Hill: University of North Carolina, 1988), chaps. 3–4.

69. Sellers, *Market Revolution,* chap. 1.

70. For the use of this language in the Revolutionary period, see Richard L. Bushman, "Massachusetts Farmers and the Revolution," in *Society, Freedom, and Conscience: The Coming of the Revolution in Virginia, Massachusetts, and New York,* ed., Richard M. Jellison (New York: W. W. Norton, 1976), 77–124.

71. The rate of growth was not unprecedented; the colonies had grown even faster in the eighty years from 1630 to 1710, but beginning from a much smaller base. For population figures, see *Historical Statistics of the United States: Colonial Times to 1970* (Washington, D.C.: U. S. Government Printing Office, 1975), 1168.

72. McCusker and Menard, *Economy of British America,* chap. 10; Aaron Fogelman, "Migration to the Thirteen British North American Colonies: New Estimates," *Journal of Interdisciplinary History* 22 (Spring 1992): 691–710.

73. Bailyn, *Voyagers to the West,* chaps. 2, 3.

74. For overviews of this expansion and conflict from differing standpoints, see Ray Allen Billington, *Westward Expansion: A History of the American Frontier*. 2nd ed. (New York: Macmillan, 1960), 154–73, and Bernard Bailyn, *The Peopling of British North America: An Introduction* (New York: Alfred A. Knopf, 1986), 93–111; Edmund S. Morgan, "Conflict and Consensus in the American Revolution," in *Essays on the American Revolution*, eds., Stephen G. Kurtz and James H. Hutson (Chapel Hill: University of North Carolina Press, 1973), 297–302; Gordon S. Wood, *The Radicalism of the American Revolution* (New York: Alfred, A. Knopf, 1992), 124–29.

75. For a discussion of eighteenth-century growth rates, see James A. Henretta, "Wealth and Social Structure," in *Colonial British America: Essays in the New History of the Early Modern Era*, eds., Jack P. Greene and J. R. Pole (Baltimore: The Johns Hopkins University Press, 1984), 269–73.

76. Marc Egnal, "The Economic Development of the Thirteen Continental Colonies, 1720–1775, *William and Mary* Quarterly 32 (1975): 208–10.

77. Carville Earle and Ronald Hoffmann, "Staple Crops and Urban Development in the Eighteenth-Century South," *Perspectives in American History* 10 (1976): 5–78.

78. Simler, "Tenancy in Colonial Pennsylvania," 542–69; Lemon, *Best Poor Man's Country*, 94–95.

79. Rowland Berthoff and John M. Murrin, "Feudalism, Communalism, and the Yeoman Freeholder: The American Revolution Considered as a Social Accident," in *Essays on the American Revolution*, eds., Kurtz and Hutson, 256–88; Gregory A. Stiverson, *Poverty in a Land of Plenty: Tenancy in Eighteenth-Century Maryland* (Baltimore: The Johns Hopkins University Press, 1977); Willard F. Bliss, "The Rise of Tenancy in Virginia," *Virginia Magazine of History and Biography* 58 (1950): 427–41.

80. Kim, *Landlord and Tenant*, chap 8; Patricia U. Bonomi, *A Factious People: Politics and Society in Colonial New York* (New York: Columbia University Press, 1971), chap. 6.

81. Daniel M. Friedenberg, *Life, Liberty, and the Pursuit of Land: The Plunder of Early America* (Buffalo, N.Y.: Prometheus Books, 1992). The Dudley Council in New England was also notorious for large land grants made to favorites. For a brief discussion of this period of large patents, see Bernard Bailyn, *Peopling of British North America*, 65–72. For New York, Kim, *Landlord and Tenant*, 129–39. For the merging of the headright system into the pattern of large grants in Virginia, see Richard L. Morton, *Colonial Virginia: Westward Expansion and Prelude to Revolution, 1710–1763* (Chapel Hill: North Carolina University Press, 1960), 420–21, 539–46; W. Stitt Robinson, *The Southern Colonial Frontier, 1607–1763*, (Albequerque: University of New Mexico Press,1979), 80, 256, n. 25.

82. Clarence W. Rife, "Land Tenure in New Netherland," in *Essays in Colonial History Presented to Charles McLean Andrews By His Students* (New Haven: Yale University Press, 1931) 41–73. While Governor of New York, Edmund Andros

issued fifty acres for each member of a family in the Duke of York's claims in Delaware. William Penn later confirmed these grants. John A. Munroe, *Colonial Delaware: A History* (Millwood, N. Y.: KTO Press, 1978), 74, 90, 94, 114.

83. John Frederick Martin, *Profits in the Wilderness: Entrepreneurship and the Founding of New England Towns in the Seventeenth Century* (Chapel Hill: University of North Carolina Press, 1991).

84. Ibid., chap. 6; Roy H. Akagi, *The Town Proprietors of the New England Colonies: A Study of Their Development, Organization, Activities, and Controversies,1620–1770* (Philadelphia: University of Pennsylvania Press, 1924).

85. Richard L. Bushman, *From Puritan to Yankee: Character and the Social Order in Connecticut, 1690–1765* (Cambridge, Mass.: Harvard University Press, 1967), 75–82.

86. Stiverson, *Poverty in a Land of Plenty*, 2.

87. Munroe, *Colonial Delaware*, 218.

88. Morton, *Colonial Virginia*, 549–50.

89. Clemens, *Atlantic Economy*, 231; Kulikoff, *Tobacco and Slaves*, 132–33; Simler, "Tenancy in Colonial Pennsylvania," 560; Jackson Turner Main, *Society and Economy in Colonial Connecticut* (Princeton, N.J.: Princeton University Press, 1985), 206–7, 225, 377–78. Main believes that improvements as much as a shortage raised land prices.

90. The maps of rural population in 1760 and 1770 graphically portray the intensification of population east of the wall formed by the mountains and by the dangers on the western side. Lester J. Cappon, Barbara Bartz Petchenik, and John Hamilton Long, eds., *Atlas of Early American History: The Revolutionary Era, 1760– 1790* (Princeton, N.J.: Princeton University Press, 1976), 22–23. For a calculation of the crowding in Virginia, see David O. Percy, "Ax or Plow?: Significant Colonial Landscape Alteration Rate in the Maryland and Virginia Tidewater," *Agricultural History* 66 (Spring 1992): 69.

91. Toby Ditz, *Property and Kinship: Inheritance in Early Connecticut, 1750–1820* (Princeton, N.J.: Princeton University Press, 1986); Christopher M. Jedrey, *The World of John Cleaveland Family and Community in Eighteenth-Century New England* (New York: W. W. Norton, 1979), chap. 3.

92. Grant, *Democracy in the Connecticut Frontier Town of Kent*, 57–58; Richard L. Bushman, *Joseph Smith and the Beginnings of Mormonism* (Urbana: University of Illinois Press, 1984), 20–24; Jack P. Greene, "Independence, Improvement, and Authority: Toward a Framework for Understanding the Histories of the Southern Backcountry during the Era of the American Revolution," in *The Southern Backcountry during the American Revolution*, eds., Ronald Hoffman, Thad W. Tate, and Peter J. Albert, (Charlottesville: University Press of Virginia, 1985), 12–13; Robert A. Gross, *The Minutemen and Their World* (New York: Hill and Wang, 1976), 79–80. Gross mentions the township of Peterborough, New Hampshire, that was granted to petitioners by the Massachusetts General Court in the mid-eigh-

teenth century. For a clear explication of the farmer's life cycle in Pennsylvania, see Schweizer, *Custom and Contract*, 21–34.

93. Bushman, *From Puritan to Yankee*, 107–23.

94. Bruce H. Mann, *Neighbors and Strangers: Law and Community in Early Connecticut* (Chapel Hill: University of North Carolina Press, 1987), 40. For a similar change in New York, see Herbert A. Johnson, *The Law Merchant and Negotiable Instruments in Colonial New York, 1664–1730* (Chicago: Loyola University Press, 1963).

95. Mann, *Neighbors and Strangers*, 33; Bushman, *From Puritan to Yankee*, 297; Main, *Society and Economy in Colonial Connecticut*, 212, 215; Szatmary, *Shays' Rebellion*, 29.

96. Mary Schweizer concludes that most of the loans from the Pennsylvania loan office between 1724 and 1756 did not go toward land purchases. Although two-thirds of the borrowers were yeomen, most of them did not buy another farm with the money. However, she believes that the money went toward development that contributed to the large amounts of financial assets held by Pennsylvania farmers. Presumably, these assets then aided farmers in the purchase of land for their children. Schweizer, *Custom and Contract*, 82, 157, 160–63.

97. Bushman, *From Puritan to Yankee*, 107–21.

98. Because of their staple crops, Southern planters less often felt the pinch of debt, and so fewer complaints are heard; but debt hung over their farms too. Emory G. Evans, "Planter Indebtedness and the Coming of the Revolution in Virginia," *William and Mary Quarterly* 19 (1962): 511–33; Beeman, *Evolution of the Southern Backcountry*, 128; T. H. Breen, *Tobacco Culture: The Mentality of the Great Tidewater Planters on the Eve of Revolution* (Princeton, N.J.: Princeton University Press, 1985), 127–29; Kulikoff, *Tobacco and Slaves*, 127–31.

99. Debt repayment was not the only reason why farmers wanted currency. It facilitated every form of exchange. Schweizer, *Custom and Contract*, chap. 4.

100. Bushman, *From Puritan to Yankee*, 107–46; Klein, *Unification of a Slave State*, 125–135; Joseph Albert Ernst, *Money and Politics in America, 1755–1775: A Study in the Currency Act of 1764 and the Political Economy of Revolution* (Chapel Hill: University of North Carolina Press, 1973); John L. Brooke, *The Heart of the Commonwealth: Society and Political Culture in Worcester County, Massachusetts, 1713–1861* (New York: Cambridge University Press, 1989), 55–65, 101–6, 192–215.

101. Clark wishes to emphasize fundamental change more than I do, but he acknowledges the continuities, just as I acknowledge the change. *Roots of Rural Capitalism*, 273–80.

2

"SAY IT! NO IDEAS BUT IN THINGS":
TOUCHING THE PAST THROUGH
EARLY AMERICAN TECHNOLOGICAL HISTORY

Judith A. McGaw

"SAY IT!" orders a powerful, recurrent voice in *Paterson*, William Carlos Williams's epic poem. "Say it! No ideas but in things."[1] Williams' words offer an apposite motto for those writing America's early technological history. As exemplified in *Paterson*, looking at the concrete particulars of early American life can help us comprehend the complex modern landscape we inhabit. Behind the signs proclaiming "No Dogs Allowed At Large In This Park", Williams shows us "the ten houses Hamilton saw when he looked (at the falls!) and kept his counsel"; the nearby "human monster" visited by the curious George Washington, among others; and the famous Jacksonian era figure, Sam Patch, who became a national hero by "diving from cliffs and masts, rocks and bridges."[2]

The poet's mode of operation is, Williams tells us in his preface, "To make a start, out of particulars and make them general, rolling up the sum, by defective means."[3] And the list of particulars begins: "Paterson lies in the valley under the Passaic Falls."[4] That boisterous reality, with its industrial potential and entertainment possibilities, its beauties and dangers, and, above all, its roar echoing even in the poet's dreams – that reality is where the poet has to begin because it is where modern Paterson, New Jersey, began. What follows includes the Society for Useful Manufactures, the ethnically heterogeneous mill population of 1870, Sam Patch jumping to his death, other daredevils and drunkards walking tightropes over the falls, Hamilton's "great beast"– the common people – disporting itself in the park, and, yes, dogs sniffing the trees and scratching. Our task as historians of early American technology is similar: to orchestrate a selection of nearly forgotten realities so as to enable our

78

contemporaries to assess the present and imagine the future. We would do well, then, to heed the peremptory command of Williams's literary conscience: "Say it! No ideas but in things."

Such counsel especially suits technological historians, because technology is about things. It is not only about things, of course. But it remains true, as Brooke Hindle, early American technology's pioneering scholar, observed that

> the "things" of technology retain a primacy that does not adhere to the physical objects associated with science, religion, politics, or any intellectual or social pursuit. The means of technology are physical; the objectives of technology are also physical or material. Three-dimensional physical objects are the expression of technology – in the same way that paintings and sculpture are the expression of the visual arts. They call for some of the same attention and celebration that is accorded to works of art"[5]

Indeed, as Hindle has demonstrated elsewhere, American technology's early history provides compelling evidence of technology's fundamental kinship with the arts.[6]

So my argument in this essay begins with the assertion that, for studying an art, there is something to be learned from an artist. "Say it! No ideas but in things." Obeying this injunction poses an immediate dilemma for the historian – one summarized by the jarring apparent contradiction in Williams's phrase "ideas . . . in things." We customarily associate ideas with words – the medium in which history took root and the stuff of which historians still habitually fabricate their wares. As people most at home with words, historians are poorly prepared to see ideas in things. Certainly, those of us who deal in American technology's early history know that "the physical things of technology in many ways remain the ultimate source for the history of technology."[7] And yet, the chief limitation in early American technological history remains the same as when Hindle surveyed the field nearly thirty years ago: we remain insensitive to ideas in things.[8]

Three decades ago Hindle took pains to reassure literarily inclined historians that the study of things would not be intellectually impoverishing. "To begin with," he noted, "there is no simple difference or conflict between words and things – words do not represent ideas alone nor things mere material accomplishment."[9] His classic essay, "The

Exhilaration of Early American Technology," delineates many ways in which things can convey ideas and techniques whereby they can be made to disclose them.

Some of those techniques have borne impressive fruit. In particular, many of the results of material analysis applied to the history of manufacturing – industrial archaeology, that is – have been woven into a coherent, persuasive refiguring of early American technology's largest story: industrialization. By giving priority to archaeological evidence and surveying it broadly from early American water mills and charcoal iron plantations to twentieth-century factory organization and mining landscapes, Robert B. Gordon and Patrick M. Malone's new book, *The Texture of Industry*, makes the fullest and most persuasive case to date for the primacy of things in technological history.

Repeatedly the authors disclose the limitations of technological ideas expressed in documents. Sometimes written accounts mislead inadvertently, reflecting the inherent limitations of words or even drawings to convey a sense of three-dimensional objects, especially objects in motion. For example, the authors tell the story of Slater Mill Historic Site's reconstruction of a breast wheel to drive mill machinery. Like many early New England water wheels, this one needed to operate partially submerged during seasonal backwater. Although local excavation and study of surviving wheels elsewhere provided many clues, of necessity the wheel's designers derived some details for the reconstruction from literary evidence: Zachariah Allen's 1829 account of New England mill engineering and mechanics. Allen discussed the problem of backwater and mentioned the inclusion of valves in the water wheel buckets, but not in a manner that conveyed their form or importance to modern designers. Only when the new wheel's submerged wooden parts swelled to create tight joints were the designers forced by the wheel's faltering rotation to reread Allen. And only through creative experimentation with the object itself did they manage to rediscover the practical details of the feature Allen mentioned in general terms. How to construct waterwheel valves must have been common knowledge among American millwrights, so this example illustrates yet another limitation of written evidence: it is generally silent on issues its intended audience could be assumed to understand.[10]

Often, though, documents deliberately deceive. The most notable example is the litany of self-serving claims by various federal contractors and armory administrators that machine tools obviated the need for traditional metal working skills, such as filing, when producing interchangeable metal parts. Whereas scholarship depending principally on literary evidence has emphasized the achievements of inventors and entrepreneurs and the "deskilling" of workers, close study of numerous gun lock tumblers revealed that interchangeability was achieved only through skillful manipulation of hand tools by armory workmen. Indeed, Gordon and Malone marshal the techniques of archaeometry, including engineering analysis, study of surficial markings, and materials analysis, to give specificity to the much-used, but rarely defined term "skill." They transform "skill" from a word that manufacturers used to designate wage level and that workers deployed to protest change, into a series of detailed descriptions that specify the abilities demanded by particular tasks. For example, they recover novel aspects of dexterity introduced when workers accustomed to filing began the new task of filing to gauge. Having specified a skill, they can proceed to demonstrate that the progressive growth of that component of skill accompanied mechanization.[11]

These are substantial accomplishments. Any real progress in understanding the central drama of early American technological history – the transition from craft to industrial production – must now rest on what Gordon and Malone have told us. And yet, it seems to me that recognizing "ideas in things" means more than acknowledging the ability of artifacts, sites, and landscapes to set the written record straight. And it goes beyond the ability of things to offer better answers to questions derived from literary sources, be they Eli Whitney's claims to interchangeable parts manufacture, craftsmen's protests that machines deprived them of their skills, or Marx's and Marxist assertions concerning the deployment of machines in class conflict. These and other traditional historical issues certainly need to be put to material test, but such uses ultimately accord things a secondary place.

The notion of ideas in things raises another, more radical possibility: that things offer a set of questions more fundamental and potentially richer than those implicit in documents, at least for the historian of technology. Hindle suggests as much when he maintains:

> The greatest need is to stand at the center of the technology – on the inside looking out. Instead, we have usually looked at technology from the outside: through the eyes of science, economics, political reflec-

tions, social results, or literary antagonisms. There is no telling what
related factors and forces will appear once the historian develops . . .
insights from the center; it has hardly been tried.[12]

At this point, given the political history of technology studies, let me
issue an unequivocal disclaimer. I am not saying – nor was Hindle saying
– that we should turn away from social, economic, political, or cultural
history. And I am certainly not calling for a return to the deadening
internalism of hardware history or chronicles of invention. Moreover,
since there is nothing inherently conservative or consensus-minded in a
materially centered history of technology, I am not suggesting that we
ignore what Hindle called technology's "dark side"– the costs inherent
in technological change.[13] As with documents, what one sees in things
depends on the eye of the beholder.

It also depends on the fingertip, the nose, the ear, and the tongue.
Perhaps the most radical aspect of seeking ideas in things is that it involves us in sensuous history. If that is where the history of early
American technology needs to go, then let us make a start. But where
might we begin such an adventure? And how should we proceed if we are
to give things the first word?

I found an initial guidepost in Hindle's provocatively entitled essay
"How Much Is a Piece of the True Cross Worth?" in which he notices
the "very important, if not transcendent, folk wisdom implicit in the
popular value accorded relics of the past. . . . They answered a deep
human need to reach beyond abstraction and myth to reality . . . to touch
the past. . . ." Whereas language is "linear, progressive, and logical . . . life
is complex, multidimensional, instantaneous, and often illogical." This
essential dichotomy, Hindle argues, is magnified in the modern world
where we are "separated more firmly from the realities" of life than were
our ancestors.[14] Similarly, Hindle observes, historians' growing use of
social scientific models, while granting intellectual advantages, comes at
the cost of increased abstraction. Acknowledging the power of abstraction to reduce illogic and irrationality, he also points to the risks.
Ultimately, "the order and rationality achieved are useful only if the
abstractions of language are penetrated by direct knowledge of life's
complex multidimensional and instantaneous character. Abstractions are
useful only when related to whatever can be found of 'the real thing.'"[15]
"This, he concludes, "is the important and valid insight which folk
culture expresses in placing high value upon not only the true cross and

the true sword of George Washington but upon the sharecropper's cabin and the manacles of a slave."[16]

The particulars inventoried in Hindle's testimonial to folk wisdom pointed me in the right direction. Tangible reality is inherently local and unique. And my locality placed me an easy walk away from one of America's "true crosses"– Independence Hall. I decided to join the tourists and see what people reaching out to touch the past could tell me about ideas in things.

Initially the encounter reminded me how deeply resistant conventional history is to the ideas in things. The park service guide, a well-prepared, enthusiastic, and hard working former history major, was committed to conveying the "important" political significance of what happened in Independence Hall in the late eighteenth century. For him, then, the objects around us served as a stage setting, a backdrop for a lecture, rather like the illustrations in most history books. Visitors also showed the adverse effects of prolonged exposure to conventional history in the nature of the questions they asked and the observations they offered. Then a small, restless boy piped up: "Where does that door go?" he demanded. "And that one?" The reedy young voice posed the question again in each room we entered and elicited brief, specific answers. Some doors led to other rooms, some afforded exits, and still others led nowhere, They were false doors, there to supply symmetry.

The implications of this exchange were underscored in my visit next door, to Congress Hall. The ranger there was free from the demands made by continuous tours; I was his only audience. I disclosed the general nature of my mission and was rewarded with a discursive account of our surroundings, including the likelihood that the reconstructed seating arrangement was incorrect. The semicircular benches had probably been horseshoe-shaped and two additional aisles had divided the benches about where the straight sides of the horseshoe met the curved section. As the ranger's hand indicated the location of the aisles, he pointed directly toward a doorway currently accessible only by a highly circuitous route from most seats. Not only would the revised arrangement ease movement, but also an aisle leading to the inaccessible door would accord it a treatment balancing that of the hall's other doorway: a symmetry, that is.[17]

Here at the nation's birthplace, then, things conveyed several ideas so obvious that they are easily overlooked. First, they reiterate the importance builders and their patrons placed on symmetry, balance – a value that could outweigh economic or functional considerations. Both in structures and in other eighteenth-century technologies such as furniture, clothing, and the implements of everyday life, we can begin by noticing that pervasive symmetry, rather than taking it for granted. What constraints did the assumption of symmetry impose on early American technologists? How did it foster or restrict invention? In what situations did technologists feel free to violate the imperative? Did the bilateral symmetry of the things around the founding fathers promote or reinforce a preference for political balance? In other words, in what senses did Enlightenment ideas reside in things?

It is even easier to miss the other obvious idea – the one that the visiting child called to my attention: doors serve to lead us somewhere. What was it like to move through eighteenth-century doorways? Although here and in other eighteenth-century park structures a few doors led me into entrance halls or passageways, most doors provided relatively sharp transitions from room to room or from inside to outside. This simple fact reminds us that technologies – doors, for example – have consequences that depend on the context in which they are used. Most technological history now focuses on *social context,* a laudable corrective to the field's earlier preoccupation with the heroic inventor. But looking at things, especially early American things, reminds us that technologies also function in a physical context.[18] Sometimes, as with the doors in Independence Park, the relevant context is the surrounding technology – the other components of the building in this case. As often, as Gordon and Malone demonstrate, the context is material, but natural, although always mediated through people's selective perception of nature.[19]

Walking through other historic buildings that have been restored and furnished by the park service to suggest their nineteenth-century uses, notably the modest, Quaker Todd House and the spacious and elegant Bishop White House, led me to develop further the idea of what one might term the kinesthetic significance of such early American technologies as buildings, furniture, and furniture arrangement. What would it be like to move through these spaces on a daily basis? How easily could one come and go to the "necessary," to a neighborhood shop, or simply out for a breath of fresh air? All of these buildings were densely inhabited by late nineteenth- or twentieth-century standards, so how freely might one have moved? How much did small rooms, few doorways, and steep, narrow stairways constrain movement, prompting inhabitants to shorten their steps, narrow their gestures, or stand very erect? Whether one moved or stayed still, did the crowded quarters accustom eighteenth-century Philadelphians to more or less continuous awareness of other people – sensing their body heat, brushing against their clothing, smelling their sweat? How might such tactile consciousness and movement patterns have differed between women and men, given their different dress and their responsibilities for different activities? How might they have differed for children? For servants? For slaves? What do the physical barriers that guided and shaped people's movement and relative proximity add to our understanding of eighteenth-century work? And, finally, what of the odors, temperature differences, and sounds that moved more readily than people between adjoining rooms or between indoors and out? How do such considerations help us understand the designs and locations chosen for the most technologically complex parts of eighteenth-century residential building: the kitchen, the cellar, and the necessary?

Walking around Independence National Historical Park, I encountered another surviving eighteenth-century technology – cobblestone pavement – that raised additional kinesthetic issues. Even in sturdy, comfortable, modern hiking boots, walking on cobblestone transmits repeated, unpredictable, uneven stress from the sole of the foot to the ankle, knee, and hip. The common eighteenth-century alternative to cobblestones – rutted dirt surfaces, especially when frozen in winter, offer much the same experience, as do dirt roads in which split logs or boards have been placed to protect the surface.[20] Did habitually walking over such uneven surfaces act to strengthen people's leg muscles, tendons, and joints or to wear them out earlier? How did the transmission of these shocks affect the health of their spines? Did it predispose them to early cervical and lumbar arthritis – a disease archaeologists commonly document when examining skeletons of prehistoric and colonial-era Native Americans presumed to have had arduous lives?[21] And how did the effects differ for those – slaves, servants, and the very poor – who carried heavy burdens over these surfaces? Did more expensive and fashionable shoes and boots make a salutary difference? Or did such footwear merely attest to the ability of the wearer to command the use of a horse, carriage, or sedan chair?

These and similar questions suggest the sort of ideas that can emerge from things when we look and wonder: what is it like to walk through that door? To use that tool? To wear that garment? They are the sorts of commonplace experiences contemporary writers felt no need to record. And they are the sorts of realities modern Americans are likely to miss given our relatively sedentary lifestyles and the limited kinesthetic stimulation associated with most modern work. Moreover, walking and symmetry are the sorts of pervasive aspects of life that it is easy to assume rather than to examine. Thus, historians have repeatedly observed that the eighteenth-century city was a walking city, but they remain silent as to how eighteenth-century bodies might have felt after a day, or a lifetime, of walking through its buildings or over its roadways.

A final set of kinesthetic issues emerges only when we are allowed to handle things or talk with employees of early American village, house, or farmstead restorations, people who work with early American tools. The arduousness of housework performed with heavy and cumbersome wooden or cast iron implements; the physically stressful repetitive motion entailed in many household and craft activities; the bending and stooping required to labor at an open hearth – each conveys ideas about traditional manufacture that differ greatly from those romanticized by the arts and crafts movement or celebrated in colonial revival images and rhetoric. They complicate the simplistic arguments of those who envision the technological changes of the nineteenth century as entailing unmitigated loss for workers or the creation of Victorian housework and housewives as the nadir of woman's relationship to technology. Things can lead us to wonder whether eighteenth-century women were generally more muscular, and if so, whether that meant that they were also more physically fit or whether, instead, their anatomy bore the marks of overworking particular parts of their bodies, especially their favored sides. Ironically, given the physical demands implied by early American tools and the likelihood that such arduous and skillful manual tasks were done primarily with the more dextrous hand, the era in which people placed a premium on bilateral symmetry in their surroundings may have been the epoch in which the symmetry implicit in the human body was most distorted. If so, were these phenomena related?[22]

Manipulation of early tools or observing their use also suggests how much room they left for error, increasing the risk of injury or of shoddy products or both. Of course, the aspect of eighteenth-century craft production least evident through surviving objects is the probable ubiquity of poorly made things. Fortunately, industrial archaeology offers a partial corrective to this bias. For example, whereas we now take craft production to mean high quality, analysis of the iron used to make various eighteenth- and early nineteenth-century artifacts exposes the unpredictable quality that must have proven fatal or crippling to many users of firearms, boilers, or bridges, to cite a few obvious examples. Although the unexpected failure of wrought iron kitchen implements or domestic hardware may have resulted merely in a spoiled meal or a door hanging ajar in wintry weather, such experiences also need to be part of the era's technological history. Instead, because we have failed to make things integral to early American technological history, we have implicitly generalized the survival of a few colonial artifacts into a presumption that all traditional goods possessed superior durability.[23]

Durability, symmetry, ease of movement – all are but facets of a larger issue for early American technological history: the issue of quality. Things make the idea of quality visible; inherent in the experience of being surrounded by the things of the past is the sense that life was once qualitatively different. As with our view of craft and household labor, our failure to incorporate things in our studies has generally resulted in a romanticized view of craft and household labor's products. Compounding the dilemma is the fact that industrialization emphasized *quantity* production. Thus, scholarly assessments of industrialization have been couched principally in quantitative terms. By contrast, our view of the industrial revolution's qualitative results has not advanced much beyond quoting the conflicting and self-serving claims of craftsmen, inventors, and manufacturers.

Things offer us a touchstone for identifying quality. They embody the genuine, if partial, reality behind that vague term as it was manifest in objects produced from the era of craft production through the transition to industrial manufacture. And, fortunately, we will not have far to look if we want guidance in appraising that reality. Unlike historians, student of material culture, especially those focusing on "workmanship," have been quite creative in probing things for what they reveal of the manner and outcomes of craft and industrial production. They have effectively laid to rest many an arts and crafts inspired myth, including the image of craft production as inherently freer, more creative, and more certain to result in diverse, individualized work. His-

torians have much to learn from them, but they have been highly
resistant to learning it.[24]

Historians can hardly be blamed for begging the question of quality;
the qualitative significance of the transition from craft and household to
factory production is exactly the sort of complex, multifaceted, human-
istic inquiry that those of us who embraced social scientific approaches
hoped to avoid. But it is the sort of question that becomes inescapable
when we begin to look at things. Take, for example, things made of
wood, the quintessential material of early American technology.[25] To the
modern eye and fingertip, accustomed to the common use of fiberboard
and veneer, solid hardwood furnishings or implements apparently testify
to the higher quality craftsmanship assured. Yet the very abundance of
wooden items urges caution.

Once we begin to scrutinize wooden things, they begin to disclose
a different grammar of quality. At best – and it is worth reiterating that
the best most often survives – wood workers evidently thought not in
terms of wood, but in terms of oak and maple, white pine and ebony.
Their qualitative concerns included relative hardness and tensile
strength, comparative weight and fire resistance, as well as more super-
ficial differences such as beauty of grain, or color, or capacity for high
finish that we customarily associate with high quality wood work. In the
wooden age, then, high quality wood was specific to the task. Moreover,
for some tasks wood was qualitatively inferior, whatever visually pleasing
qualities we may attribute to surviving items. So, for example, the
housewife might have preferred churns that were easier to clean, buckets
that weighed less, and storage vessels less prone to retain food odors.[26]

Like symmetry, ease of movement, and durability, choice of material
is precisely the sort of qualitative concern so obvious that only an intimate acquaintanceship with things forces us to notice it. Robert Friedel
highlights the obviousness in his formulation: "Everything Is Made from
Something." He also attests to the material genesis of such an insight.
He reports,

> I stumbled across this truth while working on the Smithsonian
> Institution exhibit "A Material World." Anyone who has worked on
> large, complicated exhibits . . . will appreciate this scene: A number of
> us were gathered over lunch and beginning to ask whether this exhibit
> made any sense, whether it had a theme. A number of statements were
> proposed, but somehow none of them seemed to the point or suf-

ficiently comprehensive. That's when I came up with this statement: Everything is made from something. No one could put a hole in this statement, nor could they claim it was not encompassing. I detected, however, the lingering (if unspoken) thought that no one knew what it meant.[27]

Friedel's concluding phrase is as suggestive as his axiom is true: we don't know what it means. We don't know what it implies to say that people choose particular materials from which to fabricate things, what to make of the fact that both our world and that of the eighteenth century present an indescribably complex surface as a result. Nor do we know what it signifies to say that eighteenth-century people's everyday activities entailed patterns of movement very different from ours. To be more precise, these observations cannot be reduced to succinct conclusions – not as long as we remain close to things. They can't because things force us to reckon with complexity; they preclude our simplifying the assessment of quality by confining it along a single dimension.

This is precisely the sort of idea we are forced to admit if we persist in our encounter with things: the qualitative aspects of life are hard to sum up, weigh and measure, nail down, pinpoint. "How did the quality of life change as America industrialized?" is a short question, but it requires a very long, complex answer if we are true to the material things from which the question emerges. Indeed it is almost beyond expression. As Hindle reminds us language is "linear, progressive, and logical," but things, like the life of which they are a part, are "complex, multidimensional, instantaneous, and often illogical."[28]

Almost beyond expression, but not quite. Certainly the qualities of early American objects, and of the life and work they suggest, defy expression in abstract scholarly language. But the evocative language of the poet, the historian-essayist's poetic cadences, the language appropriate to history practiced as a humanity – that language offers a possible voice. So we can either keep evading our responsibility to examine the changing quality of life or we can, like Williams, "make a start, out of particulars and make them general, rolling up the sum, by defective means"[29] And admitting the defectiveness of the means is part of it – not pretending to be able to express it all, but starting with a fragment.

Walking around Independence National Historic Park, I heard a number of sounds, some of them evoking the auditory quality of eighteenth-century life, others offering contrasting twentieth-century intrusions. On most adjacent streets, the cloppety clop of horses' hooves striking pavement echoes alongside the mechanical whine of internal combustion engines and the shrill artificial shriek of brakes, sirens, and antitheft devices. A similar irregular eighteenth-century beat might be heard in the thump of the hand press, or flail, or loom, while the modern workplace resounds with the synthetic beeps of office automation or the deafening roar of heavy equipment. At the same time, the irregular beat of the hand wielded hammer, of human speech and breathing, of the listeners' own heartbeat persist through the centuries. And yet, I bring less awareness to these persistent natural voices here in the modern city than I do when visiting a historic restoration or vacationing in the country. The car horns, jack hammers, and boom box assaults of rap music arrest my conscious hearing. Perhaps the eighteenth-century colonist also heard more clearly the strident sound: the animal cries from the shambles, for example.

Alongside the promiscuous auditory offering that we and our ancestors are or were subjected to, and of which we are and were only partially conscious – alongside these, and perhaps shaping the ear's willingness to hear and the brain's ability to interpret, are and were more formal listening experiences – musical concerts, for example. The harpsichord upstairs at Independence Hall and the tape recorded harpsichord music played there serve as reminders of a profound technological transformation taking place in this realm as well. The visible signs of this revolution are the new eighteenth-century instruments: the pianoforte originated early in the century and had largely replaced the clavichord and harpsichord by 1800, introducing a range in the volume and duration of tone that was utterly novel to listeners. The harp and clarinet joined the orchestra during the same era, while various stringed and brass instruments assumed their modern forms.

Music sounded different when it issued from these new tools of the trade. It also sang to new rules. Since the late seventeenth century, keyed instruments had been tuned to the modern scale or "equal temperament," permitting through its mathematically regular intervals a rich palette of harmonies, but simultaneously downplaying earlier music's emphasis on melody. Regular, mechanical beat had come to characterize its rhythms, whereas earlier plainsong had sounded the irregular beat of speech. By the early nineteenth century this trend reached its logical conclusion; the invention of the metronome demonstrated that clock-work could govern music as well as other human endeavors.[30]

Early music now sounds almost as alien as the melodies of South Asia. It sounds a good deal less rich, less full, less interesting than our music. That is one set of qualitative assessments. Some new age composers maintain, and some experiments in the realm of music therapy confirm, that the drone, melody, and irregular rhythms of earlier music confer both physiological and emotional benefits – as its Greek progenitors had intended.[31]

Has the auditory quality of modern life improved or declined? Is its diversity adequate compensation for its deadening volume and bone-chilling pitches? Have the model cadences of its music taught us to tolerate an unhealthy intensity and regularity elsewhere in our auditory environment? These are hard questions with no simple answers.

Has the quality of everyday life improved as a result of the technological changes that separate us from our eighteenth-century ancestors? A real answer to that materially rooted question cannot emerge from numbers or documents, although they may offer an occasional corrective observation. To say anything very meaningful about quality, we must keep a firm hold on the things that allow us to touch the past – and taste and smell and hear it as well. Quality of life is no abstraction. If we care about life's quality, historians of technology need to say our ideas in things.

Notes

The author wishes to thank Mary Kelley, Pat Malone, and Jean Silver-Isenstadt for comments on earlier versions of this work.

1. William Carlos Williams, *Paterson* (New York: New Directions, 1948), 14, 18.

2. Ibid., 77, 18–19, 25.

3. Ibid., 11.

4. Ibid., 14.

5. Brooke Hindle, *Technology in Early America: Needs and Opportunities for Study* (Chapel Hill: University of North Carolina Press, 1966), 10.

6. See especially Brooke Hindle, *Emulation and Invention* (New York: New York University Press, 1981).

7. Hindle, *Technology in Early America*, 10.

8. There are other limitations as well, but many of them are addressed effectively in Judith A. McGaw, ed., *Early American Technology: Essays in the History of Making and Doing Things from the Colonial Era to 1850* (Chapel Hill: University of North Carolina Press, 1994), see especially my "Introduction: The Experience of Early American Technology," 1–15 and Nina E. Lerman, "Books on Early American Technology, 1966–1991," 358–429. The availability of this recent overview of scholarship in the field enables me to concentrate my attention here on the single area that seems to me most promising for the future of the field. Since according centrality to objects in technological history has provoked considerable controversy and, I believe, considerable confusion over the years, giving full attention to this issue seems warranted.

9. Hindle, *Technology in Early America*, 10.

10. Robert B. Gordon and Patrick M. Malone, *The Texture of Industry: An Archaeological View of the Industrialization of North America* (New York: New York University Press, 1994), 17–20.

11. Gordon and Malone, *Texture of Industry*, 24–32, 38–41, 373–88. See also, Robert S. Gordon, "Who Turned the Mechanical Ideal into Mechanical Reality?" in *Technology and Culture* 29 (1988): 744–88.

12. Hindle, *Technology in Early America*, 24–25.

13. On the "dark side" controversy and some of the other political issues surrounding Hindle's earlier writings see Robert C. Post, "Technology in Early America: A View from the 1990s," in *Early American Technology*, ed., McGaw, 16–39. See also, David A. Hounshell, ed., *The History of American Technology: Exhilaration of Discontent?* (Wilmington, Del., 1984).

14. Brooke Hindle, "How Much Is Piece of the True cross Worth?" in *Material Culture and the Study of American Life*, ed., Ian M. G. Quimby (New York: Henry Francis duPont Winterthur Museum by W. W. Norton, 1978), 5, 10–11, 5.

15. Ibid., 11. Similarly, Gordon and Malone, *Texture of Industry*, 5, allude to the separation of contemporary American children from the experience of production, and Williams, *Paterson*, includes recurrent images of loss of voice through loss of concrete language.

16. Ibid.

17. The current arrangement, I was told, derived from a newspaper sketch featuring an altercation in Congress Hall. This is worth mentioning because, although a picture may be worth a thousand words, it is not necessarily more accurate than those words. And a picture of a thing is no substitute for the thing itself.

18. The point may be more important for early American technologies because, unlike more recent technologies, they were probably less often created as part of a system of things. The issue deserves closer attention, however, because the difference may be central to a full assessment of the long-term consequences of technological change. It is, of course, also true that social history might be

considerably enhanced by greater attentiveness to things – by recognizing the physical as integral to the social context.

19. See especially the central section of Gordon and Malone, *Texture of Industry*, 55–223, entitled "Industrial Landscapes," although an environmental perspective in the broadest sense informs the entire work.

20. These observations are based on substantial experience hiking on trails in various states of maintenance as well as on abandoned and currently used dirt roads and lumber roads.

21. John L. Cotter, Daniel G. Roberts, and Michael Parrington, *The Buried Past: An Archaeological History of Philadelphia* (Philadelphia: University of Pennsylvania Press, 1992), 23.

22. My sense is that these phenomena were, indeed, related – that things betray the inherent asymmetry that underwrote the apparent symmetry of eighteenth-century culture. Profound asymmetry of class, race, and gender is, for example, evident throughout the documents drafted in Independence Hall – hardly surprising given the characteristics of those who enunciated enlightenment ideas in that era. It seems likely that the high status accorded to symmetry reflected its comparative rarity and its association with high social status. Thus, only the colonial and early national era elite, whose bodies were not distorted by arduous labor and/or deprivation, could approximate the ideal symmetry of human form that the Greek revival celebrated.

23. A sense of the uneven quality of the craft worker's products is conveyed by handling and observing the various pieces of paper on which colonial and early national era documents are written. Because paper is preserved, not for its intrinsic qualities, but for what is written on its surface or for sentimental reasons, paper's variation in quality has been better preserved for those who care to observe it. Although my fingertips had recorded this data during my earlier study of the paper industry, I had not thought of it as a counter-example until Jim Green of the Library Company pointed out that books, for similar reasons, are often preserved irrespective of the quality of their paper and bindings.

24. See especially David Pye, *The Nature and Art of Workmanship* (Cambridge, Eng.: Cambridge University Press, 1968); and Philip D. Zimmerman, "Workmanship as Evidence: A Model for Object Study," *Winterthur Portfolio* 16 (1981): 283–307. Again, Gordon and Malone are notable exceptions in their attentiveness to workmanship.

25. Its centrality is suggested both by Gordon and Malone's choice of the title, "Wood and Water," for the section they devote to the resource base of early American manufacturing and by Brooke Hindle's two major collections of articles on early American technology, *America's Wooden Age* and *The Material Culture of the Wooden Age*.

26. Although I had the chance to view it only after drafting this text, many of the issues surrounding craft production, woodworking, and quality are addressed

with exceptional clarity in Colonial Williamsburg's exhibit, "Tools: Working Wood in 18th-Century America."

27. Robert Friedel, "Some Matters of Substance" in *History from Things: Essays on Material Culture*, eds., Steven D. Lubar and W. David Kingery (Washington, D.C.: Smithsonian Institution Press, 1993), 42–43.

28. Hindle, "True Cross," 5.

29. Williams, *Paterson*, 11.

30. It is hardly coincidental that the same poetic movement, Imagism, that echoes in Williams's phrase "no ideas in things," also called for poetry that sang to the rhythm of speech, not "to the rhythm of the metronome." Essentially this movement was a rebellion against romanticism, which, in music, had taken full advantage of all the new eighteenth-century developments discussed above.

31. For one provocative overview of the physical and emotional consequences of the changing auditory environment see Kay Gardner, *Sounding the Inner Landscape: Music as Medicine* (Stonington, Maine: Caduceus Publications, 1990). My thanks to Tom Waldman for explaining a number of the changes in early modern music in terms that I could comprehend.

3

"NO TOWNS OF ANY CONSEQUENCE?":
THE LOST URBAN HISTORY OF THE COLONIAL CHESAPEAKE

Christine Daniels

D
ESPITE THE EFFORTS of a number of historians during the last twenty-five years, we still do not know much about the process of regional settlement and urban systems in the Anglo-American colonies.[1] Probably the area that has been most successfully mapped, both geographically and economically, is the Chesapeake region between Philadelphia and Richmond, as far west as the Shenandoah Valley. Even in this region, however, our knowledge of the settlement and urbanization process is incomplete. The study of colonial towns includes many fields of inquiry; townsiting, for example, has raised a number of questions.[2] Many historians have examined the economic development of urban places; fewer have been concerned specifically with urban decline, although it remains a subtext in many studies of economic development.[3] Historians have also researched town design and architecture and the cultural meaning of spatial layout.[4] Many scholars have been intrigued by the increasing economic and social amenities towns offered to their citizens, but generally their inquiries have touched upon urbanization only tangentially.[5] Others have discussed the political processes and interchange between towns and townships.[6] Finally, an intriguing field for inquiry might be town morphology – the changes in the appearance and urban zones of a town over time, that might be best approached through visual sources – maps and depictions of colonial towns.[7]

As this discussion and the accompanying notes indicate, historians of urbanization and urbanism, more than many others, rely on the construction of models to help explain historical processes. The models they use, although they purport to be ahistorical, are in fact based heavily on historical examples, which then color the model itself. While the models are useful, therefore, they can and frequently are given too much weight as "objective" descriptions against which historical examples of urbanization are examined and, unfortunately, judged.

Many of these models contain two implicit presuppositions. The first is that only cities deemed "successful" in nineteenth and twentieth-century terms may be used to construct models for eighteenth-century urban development. Philadelphia or New York, therefore, become the models by which other instances of eighteenth-century urbanization are evaluated. This approach is teleological. It also effectively eliminates the study of hundreds of socioeconomic regions that developed villages, towns and even small cities, which were later eclipsed by metropolises like New Orleans, St. Louis, Baltimore and others.

The second presupposition, a corollary of the first, is that urban places did not exist in the colonies south of Pennsylvania. The literature that espouses this theory maintains that the production of a staple crop would mitigate against nucleated settlements, and that nucleated settlements should have been the norm.[8] The New England "town studies" of the 1960s and 1970s reinforced this view. Valuable as they were, none of the town studies concerned the economics of an urban process. Instead, their authors used town records as a logical and organized way to pose questions about politics, family structures, inheritance or land speculation.[9] The "town" records were, in fact, not those of urban places, but of political entities, similar to southern counties or townships. The church records that supported them were those of individual congregations. While more recent studies have examined the urban process and the development of economic markets in New England, the town studies emphatically did not.[10] Nonetheless, they created a vision of the seventeenth-century English colonies in which urban places *should* have existed from the beginning of settlement, whether or not they served any economic functions as towns, rather than as congregations or political entities. Thus, the New England studies, although they did not advance such queries, contributed to such illposed questions as "Why were there no towns in the colonial South?" One might answer "Why would we call a few straggling houses grouped around a church a 'town'?"

In fact, we now know more about urbanization in the colonial upper south – Virginia, Maryland, North Carolina and southern Pennsylvania – than we do about any other single colonial region. Unfortunately, this knowledge has not generally informed historians's perceptions of the urban process.[11] While colonial historians continue to ignore towns in the

Chesapeake, moreover, their neglect has fueled a great debate in nineteenth-century historical literature – the debate over the rural "transition to capitalism."

Much of this debate, as Richard Bushman points out in his essay in this volume, centers on the extension of markets into the countryside during the late eighteenth and nineteenth centuries.[12] Participants in the discussion have tried to frame it as an argument about the progress of market production in the colonies and later the United States as a whole. But a moment's reflection reveals that, in colonial terms, that contention must be false. The masters of great sugar, rice and tobacco plantations did not sit down each night to a hearty stew made solely from the products of their own farms; they participated, from the inception of the colonies, in a far-flung imperial market as they shipped produce to London, Bristol and Glasgow. The debate about farmers' failure to participate in an international market, therefore, relies on a model based heavily in New England and a few areas of the Middle Colonies.

At the same time, historians have long accepted the presence of small, very local markets for exchange in the countryside. The debate about the transition to capitalism in the nineteenth century, therefore, is as Bushman indicates, a debate, not about the presence of markets in general, but the presence of a particular type of market. We might call this a regional market, one midway in size between an imperial and a local market, where the development and penetration of stores into the countryside created market opportunities for middling and small farmers. Not surprisingly, many of these stores operated at embryonic urban places – villages and crossroads, mill complexes and iron plantations.[13]

This essay will address questions of town siting, market development and urban economic growth and decline in the colonial Chesapeake. In it, I propose to examine the process of settlement and economic differentiation in a single county in Maryland – Kent – from 1650 to 1810. This county was founded in 1648 as a tobacco outpost in the first British empire, but evolved over the next two centuries into an area in which the cultivation of wheat and other crops became essential. This change integrated Kent into a region – a very widespread region – where the economy exerted pressure in two different directions. Its reliance on tobacco pulled it toward British merchants, slavery and economically integrated plantations. Its reliance on wheat pulled it toward other European cities and New World outposts (notably the British West

Indies), colonial merchants, free and short-term bound labor, and towns, villages and crossroads.

The tobacco economy of the first British Empire was based on dispersed marketing techniques, on relatively little product processing, and on long-term bound labor – either indentured servants or slaves. Before the late seventeenth century, the economies of Virginia and Maryland were built almost exclusively on tobacco. The weed was exported to England and sold by consignment agents who capitalized the trade and who exported English goods to tobacco planters in payment. Tobacco prices (like those of sugar) exhibited a long-term decline after the first generation of settlement that continued until the end of the seventeenth century. Until the 1680s, planters in the Chesapeake, like their counterparts in the sugar colonies, had counteracted this decline by reducing costs. With the establishment of regular trade with England, credit became more accessible as the costs for imported manufactured goods fell. Mortality rates in the Chesapeake fell somewhat by the 1670s; more indentured servants therefore lived to work their masters, land, and the annual cost of labor fell. Tobacco output per worker increased as colonists learned better ways to transplant, sucker and cut it. Freight charges, levied by space rather than weight, fell as planters learned to prize more tobacco into a cask without ruining it. By the late seventeenth century, tobacco prizes, usually furnished at a local warehouse, helped pack more tobacco in each cask.[14]

After about 1685, however, planters were unable to reduce costs further due to rising land and labor prices. Much of the good land available on the Chesapeake Bay and on navigable rivers was occupied, while falling mortality rates and increasing numbers of freedmen (servants who had completed their indentures) placed more pressure on available land.[15] The price of servants rose. While more slaves were being imported, their high initial cost limited purchases to the well-to-do. At the same time, the English tobacco market stagnated.[16]

As the tobacco market faltered, trade with Britain became more hazardous; international wars almost continually disrupted shipping. The War of the League of Augsburg (1689–97), the War of the Spanish Succession (1702–13), the War of the Austrian Succession (1739–48), the Seven Years' War (1754–63), and the American Revolution all played havoc with imperial trade. Some colonial planters spent most of their adult lives coping with the exigencies of wartime. It was not uncommon for too few British ships to arrive to carry off the crop. English merchants also tripled their freight charges to 15–18 pounds sterling per ton to cover rising insurance costs, a move that cut dramatically into planters' profits.[17] The insurance, moreover, primarily covered only the merchant's vessel. Tobacco shipped on consignment was shipped at a planter's risk. If a ship sank or was captured as a prize of war, the planter, not the merchant, suffered the loss.[18]

Before 1680, some planters in Maryland sought a hedge against poor tobacco markets by selling diverse plantation products, such as cider, pork, and beef, locally. During much of the seventeenth century, however, local markets were bound to the tobacco crop. High tobacco profits created local markets for other products. During lean years, however, markets for diverse products and the tobacco market declined together.[19]

Wheat, timber and other diverse crops, on the other hand, which grew in importance in the Chesapeake economy after 1690, differed substantially from tobacco in their marketing, processing and shipping requirements. They were also almost certain to be shipped, not to England but to other colonies. These differences stimulated the growth of local economies and the clustering of people and businesses through three separate but related economic factors: first, a clustered, local mercantile community; second, forward manufacturing and transport linkages; and third, a population of free laborers who were able to consume imported goods.

The mercantile functions involved in the wheat trade, unlike those of the tobacco, sugar and to a lesser extent, rice trades, has not yet received the scholarly attention it deserves. Wheat, unlike tobacco, was not consigned by planters to specific agents in Britain. It was not a product the British crown valued sufficiently to enumerate for obvious reasons; in most years, England and Western Europe could grow enough wheat to fill their needs. The lack of a consignment system meant that either the farmers and planters who grew it or the local merchants who bought and sold it had to develop a considerable amount of product judgement and marketing expertise in wheat, flour and other grains, as they could not rely on agents. This task, unsurprisingly, devolved on merchants, as farmers and planters had other things to do. They had to be able to assess grain qualities, and juggle demand and market prices in Spain, Portugal, Ireland, the Wine Islands, the Maritimes or the British West Indies. In lean years, they might even consider small markets in the

Atlantic Islands or South Carolina. Such possible sales were always to be balanced against profits to be realized by selling to larger merchants in Delaware or Philadelphia.[20]

Wheat merchants also had to possess the administrative and financial expertise to assemble cargos quickly; insofar as they delayed, their overhead costs for storing and insuring it would cut into their profits. The same impetus would have pushed them to centralize or cluster efforts to collect grains and to build and own oceangoing ships, coasting sloops and wagons. If they did not do so, their profits, already certainly lower than those London or Bristol merchants realized on tobacco or sugar, again could plummet.[21]

Finally, credit for wheat and other diverse products with a local merchants could ultimately purchase colonial goods and services while tobacco could not. Although notes drawn against tobacco in Maryland warehouses circulated as specie, credit with a London merchant ultimately could purchase only English goods. All of these factors contributed to the growth of independent local merchants who could accelerate the development of a regional economy and urban centers, both by creating jobs and by providing local credit. These aspects of the wheat trade, however, remain unexplored.[22]

Wheat and other products destined for intercolonial markets – lumber and leather for example – also required considerably more processing than did tobacco and stimulated the development of linkage networks to ready them for export. In general, such networks in the colonies tended to develop around, and spur capital investment in, the domestic production of goods for use in the export trade and in processing, transport and storage services in intercolonial trade. Capital-intensive processing industries included lumbering, mill building and milling, tanning and others. Gristmill construction required literally dozens of specialized workers, and was infinitely more capital and labor intensive than building even a large plantation house and outbuildings. Simply acquiring and hauling the raw materials for a mill took twice as many working days as did the same task for a considerable plantation quarter.[23]

Wheat and other grains, moreover, were, because of their weight, harder to transport; tobacco could be rolled or carted by only a few servants to an agent's ship.[24] As a result, grains also required a considerable investment in short duration portage and hauling – sloops and wagons – as well as the facilities – inns and taverns – to support the boatmen and draymen who handled them. Finally, wheat, unlike tobacco, required roads that were usable even in heavy weather to render their transport profitable. Other historians have examined the effects of these requirements in meticulous detail.[25]

Third, intercolonial markets for diverse goods, as local merchants discovered, had more variable demands for goods than did the markets for staples in Britain. Merchants who supplied them often could not project their labor needs precisely, nor count on using slave laborers. A laborer who cut and hewed several thousand feet of timber for a West Indian cargo, for example, would be occupied for only four to five months. If a merchant purchased a slave for such a task, the man would be underemployed.[26] Other crops, especially European grains, which throve seasonally in a temperate climate were more predictable. But their cyclical demands for labor made free workers, who could be hired for a day or two and then released, preferable to slaves. Merchants in an area of diversified agriculture and commerce, therefore, needed free laborers, although they also benefitted from the services of short-term bound laborers, such as debt servants and some types of apprentices.

Free laborers needed merchants as well, although the work they did for them supplemented, but did not supply, their income. Few laborers even in the largest port cities – Philadelphia, New York and Boston by the mid to late eighteenth century – anticipated anything like steady employment, even in eighteenth-century terms, from commerce alone. The free workers employed by Chesapeake merchants included freedmen (indentured servants who had served out their terms); single young men and women and widows, who either did not have family responsibilities or whose responsibilities were attenuated; and tenants, who frequently fell into one of the two previous categories and did not have tenancies large enough to require their constant attention.[27]

Historians may, however, have underestimated the amount of product consumption slaves – or, more accurately, masters on behalf of their slaves – contributed to colonial economies. In Kent county, at least, one segment of the population, working women, spent between one-quarter and three-quarters of their time working for pay by performing tasks for the region's slaves. Slave women in the early eighteenth-century Chesapeake worked in the fields.[28] Slaves, however, still needed clothing and other services generally provided by women in Anglo-American society.

Free women filled these demands for pay. The argument that slaves dampen either local economic growth or urbanization ignores the contributions of women to local production.[29]

Naval wars, too, encouraged the development of mixed agriculture. Wars forced Chesapeake planters and merchants to seek new markets for diverse products, as skyrocketing insurance rates and privateers combined to make the tobacco trade with England unprofitable and dangerous. As early as the 1690s, naval wars also motivated planter-merchants to manufacture goods they otherwise would have imported, especially cloth, shoes and hats.[30] The disruption of imperial trade provided work for local residents and accelerated the expansion of the wheat trade and its resultant credit network. During eighteenth-century British naval wars, products other than tobacco frequently yielded the majority of planters' incomes.[31]

Between 1690 and 1790, therefore, many staple growing colonies that previously had been committed to tobacco were ripe for an economic surge, the results of which would include some degree of urbanization.[32] Most of Maryland, much of Virginia (especially the piedmont), western Delaware and most of North Carolina as well as the upcountries of South Carolina and Georgia were located in this agro-economic region.[33] Local merchants invested in a centralized or clustered trade based on grains and other crops that required the labor of artisans and free or short-term bound laborers, frequently in specific industrial sites, resulted in the creation of a number of ports and towns based on processing and shipping mixed agricultural products. Most of these towns never grew into cities; they retained the character of "country towns," but they were nonetheless urban spaces with rural elements in them.[34] Twentieth-century Americans tend to view cities as diametrically opposed to the countryside, and to construct models for urban processes with that implicit distinction in mind. Towns and crossroads in colonial America, however, were a logical outgrowth of regional economies and settlement patterns; towns were not imposed "on a rural landscape, but the development of highly integrated town-country settlement systems."[35]

In fact, although this change could have taken place in some of the earliest settled areas by 1690, the change itself was circumscribed, not temporally, but developmentally and generationally. A process similar to that which began on the Eastern Shore of Maryland around 1690 did not begin in Georgia, for example, until the late eighteenth century.

Economic factors alone did not create towns. Within the first British Empire, government initiatives for political and administrative functions also helped establish urban sites, while private investors' initiatives in pursuit of profit provided the initial capital and interest for town founding. The need for county seats and courthouses helped promote certain town sites, although such initiatives were not sufficient to establish them, as colonial assemblies frequently learned to their dismay. The active establishment of clustered settlements on such sites were achieved through private initiative, as individuals subdivided farm or plantation lands into lots and sold them to would-be residents.[36]

Those population and mercantile/processing clusters that grew into towns during the mid-eighteenth century virtually always exhibited more than a single purpose; simply being the county seat, or a loading point for tobacco or the site of a ferry alone was not sufficient to create a town.

Between 1683 and 1708, the legislature of Maryland tried to support the maritime needs of the tobacco trade by passing legislation designed to create towns in the colony. Many of the towns thus created by executive fiat failed to flourish, as the assembly did not always select sites based on their economic or geographic capacities to support towns. Evidence from Kent county, however, suggests that the local members of the assembly attempted to nominate areas within the county that already showed some promise of becoming population centers.[37] Kent's first county seat had been established in 1648 on Kent Island in the Chesapeake Bay. As the population of the county moved east, the court moved with it, removing to the Eastern Neck in 1652. The New Yarmouth shipyard, on Gray's Inn Creek, was created a town by the act of 1683, and the county seat moved there. By the mid–1690s, however, town act or no, New Yarmouth remained essentially a site for industry, and the population of the county had continued to move east.[38]

Accordingly, by 1696, the county had purchased a lot on the Chester River, part of Thomas Marsh's land, for a courthouse.[39] This choice was not an accident. Seagoing ships that drew more than thirteen feet of water could not proceed up the Chester River beyond Marsh's plantation, where a series of mudbanks impeded them. By the mid 1690s, therefore, the site, called "Chestertown," already served as a convenient gathering point for planters from Kent and Talbot counties who stooped or rolled their tobacco to a London merchant's ship. By 1698, Chester-town functioned as a port of entry for English (later British) goods. By 1701, Marsh had also donated some land for the county's use, where schoolmaster John Withington established a school "at a certain house near unto one Robert Marshe[']s plantation on Chester River." By 1703, the surrounding area was called "Towne Hundred" suggesting that, in addition to Marsh's own store, a tavern or a few warehouses may have already clustered there.[40]

In 1707, the site was officially established as a town by an act of the assembly, and was named as one of Maryland's six ports of export; all goods shipped out of the colony, except for timber, had to clear from one of these ports.[41] Chestertown, therefore, was established first as a village which supported the tobacco trade. It fit into a group of similar towns in tidewater Virginia and bayside Maryland that included Norfolk, Williamsburg, Yorktown, Oxford and Annapolis.[42] In 1747, the Maryland legislature passed a Tobacco Inspection Act that named Chestertown, among other places, a port of inspection. This act required that the county build a warehouse in Chestertown to house tobacco before in-spection and shipment, and contributed to the town's growing economy by requiring a certain amount of portage and travel to and from Chestertown.

Despite the Act of 1707, no town lots were sold in Chestertown until 1722 as the tobacco market stagnated. By that date, however, Thomas Marsh's heirs had conveyed the land surrounding and including the site of Chestertown to Simon Wilmer. Wilmer was an entrepreneur who took advantage of the growing interest in, and economic importance of, the town to subdivide part of his land and sell it as one-acre lots. He sold only eleven lots between 1722 and 1729, for an average price of £6.7. In 1730, he sold fifty-five more, at an average price of £7.5, as well as thirty-five more in the four subsequent years, including a lot on which he had erected an inn. This lot, with its improvements, sold for £38.[43]

As demand rose for Chestertown lots, so did their prices; sellers began to subdivide lots to realize more profits, while buyers who wanted a town lot soon had little option but to buy only a portion of an acre or go without. Between 1731 and 1750, the average lot sold in Chestertown measured 7/8 of an acre. Between 1751 and 1770, the mean lot measured only 5/8 of an acre. By the 1740s, moreover, the most valuable lots in-cluded sunk capital in the form of craft shops, inns and stores. In order to realize investment and working capital, innkeepers and craftsmen, would often sell or lease part of their lots and build on the remainder. Saddler Reuben Harding, for example, leased half a Chestertown lot to baker Jordan Steiger in 1775, reserving only "the one-eighth part of that moiety [half] whereon now stands his sadlers shop."[44] As a result, business lots were smaller than average. By 1760, the average craftsman's lot that changed hands measured only ½ an acre, and the average lot with an inn measured only 4/10 of an acre. The average price for such lots, however, had risen to £866 per acre by 1770.

But by 1750, neither the county court nor the Tobacco Inspection Act were as important to Chestertown's development as was the increasing importance of wheat and other grains in the Eastern Shore economy. By that date, about 1,300 people lived in Chestertown, and its ships carried wheat and other diverse products to Spain, Ireland, and the Maritimes as well as the West Indies.[45]

After the American Revolution, however, Kent's economy began to decline as Chestertown's urban functions were increasingly appropriated by the port of Baltimore, the fastest-growing city in America. Baltimore's location on the Western Shore gave it access to the newly opened wheat regions in Maryland, Pennsylvania, and Virginia; the mills built in Baltimore during the 1780s and 1790s were technologically superior to the older mills in Kent county. Baltimore's merchants soon captured much of the trade of the smaller towns on the Eastern Shore, and shipped virtually all of their tobacco as well.[46]

As Kent's economy sagged, artisans left the area. By 1790, some craftsmen, like shoemaker William Duncan found themselves "incapable of . . . carrying on my business as usual." Duncan asked the county court to allow his apprentice, Samuel Stoker, "to go over to Baltimore where . . . he can get another master to teach him the science I was to teach him." Stoker was pleased when the court agreed to the change, as "all his Relations now lives [sic] in Baltimore."[47] Stoker was not alone; with Chestertown's decline, many local apprentices were forced to seek masters in distant cities. They went to Baltimore, to Philadelphia and to Wilmington, Delaware.[48]

While working people departed for Baltimore, Newcastle and Philadelphia, many of Chestertown's elites sought greener pastures even further afield. After the end of the American Revolution, Kent's land records are filled with references to merchants and wealthy craftsmen "formerly of this county, now of Savannah" or "of New York" or even "of Barbados." Most of this exodus was urban in nature. Members of the socioeconomic elites who identified their destinations specified cities or towns in 52 out of 59 cases, or nearly 90 percent of the time. Table 1 describes the destinations of merchants and elite craftsmen from Kent

Table 1. Destination of Elites Departing from Kent County, 1783–1810

Destination	N	%
West Indies	3	5.1
Savannah, Ga.	8	13.7
North Carolina	6	10.2
Virginia (Alexandria, Norfolk, Petersburg)	5	8.5
Washington, D.C.	2	3.4
Baltimore	11	18.4
Newcastle, Del.	6	10.2
Philadelphia	14	23.7
Pittsburgh, Pa.	2	3.4
New York City	2	3.4
Total	59	100.0

county between 1783 and 1810, proceeding from south to north.

Surprisingly, however, the decline affected Chestertown's professional district and residences before it affected business lots. The prices for lots that had not been dedicated to crafts, nor to merchant warehouses, nor to inns or taverns fell precipitously after 1781 and never recovered. This may reflect a desire on the part of gentlemen and professionals, such as doctors and lawyers, to leave an increasingly unfashionable town for one which was more a la mode or profitable. Certainly an increasing number of houses in Chestertown, but not shops, were allowed by absentee owners to fall into ruin and were subsequently sold by the sheriff to owners who agreed to try to restore them.[49]

Business lot prices, however, followed a different trajectory. They too declined during the third quarter of the eighteenth century, but they began to do so during the Revolution, rather than afterward. This suggests that Chestertown's business men were suffering from the difficulty of shipping goods during wartime, especially because the destination for those goods lay in enemy territory. The rise of Baltimore continued to keep business lot prices low until 1794. In that year, however, those in Chestertown began to climb again, and soared to their highest point ever by the late 1790s.[50] This change may be attributed to the ratification of Jay's Treaty in 1794. The treaty certainly benefitted the United States' economy as a whole; under its terms, the value of U.S. exports rose from $33 million to $94 million by 1800. More germane to Chestertown's trade, however, Article Twelve of the treaty reopened West Indian ports to United States vessels of less than seventy tons burden. All the sloops and the vast majority of the wheat schooners that cleared Chestertown for the West Indies would have been no larger than seventy tons.[51] In fact, this development may have given Chestertown's smaller wheat merchants a short-term advantage over those in Baltimore and Philadelphia. In 1805, however, in an effort to contain American trade with France and the French West Indies, the British High Court of Admiralty announced the Essex decision. This decison permitted the Royal Navy to seize ships bound from American ports to the Caribbean who could not provide clear, but unspecified, proof that they were not carrying French goods. As many as four hundred vessels and their cargoes were thus taken, and insurance rates soared. Although the ships themselves were later returned, Chestertown's economy plummeted, never to recover. Lot prices plunged to pre-1740 levels. This drop was even more severe than it at first appears; virtually all the lots sold in Chestertown in 1810 were improved, which had not been true in 1740.[52]

The growth of wheat in the first half of the eighteenth century also stimulated the county's physical development, as more and more roads were built to accommodate the wagons that hauled it. This development particularly spurred the growth of the eastern part of the county, which did not have access to Chester River system. It also rendered part of that system less efficacious. By 1790, Kent's light soils, under the plow for at least sixty years, had silted into the river near the head of the Chester. Planters had almost completely given up attempting to sloop goods upriver, and used the roads instead.

The growth of the wheat trade also tied Chestertown more tightly into the economic nexus of Philadelphia merchants. Some independent merchant families, notably the Ringgolds, remained in Chestertown. But the growing importance of Philadelphia to the wheat trade encouraged merchants in the Quaker City to invest in retail stores and other economic sites further and further south on the Delmarva Peninsula.

One measure of the growing connection between Chestertown and Philadelphia was the increasing frequency of communications and travel between the town and the city. By the late 1740s, it was becoming routine for letters to travel quickly between the two sites, as Daniel Cunningham advertised his services as "a messenger, between Philadelphia and Chestertown in Maryland" who would "gladly serve any gentlemen, or others, by carrying their letters, or doing their business, at the accustomed Rates." By the 1770s, moreover, more then letters routinely made the trip from Chestertown to Philadelphia.[53]

John Bolton's stage wagon made the trip once a week from the beginning of May until the Delaware River froze. The wagon departed Chestertown for Newcastle, Delaware, where "a compleat stage boat" took in "the passengers and goods, and sail[ed] immediately for Philadelphia." The wagon then returned to Kent County, where another stageboat boarded the passengers and sailed for Annapolis. The boats had been "built on purpose for stageboat[s]" and had "excellent accommodations for passengers." Bolton also promised to keep them "neat and clean, in hopes thereby to induce Gentlemen and Ladies to try that method of travelling." Such services integrated country towns like Chestertown and Rock Hall by the 1770s into an economic and social region bounded by Annapolis to the west and the metropolis of Philadelphia to the northeast.

The pull of Philadelphia also affected the rural areas of Kent county. As the road system developed to the north and east of Chestertown, areas where main roads crossed became small villages in their own right. By 1740, Kent's "Great Road" from the head of the Sassafrass river to the head of the Chester was bisected by a crossroad which ran from the Sassafrass Ferry (which gave residents access to Pennsylvania) to Chestertown. This crossing became Georgetown Crossroads by the early 1750s.[54] The Great Road also gave rise to another village, London Bridge (later Bridgetown) by the late 1760s.[55] Travelers from points south of Kent county could use the ferry at the head of the Chester and continue north if they were bound for Pennsylvania.

Regional economic systems were not bounded by colonial political boundaries, of course.[56] As the road system in the eastern part of the county improved, Kent county residents dealt more and more frequently with people in western Delaware and in Newcastle. The boundary between these colonies ran through a morass of swamps and marshes; before the 1780s, it was unnavigable by water and only unpleasantly passable by land. By the mid-1790s, however, at least one road, the Duck Creek Road, named for its termination point in Delaware, bisected the Great Road, and encouraged the development of a crossroads village named Gilpintown.[57]

The growth of all three of these crossroad villages – Georgetown Crossroads, Bridgetown and Gilpintown – like Chestertown, were spurred by the entrepreneurial efforts of landowners. Robert Street, a wealthy blacksmith from Newcastle, Delaware, miller Joshua VanSant, tanner Henry Holman and planter Charles Pearce all subdivided their lands to provide the lots at Georgetown Crossroads; John Nimmo, a former indentured servant and innkeeper bought the first of these for a tavern in 1752.[58] The market for lots in Georgetown Crossroads was fairly sporadic; there were brief flurries after the end of the Seven Years' War and again after the American Revolution. Between 1793 and 1804, however, the village entered a period of sustained growth, as thirty-one lots changed hands. In Bridgetown, entrepreneurial merchant Gilbert Falconer subdivided and leased his land; he doubtless expected land values to rise precipitously as the area was developed. In November, 1769, for example, Falconer leased a two-acre lot to blacksmith David Jones for £1 yearly, with the provision that "there shall be no wet or dry goods sold" except that "Jones may sell iron worked or unworked."

Falconer was anxious to preserve any "wet or dry goods" market for another lessor, merchant Thomas Gilpin. Gilpin leased the northern half of Falconer's tract (about 20 acres) in March, 1770, for £3 yearly. He received a low rent in return for his promise to build "a landing and to Build Ware Houses or other necessary Buildings to accommodate trade" as well as "a Commodious Rode." He also built a smith's shop and a shoemaker's shop, as well as several houses which he leased to artisans. They, in turn, promised "not to engage in any business without the permission of Thomas Gilpin or his Heirs" except their individual craft pursuits.[59] In 1774, Gilpin moved to Philadelphia, although he, and later his widow, Lydia, (who established Gilpintown) maintained stores and shops in Kent county's crossroad villages.[60] In fact, fifteen merchants, at least four of whom lived in Philadelphia, purchased lots in Kent county's crossroad villages between 1769 and 1810, and established stores and a local market presence in rural northern Maryland.

The northeast crossroads supported a number of other businessmen (and women) as well. Most were artisans. They included free black shoemaker Isaac Harris and seamstress Rebecca Maxwell. Nearly half of these craftsmen served the wagonning trade as blacksmiths, wagon-chaise- and wheelwrights, joiners and carpenters (who sometimes re-

Table 2. Crafts Followed by Forty Artisans in the
Northeast Crossroads Villages, 1769–1810

Craft	Number of Artisans	%
Wagonning Trades		
Blacksmith	9	
Chaisemaker	1	
Harnessmaker	2	
Saddler	2	
Wagonwright	2	
Wheelwright	2	
Subtotal	18	45.5
Primary Processing		
Fuller	1	
Tanner	1	
Miller	1	
Subtotal	3	7.5
Inexpensive Consumer Trades		
Hatter	1	
Seamstress	1	
Shoemaker	2	
Tailor	4	
Weaver	2	
Subtotal	10	25.0
Building Trades		
House Carpenter	3	
Joiner	3	
Carpenter	3	
Subtotal	9	22.5

paired wagon bodies), harnessmakers and saddlers. A few others were primary processors for other craftsmen and consumers – fullers, tanners, millers. Others were in the construction trades. A surprisingly small number followed inexpensive consumer trades, and worked as weavers, tailors or shoemakers. Half of these, moreover, were tailors and a seamstress, who processed ready-made cloth into garments. None made items for conspicuous consumption. Table 2 illustrates the crafts followed by artisans in the northeast crossroad villages.

By 1810, therefore, the crossroads villages did not have broad-based economies; they existed primarily to serve traffic going to Philadelphia and Newcastle. Nor did they, unlike Chestertown, serve other political or administrative purposes. The Philadelphia merchants who built stores and warehouses there, moreover, engrossed the demand for craftsmen's services and products that had spurred the growth of Chestertown a half century earlier. Their "necessary Buildings to accomodate trade" provided manufactured cloth, ceramics, hats and shoes to area residents. They did not, of course, provide ready-made clothing – tailors and seamstresses could still follow their callings in the Northeast Crossroads. Georgetown Crossroads, Bridgetown and Gilpintown developed as very different places than Chestertown had earlier, in part because of their location, in part because of the increasing importance of Philadelphia, and in part because merchants who dealt in manufactured goods had elbowed some craftsmen aside by the end of the eighteenth century.

The lot prices in the Northeast Crossroads reflect this change. The prices of craftsmen's lots, unlike those in Chestertown, always remained very low in the crossroads. The little villages could support an optimal number of tradesmen who served travelers and draymen, and required no others. At the same time, the demand for craftsmen's work was further dampened by merchants' goods. The average price for craftsmen's lots at the northeastern crossroads between 1770 and 1810 peaked at only £43 18s in 1800.

Merchants' lots were another story. Their price began to rise slightly after the American Revolution, and peaked in the years following the Essex decision, as the prices of merchants' lots in Chestertown plummeted. Between 1805 and 1810, the average price per acre for a merchant's lot in Georgetown Crossroads, Bridgetown or Gilpintown was £577 12s, while the equivalent price in Chestertown was only £124 12s.

Urban development in Kent's northeastern crossroad villages was a very different process than it had been for the tobacco and wheat port of Chesterown some fifty to seventy-five years earlier. The world of urban and rural markets and marketing had changed considerably by 1800, although the nuances and direction of the change is obscured, rather than clarified, by the unwieldy appellation of "transition to capitalism."

The evidence from Kent county also suggests that the process of urbanization during the eighteenth century depended heavily on timing, on region and site, on the investment of capital (or lack thereof) by local or absentee developers, on the extent to which premanufactured goods could replace the work of artisans and so on. While various models may help us understand the theory behind such developments, they are much more restricted in explaining the process than many scholars have heretofore realized.

Finally, by the middle of the eighteenth century, the southern colonies clearly possessed a multitude of towns of various sizes and shapes. Many of these towns eventually stopped growing or began to shrink after nearby cities expropriated their urban functions. But to fail to consider their purpose and importance during the colonial period is to oversimplify and ignore the historical process of urbanization. For every Baltimore or Philadelphia, there were almost certainly dozens of Chestertowns and hundreds of Northeast Crossroads. If urban historians persist in studying only winners, our understanding of economic growth and the tapestry of colonial urban history will be the loser for it.

Notes

1. Throughout this essay, I have unabashedly employed the models of urbanization employed by Robert D. Mitchell and Warren Hofstra, "How do Settlement Systems Evolve? The Virginia Backcountry during the Eighteenth Century," *Journal of Historical Geography* 21 (1995) 123–47.

2. See, for example, Brian Holder, "The Importance of Site in Urban Development: A Synopsis of the Economic Geography of Kingston, Ontario," *The Southern Quarterly* 4 (1966): 319–30; Mitchell and Hofstra, "How Do Settlement Systems Evolve?"; James O'Mara, *An Historical Geography of Urban System Development: Tidewater Virginia in the Eighteenth Century* (Downsview, Ontario: Dept. of Geography, Atkinson College, York University, 1983); and Darrett B. Rutman with Anita H. Rutman, "The Genesis of a Chesapeake Town," in *Small Worlds,*

Large Questions: Explorations in Early American Social History, 1600–1850 (Charlottesville: University Press of Virginia, 1994).

3. Current models of urbanization rely primarily on three economic models to explain town growth. Long distance trade theory addresses the development of towns at a regional or imperial level; an example of this approach might be Warren R. Hofstra and Robert D. Mitchell, "Town and Country in Backcountry Virginia: Winchester and the Shenandoah Valley, 1730–1800," *Journal of Southern History* 54 (1993): 619–46. Staple theory discusses the development of central places in terms of their economic and manufacturing functions. An excellent example of this literature is Carville Earle and Ronald Hoffman, "Staple Crops and Urban Development in the Eighteenth-Century South," *Perspectives in Economic History* 10 (1976): 7–78. Central place theory addresses the relationship between urban places and rural populations at local and regional levels. Possibly the best known example of the application of central place theory to town development in eighteenth-century America is James T. Lemon, *The Best Poor Man's Country: A Geographical Study of Early Southeastern Pennsylvania* (Baltimore: The Johns Hopkins University Press, 1972). A more accessible piece is Simeon P. Crowther, "Urban Growth in the Mid-Atlantic States, 1785–1850," *Journal of Economic History* 36 (1976): 624–44. For inquiries specifically concerned with cities south of Philadelphia, see Leonard Curry, "Urbanization and Urbanism in the Old South: A Comparative View," *Journal of Southern History* 40 (1974): 43–60; David R. Goldfield, "The Urban South: A Regional Framework," *American Historical Review* 86 (1981): 1009–34; and Darrett B. Rutman with Anita H. Rutman, "The Village South," in *Small Worlds, Large Questions.* See also Jacob Price, "Economic Function and the Growth of American Port Towns in the Eighteenth Century," *Perspectives in Economic History* 8 (1974): 121–86.

4. For example, Henry M. Miller, "Baroque Cities in the Wilderness: Archeology and Urban Development in the Colonial Chesapeake," *Historic Archeology* 22 (1988): 57–73; Laura Palmer Bell, "A New Theory of the Plan of Savannah," *Georgia Historical Quarterly* 48 (1964): 147–65.

5. One example of such a work that does not treat the urban setting as of secondary importance is Gary B. Nash, "The Social Evolution of Preindustrial American Cities, 1700–1820: Reflections and New Directions," *Journal of Urban History* 13 (1987): 115–45. One that does is Diana Rockman and Nan A. Rothschild, "City Tavern, Country Tavern: An Analysis of Four Colonial Sites," *Historical Archeology* 18 (1982): 112–21.

6. For example, Kenneth A. Lockridge, *A New England Town: The First Hundred Years, Dedham, Massachusetts, 1636–1736* (New York: W. W. Norton, 1970.)

7. This topic seems to intrigue geographers and archeologists, perhaps because they think visually, more than historians. See, for example, James E. Vance, "Housing the Worker: The Employment Linkage as a Force in Urban Structure," *Economic Geography* 42 (1966): 294–325.

8. Kevin P. Kelly, "'In Dispers'd Country Plantations': Settlement Patterns in Seventeenth-Century Surry County, Virginia," in *The Chesapeake in the Seventeenth Century: Essays in Anglo-American Society*, eds. Thad W. Tate and David L. Ammerman (New York: W. W. Norton, 1979): 183–205.

9. Lockridge, *New England Town*; Philip J. Greven, Jr., *Four Generations: Poloulation, Land and Family in Colonial Andover, Massachusetts* (Ithaca, N.Y.: Cornell University Press, 1970); John P. Demos, *A Little Commonwealth: Family Life in Plymouth Colony* (New York: Oxford University Press, 1970); Charles S. Grant, *Democracy in the Connecticut Frontier Town of Kent* (New York: Columbia University Press, 1961); John Frederick Martin discusses the ways in which seventeenth-century New England settlement processes relied on entrepreneurs in *Profits in the Wilderness: Entrepreneurship and the Founding of New England Towns in the Seventeenth Century* (Chapel Hill: University of North Carolina Press, 1991). In this, they resembled Chesapeake settlements.

10. See, for example, Winifred B. Rothenberg, "The Market and Massachusetts Farmers, 1750–1855," *Journal of Economic History* 41 (1981): 283–314.

11. I group southern Pennsylvania with the upper south as its agroeconomy, labor requirements and other economic factors closely resembled those of Maryland and Virginia, particularly the Eastern Shore and the Shenandoah Valley. See also Robert J. Gough, "The Myth of the 'Middle Colonies': An Analysis of Regionalization in Early America," *Pennsylvania Magazine of History and Biography* 103 (1979): 392–419. Leonard P. Curry points out the fallacies in perceiving the southern region as qualitatively different in the antebellum era in "Urbanization and Urbanism in the Old South."

12. Early proponents of a transition from communal to capitalist society included Michael Merrill, "Cash is Good to Eat: Self-Sufficiency and Exchange in the Rural Economy of the United States," *Radical History Review* 4 (1977): 42–71; James Henretta, "Families and Farms: *Mentalité* in Pre-Industrial America," *William and Mary Quarterly* 35 (1978): 3–32; and Christopher Clark, "The Household Economy, Market Exchange and the Rise of Capitalism in the Connecticut Valley, 1800–1860," *Journal of Social History* 13 (1979): 169–89. Early proponents of the continuity of capitalism included Rothenberg, "Market and Massachusetts Farmers;" and Lemon, "Early Americans and Their Social Environment," *Journal of Historical Geography* 6 (1980): 115–31. Stephen Innes argues for both concepts in *Labor in a New Land: Economy and Society in Seventeenth Century Springfield* (Princeton, N.J.: Princeton University Press, 1983).

13. Richard Bushman in this volume; Christine Daniels, "'Wanted: A Blacksmith Who Understands Plantation Work': Artisans in Maryland, 1700–1810," *William and Mary Quarterly* 50 (1993): 743–67; Michael V. Kennedy, "An Alternate Independence: Craft Workers in the Pennsylvania Iron Industry, 1725–1775," *Essays in Economic and Business History* 16 (1998); and Kennedy, "'Debtr to the Store': The Central Place of Ironworks and Mill Stores in the

Pennsylvania Market, 1725–1789," unpublished paper presented to the Michigan Seminar in Colonial History, March, 1998.

14. Russell Menard, "The Tobacco Industry in the Chesapeake Colonies, 1617–1730," *Research in Economic History* 5 (1980): 109–77. Lorena Walsh, *To Labour for Profit: Plantation Management in the Chesapeake, 1617–1820* (forthcoming), chap. 3. I am very grateful to Dr. Walsh for sharing her manuscript with me. John J. McCusker and Russell Menard, *The Economy of British America, 1607–1789* (Chapel Hill: University of North Carolina Press, 1985), 120–23.

15. Lois Green Carr and Russell Menard, "Immigration and Opportunity: The Freedman in Early Colonial Maryland," in *The Chesapeake in the Seventeenth Century*, eds., Thad Tate and David Ammerman, 206–42.

16. Russell Menard, "From Servants to Slaves: The Transformation of the Chesapeake Labor System," *Southern Studies* 16 (1977): 355–90, esp. 360–74. Demand in England was almost saturated when Parliament raised the duties on tobacco in 1685 from 2d to 5d per pound and raised them again by 1703 to more than 6d. These duties were passed on to consumers by English merchants. Rising costs and a saturated demand led to a stagnant tobacco market in England by the 1690s.

17. Menard, "Tobacco Industry," 138–40.

18. Arthur Pierce Middleton, *Tobacco Coast: A Maritime History of the Chesapeake Bay in the Colonia Era* (Newport News, Va.: Mariners' Museum, 1953; reprint: Baltimore: The Johns Hopkins University Press, 1984), 175–77; Marcus Rediker, *Between the Devil and the Deep Blue Sea: Merchant Seamen, Pirates and the Anglo-American Maritime World, 1700–1750* (Cambridge, Mass.: Cambridge University Press, 1987), 32–33; Menard, "Tobacco Industry," 139–40; Jacob Price, "The Economic Growth of the Chesapeake and the European Market, 1697–1775," *Journal of Economic History* 24 (1964): 506–7.

19. Russell Menard, Lois Green Carr and Lorena Walsh, "A Small Planter's Profits: The Cole Estate and the Growth of the Early Chesapeake Economy," *William and Mary Quarterly* 40 (1983) : 171–96, esp. 182–83.

20. Christine Daniels, "Alternative Workers in a Slave Economy: Kent County, Maryland, 1675–1810" (Ph.D. dissertation, Johns Hopkins University, 1990), 11–57; Paul Clemens, *The Atlantic Economy and Colonial Maryland's Eastern Shore: From Tobacco to Grain* (Ithaca, N.Y.: Cornell University Press, 1980), 168–205.

21. The wheat trade shared some, but not all, of these factors with the rice trade of South Carolina as described by R. C. Nash, "Urbanization in the Colonial South: Charlestown, South Carolina as a Case Study," *Journal of Urban History* 19 (1992): 3–29.

22. The wheat trade needs a historian to test these theses, as Jacob Price has done for tobacco, Richard Sheridan for sugar and Peter Coclanis for rice.

23. Daniels, "Alternative Workers," 58–114.

24. Earle and Hoffman, "Staple Crops and Urban Development," 32–36, 39; Carville Earle, "A Staple Interpretation of Slavery and Free Labor," *Geographical Review* 68 (1978): 51–65.

25. McCusker and Menard, *Economy of British America*, 19–34; Daniel Vickers, *Farmers and Fishermen: Two Centuries of Work in Essex County, Massachusetts, 1630–1850* (Chapel Hill: University of North Carolina Press, 1994), 7–8; Earle and Hoffman, "Staple Crops and Urban Development." By the nineteenth century, many new industries also employed slaves. See T. Stephen Whitman, "Industrial Slavery at the Margin: The Maryland Chemical Works," *Journal of Southern History* 59 (February 1993): 31–62.

26. Lois Green Carr, "Diversification in the Colonial Chesapeake: Somerset County, Maryland in Comparative Perspective," and Jean B. Russo, "Self-Sufficiency and Local Exchange: Free Craftsmen in the Rural Chesapeake Economy" in *Colonial Chesapeake Society*, eds., Lois Green Carr, Philip Morgan and Jean Russo (Chapel Hill: University of North Carolina Press, 1988); Christine Daniels, "'Without any Limitation of Time': Debt Servitude in Colonial America," *Labor History* 36 (1995): 232–50.

27. Lorena S. Walsh, "Land, Landlord and Leaseholder: Estate Management and Tenant Fortunes in Southern Maryland, 1642–1820," *Agricultural History* 59 (1985): 373–96; Christine Daniels, "'Getting His [or Her] Lively Hood': Free Laborers in Slave Anglo-America, 1675–1810," *Agricultural History* 69 (1997): 125–61; Vickers, *Farmers and Fishermen*, 52–53, 77–82, 249–50, 302–3; Laurel Thatcher Ulrich, *A Midwife's Tale: The Life of Martha Ballard, Based on her Diary, 1785–1812* (New York: Alfred A. Knopf, 1992), 80–82, 160–62.

28. Daniels, "'Getting His [or Her] Lively Hood'"; Carr and Walsh, "Economic Diversification and Labor Organization"; Carole Shammas, "Black Women's Work and the Evolution of Plantation Society in Virginia," *Labor History* 26 (1985): 5–28.

29. This argument also ignores the work of artisans, such as tailors and shoemakers, who made consumer goods in a slave economy. Planters in the Chesapeake only rarely imported such consumer goods for their slaves' use, as they were less costly when commissioned from local craftsmen.

30. Jacob Price, *Perry of London: A Family and A Firm on the Seaborne Frontier, 1615–1753* (Cambridge, Mass.: Harvard University Press, 1992) 36; Christine Daniels, "Gresham's Laws: Labor Management on an Early Eighteenth Century Chesapeake Plantation," *Journal of Southern History* 54 (1997): 205–38.

31. Daniels, "'Wanted: A Blacksmith'"; Daniels, "Gresham's Laws." Also Robert D. Mitchell, "Agricultural Change and the American Revolution: A Case Study," *Agricultural History* 47 (1973): 119–32.

32. In fact, I suspect this would have been the case with any staple less profitable than sugar, or with fewer sunk-capital requirements than rice. Rice's complex and expensive irrigation system mitigated against changing or diversifying crops.

33. Of course, the presence of an emphasis on mixed products alone could not create a successful town, as Charles L. Paul indicates in "Factors in the Economy of Colonial Beaufort," *The North Carolina Historical Review* 44 (1967): 111–34. In Beaufort's case, although it was named as a British port of entry, its geographic location prevented in from ever becoming much of a town.

34. David Goldfield, "Urban South," 1012–16.

35. Mitchell and Hofstra, "How Do Settlement Systems Evolve?" 124.

36. Ibid., 135; Paul, "Factors in the Economy of Colonial Beaufort, 111–12; Holder, "Importance of Site in Urban Development," 319–21. Some such investors, such as James Oglethorp, have become legendary for their efforts. See Bell, "A New Theory on the Plan of Savannah." For a highly theoretical look at this process, see Hermann Wellenreuther, "Urbanization in the Colonial South: A Critique," *William and Mary Quarterly* 31 (1974): 653–68. Wellenreuther was responding to Joseph Ernst and H. Roy Merrens, "'Camden's Turrets Pierce the Skies!': The Urban Process in the Southern Colonies During the Eighteenth Century," *William and Mary Quarterly* 30 (1973): 549–74.

37. John W. Reps, *Tidewater Towns: City Planning in Colonial Virginia and Maryland* (Williamsburg, Va.: Colonial Williamsburg Foundation through The University Press of Virginia, 1972), 100–101; Joseph Brown Thomas, "Settlement, Community and Economy: The Development of Towns in Maryland's Lower Eastern Shore, 1660–1775" (Ph.D. dissertation, University of Maryland, 1994), 56–85.

38. Kent County Court Proceedings (hereinafter Proceedings), Maryland Hall of Records, Annapolis, Maryland, (hereinafter MHR), 1675–96, 597; George Hanson, *Old Kent*, (reprint, Baltimore: Regional Publishing Co., 1967), 22; Morris Radoff, *The County Courthouses and Records of Maryland* (Annapolis, Md.: Maryland Hall of Records Commission, 1960), 107; Reps, *Tidewater Towns*, 98–99. All manuscript sources are located at the Maryland Hall of Records unless otherwise noted. Reps, *Tidewater Towns*, 92, commissioned a map on which the cartographer sited Chestertown near its modern site, and indicated it was created by the legislative act of 1668. I believe he is in error, as the act states the town is to be located in "Talbott county afore the Town Land in Chester River," William Browne Hand, et. al., *The Archives of Maryland* (Baltimore: Maryland Historical Society, 1887), v, 47–48; (hereafter *Archives*). While Kent County at one point extended south of the Chester, Talbot County never extended north of it, where Chestertown is now located, nor does the act name the site "Chestertown."

39. Proceedings, 1675–96, 704; Morris Radoff, *County Courthouses and Records of Maryland*, 107.

40. Colonial Office Port Records, volume 5/749, part 1/208–210, part 4/184 (photostats, Library of Congress, Washington, D. C.); Charles Ringgold to Galloway, 3/9/1766, Galloway Papers, (New York Public Library, Special Collections); Proceedings, 1701–05, 473–74; Proceedings, 1700–05, 199; Proceedings, 1708–09, 4.

41. Reps, *Tidewater Towns*, 100.

42. Mitchell and Hofstra, "How Do Settlement Systems Evolve?" 126.

43. These and all susequent statements regarding lot sales, prices, purchasers and sellers are based on my "Town Lot" file for Kent County. This file, compiled from the county land records, includes information on recorded sales for town and other lots sold in Kent County from the county's founding until 1810. The file has 940 entries; 488 for Chestertown lots; 252 for Georgetown lots; and and 200 entries for crossroads and villages including Stepney, Georgetown Crossroads (McKey's Purchase), Gilpintown, London Bridge (Bridgetown) and Newmarket. Here and throughout this essay, all prices are stated in local currency, constant value. Prices have been deflated by the price series developed by Lois Green Carr and Lorena Walsh for prices to 1765, and by the price series developed by P. M. G. Harris for prices after that date.

44. In other words, Harding retained only 1/16 of an acre for his own use. Kent County Land Records (hereinafter Kent Land Records) DD 5, 113.

45. In 1749, Kent had 2852 taxables, of whom 437 (15.3 percent) lived in Chestertown Hundred. The partial tax list of 1749 is organized geographically by household. *The Kent County Levy Books* (hereafter *Levy Books*) are aggregate counts of the population for each hundred in the county. They do not describe household size or location. Total population estimated using a nontaxable to taxable ratio of 1:1.94. To obtain this number, I compared the total Kent County population of 1755, enumerated in "An Account of the Number of Souls in the Province of Maryland," *Gentleman's Magazine* 34 (1764): as 9,443 persons, with the levy list made that year, which included 3,213 taxables. This yielded a taxable to nontaxable rato of 1:1.94. The tax list of 1749 lists each hundred separately; by 1749, Chestertown Hundred had been separated from adjoining Chester Hundred.

46. G. Terry Sharrer, "Flour Milling in the Growth of Baltimore, 1750–1830," *Maryland Historical Magazine* 71 (1976): 322–33; Charles Steffen, *The Mechanics of Baltimore: Workers and Politics in the Age of Revolution*, 1763–1812 (Urbana: University of Illinois Press, 1984), 7; Thomas Doerflinger, *A Vigorous Spirit of Enterprise: Merchants and Economic Development in Revolutionary Philadelphia* (Chapel Hill: University of North Carolina Press, 1986), 335–37; Edward Papenfuse, *In Pursuit of Profit: The Annapolis Merchants in the Era of the American Revolution, 1763–1805* (Baltimore: The Johns Hopkins University Press, 1975), 215–17; Tina Sheller, "Artisans, Manufacturing and the Rise of a Manufacturing Interest in Baltimore Town," *Maryland Historical Magazine* 83 (1988): 3–17; Daniels, "Alternative Workers," 115–53. Bayly Marks argues that the rise of Baltimore had a similar effect on other regional economies in "Rural Response to Urban Penetration: Baltimore and St. Mary's County, Maryland, 1790–1840," *Journal of Historical Geography* 8 (1982): 113–27.

47. The death of Duncan's wife contributed to his difficulties. *Minutes*, 1789–1797, 47.

48. Quaker parents in Kent County who apprenticed their sons to distant masters requested Certificates of Removal, which noted the boys, destinations, from the local meeting. These requests began to appear regularly in the 1780s, and were commonplace by the first decade of the nineteenth century. *Minutes of the Cecil Monthly Meeting,* 1780–1803, 181, 198, 206, 233, 312, 314, 315; and *Minutes of the Cecil Monthly Meeting, 1803–1840,* 47, 50, 55, 56, 95, and (Friends Historical Library, Swarthmore, Pa.).

49. The sheriff, Cuthbert Hall, sold one such lot in 1797, three in in 1802, and six in 1806.

50. Between 1790 and 1795, the average price per acre for improved craft lots in Chestertown was £921 19s, and the average price per acre for improved merchants' lots was £949 2s. In contrast, between 1770 and 1775, another period of economic prosperity the average price per acre for improved craft lots in Chestertown was £367 17s, and the average price per acre for improved merchants' lots was £157 5s.

51. Donald Hickey, *The War of 1812: The Forgotten Conflict* (Urbana: University of Illinois Press, 1989), 6– 7; Samuel Flagg Bemis, *Jay's Treaty: A Study in Commerce and Diplomacy* (reprint, New Haven: Yale University Press, 1962), 467–69.

52. I used a five year moving average in all the graphs to smooth out the curves. As a result, Chestertown's recovery appears to begin before 1794. In fact, the change between prices in 1793 and 1794 was abrupt and dramatic.

53. *Pennsylvania Gazette,* 1 March1748; 19 January1757; 21 May 1772.

54. Kent Land Records, JS22, 254; JS 27, 126; JS 29, 459. The name Georgetown Crossroads, however, was evidently not much in use before the 1770s. See Kent Land Records, DD5, 519; BC4, 88.

55. Ibid., DD3, 284; DD 4, 21–24, 71.

56. As Mitchell and Hofstra point out, one problem with analyzing regional settlement systems is that the "boundaries of local government units – the bases for record keeping" are not equivalent to those of the settlement systems. Mitchell and Hofstra, "How do Settlement Systems Evolve?" 126.

57. Kent Land Records, BC4, 9; TWI, 154.

58. Ibid., JS27, 126.

59. Ibid., DD3, 294, 343–46; DD4, 24–5; DD4 30–31; DD4, 71.

60. Ibid., DD4, 205, 339; DD5, 1–4, 25–27, 43–44, 414. Purchase prices have been deflated.

4

"LOOKING INTO THE NIGHT":
SLAVERY, FREEDOM, AND AFRICAN CULTURES IN AMERICA

David Hackett Fischer

Slavery time was tough, it like looking back into de dark, like looking into de night.
> – Amy Chavis Perry, former slave in Charleston, S.C.

The slave is in chains; but how is one to eradicate his love of liberty?
> – Gustave de Beaumont, a French aristocrat in America, 1835

ON 11 MAY 1831, two young French aristocrats strolled down the gangway of the steamship *President* into the swirling chaos of lower Manhattan. Alexis Charles Henri Clerel de Tocqueville and Gustave Auguste de Beaumont de La Bonninière had come officially to inspect the celebrated penitentiary systems of the United States – unofficially, to stay out of a French prison themselves after the Revolution of 1830.

For nine months these remarkable young men made an intellectual tour of the American republic. Together they visited the same places, saw the same sights, and talked with the same people. Afterward, each of them published a general work about American society. Tocqueville wrote his great treatise about freedom and democracy; Beaumont produced an ambitious novel with elaborate appendices about slavery and race.[1]

Both men were amazed by the contradictions that they observed in the same society, and even in the same scenes. In America they had observed savage violence and a deep concern for the rule of law. They found equality of manners and extreme inequality of material condition. Most puzzling of all, they were fascinated by the coexistence of slavery

120

and freedom. "Surely it is a strange fact," Beaumont remarked, "that there is so much bondage amid so much liberty."[2]

In their concern for the future, these remarkably prescient young men attempted many predictions, especially about American freedom and American slavery. On the subject of freedom they were highly optimistic, but in regard to American slavery they expected the worst. The problem seemed to them primarily a matter of race relations. "These two races," Tocqueville wrote, "are bound one to the other without intermingling; it is equally difficult for them to separate completely or unite."[3] In the same spirit, Beaumont wrote of "two inimical races, distinct in color, separated by invincible prejudice, one returning hatred for the other's scorn. There, it must be realized, is the great cancer in American society."[4]

Both men agreed that, "The most formidable evil threatening the future of the United States is the presence of the blacks on their soil."[5] They felt absolutely certain that two races could never live peacefully together in the United States. As early as 1835, they predicted that the Union would break apart over this great question, that a bloody civil war would follow, that slavery would inevitably come to an end, and that afterwards relations between the races would grow worse rather than better. They forecast an increase in racial hatred and racial violence. In the end, both men prophesied a great and terrible war between the races, ending in the complete extermination of former slaves in America. "The storm is visibly gathering," Beaumont wrote, "one can hear its distant rumblings; but none can say whom the lightning will strike."[6]

Some of these many predictions have come true. The Civil War broke out more or less as they expected, and it was violent beyond their worst fears. Slavery came to an end as they predicted, and for a long period relations between the races grew worse rather than better, just as they foresaw.

But the war of extermination between the races has not come to pass. In the late twentieth century most Americans believe as a matter of faith that different races can live peacefully together in the same country. With dramatic exceptions that dominate racial reporting in American newspapers (and academic monographs), the great majority of Americans today are truly at peace with one another, however difficult many of their problems may be. When we recall the bleakness of the vision that Tocqueville and Beaumont shared, and when we think clearly and dispassionately about what has actually happened in American history, we begin to understand where we have been, and how far we have come. We also rediscover the stubborn and triumphant fact that even after four centuries the American Republic continues to be an opening society, still painfully committed to the task of realizing its own expansive ideas of a free and just society.

The Problem Framed

A major task for historians is to understand the origin of this opening process. Through many generations this has been the central problem in American historiography. But for some years now this problem has passed out of fashion in American universities. Many scholars, particularly those who came of age in the traumatic period that followed the Vietnamese War and Watergate, prefer to ask not why America is an opening society, but why it is not more open. The very intensity of that concern is evidence that the opening process still continues, and that the central problem of American historiography – the problem of Tocqueville and Beaumont, Bancroft and Parkman, Turner and Beard, Hofstadter and Perry Miller – retains its old importance in American history. Today it is increasingly a world-historical problem, as many other societies are opening around the globe.

Historians have tended to explain the origins of an opening society in America in one of three ways – by reference to the American environment, or to the cultures that migrated to it, or to the process of migration itself. My own interest centers mainly on cultures and migrations, developing within the environment, but with an emphasis very much on cultural migrations.

In an earlier work I reported evidence that our opening society began with four great migrations from the British Isles to America in the period from 1629 to 1775.[7] As that story is the foundation of this inquiry, let me summarize it in a few paragraphs.

The four great migrations were those of: the Puritans, who came mostly from the east of England to Massachusetts Bay in 1629–40; the distressed cavaliers and indentured servants who migrated from the south and west of England to the Chesapeake (1640–75); the Quakers who moved from the English midlands to the Delaware Valley (1675–1725); and the North British Borderers who went from northern Ireland, the Scottish lowlands and the north of England to the southern back country (1717–75).

These migrants shared much in common. Most were Protestant in their religion and English in their language. They cherished a common heritage of British laws and liberties. But they came from different British regions, different religious denominations, different social ranks, and different historical generations. In the new world, they founded regional cultures that were defined by those differences.

These four groups did not divide all of America between them; other English-speaking cultures were also planted from the coast of Maine to the low country of South Carolina and Georgia. Dutch, French and Spanish cultures in the Hudson Valley, the lower Mississippi, and Florida were annexed to English-speaking America. But by 1790, the four major cultural regions were dominant, each with populations of 400,000 to 500,000 people. The other regions were much smaller. The cluster of Dutch culture in the Hudson valley included no more than 100,000 people. The transplanted white population of the South Carolina low country was 28,000 in 1790.

When these various groups came to organize new societies in America, they did most of the ordinary business of life in very different ways. They built their houses differently, organized their families on different principles, and raised their children by different methods. They had distinctive customs of sex and death, religion and magic, work and play, dress and diet. Most important they had different ideas about order, power and especially freedom.

At least four ideas of freedom developed in what is now the United States. The result was the "ordered freedom" of New England, the "hegemonic freedom" of the Chesapeake gentry, the "reciprocal freedom" of Quakers in the Delaware Valley, and the "natural freedom" of the back country. These various ideas of freedom were profoundly different from one another. They developed in America not as theoretical constructs or reflexes of material conditions, but as inherited customs and traditions. The politics of the new nation was dominated by their complex interplay. After independence, leaders from these various regions created a common frame for the coexistence of their cultural differences. That new framework became more libertarian than any one culture had ever been, or wished to be.

Those Anglo-American cultures, and their common frame, have persisted in America, even as the ethnic origins of the population changed. The Bureau of the Census reports that as the twentieth century comes to a close only about one in five Americans claim British ancestry. But nearly all Americans are British in our language, British in our laws and British in the origins of many institutions. At the same time we cherish our regional identities, and in our regional roots most of us are still Albion's seed, the heirs of four British folkways in early America.

African Cultures in America

This essay, however, is about another part of our cultural inheritance – the legacy of African folkways in America. Here the dynamics were very different. The major British migrations were for the most part voluntary, and they created cultural hegemonies in the new world. African immigrants who helped to build this voluntary society did not come as volunteers. Except in a few areas, they did not create hegemonic cultures. Nevertheless, distinctive Afro-American cultural patterns began to appear in some colonies as early as the mid-seventeenth century and have continued powerfully to our time.

The first question is conceptual – a question about how we might begin to understand the origins and development of Afro-American cultures. We find many competing models. They tend to overlap, like circles in a Venn Diagram; but each model has its own distinct center.[8]

Models of Cultural Destruction

First, a number of scholars have argued that African immigrants were unique in the degree to which they were separated from their cultural past. The classic statement of this thesis came from Franklin Frazier, who wrote that "probably never before in history has a people been so nearly stripped of its social heritage as were the Negroes who were brought to America."[9]

This belief was shared, in one form or another, by most historians of American slavery until only a few years ago. It lay behind Ulrich Phillips's conservative understanding of the plantations of the old

South as "the best schools yet invented for the mass training . . . of backward people."[10] It was shared by Phillips's liberal critic Kenneth Stampp, who devoted only two paragraphs to African culture, and organized his history of slavery around an idea of integration and assimilation, retarded only by racism and exploitation.[11] It was explicit in the work of Stanley Elkins, who described the history of Africans in America as a process of "shock and detachment" from their own culture. Of African slaves in general, he wrote, "Much of his past had been annihilated; nearly every prior connection had been severed."[12] Most writing on the history of slavery from 1918 to the 1960s shared these assumptions and beliefs.

Models of Cultural Persistence

A very different model stressed the persistence of African culture in the United States. This approach was developed by anthropologists who had worked in West Africa, particularly, Melville Herskovits in the United States and Arthur Ramos in Mexico.[13] But in the 1950s and early 1960s, liberal scholars in American universities condemned this model as politically incorrect. In a period of integration, the idea of a persistent African culture in America was regarded by liberal and radical historians as racist, wrong-headed, and deeply threatening to the progress of civil rights. During the course of 1960s, however, the criteria of political correctness on this question suddenly reversed. With the splintering of the Civil Rights movement and the emergence of Black Power, liberal and radical scholars began to celebrate continuity-models of African culture in America with the same passion that they condemned them only a few years before.

This new impulse became an important spur to research. Some of this work took the form of a demonstrating the persistence in America of specific cultural traits that Joseph Holloway has called, "Africanisms." Other scholars, for example, the art historian Robert Farris Thompson, stressed the transmission of entire constellations of cultural value from Africa to America. Some celebrated the fact of persistence itself. Others developed pluralist interpretations, but agreed that what distinguished Afro-American folkways were its African elements.[14]

Models of Cultural Interaction

A third approach argued that what was most distinctive about Afro-American culture was its interactive nature. Some scholars conceptualized it as a cultural hybrid, and located its beginnings at the meeting point of African and Eurpoean cultures on the coast of Africa during the period of the slave trade. One of these approaches is what might be called the Pidgin-Creole model, drawn mainly from the study of pidgin languages in China, Melanesia and West Africa. A pidgin is a language that nobody speaks as a native tongue. It is a highly functional means of communication that tended to develop for trading purposes, combining elements from two or more native languages with highly simplified rules of syntax, restricted vocabulary, and a narrow range of expression. Some linguists believe that Afro-English dialects on both sides of the ocean began as a pidgin, and derivative forms came to be spoken as a native or creole language.[15] This Pidgin-Creole model has been taken as a clue to the history of Afro-American culture in general. It was an important element of one of the best ethnographic histories that we have been given so far, Charles Joyner's *Down By the Riverside*, on the slave communities that formed along the Waccamaw River in coastal South Carolina.[16]

Interaction in the Middle

Another model, while incorporating elements of the Pidgin-Creole construct, takes another approach that centers less on the African coast, and more on the middle passage. In 1973, anthropologists Sidney Mintz and Richard Price developed a highly complex model of this sort. They began with the assumptions that the cultures of western and central Africa were highly diverse, that the slave trade was so structured as to block the direct movement of specific African culture to the new world, and that slaves from many different ethnic regions in Africa were scattered through many parts of America. They hypothesized that in the middle passage, and on the earliest American plantations dyadic relations began to develop among individual slaves who began to create for themselves a new syncretistic Afro-American culture that combined various African elements. Mintz and Price gave particular importance to what they called "deep-level cultural principles" that were widely shared in west and central Africa. They argued that "people in Afro-American societies, even within the context of oppression that pervaded them, quite literally built their lifeways to meet their daily needs."[17]

Yet another approach appears in the work of John Thornton, an African historian who agrees with Mintz and Price on some questions, but believes that they were mistaken in several of their major assumptions. From much pathbreaking research in African historical materials, Thornton concluded that the Mintz-Price model (and other work in the field) overstated the diversity in African cultures, and exaggerated the extent to which the slave trade disrupted the transmission of specific African cultures.

While agreeing that the nature and rate of demographic change are relevant, Thornton argues that "wherever more than a few slaves from the same nation were concentrated in towns or estates, cultural transfer was possible." He describes the development in Afro-American culture as a process that included stronger and more specific links to specific African cultures, and stronger interactions between African and European cultures, an interaction that he believes to have begun in Africa itself, and to have gone very far before the middle passage. Thornton's essay on the Stono Rebellion finds evidence that it was led by Angolan slaves who had been converted to Catholicism in Africa and were unhappy to find themselves not only enslaved in South Carolina, but slaves to Protestant masters.[18]

Models of Cultural Interaction in America: Accommodation and Resistance

Still other scholars have followed the interactive theme into later periods of American history from the eighteenth to the twentieth centuries, particularly with regard to the interplay of African and European cultures in America. The path-breaking work was done by John Blassingame, Eugene Genovese and Herbert Gutman in the 1970s showed a distinctive Afro-American culture developed within strong slave communities and families as an instrument of accommodation and resistance.[19] Mechal Sobel, in her work on Afro-American religion and on the interplay of African and European values among individuals in eighteenth-century Virginia, extended this general model, which continues to yield important results, especially when integrated with other lines of inquiry.[20]

A Problem for Research

Each of these approaches has expanded our understanding of their common problem. All of them, even those that are out of fashion, have things to teach us. But none has given general satisfaction, and as organizing models their claims are mutually contradictory. One can attempt to resolve these contradictions by thinking of the task as a conceptual problem to be resolved by an effort at reconciliation or refinement. Another approach is to think of the relative merit of these competing claims as an empirical question, to be resolved by historical research.

This inquiry takes the empirical approach. The evidence is now very abundant. In the past generation, a revolution has occurred in the range and depth of the sources that are available to the historian of slavery and Afro-American culture. Phillips and Stampp were among the first to collect and exploit systematically the plantation records that Stampp's microfilm edition is just now making generally available to students throughout the country. New plantation records continue to be discovered and made available – for example, in 1997 the remarkable Davison-McDowell collection was added to the Carolinian Library in Columbia, South Carolina.[21]

The records of the domestic slave trade and correspondence of white slave traders and overseers are also being exploited by historians and economists such as Edmund Drago who has compiled and edited the extensive correspondence of a Carolina slave trader.[22] A surprisingly large number of letters written by American slaves have been found, and many have been published by Robert Starobin and Randall Miller.[23] Similarly, the efforts of George Rawick, Charles Perdue, Thomas Barden, Robert Phillips and other historians have made the slave narratives generally available to scholars. Their quality has been assessed empirically by historian Paul Escott, who finds that many of criticisms made against them are invalid.[24]

Another and very different corpus of source material appears in the slave autobiographies that began to be published in the eighteenth century. These sources permit life cycle analysis, even from one cohort to the next, and makes it possible to answer such questions as how family cohesion through the life cycle actually changed through time. For example, a study of more than one hundred of these autobiographies shows that in them the proportion of families that remained intact until the author reached the age of sixteen was zero! From this the startling conclusion must be drawn that every slave child suffered a broken family – every one, from the beginning to the end of slavery.[25]

In our own time, the evidence of historical archeology and material culture is rapidly coming available. Other categories of source materials that have long been used in an anecdotal way are now being exploited systematically – advertisements for fugitive slaves, legal records, travelers accounts and much more.[26]

The Diversity of Afro-American Slavery

When one studies these materials the first finding – and one of the most important – is the diversity of Afro-American cultures. Much scholarship has tended to discuss Afro-American culture as if it were a single entity. Powerful political imperatives have tended to support interpretations that stressed cultural unity in this way. This unitary interpretation is historically incorrect. The Afro-American cultural heritage in the United States is at least as diverse as that of Anglo-America. We have tended to understate the astonishing richness and variety of Afro-American cultures. In the process, we have missed something profoundly important in its history.

Within the present boundaries of the United States, at least ten distinctive Afro-American cultures developed by the early nineteenth century. The first and largest in the mid-seventeenth century was not in what we call the South today, but in New Netherlands, where the maps of the West India Company in 1639 showed a separate settlement called the slave camp, on Manhattan Island, north of New Amsterdam. The second largest in 1650 was in New England, later expanding through the northern tier and in the eighteenth century assimilating with the various remnants of native American groups. Among the most creative was the Afro-American culture that emerged during the late seventeenth and early eighteenth centuries in the Quaker colonies of the Delaware Valley, which in time extended through midland America, leaving behind trace elements that also intermarried with both Europeans and more often Indians.

By far the most expansive regions were the cultures developed at the same time in tidewater Chesapeake and Carolina low country. Both of these cultural regions grew so rapidly in the early and mid-eighteenth century, that on the eve of the Revolution they included 70 percent of Afro-Americans in mainland British America. Other distinctive Afro-American cultures also crystallized within the present boundaries of the United States in French Louisiana (where many Cajuns are bi- or tri-racial) and in Spanish Florida.

The most interesting and most obscure system of bondage in America was Afro-Indian slavery, which existed on a larger scale than most historians of slavery have recognized. Southern Indians were traders in slaves, but had none of the racial sense of the Europeans – or at least a different racial sense. They adopted blacks into their families and on occasion elevated them to the role of chief while at the same time they enslaved and sold Indians from other groups. The Afro-Indian communities that formed along the Florida border and were attacked by Andrew Jackson and Francis Gaines in 1816 and 1818 during the First Seminole War, had populations reckoned in thousands. Many other small cultures of the sort called triracial isolates still exist today from New England to Florida.

After the American revolution, two other very large regional Afro-American cultures began to develop in the early republic. One of them formed in Kentucky and Tennessee, while another took root in the southern highlands, especially on that fertile crescent of rich cotton land stretching from upcountry Carolina through Georgia and Alabama to the Mississippi Delta. By the time of the Civil War, it had become the largest regional Afro-American culture (or set of cultures) in the United States. Many works that generalize about Afro-American slave culture in a unitary way refer primarily to the Black Belt.

These cultural entities could be variously consolidated or subdivided, depending on one's taste for lumping or splitting. There is an empirical basis for a taxonomy of Afro-American regions, mainly in the evidence of regional patterns of speech, which for example suggests that the cotton belt culture from upcountry South Carolina to Mississippi Delta was a linguistic unit, however large and diverse.[27] These ten cultures, however, represent only the largest identifiable groups and my no means exhaust the subject. One could multiply other examples of small distinctive cultures. In the Cape Fear Valley of North Carolina, a small but highly distinctive Afro-Scottish culture developed among Gaelic-speaking African slaves. In the lower Delaware Valley there was an Afro-Swedish culture.

Determinants of Diversity: Hegemonic
European and American Cultures

All of these regional cultures began in slavery. Even in the northern colonies before the Revolution, more than 95 percent of the Afro-Americans were slaves. It is easy for cultural historians to forget the fundamental fact that slavery was everywhere a system of forced labor, maintained always by the threat of violence, and often by its application. Slavery in that sense existed in every part of North America before the American Revolution, and throughout most parts of the world. But its existence took different forms. Before the American Revolution there were many different systems of slave law within the present limits of the United States. These legal systems differed from one another. In some of them, slaves were chattels; in others, real estate. Some allowed slaves virtually no legal rights; others guaranteed their right to marry, to hold property, to execute contracts, and go to law. Some systems of law discouraged religious observance by slaves; others required it.[28]

These differences were not merely a matter of individual provisions, but of fundamentally different ideas of slavery itself, and of different structures of cultural value and material order. The laws of New England made slaves into biblical bondservants in ways that were linked to the founding purposes of the Puritan colonies. The black codes of Louisiana envisioned slaves as wards and servants of an absolutist state. The bylaws of New Netherlands made bondage into a negotiable instrument, subject to complex processes of commercial bargaining between master and slave which created conditions of quasi-freedom.

Behind these different systems of slave-law lay different social imperatives that flowed from the hegemonic European cultures in each American region. Nowhere did slavery create these environing cultures. Everywhere, even in Virginia and South Carolina, these cul-

tures created slavery according to their own special purposes and
needs. While the legal forms of slavery codified by the Euro-American
cultural polities, the institution of slavery as it evolved and the response of the slaves themselves in the various regional labor forces
effected the process to varying degrees.

Determinants of Diversity: African Cultural Origins and Demography

If one dimension of difference was to be found in hegemonic European cultures, a second differentiating factor arose from place of African
origin. This is a subject of high complexity, but some things are clear
enough. Beyond doubt, patterns of African migration differed from
one American region to another, not in the way of a simple identity of
African and American regions, but in more complex ways. Virtually all
Afro-American regions drew from a broad range of African cultures
from Senegambia to Angola, and a small scattering even from Mada-
gascar and Mozambique as well. But each region had its own distinctive mix, in which a few cultures were predominant.

What is important here is not merely the aggregate pattern of
African origins but other things as well. In many regions, some African
cultures had an importance out of proportion to their numbers by
reason of the timing of their arrival, or their place of settlement, or
patterns of gender, occupation or special skills. Here again, as in
Anglo-American migrations, there were also African groups that established cultural ascendencies and preserved them for many years. A
case in point is an excellent book on French Louisiana by Gwendolyn
Hall, who makes a strong and persuasive case for the critical importance of Bambara slaves in the Afro-American culture of that colony,
even though other African nations were more numerous in subsequent
migrations.[29]

Yet another factor was the response of European masters to the
diversity of African cultures. In some colonies, slaves were encouraged
to find spouses of the same nation, and to settle and assemble together. In other regions this did not happen, and in some places it was
actively forbidden. Here was another determinant of regional development.[30]

If one differentiating factor was the hegemonic European culture and another was the pattern of African origin and settlement, a third was the demographic ratio of Africans to Europeans in each American region. The actual range of variations was as broad as the limit of possibility. In many parts of New England, Africans were less than 1 percent of the colonial population. On Butler Island, Georgia, Africans were more than 99 percent of the inhabitants in most seasons. This ratio made a fundamental difference in cultural development.[31]

These differences were further reinforced by other related demographic, social and economic factors: the size of slave-holdings, units of residence; methods of farm management; the extent of cultural relations and assimilation; and the patterns of sexual contact between Americans of African and European dissent. All of these patterns varied greatly from one region to another in ways that made a difference for the formation of African-American culture.[32]

Dynamics of Cultural Development

The second stage of the inquiry involves the question of cultural development from these determinants. Although the details will consume a large part of my forthcoming volume on this subject, the major findings can be summarized in a few sentences. First, Afro-American culture was no more monolithic than Anglo-American culture. It has left a heritage that is far more rich and complex than most general accounts suggest. This richness and complexity was elaborately patterned in historical and regional terms. Second, Afro-American cultures developed from the interplay of different elements. It cannot be understood in monolithic terms, either in terms of the assimilation of European culture or of the persistence of African patterns. These were syncretistic systems that developed from the meeting and mingling of European and African cultures in an American environment. Third, and finally, the African inheritance was profoundly important – more so than historians of earlier generations imagined.

These three components were brought together in many different ways depending on the impact of the hegemonic European cultures with which they interacted, and the nature of the American environment that provides the natural context for the development of these diverse cultural patterns.

Patterns of Change Through Time

An important empirical task is to create a chronology of Afro-American cultural development. On this problem very little progress was made in pioneering works. The abundant primary evidence casts its light upon the subject mostly in the form of spotlights which illuminate small segments of the question with great intensity, but leave other parts in darkness.

To solve this problem, we need empirical indicators that might test the timing and rhythm of assimilation and acculturation in Afro-American cultures as a historical variable. Such a time series can be derived from advertisements for fugitive slaves, on questions such as literacy and occupation. In most regions they show a very interesting pattern of nonlinear change. During the eighteenth century, literacy and skilled occupations increased among African slaves, reaching a peak in the early nineteenth century, then declining from 1830 to 1860.

The evidence suggests that southern attempts to forbid slave literacy became more effective after the advent David Walker, Nat Turner and William Lloyd Garrison. They also confirm much individual testimony (by Frederick Douglass for example) that both slaves and free blacks were being driven out of skilled occupations by increasing competition from whites. One might combine these findings with other evidence for later periods which shows an enormous surge of interest in formal education among freedmen during Reconstruction, followed by a strong countermovement thereafter. A further reinforcement appears in the twentieth century, with its recurrent rhythm of integrationist and separatist movements in America.

This evidence suggests a series of strong wave-like assimilation movements, punctuated by sweeping reactions in which Afro- Americans were cruelly punished for rapid acculturation. Similar wavelike movements continued into the twentieth century, not so much in the form of surge and decline but surge and stasis.

All of this suggests of a distinctive chronology of Afro-American cultural history, one that is closely keyed to major historical events, and to elements of contingency. Further, to study Afro-American proverbs and music and literature is to find that this nonlinear chronology is much stronger as a folk memory among young people in our urban ghettos today than it is in academic historiography – a fact of high relevance to our present discontents.

The Articulation of Afro-American Cultures

The next step in comprehending the opening process is to explore the substantive content of Afro-American regional cultures. Each of these regional cultures might be understood, equally with various Anglo-American cultures, as constituting a distinctive set of folkways which collectively express a coherent structure of cultural values. Where possible, one might use the same indicators as in *Albion's Seed* – language, vernacular architecture, and onomastics – plus others that are particularly helpful when one is studying predominantly oral cultures, such as material artifacts, music, and dance.

It is not possible to summarize in this short essay the results in a comprehensive way, but a few illustrative examples might be discussed briefly to indicate the texture of our findings. In regard to language, we find many different Afro-American speechways. In the South during the mid-twentieth century, Black radio stations sponsored contests in which examples were given of Afro-American speech, and prizes were given to listeners who could identify what part of the country the speaker came from. Evidence is accumulating of the existence of a broad variety of regional Afro-American speechways – some evidence from current study, some from linguistic analysis of slave narratives, and some from earlier historical sources.[33]

All of these regional speech patterns were distinctively Afro-American, but some (notably in New England) were very close to the hegemonic Anglo-American speech. Others were more distant – especially Gullah, and the Afro-French speechways of Louisiana that is sometimes called "Gombo." Somewhere in between was what Frederick Douglass called the "Guinea speech" of the Chesapeake colonies.

To study these speechways is to discover that the pioneering work by Charles Joyner and others has established that some of linguistic dynamics of Pidgin-Creole languages operated powerfully in Afro-American speech. In general, Afro-American speechways were like Pidgins in the fact that they were predominantly oral languages which bridged between cultural worlds.

But in other ways they were very different from Pidgins. Though some of their grammar and syntactical forms may have been simplified as Pidgins are, the range of expression became in some dimensions broader and more complex than Pidgins – and also broader than either African or European languages alone had been. They were also in some ways more creative. This process of linguistic creativity was invigorated by a process of crossfertilization. The mixture of linguistic forms created structures more open, more flexible, more friendly to invention. One thinks in particular of the extraordinary richness of Afro-American languages in metaphorical constructions, and also in other forms of imagery that do not exist so strongly in European rhetoric. Other examples are the heavy use of accent, rhythm, and rhyme (as in many oral languages), and the reconstruction of vocabulary and syntax not for purposes of precise meaning and rational content as in most written languages, but for aural impact, and emotive meaning. An example would be the word for bird in Louisiana Gombo, where the gentle French *l'oiseau* becomes the explosive *zozo*, with much stronger broader range of aural impact, and an impact that could be directed in many different emotive directions.

The mix of European and African ingredients varied broadly from one of these Afro-American speechways to another, more or less in a ratio to the composition of population, and other determinant factors mentioned above. In general all of these speechways were predominantly European in their linguistic materials. Even in Gullah or Gombo, as Africanists argue about the various weights of Bantu and West African languages, a good 90 percent of Gullah vocabulary was English; and a similar proportion of Gombo words were French. Here the hegemonic cultures showed their power.

But the true test can never be a simple count of symbols. The genius of these Afro-American speechways was to put European and African materials to new uses that went far beyond the parent languages and created something genuinely new. This happened everywhere that Africans settled in America – in New England and New Netherlands, as well as in South Carolina and Louisiana where African elements were stronger. The important thing was the creativity of cultural interactions, not the relative proportion of one set of cultural ingredients to another.[34]

This interaction put in motion a set of linguistic processes that are today more creative than ever. Their creativity derives not predominantly from Africa or Europe, but from the interplay between the two in the new world. Further, this creativity once formed in the slave cultures of early America spread also into hegemonic linguistic cultures, and today is transforming many languages throughout the world.

As it was with speech, so also with vernacular architecture, many forms of material culture, diet, dress, and body language – and not merely discrete traits alone, but something much deeper. Similar trends appeared in the remodeling of social institutions such as the family. It also developed in the reconstruction of social values which convert an array of cultural traits into a functioning ethical system. Among these values were ideas of order, power, and especially freedom.

Freedom as an African American Folkway

In *Albion's Seed* I argued that the four British folkways in America developed different ideas of order, power and freedom. Precisely the same thing also happened in Afro-American cultures. Consider the problem of freedom. This I believe to have been a western idea, which developed in Europe and was carried to America as a living process of folk tradition – not a fixed set of formal academic doctrines that were the rationales of freedom. Ironically, the people of Africa first met western traditions of freedom when they were in chains. They instantly appropriated these ideas and changed them profoundly in that process. Orlando Patterson, however, has recently suggested that slaves created their own ideas of personal liberty in the ancient world.[35]

I would suggest two related possibilities. The evidence is very strong that slaves in the new world transformed the meaning of freedom in at least two very different ways. First, their presence in America challenged some people to transform the old folk traditions of western freedom from tribal possessions to universal ideas. This happened most of all in British America, and especially in those colonies that were planted by Quakers and Puritans. It is presently fashionable to write of the history of slavery as evidence of the moral obliquity of western and especially American society. Nothing could be further from the truth. The English-speaking people of the British Empire were not distinctive in keeping slaves, but they were the first people to end slavery. The abolition of forced bondage in England itself and nine states of English-speaking America were the first emancipations anywhere in the world. Americans of African and European descent worked together in this effort.

At the same time, African Americans themselves transformed freedom in another way. In various regional cultures, African slaves developed new ideas of freedom that were meaningful even when they were still in chains. They extended western ideas of freedom into a new realm of consciousness and being. They extended it to freedom of the spirit, freedom of the soul, freedom of the senses, freedom of the body.

These new ideas of freedom expressed themselves not only in new forms of expression, but also in new ways of inventing these forms, and new ideas of invention itself. All this appeared simultaneously in the creativity of African-American speech, dance, worship, music, and many other forms of thought and expression. This new freedom of thought, feeling, and expression appeared everywhere that Africans settled in the new world. It took many different forms, and flourished in the regional complexity of African-American cultures. The variety of syncretistic African folkways made these processes more open and creative than any unified culture alone could have.

In time, this new ferment of thought and expression spread rapidly from African-American slaves to their masters and mistresses. After slavery, this new dimension of freedom presented an ethical challenge to hegemonic cultures of White America. Afro-American ideas of freedom were not easily reconciled with the ordered freedom of the Puritans, or the hegemonic freedoms of the cavaliers. After slavery, segregation was a functional system for keeping separate not merely two races but two cultures, and not merely two cultures but two ethics. Not until the appearance of the civil rights movement in the 1950s and 1960s were these traditions of freedom reconciled. The first work in this series, *Albion's Seed*, concluded that we are all English in parts of our culture. At the same time, we are all African in others. These folk traditions that confronted one another in colonial America are still mixing and merging in unexpected ways, and transforming ethical systems throughout the world.

Notes

1. Alexis de Tocqueville, *Democracy in America*, ed. J. P. Mayer, and trans. George Lawrence (Garden City, N.J.: Doubleday, 1969); Gustave de Beaumont, *Marie or Slavery in the United States, A Novel of Jacksonian America*, ed. Alvis L. Tinnin and trans. Barbara Chapman (Stanford: Stanford University Press, 1958), which unhappily omitted historical and sociological appendices integral to the work. For the originals see Alexis de Tocqueville, *De la Démocratie en Amérique*, 2 vols. (Paris, 1835); and Gustave de Beaumont, *Marie, ou l'Esclavage Etats-Unis, Tableau de Moeurs Américaines,* 2 vols. (Paris, 1835).

2. Beaumont, *Marie*, 4; epigraph from 191.

3. Tocqueville, *Democracy in America*, 340.

4. Beaumont, *Marie*, 216.

5. Tocqueville. *Democracy in America*, 340.

6. Beaumont, *Marie*, 216.

7. David Hackett Fischer, *Albion's Seed: Four British Folkways in America* (New York: Oxford University Press, 1989).

8. For general surveys see Peter J. Parish, *Slavery: History and Historians* (New York: Harper & Row, 1989); Peter Kolchin, *American Slavery, 1619–1877* (New York: Hill and Wang, 1993).

9. E. Franklin Frazier, *The Negro Family in the United States* (Chicago: University of Chicago Press, 1939), 20.

10. Ulrich B. Phillips, *Life and Labor in the Old South* (Boston: Little Brown, 1929), 4, 198; *American Negro Slavery: A Survey of the Supply, Employment and Control of Negro Labor as Determined by the Plantation Regime* (New York: D. Appleton & Co., 1918), 291, 309, 313, 325, 342–43.

11. Kenneth M. Stampp, *The Peculiar Institution; Slavery in the Ante-Bellum South* (New York: Alfred A. Knopf, 1956), 12–14.

12. Stanley M. Elkins, *Slavery: A Problem in American Institutional and Intellectual Life* (Chicago: University of Chicago Press, 1959), 101–2.

13. Melville J. Herskovits, *Acculturation: The Study of Culture Contact* (New York: J. J. Augustin, 1938); idem., "The Negro in Bahia, Brazil: A Problem in Method," *American Sociological Review* 8 (1943): 394–402; *The Myth of the Negro Past* (1941; rev. ed., Boston: Beacon Press, 1958); Arthur Ramos, *Las culturas negras en el nueva mundo* (Mexico City: Fondo de Cultura Economica, 1943).

14. Joseph E. Holloway, ed., *Africanisms in American Culture* (Bloomington: Indiana University Press, 1990); Robert Farris Thompson, *Flash of the Spirit: African and Afro-American Art and Philosophy* (New York: Random House, 1983).

15. Molefi Kete Asante, "African Elements in African-American English," in *Africanisms in American Culture*, ed., Holloway, 19–33.

16. Charles Joyner, *Down by the Riverside: A South Carolina Slave Community* (Urbana: University of Illinois Press, 1984).

17. Sidney W. Mintz and Richard Price, *An Anthropological Approach to the Afro-American Past: A Caribbean Perspective* (Philadelphia: Institute for the Study of Human Issues, 1976), 7.

18. John Thornton, *Africa and Africans in the Making of the Atlantic World, 1400–1680* (Cambridge, Eng.: Cambridge University Press, 1992), 180–92, 204.

19. John W. Blassingame, *The Slave Community: Plantation Life in the Antebellum South* (1972; rev. and enl., New York: Oxford University Press, 1979); Eugene Genovese, *Roll, Jordan, Roll: The World the Slaves Made* (1972; reprint, New York: Pantheon Books, 1974); Herbert G. Gutman, *The Black Family in Slavery and Freedom, 1750–1925* (New York: Pantheon Books, 1976).

20. Mechal Sobel, *The World They Made Together; Black and White Values in Eighteenth Century Virginia* (Princeton, N.J.: Princeton University Press, 1987).

21. Kenneth M. Stampp, comp., "Records of Ante-Bellum Southern Plantations from the Revolution through the Civil War," University Publications of America, now nearly 1000 reels of microfilm.

22. Edmund L. Drago, ed., *Broke by the War: Letters of a Slave Trader* (Columbia: University of South Carolina Press, 1991).

23. Robert S. Starobin, ed., *Blacks in Bondage: Letters of American Slaves* (New York: New Viewpoints, 1974); Randall M. Miller, ed., *"Dear Master": Letters of a Slave Family* (Ithaca, N.Y.: Cornell University Press, 1978).

24. George P. Rawick, ed., *The American Slave: A Composite Autobiography*, 39 vols. (Westport, Conn.: Greenwood Press, 1972–79); Charles L. Perdue, et al., *Weevils in the Wheat; Interviews with Virginia Ex-Slaves* (Charlottesville; University Press of Virginia, 1976); Paul D. Escort, *Slavery Remembered: A Record of Twentieth Century Slave Narratives* (Chapel Hill: University of North Carolina Press, 1979).

25. This research was carried out by Jane Reynolds in the author's seminar at Brandeis University, and a copy of the resulting paper is in the possession of the author.

26. Leland Ferguson, *Uncommon Ground: Archeology and Early African America, 1650–1800* (Washington, D.C.: Smithsonian Institution Press, 1992); Theresa A. Singleton, ed., *The Archeology of Slavery and Plantation Life* (Orlando, Fla.: Academic Press, 1985).

27. Edgar W Schneider, *Morphologische und syntaktische Variablen im amerikanischen Early Black English* (Frankfurt am Main: Lang, 1981).

28. On how the legal forms of slavery were framed and evolved see: Ira Berlin and Philip D. Morgan, eds., *Cultivation and Culture: Labor and the Shaping of Slave Life in the Americas* (Charlottesville: University Press of Virginia, 1993); Philip D. Morgan, "British Encounters with Africans and African Americans, circa 1600–1780," in *Strangers within the Realm: Cultural Margins of the First British Empire*, eds., Bernard Bailyn and Philip D. Morgan (Chapel Hill:

University of North Carolina Press, 1991), 157–219; and Thomas D. Morris, *Southern Slavery and the Law, 1619–1860* (Chapel Hill: University of North Carolina Press, 1996).

29. Gwendolyn Midlo Hall, *Africans in Colonial Louisiana; The Development of Afro-Creole Culture in the Eighteenth Century* (Baton Rouge: Louisiana State University Press, 1992).

30. A controversial new interpretation appears in Brenda Stevenson, *Life in Black and White: Family and Community in the Slave South* (New York: Oxford University Press, 1996).

31. Malcolm Bell, Jr., *Major Butler's Legacy; Five Generations of a Slaveholding Family* (Athens: University of Georgia Press, 1987).

32. For attention to regional differences the most useful work is still Lewis Cecil Gray, *History of Agriculture in the Southern United States to 1860*, 2 vols. (1932, reprint, Washington, D.C.: Carnegie Institution of Washington, 1958), but see also Robert W. Fogel and Stanley L. Engerman, *Time on the Cross: The Economics of American Negro Slavery*, 2 vols. (Boston: Little Brown and Co., 1974); and Paul David, et al., *Reckoning with Slavery: A Critical Study in the Quantitative History of American Negro Slavery* (New York: Oxford University Press, 1976). On sexual relations: Joel Williamson, *New People: Miscegenation and Mulattoes in the United States* (Baton Rouge: Louisiana State University Press, 1995).

33. Salikoko S. Mufwene, ed., *Africanisms in Afro-American Language Varieties* (Athens: University of Georgia Press, 1993).

34. Michael Montgomery, ed., *The Crucible of Carolina: Essays on the Development of Gullah Language and Culture* (Athens: University of Georgia Press, 1994).

35. Orlando Patterson, *Freedom in the Making of Western Culture* (New York: Basic Books, 1991).

5

"BETWEEN THE TIMES":
POPULAR RELIGION IN EIGHTEENTH-CENTURY
BRITISH NORTH AMERICA

David D. Hall

O N A MARCH DAY IN 1705, the townspeople of Taunton, Massachusetts, gathered in their meetinghouse for a ceremony of covenant renewal. "We gave Liberty to all Men and Women Kind, from sixteen years old and upwards to act with us," the minister of the town reported, "and had three hundred Names given in to list under Christ." Remarkable in and of itself, the ceremony also stirred up powerful feelings among a particular group of participants; in the words of the same narrator, the scene included "Parents weeping for Joy, seeing their Children give their names to Christ.[1] A century later, on a cold January day in 1801, Nathan Barlow, a farmer living in frontier Maine, returned home from hearing an evangelical minister depict "hell's horrors" and suddenly found himself in the presence of the risen Christ, who "carried me away as quick as a flash of lightning (my spirit I mean, for I was sensible at the time that I had left my body behind, and had no feeling of weight, but light as air.)" Barlow was taken on a tour of hell and then to the very "gates of heaven to see God and the saved in all their ecstatic glory."[2]

These episodes invite us to reflect on what constituted "the religious" for the English-speaking colonists in eighteenth-century America.[3] That invitation gains its force from juxtaposing such forms of spiritual experience with the standard religious narratives and church history for this period. Is there room within these narratives for Barlow and the parents overcome with joy? And if not, what must we do to fashion a more inclusive story? To answer this question, I will apply three major frameworks of interpretation.

The longest-lasting of these frameworks is the narrative of declension, which antedates the eighteenth century. Familiar to most of us through the second volume of Perry Miller's *The New England Mind*, this tale of how Puritanism (read: Calvinism) lapsed into "hypocrisy" and "formality" may be traced back through evangelical historians in the nineteenth century to clerical voices among the second-generation colonists.[4] Its appeal seems undiminished in our day, for it has turned up anew in the work of William McLoughlin, Edmund S. Morgan, and C. C. Goen, among many others. Thus in an introduction to Edwards's writings about the Great Awakening, Goen indicted the halfway covenant of 1662 for contributing to "New England's departure from the experiential [Calvinist] tradition," steps that Goen interpreted as hastening the rise of "Arminianism."[5] The whole of this interpretative tradition is epitomized in a rhetorical gesture that James Carse makes in setting the scene for Jonathan Edwards's emergence as a minister: "What sparks were left of the once vivid fires of Puritanism had been stamped out by such modern men as Solomon Stoddard."[6]

Almost as long-lived is a narrative that focuses on the emergence of toleration and the disentangling of church and state. Detached from these specifics, this narrative has a larger meaning that we may term "emancipation": the eighteenth century becomes a moment of redefinition as the colonists learn to discard certain ways of doing things and to affirm others. In a casual piece of writing from 1920, Carl Van Doren thus linked emblematically "the defeated" Jonathan Edwards and the triumphant Benjamin Franklin; the one man looked backward even as the other helped fashion the pragmatically secular and progressive ethos of a new America.[7] As in Van Doren's version of the eighteenth century, so in many others its significance is that the spirit or genius of "American" culture emerged from the shell of European ways. As in his scheme, so elsewhere the eighteenth century becomes the moment when immigrant, hierarchical or exclusivist religious bodies accommodated themselves to plurality, a process that generated a new institutional structure, the denomination.[8] In combination, the emergence of the denomination and the separation of church and state signify the "Americanization" of Protestantism, a refashioning of religious structures in keeping with the broader structures of American nationhood. The convergence between the religious and the sociopolitical (that is, a politically independent, proto-democratic nation) culminates in the argument that, on the very eve of the Revolution, "civil religion" made its first appearance. [9]

A third narrative is close cousin to the first two enumerated. Focusing on the evolution of ideas within learned culture, it traces the emergence of a utilitarian ethics understanding of providence, and a concept of "natural religion,"or a universal capacity within humankind to discern the rules of virtue and the existence of God.[10] Such ideas, which first gained favor in England after 1690, were becoming influential in the colonies by midcentury. The traditional name for them is "the Enlightenment," though in the New England (and American) context we are just as apt to speak of "liberalism." Liberalism redefined religion as a system of ethics, a system grounded on (mostly) natural and utilitarian principles or faculties. Because it became the religion of choice among some of the Founding Fathers, and notably so in the case of Thomas Jefferson, liberalism lends itself to being subsumed within the story line of emancipation. And it can also be represented as providing the substance of the American version of the Enlightenment, with all the overtones of well-merited progress that the very term "Enlightenment" can convey.[11]

Each of these narratives has its critics; each has properly been challenged as inadequate or even incorrect.[12] For present purposes, however, I want to sidestep these currents of historiography and return to the matter of "the religious." A simple observation will suffice: the three paradigms I outlined do not encompass the visionary experiences of Nathan Barlow or the emotions released by the ceremony of covenant renewal. To account for them we must look elsewhere.

We come closer to the fabric of religion for the Barlows of eighteenth-century America when we turn to the pietists and evangelicals on both sides of the Atlantic – John Wesley and George Whitefield in England, John Willison in Scotland, and Jonathan Edwards in New England, to name a handful of the leading figures – who insisted that true religion was a matter of inner experience occasioned by the supernatural action of the Holy Spirit. Thanks to a recent cluster of studies carried out by historians who share a "neo-evangelical" perspective, these eighteenth-century figures have taken on a fresh importance in our understanding of American religious history.[13] Yet we can be certain that Edwards and company would have shared the sentiments of an ordained Congregational minister who, encountering men like Barlow on the Maine frontier at the beginning of the nineteenth century, described them as persons "to be pitied and prayed for, who take the flights of a wild and disordered brain for the genuine dictates of wisdom."[14] Keeping in mind, as we must, Jonathan Edwards's vigorous critique of "New Light" anticlericalism and spirituality,[15] it may be that evangelicalism should be understood less as a unitary phenomenon than as a movement charged with contradictory possibilities in theology and ecclesiology. Only if we open up the meaning of evangelicalism does it begin to account for the practices and emotions of Barlow and the people who assembled in Taunton.

By way of opening things up, a strategy for making sense of Nathan Barlow and the events of Taunton and Cranbury is to broach the term "popular religion." In so doing my purpose is twofold: to place at the center of inquiry the agency of ordinary people in fashioning what for them constituted "the religious," and equally to direct attention to practices around which tensions accumulate, practices that often make visible the varying expectations of the laity and the clergy. That which constitutes "the religious" can be framed schematically as follows:

(1) The boundaries of the religious are wider and more permeable than is often acknowledged. Within every religious system certain religious specialists take on the task of "polarizing authority, knowledge, ritual, and religious belief between true and authentic on the one hand, erroneous and counterfeit on the other."[16] The historian of popular religion must step outside this process and the categories that it generates: the forms of hierarchy that (explicitly or implicitly) valorize "reason" over "enthusiasm" and "superstition," literacy and learning over "illiteracy,"[17] orthodoxy over heterodoxy. In openirig up these boundaries, we may need to pass beyond the method of intellectual history, which tends to privilege systems of "beliefs."

(2) The religious inheres in what people practice or perform.

(3) Lay people participate unevenly in official ("orthodox") forms of religious practice. Some rhythms of participation are related to gender and the stages of the life cycle. The intermittancy of participation may also be understood as arising from any of several forms of dissatisfaction.

(4) One form of dissatisfaction is expressed in the behavior of persons we may term "Seekers." Rejecting the authority of the institutional church, these people affiliate with alternative forms of authority and stringent ritual practices. Or they may become persistent improvisers.

(5) The religious has close relations to healing, understood not only (or even primarily) as physiological but as spiritual, moral, and social. Here we encounter the paradox that certain forms of the religious engender "perplexities" (to use a term current in the eighteenth century) that are addressed and possibly resolved or alleviated by other forms of the religious.

Though I am hesitant to provide a single name for this several-sided description, the phrase "popular religion" may do well enough. It is advantageous in shifting our attention away from the clergy and toward the laity. A further advantage is that it stimulates a rethinking of how, so often, we privilege certain forms of religion and relegate others to the periphery; to paraphrase William James's characterization of pragmatism, the category of popular religion can unstiffen our habitual ways of doing cultural and religious history. In particular, it encourages us to acknowledge the multitude of meanings and practices that we encounter at every turn. And because the term implies a particular social location, "the people," it challenges us to discern the connections between religion and society.

Yet another justification of the term is that the rethinking of religion and society it inspires has sharply affected our understanding of seventeenth-century America. The payoff has been high, as two or three examples will indicate. At the beginning of the 1970s a crisis beset intellectual history and the history of religion when proponents of the "new social history" jettisoned Perry Miller's unitary "mind." Darrett Rutman, who led the charge against Miller, scornfully dismissed "declension" as something the ministers conjured up. He went on to argue in *Winthrop's Boston* that the Puritan vision of an ordered, religiously observant society disintegrated almost immediately in the social experience of the colonists who arrived in the 1630s. In retrospect we realize that Rutman's was a restrictive definition of religion; for him, if people disagreed on how to organize a congregation or did not always go to church, they were not religious. These restrictions figured in his very definition of Puritanism, which he interpreted as a top-down movement that arose among the clergy. Others were quick to draw the conclusion that "the people" were indifferent to ideas expressed by the clergy.[18] Hence the crisis, or better yet, the impasse of allowing social history to become antagonistic to intellectual history.

That crisis disappeared once the phrase "popular religion" came on the scene, for it filled in the void between the clergy, who from the vantage of the social historian were monopolizing religion, and the people, who seemed otherwise occupied. The new category, with its underlying postulate of agency, opened up the possibility that lay people were actively religious in ways that did not fully coincide with the forms of religion favored by the clergy. I have argued this point more fully in *Worlds of Wonder, Days of Judgment*, where I go on to specify a repertory of practices and story frameworks that constituted the stuff of religion for ordinary people.[19] The same shift of perspective has transformed our understanding of witchhunting, the origins of Congregationalism, and the currency of millennialism. To cite but one example, the disagreements between juries and magistrates in cases of witchcraft that went to trial have much to do with two competing frameworks of understanding, the one that dominated the thinking of the magistrates and ministers, the other that prevailed among the lower orders.[20]

Before I turn to the eighteenth century and speculate about the consequences of setting the term popular religion in motion during that period, let me note that this strategy owes much to the literature on religion and society in early modern Europe and Britain. From that literature I take the basic question of what constitutes the religious, a question the British historian John Bossy made central to his work on the two Reformations, Catholic and Protestant, and on late medieval Christianity.[21] The significance of healing in the everyday practice of religion was established by Keith Thomas in *Religion and the Decline of Magic*, though his portrait of "cunning" men and women offering forms of healing that competed with the "godly" methods of the clergy must be supplemented by Michael MacDonald's study of the multiple healing strategies employed by the clergyman-physician Richard Napier.[22] The uses of ritual loom large in a number of Natalie Z. Davis's essays of the late 1960s and early 1970s.[23] And her insistence that the laity or the lower orders were active makers of culture, not merely the passive or subordinated recipients of what others had created, became a fundamental premise of the new cultural history.[24]

How does this way of thinking affect our understanding of religion and society in eighteenth-century America? Let me begin to answer this question by turning to attitudes and practices in two New England communities, East Windsor, Connecticut and Northampton, Massachusetts. The two are linked in having a religious culture that descended from Puritanism, and in having a father and son as their respective clergy.

Timothy Edwards, Harvard College class of 1691, went to East Windsor, Connecticut in 1694 as trial minister for a community that had finally been permitted to separate from the parent town on the other side of the Connecticut River. There he remained for some sixty-four years. From early in this pastorate and from midway through, in the 1720s, we possess a collection of the narratives or "relations" made by persons seeking admission as adults to the congregation. In these narratives the minister seems omnipresent. The people offering a relation remembered passages from specific sermons they have heard, and especially sermons that proved "awakening." Once started on the path to conversion, they seem to have frequented the minister's house, seeking his advice "in private" and "making known" their "case." We can hear the voice of Timothy Edwards in these exchanges: "[I] was told that there was hope, if I would go on in the use of means." But the voice that offered hope could also intimidate, or be perceived as intimidating: "going for counsel in private I was advised still to keep on, but thought if the minister did but know how I found my self to be he would give me no encouragement." It was surely the minister who induced these people to indict themselves for being "so slighty . . . in the use of means" and to worry whether they came to the meeting house in the proper mood: "And I was told that I must be very much in earnest . . . which made me purpose to be more . . . diligent in the use of means." Someone who attended an ordination service for a neighboring minister had heard a sermon on the text, "we then are ambassadors for Christ [II Cor. 5:20]," a text that opened out into a defense of hierarchy and a plea for deference: "wherein it was showed that ministers were Christ's ambassadors . . . and what a great sin it was to despise them, and the messages that Christ sent by them. And I saw then I had committed that sin." Joseph Loomis, whom I have been quoting, went on to remember a sermon by someone other than Timothy Edwards, a minister who, "applying himself to the unconverted, showed what a great sin it was to live in an unconverted state, and how greatly those were to blame . . . [who] were not earnest in the use of means. . . ."[25]

Sometimes in their own voice, sometimes through the medium of Scripture passages they quote, the men and women of East Windsor proceeded to narrate the classic sequence – classic within the "practical divinity" of evangelical Calvinism – of achieving a true sight of sin, acknowledging their worthlessness and the merits of God's anger, and, in an abrupt turn of emotions, recalling Christ's mercifulness and his invitation to sinners: "for then I thought I saw that Christ invited me and died for me, which quite broke my heart all to pieces so that I was I thought like a heap of snow when it is melting away."[26]

Conversion was a matter of "now or never," and, like his colleagues elsewhere in New England, Edwards exhorted his flock that the proper time for conversion was the very instant they heard him preach the gospel. Edwards also tied the motif of now or never to certain forms of experience – the onset of unexpected illness, the coming of unexpected death, the waves of disease that seem to have swept over the community. Not surprisingly, several men and women linked their awakening to spells of sickness, or to the death of relatives or someone their age. Ann Fitch told of being "more afraid of hell than before" the first time she was sick. She "thought that [her] sickness was sent as a warning to me to prepare for death, and that if I did not improve it another severe sickness would come."[27]

Yet these people had within their consciousness another and quite different sense of time. They seem to have worked out for themselves that the proper time to affiliate with the church – to take the steps that signified commitment to the means of grace – should occur before age thirty, but after they had passed out of the stage of youth. For them the experience of making a relation was closely related to the social facts of marriage and family formation, which for most of them happened at some point in their twenties. Thus it was common in these narratives for men and women to speak of "convictions" they experienced while in their teens, but to append the reflection, quite contrary to their minister's way of thinking, that young people had "time enough to mind their soul[s] afterwards." Hannah Bancroft remembered hearing a sermon (perhaps not by Edwards) in which the minister said "that men or persons were usually converted before they were thirty years of age." She herself was "told that though I was so old . . . there was hope for me." The people who had crossed the magic divide of thirty were, however, of a different mood: as one man put it, the thought that it was more difficult to gain an interest in Christ for those beyond that age "very much terrified me."[28]

These stories thus embody contrasting and indeed conflicting schemes of time, one that we may term "evangelical" and another that can be designated "social," in the sense of the life stages. The tension between these two schemes is palpable in the narratives. Much of that tension arose from and affected the relation between minister and people. A congregation that was being asked to recognize the minister as ambassador of Christ also knew him as someone who could "offend them," indeed so strongly that one women "went away so displeased I thought I would never come any more." Seeking to explain a tension that the minister himself interpreted as signifying their alienation from God, lay people reversed the accusation and insisted that it was "not their fault that they were not converted." Religion as represented by the minister was uncomfortable and possibly harmful; Josiah Loomis remembered neglecting the worship of God "because I thought the Word preached did me more hurt than good." Alternatively, some reasoned that they were not damned, an interpretation of God's workings that effectively shielded them from the message of now or never.[29]

Taking the narratives as a whole, and always keeping in view the deference of lay people to the clergy, in them we observe the people of East Windsor negotiating between their needs and the prescriptive statements of Timothy Edwards. These people sought a middle ground that accommodated his understanding of religion, and theirs; or more properly, the fusion of the religious and the social that for them *was* religion. That middle ground concerned the uses of time: only partially acceding to their minister's cry of "now or never" and to his insistence that their salvation depended on constant, continuous "waiting on the means of grace," these people sometimes stayed away from church and, more crucially, waited to become members until they were about to be married or become parents.

Jonathan Edwards entered the pastorate in Northampton in 1726 as junior minister to his grandfather Solomon Stoddard. We remember Edwards for his remarkable skills as a theologian and his role in the fashioning of revivals. But the church members, who constituted a majority of the adult townspeople, knew him as someone who, in 1749, confronted the structures of popular religion. He did so by refusing any longer to baptize the children of adults whom he deemed insincere in their professions of religion. His definition of insincerity has to do with time: when was it, he asked, that persons came forward to profess a commitment to religion? Answering the question in the same breath, he noted that lay people did so when they were about to be married or become parents. The coincidence of family formation and statements of religious commitment struck him as prima faciae evidence that sincerity was absent. The church members thought otherwise. All too familiar with the "perplexities" that surrounded the question of assurance of salvation, and having struggled, some of them, with "scruples" about whether they were worthy to participate in the sacrament of the Lord's Supper, they rejected Edwards's interpretation of popular religion. When he refused to negotiate, the outcome was dismissal: by a vote of some two hundred to twenty, the adult men voted to terminate his pastorate.[30]

The workings of popular religion in Northampton explain the high emotions of the parents in Taunton who rejoiced as their near adult-age "children" joined in the church covenant. In effect, these parents were celebrating the incorporation of the next generation into a certain mode of family culture. The very nature of the ceremony and, within a few decades, the emergence of a youth-centered revivalism, suggest that the customary mechanisms of incorporation were not working quite as well as parents hoped they would.[31] It may be that some of the contemporary talk of "declension" arose out of parental anxieties. From other data on the rhythms of affiliation with the church we learn that wives and mothers initiated the process of incorporation – joining the church before their husbands, and often coming forward to renew the covenant at the moment when they held a new-born in their arms.[32] The practices of covenant renewal and participation in the sacrament of baptism thus brought together the religious and the social, with the social here being understood as the web of relationships within the intergenerational family. Indeed the word "covenant" was perfectly suited to this convergence of the theological and the social.

The two case histories that involve the Edwardses are helpful in another respect. They impose on us the recognition that the nature of "the religious" within a given historical context is always and everywhere negotiable. The two Edwardses articulated a certain understanding of the religious to their congregations, an understanding summed up best, perhaps, in the lengthy covenant wherein Jonathan's parishioners agreed in 1742 to "devote our whole lives to be laboriously spent in the business of religion: ever making it our greatest business." (The covenant includes clauses aimed at preventing, among other practices of normal people in an eighteenth-century town, premarital sex, tavern haunting, and social conflict!)[33] But the historian must step outside this understanding of religion, with its attendant dichotomizing of "sincerity" and "hypocrisy," and accept as fully religious the attitudes and practices of the laity. Otherwise, we fall into the perspective of declension, which is to say, we see things only from the vantage of the clergy.

Jonathan Edwards came into conflict with popular religion on another front. Here the enemy was not so much within Northampton as without, in the person of the numerous "New Lights" (a pejorative term) who emerged out of the revivals of the 1740s. Historians of the Great Awakening teach us that the great debate of the 1740s pitted the Calvinist Edwards against the proto-Arminian Charles Chauncy. But this axis ignores what Edwards and Chauncy had in common, a distaste for "enthusiasm" and for any and all challenges to the authority of a learned, well-paid clergy. To the historian of popular religion, the phenomenon of "unlearned" persons acting on their own to voice and validate appropriations of the Bible and ecstatic forms of spiritual experience has a different significance, a significance enhanced by the parallel rejection among New Lights of clericalist pretensions to authority.[34]

Indeed, revivalism became a transgressive moment. Itinerants, some of them ordained ministers, and others not, transgressed on the parish system and its civil state supporters. Persons giving way to ecstatic experience transgressed on the usual routines of conversion. Some women felt empowered to speak out, and people of color entered into mixed-race congregations.

Viewed from a longer perspective, the Great Awakening grew out of and simultaneously set in motion a restlessness with institutionalized religion. Historians of "radicalism" in the seventeenth century are well aware of this restlessness, which sometimes ran in families. In that century contemporaries had a name for some who seemed so discontented; these were "Antinomians" or "Seekers" who questioned the legitimacy of any church's claims to truth. The two most famous seekers in early America were Roger Williams and Anne Hutchinson. Hers is the spiritual history that I want to foreground, for it is a history of someone who, becoming "much troubled" about the "unfaithfulness" of ministers who remained within an unreformed Church of England, broke with them and turned to the direct "voice" of God.[35] Others like her abounded in England during the period of the Civil War and Commonwealth, and in smaller numbers left their traces in and on the colonies – early Quakers, certain Baptists, the Rogerenes.[36]

No historian has systematically tracked their eighteenth-century heirs. But the possibilities for doing so are many. Two major studies of "spirit possession" and attendant practices (dreams, visions, and a new language of the body) are, in effect, studies of disaffection with the established order of things, a disaffection that rose to the surface among the early Methodists before that movement achieved denominational definition, and found expression equally among the Universalists, the Shakers, and the Freewill Baptists.[37] Alan Taylor explicitly employs the term "Seeker" in describing religious activity on the Maine frontier at the end of the century. (It is from his narrative that I have taken the story of Nathan Barlow.)[38] The possibilities expand to include the varieties of Pietism that German immigrants brought with them to Pennsylvania.[39] And as Clarke Garrett has noted, this framework is necessary to make sense of the Connecticut New Light Nathan Cole, who spent seventeen years restlessly working out a path between official and unofficial forms of the religious.[40] Interspersed among these movements and spiritual histories were healing practices that have yet to find their historian. Remembering that in the liminal stage of Quakerism George Foxe performed "miracles," we should not be surprised to learn that the founder of the Rogerenes laid claim to the power of spiritual healing.[41] How it is that early Methodists, Shakers, and followers of Wilkinson practiced healing may be gleaned from J. F. C. Harrison's *The Second Coming*. John Brooke has studied the intertwining of perfectionist and alchemical ideas within the German communities in eighteenth-century Pennsylvania, ideas that recurred in the practices of treasure hunting and counterfeiting that extend into the social and religious formation of Joseph Smith, Jr., who himself performed as a healer.[42]

By their very nature Seekers in eighteenth-century America left fewer traces than did persons affiliated with an institution. But in reckoning with this tendency I would not want historians of religion in early America to rule out the possibility that some persons were, at one and the same time, members of a formal church and sympathetic to ecstatic or transgressive practices. In our own times the phenomenon of multiple religious affiliations and even of multiple identities has become commonplace. Historians of Spiritualism have alerted us to the same phenomenon in the third quarter of the nineteenth century.[43] These realities should encourage us to acknowledge analogous situations in early America. What can be said conclusively is that some of the colonists, some of the time, were attracted to and engaged in ecstatic experiences and healing methods of which the orthodox clergy disapproved. The eschatological or primitivist expectations that nurtured such practices also led many of the colonists away from what they regarded as "tyranny" and "human inventions": creeds, learnedness and a salaried and perpetual ministry that depended on the civil state for certain kinds of support.[44]

Religious practice in eighteenth-century America encompassed certain forms of ritual. Rituals (as we might better learn to say, modes of ritualization) emerge, ripen, and decay. Witch-hunting came to an end at the close of the seventeenth century, and within New England Congregationalism the efficacy of public "confession" of sins steadily diminished, overtaken in part by gender norms that privileged men. Fast days, public executions – these and other ritual practices persisted. What was new to the colonists was the practice of revivalism. Its origins were several, including an event in the Presbyterian religious calendar, the sacramental feast, that immigrating Scotch-Irish brought with them to the new world. Unfolding over a three day sequence, the sacramental feast transformed ordinary space and time into an encounter with the sacred. At its most intense, at the climax of the ritual, this encounter was embodied in near-ecstatic spiritual experience as the participants felt themselves' transformed by the presence of the Holy Spirit.[45]

The category of popular religion brings into view other examples of ritual practice or, as some analyists would prefer to say, "performance." Here I am thinking of Rhys Isaac's description of the Baptist insurgency in prerevolutionary Virginia, a description keyed to a theory of performance Isaac owes to cultural anthropology. Isaac is mainly interested in the social and political uses of ritual, or how the Baptists "performed" in ways that challenged the hegemonic culture of the Virginia gentry.[46] A similar interest in social antagonism pervades Gary Nash's description of the Great Awakening in Boston, a description that translates religious symbolism into the language of unrest and inversion among the lower orders.[47] The historian of religion (popular or otherwise) can suggest in response that the essential issue in these two insurgencies was the nature of the religious considered in and of itself. But perhaps the point to emphasize is that, with such studies, we shift our attention from systems of belief and the history of institutions to religion as performed or practiced: something people "do." As in the rhythms of affiliation in East Windsor and Northampton, so in the sacramental feast and the revival the religious and the social converge in practices.

I have gathered several disparate lines of scholarship under a single heading, "popular religion." My point has been to suggest that scholarship both old and new offers us an alternative understanding of the eighteenth century. Employing the methods of social and intellectual history, this alternative is, however, more indebted to anthropologically-grounded studies and to a European scholarship attentive to *mentalité*, popular culture, and the changing forms of the religious.

The possibilities for expanding and enriching this alternative are many, and I construe this essay as a call for further work along such lines. Yet it would not be honest of me to ignore certain contradictions that accompany the term popular religion. Although it may open certain doors, it does so at a price.

Consider the question of "dechristianization." A salutary shock ran through studies of the Reformation when historians began to question whether we should take at face value the triumphalism of the Protestant reformers. Asking whether the mass of the people particiated in either of the Reformations, Protestant or Catholic, or persisted in forms of folk belief (at best but partially accommodated to Christianity), these historians strongly preferred the latter interpretation.[48] The American historian Jon Butler has borrowed this skepticism and applied it to the presence of Christianity in the English-speaking colonies. He argues that Christianity was much less visible in the first two centuries than church historians have supposed. To this provocative thesis he adds (a la Keith Thomas) the proposition that beliefs stemming from a pre-Christian folklore or the lore of the occult were in broad circulation. The Butler thesis borrows another premise from the European literature, that the culture of the elite or the clergy was sharply differentiated from that of the people.[49]

These two interrelated propositions must be addressed by anyone who deploys the term popular religion. Does it designate (a) modes of belief other than Christianity; and (b) a culture that was more autonomous or set apart than permeable in its boundaries? To say that the historical literature is divided on how to answer these questions is an understatement. Yet we can gain some ground by turning back to the records, as Patricia Bonomi and Peter Eisenstadt did in reappraising the extent of church adherence among the colonists.[50] And we can benefit from the sharp attacks within the European literature on the "autonomy" and non-Christian models of popular religion.[51] Elsewhere I have reviewed and criticized the dichotomies that inform those models, concluding that, on the whole, they are irrelevant to seventeenth-century New England, a point that surely holds for the eighteenth century as well.[52] And I venture the proposition that the recent literature on both sides of the Atlantic tells a story of interchange, negotiation, and commonalities far more than it does one of autonomy and conflict. More generally, we may suppose that exchange is always taking place within culture as part of the process of fashioning and refashioning boundaries.[53]

This principle (at once practical and theoretical) of exchange or negotiation leads to the recognition that popular religion is not a thing in and of itself. It is a category fashioned out of a dialectical process, the terms of which keep changing. The imprecision that accompanies the category is also a consequence of our wanting to have things both ways. As in the instance of Jonathan Edwards's dismissal, we deploy popular religion to bring conflict or difference into view even as we

affirm the permeability of all boundaries and the interchanges between "high" and "low." Similarly, we want it both ways when we
allow popular religion to stand for the illicit, the disruptive, or the
esoteric while at the same time observing how it inscribes firm
boundaries of its own, as in the fierce hostility of Virginia Baptists to
the cultural practices of the gentry. Let me acknowledge that my own
understanding of popular religion encompasses what may seem
opposites: on the one hand, disaffection with well-organized ecclesiastical bodies, and, on the other, stabilizing rituals of incorporation into
such groups.

Popular religion as I have sketched it in this essay is deeply
marked by the tensions between clergy and laity. In some regions of
early America, however, the clergy were too few to play an effective
role in constraining the choices of the laity – Maryland and Virginia for
much of the seventeenth century; the back country for most of the
period up to the American Revolution, and perhaps beyond. Nor did
clericalism have much importance for groups like the Quakers, who
never had a formal clergy. And within a society that lacked a center or
metropolis, religious structures accommodated themselves to a dispersed and decentralized society; Christianity in eighteenth-century
America became so many versions of "local" religion in ways that
worked to the advantage of the laity.[54] Nonetheless I would propose
that contests over the meaning of the religious continued to arise in
these local settings and within groups such as the Quakers.

A final problem is how to incorporate change over time within the
framework of popular religion. Analyzing the category of the "folk" as
it emerged within European Romanticism, Peter Burke has noted how
the folk became identified with an unchanging, near timeless culture.
This representation of the folk was premised on the assumption that
modernity had doomed folk ways to extinction.[55] Were we to render
popular religion as that which was being left behind, the category
would serve only to reinscribe the very dichotomies – as in the opposition between "reason" and "superstition"– that it seeks to overturn.
Granting popular religion its full complexities of meaning, we must
also grant it the flexibility to absorb and even to initiate change.

These possibilities bring us back around to the grand themes of
American religious history that I listed at the outset: "declension,"
Americanization, the coming of liberalism. Thinking broadly about the

evolution of popular religion over time, we may find that other processes and periodizations are more relevant than these. One major
phase originated with the Protestant Reformation, and especially with
its English version, which eventuated in the Puritan movement. The
creative and transformative energies of that movement fashioned a
version of popular religion that became institutionalized in the
"Congregational Way" and in practices such, as Sabbatarianism and
public rituals of confession. At the middle of the seventeenth century,
other Puritans passed over into Quakerism. By the end of that century
the rigorist and ecstatic forms of the religious within Puritanism were
giving way to strategies of familial incorporation among the laity and to
stronger affirmations of clericalism, together with a critique of enthusiasm, among the ministers. The awakenings of the 1740s and
beyond were the seedbed of a new rigorism (as in Methodism) that,
by the early nineteenth century, was working major changes in practice: temperance, a renewed sabbatarianism, a new evangelism to
those who were not Christians. The Sunday school emerged as a new
tool of the nineteenth century, the full apparatus – educational, political, financial, ecclesiastical – of the denomination was in view, an apparatus that included seminaries capable of providing ample numbers
of clergy. Thereafter, for most American Protestants popular religion
became subsumed within the denominational framework. When and
why negotiations over the religious resumed within this framework is
a matter for other historians to describe.

This way of telling the longer story translates liberalism into what
Peter Burke has named the "reform of popular culture,"[56] recasts
declension into shifting modes of incorporation, and relegates the
question of Americanization to the sidelines. Would it not be re-
warding for us all if historians of popular religion led the way in
turning away from the nation state and committed themselves to
exploring persistence and change in the nature of the religious?

Notes

1. Thomas Prince, ed., *The Christian History . . . for the Year 1743* (Boston, 1744), 110–11.

2. Alan Taylor, *Liberty Men and Great Proprietors: the Revolutionary Settlement on the Maine Frontier, 1760–1820* (Chapel Hill: University of North Carolina Press, 1990), 123.

3. I say "America" recognizing, however, that I deal far more fully with New England than with other regions.

4. Perry Miller, *The New England Mind: From Colony to Province* (Cambridge, Mass.: Harvard University Press, 1953); ch. 5, on the half-way covenant, is entitled "hypocrisy."

5. C. C. Goen, ed., *Works of Jonathan Edwards 4: The Great Awakening* (New Haven, Conn.: Yale University Press, 1972), 10–1ε (quotation p. 12). See also William G. McLoughlin, *New England Dissent, 1630–1833: The Baptists and the Separation of Church and State*, 2 vols. (Cambridge, Mass.: Harvard University Press, 1971), 1:47; Edmund S. Morgan, *The Gentle Puritan: A Life of Ezra Stiles, 1727–1795* (New Haven, Conn.: Yale University Press, 1962), 185. Morgan's second thoughts are embodied in *Visible Saints: the History of a Puritan Idea* (Ithaca, N.Y.: Cornell University Press, 1963).

6. James Carse, *Jonathan Edwards and the Visibility of God* (New York, 1967), 46.

7. Carl Van Doren, ed., *Benjamin Franklin and Jonathan Edwards: Selections from Their Writings* (New York: C. Scribner's Sons, 1920), ix.

8. Sidney Mead, *The Lively Experiment: The Shaping of Christianity in America* (New York: Harper & Row, 1963); Leonard J. Trinterud, *The Forming of an American Tradition: A Re-Examination of Colonial Presbyterianism* (Philadelphia: Westminster Press, 1949).

9. Nathan Hatch, *The Sacred Cause of Liberty: Republican Thought and the Millennium in Revolutionary New England* (New Haven, Conn.: Yale University Press, 1977).

10. Norman Fiering, *Jonathan Edwards's Moral Thought and Its British Context* (Chapel Hill: University of North Carolina Press, 1981); Peter Byrne, *Natural Religion and the Nature of Religion: The Legacy of Deism* (New York: Routledge, 1989); Leslie Stephen, *History of English Thought in the Eighteenth Century* (1876; reprint, New York: Harcourt, Brace & World, 1962).

11. Eugene Sheridan, Introduction to *Jefferson's Extracts from the Gospels: The Papers of Thomas Jefferson*, second series ed., Dickinson W. Adams (Princeton, N.J.: Princeton University Press, 1983); G. Adolph Koch, *Republican Religion: The American Revolution and the Cult of Reason* (New York: H. Holt & Co., 1933).

12. The scheme of "declension" is challenged in Stephen Foster, *The Long Argument: English Puritanism and the Shaping of New England Culture, 1570–1700*

(Chapel Hill: University of North Carolina Press, 1991), and in scholarship I refer to "On Common Ground: The Coherence of American Puritan Studies," *William and Mary Quarterly* 44 (1987): 210–11, 221. The "Americanization" and church-state frameworks are questioned in Jon Butler, *The Huguenots in America: A Refugee People in New World Society* (Cambridge, Mass.: Harvard University Press, 1983), and in chs. 4 and 9 in Butler, *Awash in a Sea of Faith: Christianizing the American People* (Cambridge, Mass.: Harvard University Press, 1990). Henry May has greatly complicated the working of the Enlightenment on our shores in *The Enlightenment in America* (New York; Oxford University Press, 1976). Melvin Endy challenges the too-facile conflation of church and nation in "Just War, Holy War, and Millennialism in Revolutionary America," *William and Mary Quarterly* 42 (1985): 3–25.

13. Mark A. Noll et al., *Evangelicalism: Comparative Studies of Popular Protestantism in North America, the British Isles, and Beyond, 1700–190* (New York: Oxford University Press, 1994); David W. Bebbington, *Evangelicalism in Modern Britain: A History from the 1730s to the 1980s* (London: Allen & Unwin, 1989).

14. Taylor, *Liberty Men*, 136.

15. As expressed in *A Treatise Concerning Religious Affections* (1746).

16. Sabine MacCormack, *Religion in the Andes: Vision and Imagination in Early Colonial Peru* (Princeton, N.J.: Princeton University Press, 1991), 38.

17. The meaning of "illiteracy" in eighteenth-century polemics, when it designated persons who, regardless of their learning, appealed to the Holy Spirit as the source of all true knowledge, must be differentiated from its almost wholly technical meaning in our own time.

18. Darrett B. Rutman, *Winthrop's Boston: Portrait of a Puritan Town 1630–1649* (Chapel Hill: University of North Carolina Press, 1965); Rutman, *American Puritanism: Faith and Practice* (Philadelphia: Lippincott, 1970). The same point of view is present in John Demos, *A Little Commonwealth* (New York: Oxford University Press, 1970). For an early sketch of an alternative, see David D. Hall, "Toward a History of Popular Religion in Early New England," *William and Mary Quarterly* 41 (1984): 49–55.

19. David D. Hall, "The World of Print and Collective Mentality in Seventeenth-Century New England," in *New Directions in American Intellectual History*, eds., John Higham and Paul Conkin (Baltimore, Md.: The Johns Hopkins University Press, 1979), 166–80; David D. Hall, *Worlds of Wonder, Days of Judgment: Popular Religious Belief in Early New England* (New York: Alfred A. Knopf, 1989).

20. Richard Weisman, *Witchcraft, Magic, and Religion in 17th Century Massachusetts* (Amherst: University of Massachusetts Press, 1984); Richard Godbeer, *The Devil's Dominion: Magic and Religion in Early New England* (New York: Cambridge University Press, 1992).

21. John Bossy, *Christianity in the West, 1400–1700* (New York: Oxford University Press, 1985); John Bossy, "Holiness and Society," *Past and Present*

75 (1977): 119–37; John Bossy, "Blood and Baptism: Kinship, Community, and Christianity in Western Europe from the Fourteenth to the Seventeenth Centuries," in *Sanctity and Secularity: The Church and the World*, Studies in Church History, 10, ed., Derek Baker (Cambridge, Eng.: Cambridge University Press, 1973), 129–43. Bossy relied on Wilfred Cantwell Smith, *The Meaning and End of Religion: A New Approach to the Religious Traditions of Mankind* (New York: Macmillan, 1963).

22. Keith Thomas, *Religion and the Decline of Magic* (New York: Oxford University Press, 1971); Michael MacDonald, *Mystical Bedlam: Madness, Anxiety, and Healing in Seventeenth-Century England* (New York: Cambridge University Press, 1981).

23. These studies are collected in Natalie Zemon Davis, *Society and Culture in Early Modern France* (Stanford, Calif.: Stanford University Press, 1975).

24. Natalie Z. Davis, "Some Tasks and Themes in the Study of Popular Religion," in *The Pursuit of Holiness in Late Medieval and Renaissance Religion*, eds., Charles Trinkaus and Heiko A. Oberman (Leiden: Brill, 1974), 307–36.

25. Kenneth P. Minkema, ed., "The East Windsor Conversion Relations 1700–1725" *Connecticut Historical Society Bulletin* 51 (1986): 24, 27, 33, 30, 36.

26. Ibid., 37.

27. Ibid., 33.

28. Ibid., 45, 42, 27, 45.

29. Ibid., 25, 28, 40.

30. This paragraph condenses the argument of the introduction to *The Works of Jonathan Edwards, 12: Ecclesiastical Writings*, ed., David D. Hall (New Haven, Conn.: Yale University Press, 1994), where the necessary documentation is provided.

31. Patricia J. Tracy has suggested that the strain on mechanisms of incorporation was linked to increasing inadequacy of property inheritance: *Jonathan Edwards, Pastor: Religion and Society, in Eighteenth-Century Northampton* (New: York: Hill and Wang, 1980). Newer work makes the "deprivation thesis" seem less probable.

32. This statement is based in part on research in progress by Anne S. Brown for a Boston University Ph.D. thesis on church and society in eighteenth-century Essex County, Massachusetts.

33. Goen, ed., *Works of Jonathan Edwards*, 4, 550–54.

34. See in general C. C. Goen, *Revivalism and Separatism in New England, 1740–1800* (New Haven, Conn.: Yale University Press, 1962).

35. David D. Hall, ed., *The Antinomian Controversy, 1636–1638: A Documentary History* (Middletown, Conn: Wesleyan University Press., 1968), 271–72.

36. For such persons in New England before 1660 see, in general, Philip F. Gura, *A Glimpse of Sion's Glory: Puritan Radicalism in New England, 1620–1660* (Middletown, Conn.: Wesleyan University Press, 1984).

37. Clarke Garrett, *Spirit Possession and Popular Religion: From the Camisards to the Shakers* (Baltimore: The Johns Hopkins University Press, 1987); Stephen A. Marini, *Radical Sects of Revolutionary New England* (Cambridge, Mass.: Harvard University Press, 1982).

38. Taylor, *Liberty Men*, ch. 5.

39. Elizabeth Fisher, "Prophesies and Revelations: German Cabalists in Early Pennsylvania," *Pennsylvania Magazine of History and Biography* 109 (1985): 299–333.

40. Garrett, *Spirit Possession*, 111–12.

41. Henry J. Cadbury, ed., *Book of Miracles* (Cambridge, Eng.: Cambridge University Press, 1948); See also Hall, *Worlds of Wonder*, ch. 4.

42. J. F. C. Harrison, *The Second Coming: Popular Millenarianism, 1780–1850* (New Brunswick, N.J.: Rutgers University Press, 1979); John L. Brooke, *The Refiner's Fire: The Hermetic Tradition and the Origins of Mormon Cosmology* (New York: Cambridge University Press, 1994).

43. Ann Braude, *Radical Spirits: Spiritualism and Women's Rights in Nineteenth-Century America* (Boston: Beacon Press, 1989).

44. Hall, *Worlds of Wonder*, ch. 4; Daniel A. Cohen, *Pillars of Salt, Monuments of Grace: New England Crime Literature and the Origins of American Popular Culture, 1674–1800* (New York: Oxford University Press, 1993).

45. Leigh Eric Schmidt, *Holy Fairs: Scottish Communions and American Revivals in the Early Modern Period* (Princeton, N.J.: Princeton University Press, 1989).

46. Rhys Isaac, *The Transformation of Virginia, 1740–1790* (Chapel Hill: University of North Carolina Press, 1982), ch. 8 and the concluding "Discourse on the Method: Action, Structure, and Meaning."

47. Gary Nash, *The Urban Crucible: Social Change, Political Consciousness, and the Origins of the American Revolution* (Cambridge, Mass.: Harvard University Press, 1979), ch. 8.

48. See, e.g., Jean Delumeau, *Catholicism between Luther and Voltaire: a New View of the Counter-Reformation* (Philadelphia: Westminster Press, 1977).

49. Butler, *Awash in a Sea of Faith*, chs. 2–3.

50. Patricia Bonomi and Peter Eisenstadt, "Church Adherence in the Eighteenth-Century British American Colonies," *William and Mary Quarterly* 39 (1982): 245–86.

51. See, e.g., Eamon Duffy, *The Stripping of the Altars: Traditional Religion in England, 1400–1580* (New Haven, Conn.: Yale University Press, 1992).

52. Hall, *Worlds of Wonder*, introduction.

53. Stephen Greenblatt, "Culture," in *Critical Terms for Literary Study*, eds., Frank Lentricchia and Thomas McLaughlin (Chicago: University of Chicago Press, 1990), esp. 228.

54. I borrow this term from William Christian, Jr., *Local Religion in Sixteenth-Century Spain* (Princeton, N.J.: Princeton University Press, 1981).

55. Peter Burke, *Popular Culture in Early Modern Europe* (London: Temple Smith, 1978), ch. 1.

56. Ibid., ch. 8.

6

WRITING THE LITERARY HISTORY OF
EIGHTEENTH-CENTURY AMERICA:
A PROSPECT

Philip F. Gura

IN 1988 I PUBLISHED a lengthy piece that initiated a "Forum" in the William and Mary Quarterly.[1] That effort took the form of a wide-ranging survey of scholarship in the field of early American literature over the previous two decades and ended with a prospectus for future study. I defined my topic as scholarship about the literature of British America from settlement to the year 1763 and thus did not treat exploration literature in any depth, nor the writing of the Revolution and the New Nation. By stopping my survey when I did, I trimmed about forty years from the field of early American literature as it usually is defined, but I did so for what I believed sound scholarly reasons. In any event, I thought that an assessment of the scholarship on the later eighteenth-century was best treated in a separate essay, because the subject was not treated in Jack P. Greene and J. R. Pole's landmark volume, *Colonial British America*.[2] This rich and wide-ranging collection has helped to set the agenda for historians of colonial British America, yet there is nary a word to guide us in the belle-lettristic literature or (to define matters more broadly) the written discourse of British America. As I planned my idea for the "Forum," I kept uppermost in mind my wish to supply the sorely missing piece. The present essay is intended as an extension of that original project, to consider recent scholarship in American literature between, roughly, 1763 and 1815, when, most scholars agree, hints of what later was termed an "American Renaissance" are evident.[3] But before I venture into the subject, let me indicate how I have conceived the topic.

First, to better understand the development of literature in this period, I will summarize what I have observed elsewhere about the various trends in scholarship on the literature of British America between its settlement and the mid-eighteenth century. Obviously, no matter what the changing conditions of the British empire at mid-century, old forms of discourse were not simply superseded. The literature of American religion in this period, for example, cannot be understood without reference to Jonathan Edwards and other of those affected one way or another by the religious upheaval of the 1740s and 1750s; nor can the achievement of Benjamin Franklin be strictly separa-ted from that of Puritans like Samuel Sewall and Cotton Mather.

Second, I claim the same prerogative given me in my capacity as editor of the journal *Early American Literature* to treat literature up to about 1815. Although the canon and, in consequence, the periodization of American literary history are rapidly changing, I think it valuable to consider herein some early American writers, particularly novelists like Charles Brockden Brown, Hannah Foster, and Susannah Rowson, and such poets as the Connecticut Wits, those with feet squarely in two centuries. Although I do not intend to discuss such well-known writers as Irving, Cooper, or Bryant, who by some are considered "early American," by others "Romantic," there are some authors who wrote between the turn of the century and 1815 who help us better chart directions in literature prior to the emergence of such major voices as Emerson, Hawthorne, and Stowe.

Finally, I note that in this essay I take a different tack than I did in my earlier effort, in which I surveyed in great detail twenty years of scholarship on different aspects of the subject. Herein I intend to focus on what might be termed "prospective scholarship": that which allows us to reconsider and redraw the boundaries of literary discourse in eighteenth-century America. Thus, behind and beneath what I say lies the work of a great number of other literary critics, and cultural and intellectual historians on whose work we all will continue to build.

Let me quickly summarize where we have been, that is, what I take to be the problematic ways in which eighteenth-century British American literature in general hitherto has been treated. First, like the writing of the seventeenth century, it often has been viewed as a mere prologue to the literature of the United States of America and thus has not been considered in its own right and on its own terms. Thus, until very recently one of the most striking things about the

study of colonial American literature was the persistence, even among
the most sophisticated critics, of the notion of profound continuities
between early American literary expression and the canonized
literature of the United States in the mid-nineteenth century, and of
the concomitant belief in American "exceptionalism," both literary
and cultural.[4] This is especially surprising because for many years now
in the historical profession assumptions about the uniqueness of
American culture in the colonial period have been considered wrong-
headed, a hangover, as Greene and Pole put it, from the heyday of the
"American Studies" movement of the 1950s whose champions assidu-
ously analyzed "colonial developments largely in terms of the extent
to which they exhibited a process of Americanization." But, despite
growing evidence to the contrary, most recently provided by Richard
Bushman, many literary historians continue to assume that "America,
at least in its continental British-American variant, was and had been
always fundamentally different from Europe."[5]

Indeed, to many scholars, particularly those who wrote before the
1980s, eighteenth-century British American writing often was seen as
dull, at best transitional, something one had to work through to get
from the Puritans to Hawthorne and Emerson, unless one had a
particular interest in religious or political polemics. Parrington's quip
about the Connecticut Wits, who for many still epitomize American
belles-lettres in this period, is emblematic: the best one can say of
them is that "they are annually recalled by a considerable number of
undergraduates on the eve of an examination" in American literature!
And if one sought to hang more on their shoulders, to suggest, for
example, that some of Freneau's verse anticipated that of Bryant the
Romantic, one still understood that the progenitor was inferior in accomplishment and sophistication to those whom he served as a type.

William C. Spengemann, one of the few to criticize the use of
such a "continuities" thesis, puts it more sharply. In his view, scholars
engaged in this enterprise often are motivated more by their desire to
find ways to refertilize the overworked fields of nineteenth-century
American literature than by any genuine interest in earlier discourse.
He claims their final inability to explain how "pre-Revolutionary
American writing can have [anything] to do, immediately, with the
shape and meaning of North America in the nineteenth century
supports this point."[6] Scholars who peruse the continuities theme, he

continues, come to their conclusions by "a kind of verbal shell game, in which the prestidigitator places his thematic pea under one shell labeled 'Puritan,' makes a lot of rapid movements on the typewriter, and then produces the pea from under another shell marked 'American literature.'"[7]

Those who take eighteenth-century American writers more seriously always seem to want to get *beyond* them, to go *from here to there*; that is, to say, from Bartram's natural history writing to Thoreau's, or from Charles Brockden Brown's quasi-psychological fiction to Poe's. If the earlier literature is thought important, it is because of how it, too, announced themes that somehow seemed, in retrospect, archetypically "American." Thus, while most historians now agree with Pole and Greene, that the American colonies, "no matter how distant they might be from Britain or how much latitude they may have had in their internal development," were all "cultural provinces of Britain," literary historians who treat the eighteenth century, particularly those who reside, intellectually or otherwise, in New England, stubbornly maintain the primacy of this literature in the formation of an "American mind."[8]

In large measure the ascendancy of such views derives from the provocative work of Sacvan Bercovitch, who has taken up where Perry Miller left off in his claims for the uniqueness of colonial American literature. Particularly in his book *The American Jeremiad*, Bercovitch argues that America's religious and civil leaders institutionalized a rhetorical mode that can be traced throughout American literary history. His, and his disciples', generalizations have not gone unchallenged, but as yet no one has seriously shaken their belief in the notion of consensus or hegemony that he sees at the heart of the American way.[9]

Further, often such studies as Bercovitch's become more problematic because they persist in treating the literature of colonial America as though it is that of New England writ large, with the result that the literature of other areas does not get its due, a tendency we might term "Novanglophilia." But as Greene has pointed out most strikingly in his *Pursuits of Happiness*, during the colonial period the New England colonies were hardly normative of British North American settlement.[10] Rather, in the region's initial resistance to the market economy and its heightened moral fervor, it was something of an

oddity. But until very recently few scholars of early American literature have concerned themselves with how the experience of people in
other of the British North American regions, particularly the Chesapeake, may have drawn from different traditions of discourse for its
explication and so contributed to the development of literature quite
different from New England's. Instead, most literary historians, ignoring the varied regions of the mid-Atlantic and Southern colonies,
have continued to think and write as though colonial America were
divided into only two regions, New England and the South, and for
decades have assigned primacy to the literature of the former, again,
often as part of their attempt to display the supposed continuities
between the colonial period and the American Renaissance. Despite
the monumental work of Richard Beale Davis and the directions
charted by Leo Lemay and Lewis Simpson, hitherto most of the "action" in early American literature written before 1763 focused on New
England.[11]

The center of many studies of eighteenth-century British-American literature thus continues to reside in the supposed continuities
between it and that of the Early National and Romantic periods, or,
more specifically, between the language and rhetoric – primarily religious discourse – of Puritan New England and those of the late eighteenth and early nineteenth centuries in the United States as a whole.
Although the precise nature of these continuities still rouses vigorous
debate, an interest in the persistence for at least two centuries of a
special language and set of symbols – the most vivid of which is
"America" itself – derived from the New England settlers has superseded questions of region, canonicity, and even critical methodology.

In other words, a majority of the scholars of colonial American
literature continue to seek the roots of American exceptionalism in a
historical period in which the colonies were cultural and linguistic
appendages of European countries. Even the best studies of individual
writers or genres, in which the author has the time and space to explore the literature contextually, frequently manifest a compulsion to
put scholarship to the use of the larger project – the description of a
unique national literature whose foundation lies solidly in the previous two centuries. Patricia Caldwell's sophisticated treatment of the
Puritan conversion narrative, subtitled *The Beginnings of American
Expression*, epitomizes this mode, as does Leo Lemay's recent treat-

ment of John Smith, exceptional only in that Lemay, perhaps taking a cue from Greene, places a Southerner rather than a New Englander at the *omphalos* of American literature and culture.[12]

But matters have begun to change. Perhaps the single most important development in recent studies of eighteenth-century American literature is the redefinition and expansion of the canon that is taking place through the recovery of the hitherto unstudied manuscript culture of the period. To understand the significance of this work we must remember how until very recently literary historians basically derived their guide to the period either from the same assumptions and information used by their nineteenth-century predecessors, men like Samuel Knapp, Samuel Kettell, Moses Coit Tyler, or that subsequently provided by the great bibliographer Charles Evans. Put simply, until very recently we have understood the "literature" of colonial America primarily in terms of what was published for circulation in print culture.

But the point of recent scholarship by David Shields and Wilson Somerville, among others, is that eighteenth-century America had an elaborate "club" culture derived from and comparable in sophistication to that which thrived contemporaneously in England and on the Continent – miniature, self-contained worlds in which gentlemen, and their ladies, shared each other's company for conversation, wit, music, and *literature* – literature written expressly for and read exclusively to the club, and thus never intended to be printed for a wider audience, either then or subsequently.[13] Acknowledgment and exploration of this literary archive is revising our understanding of eighteenth-century British-American literature and culture. The monument to this social activity found in virtually every major British-American seacoast community – Boston, Newport, New York, Trenton, and Philadelphia all had theirs – is Dr. Alexander Hamilton's *History of the Ancient and Honorable Tuesday Club* (1745–56), an immense manuscript recently published in its entirety in three elegant volumes edited by Robert Micklus, and the focus of a separate book-length study by him as well as of a recent dissertation by Somerville.[14]

Micklus views Hamilton's sprawling mock-history as virtually the first novel written on these shores, something to be measured without embarrassment against Sterne's *Tristram Shandy* and Fielding's works.

But in a sense Micklus's study, particularly in the current climate of literary criticism which seeks to incorporate more historicism, is too narrow and not quite what Hamilton and his group deserve. They are better served by Somerville's work, *The Tuesday Club of Annapolis, Maryland (1745–56) as Cultural Theatre*. Therein he reads not only the *History* but all the varied activities – music, ritual, dance, letter writing, dining, formal publications in newspapers and books, etc. – of the entire Annapolis circle through the kind of cultural anthropology Rhys Isaac used in his *Transformation of Virginia*.[15] Thus, Somerville focuses the Tuesday Club like a lens on various facets of Anglo-American culture, particularly the relationship of provincial periphery to cultural center, and the development of a uniquely Chesapeake version of the British-American self.

The larger point, of course, is that the Tuesday Club and its manifold remains are but the tip of an iceberg. As Shields, following Leo Lemay's lead, puts it in his path-breaking study of British-American poetry, *Oracles of Empire: Poetry, Politics, and Commerce in British America, 1690–1750*, "The discovery of the literature of British America depends upon an understanding of the *mixed print and manuscript culture* that operated in the provinces."[16] Study of the literary production, as well as of the many other activities, of these various groups is providing new ways both to understand how closely linked the colonies were to their imperial center, and, as Somerville has demonstrated, to view the nascent sense of identity that emerged through the participants' knowledge that they indeed were somehow different from those whom they so strenuously emulated and whose approval they sought. But because most literary historians, beginning with Knapp and Kettell in the 1820s, defined *literature* as that which was published in print and thus could conceivably have contributed to the development of something called "American" identity, most aspects of this complex manuscript culture have remained hidden from all but the most intrepid and imaginative scholars.

Such work epitomizes another important dimension of the new literary study of eighteenth-century British America, a sophisticated integration of history and literature. Pioneered by Jay Fliegelman in his indispensable *Prodigals and Pilgrims: The American Revolution against Patriarchal Authority, 1750–1800*, most recently such work is epitomized by William C. Dowling in his *Poetry and Ideology in Revolutionary Connect-*

icut and Fliegelman's own student, Thomas Gustafson, in his *Representative Words: Politics, Literature, and the American Language, 1776–1865*. Fliegelman was among the first literary scholars to plant and harvest in the ground turned by Bernard Bailyn and Gordon Wood, to address the question, that is, of how literary discourse both derived from and contributed to the ideological complexity of the Revolutionary and early national periods that these eminent scholars have so meti-culously described. Fliegelman's novel treatment of such long-canon-ized literary figures as Benjamin Franklin and Charles Brockden Brown, among others, as well as of such outsiders as Stephen Burroughs, has allowed literary historians to enter what seemed the most significant historiographical debates concerning the originary moment of American nationhood.[17]

But *Prodigals and Pilgrims* primarily falls under the rubric of what once was called "intellectual history" (now it would be "cultural studies") and thus belongs more with the work of Alan Heimert than that of any literary critic. Not so Dowling's recent study of the Connecticut Wits. This group of New England writers, the first self-consciously to think of themselves as writing American literature, too long have been relegated to the slag heap of literary history. But Dowling fully rehabilitates them, particularly if we link his work to Shields's, and enables us to understand the poetry of the full century in ways we hitherto have not appreciated.

Like Shields, Dowling is at home on both sides of the Atlantic, and this allows him to see the Wits as more than pitiful provincials emulating classical modes. Rather, in his view they are "literary Augustans" whose "notion of poetry as ideological intervention, and actual belief in the power of language to remake the world" marked them as key players in attempts to forge the ideological underpinnings of the New Nation.[18] No longer cultural dinosaurs whose epic verse is a literary curiosity but writers fully engaged in attempts to mold the New Nation, the Wits are best understood in the context of the debates over classical republicanism that have brought intellectual historians back in droves to the late eighteenth century. By making us understand that New England Federalism was itself a "transmutation of the classical republican tradition" at the center of so much late-eighteenth-century verse, Dowling awakens us to Federalism's essence as a "positive ideology, a vision of order, peace, and harmony in which the settled life of the original Puritan colonies . . . is seen as nothing other than the *ricorso* demanded by classical republicanism in its post-Machiavellian mode." He concludes that what continued to unite the Wits, even after Joel Barlow had embraced the revolutionary order in France, was a "strong tendency toward demystification or unmasking," a "tremendous power to deny ideological legitimacy" to those whom they viewed as "agents of social decline."[19] Thus, through their poetry the Wits offered variously the cautionary examples and reflective celebrations of those people and places that either aided or hindered the development of the liberal republic.

The book is a tour-de-force of intelligence *and* common sense, for Dowling's allusions are so "right" that we wonder why such observations were not made years ago. *Of course* we should view the achievement of Timothy Dwight and David Humphreys against the background limned by Bushman in *From Puritan to Yankee*, just as Bailyn and Wood should be the reference points for elucidation of the politics that used to deaden our interest in the Wits' poetry. Through this new appreciation of what Dowling calls the "Connecticut georgic," which represents at one level "Country ideology transformed from a revolutionary doctrine into a permanent ethic of republican virtue," we thus have another set of voices that registers the intersection of language, politics, and time in late eighteenth-century America.[20]

The larger point here is that in the past decade literary historians have begun to place literature much more deeply in the political culture of eighteenth-century British America, and have done it so well that the study of even the seemingly most derivative, and thus moribund, genre – neoclassical poetry – has been revitalized. By moving beyond the formalist, belle-lettristic understanding of eighteenth-century literature that for decades ruled our profession, scholars like Shields, Dowling, and a handful of others – I think here particularly of Carla Mulford's forthcoming work on the New Jersey poetess Annis Stockton and Pattie Cowell's on other women poets of the period – have revivified the century's literary production and made us better understand the seamless web of culture.[21] And Gustafson's recent work on meaning of language and interpretation epitomizes how exhilarating such work can be when it is explored without self-consciousness in the new mode of "cultural studies."

In his *Representative Words*, Gustafson exhaustively demonstrates how questions of language and interpretation were at the center of the American political experiment. In particular, he addresses how questions of language and its proper signification emerged from the constitutional wrangling of the 1780s and further engaged the nation in the sectional crisis over slavery. To set this scene properly, the author, like Dowling, contextualizes matters for us, and thus traces the relation of language to political culture in classical, Renaissance, and Enlightenment thought before delivering us at our own doorstep in the mid-eighteenth century, to demonstrate "how political events and a republican form of government helped shape linguistic theories and practices in America."[22]

At home with the complex debates over the political, judicial, and linguistic meanings of interpretation as they derived from the constitutional debates, Gustafson provides new ways to understand why later thinkers like Emerson or Melville were so obsessed with the word, what it meant and what it could do. His *leitmotif* is what he terms the Thucydidean moment, "when as occurs in Thucydides' famous description of the *stasis* at Corcyra, political and linguistic disorders – the corruption of people and language – become one and the same."[23] The power of Gustafson's work lies in his demonstration that from the 1770s on in America, intellectuals dealt with one crisis after another that originated in just such a fear, putative or real, of corruption of how meaning is established and maintained. In other words, he has linked the literary critics' interest in language to the cultural historians' in the ideological origins of America.

Such fruitful conjunction of literature and history underlines the centrality of ideology to our mapping of the literary culture of eighteenth-century America, the topic as well of another recent seminal work, Michael Warner's *The Letters of the Republic: Publication and the Public Sphere in Eighteenth-Century America*. Part of the larger, now collaborative, project of charting the history of the book in American culture, Warner's work derives its power from an extension of Jurgen Habermas's observations on *The Structural Transformation of the Public Sphere*, that is, as Warner parses the master, of his notion of a set of institutions in which "political discourse could be separated both from the state and from civil society, the realm of private life." And the story of this new sphere of activity is largely that of the "new uses of texts." "Newspapers, literary salons, coffeehouses, novels, art criticism, and magazines," Warner goes on, "all play an important role in Habermas's account of how the fundamental structure of politics changed in this century."[24]

For many who work in eighteenth-century literature – Shields, for example – as well as for those like Warner who study the history of print culture, Habermas offers something like a *passepartout* into many different rooms in British America and the early United States. For Warner specifically, he provides ways to understand the wide spectrum of literary activity on these shores; and thus Warner's book is an inquiry into what he rightly terms "the conditions of meaning that inform the bulk of American writing in the period." In chapters that range from summaries of what we know of print activity in eighteenth-century America, to Franklin as a man of letters, to "Textuality and Legitimacy in the Printed Constitution," to the early American novels of Charles Brockden Brown, Warner illustrates the utility of understanding the cultural uses of print over the course of the century, particularly in the crucial period just before the Revolution itself, when printing finally "began to sustain a continuous local discourse" rather than merely to reflect the culture of the learned classes.[25] The larger point is that by 1765 the individual, the citizen himself, had frequent and easy access to the new discourse. Indeed, its very authority was dependent on just such engagement. This was the crucible from which, among other things, revolutionary politics emerged.

In brief compass it is difficult to convey the provocation of Warner's book; suffice it to say that many in literature now consider it as seminal as Fliegelman's was a decade ago. Much of its power stems from Warner's ability to link Habermas to Bailyn, Wood, et al. – for example, in his observation that, "Developed in practices of literacy that included the production and consumption of newspapers, broadsides, legal documents, and books, the republican ideology of print elevated the values of generality over those of the personal." Thus, "in this cognitive vocabulary the social diffusion of printed artifacts took on the investment of the disinterested virtue of public orientation, as opposed to the corrupting interests and passions of particular and local persons."[26] Print culture, in other words, functioned to create, in its own textuality, the perfect Republican who would guarantee America's virtue.

Not surprisingly, given that he is a professor of English, Warner ends with a challenging discussion of the early American novel, a genre that did not emerge on these shores until the 1780s and which, to his mind, took its unique form because of its very embeddedness in the ideology of the public sphere he so carefully delineates. The seemingly mixed motives of early American novelists, their confusion over how their work was to fit into some ideal of "American" literature, their unwillingness to admit without equivocation that their work was fiction rather than truth – all these matters derived from the fact that before 1810 American writers continued to regard their work primarily as a contribution to the ideology of Republicanism, not to some subjective "national identity" or, as in Poe's case, an abstraction called "art." As Warner puts it, the novelists imagined "the readers of their publications as participants in public discourse rather than as private consumers of luxury goods," which the readers were indeed becoming. For with the rise of the novel and the leisure time to read extensively in it, even if the reader had "a virtuous orientation" to his activity, such virtue more and more came to be "experienced privately rather than in the context of civic action."[27] By century's end, in other words, print culture had become more than an inextricable part of the public sphere. It was beginning to define subjectivity itself.

To date, the most exciting discussion of such cultural work of the early American novel occurs in Cathy S. Davidson's *Revolution and the Word: The Rise of the Novel in America*. Moreover, her book also stands as the most sophisticated example in America of work that has come to be called "the history of the book."[28] Researched in good part in the unparalleled library of the American Antiquarian Society, which itself is sponsoring a multivolume, collaborative history of the book in American culture, *Revolution and the Word* is particularly significant because, like Dowling's work, it resuscitates interest in a group of early American novels hitherto quickly passed over, usually in favor of the work of Charles Brockden Brown, who in the old genealogy of American literary history connects nicely to the gothicism of Poe and the psychological fiction of Hawthorne – i.e., as part of the infamous "continuities" thesis. Moreover, Davidson argues the centrality of women writers and readers to the emergence of the American novel;

though she spends time with Brown, his predecessor William Hill Brown, Royall Tyler, and other less frequently studied male novelists, her main interest lies in the large body of fiction written by and for late-eighteenth-century American women.

Davidson's work engages many of the questions Warner raises in passing at the conclusion of his work, most importantly concerning the changing meaning of textuality at a time when certain forms of literature, particularly the novel, began to be considered commodities for middle-class, primarily female, consumers rather than as the locus of public discourse. But while Warner's grounding is in Habermas, hers is in European practitioners of *l'histoire du livre* and, in terms of critical theory, in Mikhail Bakhtin's notion of prose fiction as a profoundly subversive literary form, "subversive," as she glosses him, "of certain class notions of who should and should not be literate; subversive of notions of what is or is not a suitable literary matter and form and style; subversive of the term *literature* itself."[29]

In her earlier chapters Davidson neatly synthesizes what we know of the early book trade in the Northeast, discussing everything from printing costs to the costs of books, the numbers of books issued in print runs, financial arrangements made among authors, printers, and publishers, the nature of the book distribution network, the formal and informal means through which books circulated through society, and the public reception of various early American novels – about a hundred of them in all, before 1820. But subsequently she moves into territory reconnoitered as well by Warner when he ponders the development and importance of early American fiction.

For one thing she clarifies the relationship between early American fiction and the reader who, through his or her own relationship to the public sphere, began to understand better the limits of its ideological underpinnings. Reminding us that contemporary educational reformers themselves emphasized "the need for the *active* production of meaning both in the free play of the mind that comes from reading imaginative literature and in the active production of meaning that arises from writing out one's thoughts," Davidson demonstrates how the early American novel sought to address its readership in quite the same ways, assisting in their education even as its messages carried more weight for those, particularly women, hitherto left out of elite culture, and thus out of the public sphere.[30]

Davidson's larger point is that for women of the republic, reading novels was profoundly subversive. Because, as she notes, "the very act of reading fiction asserted the primacy of the individual as reader and the legitimacy of that reader's perceptions and responses," it offered as well subjective empowerment, a validation of one's individual identity and worth, even if these were not yet acknowledged in the Republican ideology that dominated the public sphere.[31] Treating in turn most of the major American novels of the period, from William Hill Brown's *Power of Sympathy* to Foster's *Coquette* to Tyler's *Algerine Captive*, as well as others that she rediscovered in the course of her research, Davidson explores the plight of young women in the new republic, particularly their domination by a patriarchy that strictly circumscribed their behavior and freedom of choice, and how such frustrations were addressed and illuminated in fiction by women. Reading, in other words, now offered a place – an interior sphere – of personal freedom in which the reader, through her imaginative identification with fictional characters, could better understand who she was and what she was allowed to become. What had begun as an extension of the public sphere now allowed women readers to question their estrangement – indeed, their banishment – from its activity – to question, in other words, the patriarchy's attempt to imprison them in the silken bonds of domesticity.

Davidson concludes her work with a lengthy chapter on Charles Brockden Brown, in whose gothic romances one finds perhaps more than anywhere else in the new republic a challenge to "the Age of Reason's ruling premises about the purposes of discourse, the status of knowledge, and the limits of both realism and rationality," an emergent criticism, in other words, of the commodity capitalism that was beginning to sweep the American strand.[32] In a sense, in his novels the kind of cultural work being done by writers like Foster, Tenney, and Rowson for their women readers was extended to the entire reading populace. Literature had become, through its ability to help define one's subjectivity, a proposition potentially yet more subversive of the Republic.

We thus see that the best recent criticism on eighteenth-century British American literature addresses more and more directly the complex relation of the public to the private spheres. This work is a breath of fresh air, a welcome escape from the iron cages of ideological readings that hitherto have dominated our discussions of colonial American literature, particularly in the wake of Bercovitch. The movement, visible to some degree both in Shields's explorations of the poetry of empire and Dowling's of the literature of Republicanism, and very apparent in Warner's and Davidson's work, toward a more profound understanding of the sociology of texts, clearly indicates where the new action is. And the debates, as they are shaping up, probably will center on the relationship of republican ideology to gender, and of liberalism to the rise of sentiment. We will be backing up, in other words, into the late eighteenth and early nineteenth centuries such landmark studies as Ann Douglas's *Feminization of American Culture*, which for all its hyperbole, remains central to our understanding of nineteenth-century women authors, as well as the more recent revisionary work on the development of the American novel from the 1830s on.[33]

We are seeing, then, a significant paradigm shift, away from the assumptions of continuities and American exceptionalism that so marks the ideological critics as well as the earlier "American Studies" scholars, to those derived from an understanding of the immense transformation wrought in the late eighteenth- and early nineteenth-centuries by what Charles Sellers, in his recent synthetic book calls the "market revolution."[34] And, once we understand that in late eighteenth-century America texts more and more were becoming artifacts for consumption in private rather than, as in Warner's formulation, a means first to define and then to extend one's activity in the public sphere, we can begin to break free of the restrictive and predictable literary histories that have dominated our field.

To conclude let me focus on this larger question of how literary history now should be written, keeping in mind what I have argued about the general development of studies of eighteenth-century American literature. In his recent book *The American Ideal* and in a subsequent essay in *American Literary History*, Peter Carafiol takes to task literary historians who continue the same idealistic and quixotic venture, the composition of yet more "historical" narratives that privilege the notion of a peculiarly "American" literature, a project that he unmasks as naively ahistorical in its conception and various incarnations. He tries to shake us into considering a "post-American literary studies" in which "critical accounts would be shaped not by a pre-venient ethos or metanarrative [that is, by the transcendent notion of 'America' that lies at the heart, say, of Bercovitch's formulation] but by the changing conditions of their unfolding inquiry, their process of articulation"; and he cites as pioneers of this mode of inquiry such writers as Coleridge, Emerson, Thoreau, Henry James, and Wittgen-stein.[35]

Carafiol's notions about American literature are seconded by David Perkins in his similarly provocative and more wide-ranging *Is Literary History Possible?* in which he concludes that the sort of thing to which Carafiol objects is simply endemic to the project itself. "Liter-ary history," he writes, "is and perhaps must be written in metaphors of origin, emergence from obscurity, neglect and recognition, conflict, hegemony, succession, displacement, decline, and so forth." But more willing than Carafiol to accept the genre's limitations, he also notes that while many of us find it impossible to write literary history with any conviction," we still "must read it." He means that though we cannot achieve the ideal of objective knowledge, we still must pursue it, "for without such pursuit the otherness of the past would entirely deliquesce in endless subjective and ideological reappropriations." "A function of literary history is, then," he concludes, "to set the litera-ture of the past at a distance, to make its otherness felt."[36]

Despite their suspicions – different as they are – of the project of literary history, both Carafiol and Perkins open a space for the work of new cultural historians. The embrace by literary historians of this new cultural history for the early national period – embodied in works like Christopher Clark's *The Roots of Rural Capitalism*, John Brooke's *The Heart of the Commonwealth*, and William J. Gilmore's *Reading Becomes a Necessity of Life* – will move us further from those Whiggish narratives, ways merely of getting from *there* to *here* in our teaching and scholar-ship, that Carofiol (and his mentor Spengemann before him) rightly condemns.[37] We are at the point when we are moving away from studies centered on literary figures per se and toward excavations of large-scale cultural sites – like the book distribution network, mass advertising, the centralization of publishing in urban areas, the relation of gender to authorship and readership, and the like. Not the least significant result of this work will be our ability to compare such phenomena to those in other cultures being similarly transformed by the market. In such new histories "America" will become merely one example among many of how modernization occurred. Put another way, the chief prospective task of the new literary historian of eighteenth- and early nineteenth-century America is to explore the ways in which individuals at different points in time made sense of their lives through texts, all manner and all number of them, and all placed solidly within the larger extratextual archive that historians of culture, and, like Gilmore and Richard D. Brown, of knowledge itself, provide.[38] Then we will better be able to speak of the past's "otherness."

Nathaniel Hawthorne, among his generation of writers not the least interested in the relation of history to literature, introduced his collection of stories, *Mosses from An Old Manse*, with his charming reminiscence, "The Old Manse," a leisurely discussion of an attic room in his Concord home where young scholars who came to study with Emerson's grandfather William Emerson and, later, the venerable Ezra Ripley, had boarded.[39] Therein Hawthorne found many old volumes; presumably the remains of the clerical library; and, good historian that he was, he "burrowed among these venerable books, in search of any living thought, which should burn like a coal of fire, or glow like an inextinguishable gem." But to his surprise he found "no such treasure" among the leather-bound books. "All was dead alike," and he "could not but muse deeply and wonderingly upon the humiliating fact, that the works of man's intellect decay like those of his hands." "Thought grows mouldy," he continues. "What was good and nourishing for the spirits of one generation, affords no sustenance for the next."

After examining some works that pertained to the more recent Unitarian controversy and noting that these had an effect even more depressing than the more "venerable" tomes, which at least were "earnestly written" and "might be conceived to have possessed warmth, at some former period," Hawthorne lit upon some old newspapers and almanacs. These genuinely excited him, he wrote, for they "reproduced, to [his] mental eye, the epochs when they had issued from the press, with a distinctness that was altogether unaccountable." "It was as if," he continued, "I had found bits of magic looking-glass among the books, with the images of a vanished century in them." Interrogating a tattered portrait of an eighteenth-century divine who had lived in the Manse, Hawthorne wondered why it was "that he and his brethren, after the most painful rummaging and groping in their minds, had been able to produce nothing half so real, as these newspaper scribblers and almanac-makers had thrown off, in the effervescence of the moment."

These "newspaper scribblers and almanac-makers" epitomize nothing less than the all-encompassing transformation of the market economy that marked the late-eighteenth and early-nineteenth-centuries; and further, the immense changes in print culture and the transfer of knowledge initiated and encouraged by this revolution. To recenter American literary history in this period we must come to terms with the significance of what Hawthorne, good historian that he was, already knew. The best work of the last decade – canon revision, recovery of voices hitherto locked in dusty archives, New Historical explorations of American ideology, investigations of race and gender, indeed, even traditional biographies and source studies – all falls into line around these magnetic poles.

No one will ever get literary history, or for that matter any history, just "right" because the past finally is, as Perkins simply but eloquently observes, so different from us. He might have found confirmation of this in Thoreau, who reminds us that "Critical acumen is exerted in vain to uncover the past; the past cannot be presented; we cannot know what we are not." Yet, he goes on to say, "one veil hangs over past, present, and future, and it is the province of the historian to find out, not what was, but what is."[40] As long as we recognize that in writing literary history we write as much about our difference from the past as about the past itself, the project remains honest and worthwhile. And as we move in our studies of eighteenth- and early nineteenth-century American literature precisely in this way; as we write, in other words, more self-consciously aware of what premises underlie our attempts to recover and narrate the past, we move toward a deeper understanding of that otherness. Ours finally has become, I think, a wide and exhilarating prospect.

Notes

1. Philip F. Gura, "The Study of Colonial American Literature, 1966–1987: A Vade Mecum," *William and Mary Quarterly* 45 (1988): 305–41.

2. Jack P. Greene and J. R. Pole, eds., *Colonial British America: Essays in the New History of the Early Modern Era* (Baltimore: Johns Hopkins University Press, 1984).

3. The term "American Renaissance" gained its currency following F. O. Matthiessen's magisterial book, *American Renaissance: Art and Expression in the Age of Emerson and Whitman* (New York: Oxford University Press, 1941). Recently, his canonization of certain authors has been challenged by revisionists who argue that his criteria excluded much important and interesting writing, particularly by women and African-Americans. See, for example, Walter Benn Michaels and Donald Pease, eds., *The American Renaissance Reconsidered* (Baltimore: The Johns Hopkins University Press, 1985).

4. See Greene and Pole, eds., *Colonial British America*, 2–7.

5. Ibid., p. 3. Richard L. Bushman, *The Refinement of America: Persons, Houses, Cities* (New York: Alfred A. Knopf, 1992).

6. William C. Spengemann, "Discovering the Literature of British America," *Early American Literature* 18 (1983): 7, and "Review Essay,"*Early American Literature* 16 (1981): 184. Spengemann's many provocative essays recently have been collected in his *A Mirror for Americanists: Reflections on the Idea of American Literature* (Hanover, N.H.: University Press of New England, 1989).

7. Spengemann, "Review Essay," 179.

8. Greene and Pole, *Colonial British America*, 14.

9. See in particular, Sacvan Bercovitch: *Typology and Early American Literature* (Amherst: University of Massachusetts Press, 1972), *The Puritan Origins of the American Self* (New Haven, Conn.: Yale University Press, 1975), *The American Jeremiad* (Madison: University of Wisconsin Press, 1978), and *The Rites of Assent: Transformations in the Symbolic Construction of America* (New York: Routledge, 1993), this last a work assembled from essays composed over the course of his career. For the challenges to Bercovitch's undeniably powerful influence, see David Harlan, "A People Blinded from Birth: American History According to Sacvan Bercovitch," *Journal of American History* 78 (1991): 949–71; Andrew Delbanco, "The Puritan Errand Re-Viewed," *Journal of American Studies* 18 (1984): 343–60; and Dwight Bozeman, *To Live Ancient Lives: The Primitivist Dimension in Puritanism* (Chapel Hill: University of North Carolina Press, 1988).

10. Jack P. Greene, *Pursuits of Happiness: The Social Development of Early Modern British Colonies and the Formation of American Culture* (Chapel Hill: University of North Carolina Press, 1988), 7–80.

11. See Richard Beale Davis, *Intellectual Life in the Colonial South, 1585–1763*, 3 vols. (Knoxville: University of Tennessee Press, 1973); Lewis Simpson, "The Act of Thought in Virginia," *Early American Literature* 14 (1979–80): 253–68; and J. A. Leo Lemay, *Men of Letters in Colonial Maryland* (Knoxville: University of Tennessee Press, 1972).

12. Patricia Caldwell, *The Puritan Conversion Narrative: The Beginnings of American Expression* (New York: Cambridge University Press, 1983); J. A. Leo Lemay, *The American Dream of Captain John Smith* (Charlottesville: University Press of Virginia, 1991).

13. See David S. Shields, "Anglo-American Clubs: Their Wit, Their Heterodoxy, Their Sedition" *William and Mary Quarterly* 51 (1993): 293–304; idem., *Civil Tongues & Polite Letters in British America* (Chapel Hill: University of North Carolina Press, 1997), and A. Wilson Somerville, *The Tuesday Club of Annapolis (1745–1756) as Cultural Theatre* (Athens: University of Georgia Press, 1996).

14. Dr. Alexander Hamilton, *The History of the Tuesday Club*, ed. Robert Micklus, 3 vols. (Chapel Hill: University of North Carolina Press, 1990); and Robert Micklus, *The Comic Genius of Dr. Alexander Hamilton* (Knoxville: University of Tennessee Press, 1990).

15. Rhys Isaac, *The Transformation of Virginia, 1740–1790* (Chapel Hill: University of North Carolina Press, 1982).

16. David S. Shields, *Oracles of Empire: Poetry, Politics, and Commerce in British America, 1690–1750* (Chicago: University of Chicago Press, 1990), 6.

17. Jay Fliegelman, *Prodigals and Pilgrims: The American Revolution against Patriarchal Authority, 1750–1800* (New York: Cambridge University Press, 1982). Fliegelman's most recent work, *Declaring Independence: Jefferson, Natural Language, and the Culture of Performance* (Stanford, Calif.: Stanford University Press, 1993), is equally provocative. See also Bernard Bailyn, *Idological Origins of the American Revolution* (Cambridge, Mass.: Harvard University Press, 1967); and Gordon Wood, *The Creation of the Republic, 1776–1787* (Chapel Hill: University of North Carolina Press, 1969).

18. William C. Dowling, *Poetry and Ideology in Revolutionary Connecticut* (Athens: University of Georgia Press, 1990), ix.

19. Ibid., 14, 17, 18.

20. Ibid., 81. See Richard L. Bushman, *From Puritan and Yankee: Character and the Social Order in Connecticut, 1690–1765* (Cambridge, Mass.: Harvard University Press, 1967)

21. Carla Mulford, *"Only for the Eyes of a Friend": The Poetry of Annis Boudinot Stockton* (Charlottesville: University Press of Virginia, 1995); and Pattie Cowell, *Women Poets in Prerevolutionary America, 1650–1755: An Anthology* (Troy, N.Y.: Whitston, 1981).

22. Thomas Gustafson, *Representative Words: Politics, Literature, and the American Language, 1776–1865* (New York: Cambridge University Press, 1993), 12.

23. Ibid., 13.

24. Michael Warner, *The Letters of the Republic: Publication and the Public Sphere in Eighteenth-Century America* (Cambridge, Mass.: Harvard University Press, 1990), x.

25. Ibid., xi, 32.

26. Ibid., 108.

27. Ibid., 150.

28. The history of the book and of reading in America is a field still in its infancy, though there currently is under way a multivolume, collaborative *A History of the Book in America*, under the general editorship of David D. Hall to be published by Cambridge University Press. For examples of work in this field, David D. Hall, ed., *Cultures of Print: Essays in the History of the Book* (Amherst: University of Massachusetts Press, 1996); Cathy N. Davidson, *Revolution and the Word: The Rise of the Novel in America* (New York: Oxford University Press, 1986); idem, ed., *Reading in America: Literature and Social History* (Baltimore: The Johns Hopkins University Press, 1989); and Ronald Zboray, *A Fictive People: Antebellum Economic Development and the American Reading Public* (New York: Oxford University Press 1993).

29. Davidson, *Revolution and the Word*, 13. See M. M. Bakhtin, *The Dialogic Imagination: Four Essays* (Austin: University of Texas Press, 1981).

30. Ibid., 68

31. Ibid., 52.

32. Ibid., 237. Recently, important new work on the early American novel has appeared. See Julia A. Stern, *The Plight of Feeling: Sympathy and Dissent in the Early American Novel* (Chicago: University of Chicago Press, 1997); Elizabeth Barnes, *States of Sympathy: Seduction and Democracy in the American Novel* (New York: Columbia University Press, 1997); and most important, Grantland S. Rice, *The Transformation of Authorship in America* (Chicago: University of Chicago Press, 1997), which strongly challenges Warner's influential thesis concerning literature and the emergence of the public sphere.

33. Ann Douglas, *The Feminization of American Culture* (New York: Alfred A. Knopf, 1977). See also Nancy Cott, *The Bonds of Womanhood: "Woman's Sphere" in New England, 1780–1835* (New Haven, Conn.: Yale University Press, 1977); Shirley Samuels, ed., *The Culture of Sentiment: Race, Gender, and Sentimentality in Nineteenth-Century America* (New York: Oxford University Press, 1993), Susan K. Harris, *Nineteenth-Century American Women Novels: Interpretive Strategies* (New York: Cambridge University Press, 1990), and Susan Coultrap-McQuin, *Doing Literary Business: American Women Writers in the Nineteenth Century* (Chapel Hill: University of North Carolina Press, 1990).

34. Charles G. Sellers, *The Market Revolution: Jacksonian America, 1815–46* (New York: Oxford University Press, 1991).

35. Peter C. Carafiol, "After American Literature," *American Literary History* 4 (1992): 546. Also see idem, *The American Ideal: Literary History as a Worldly Activity* (New York: Oxford University Press, 1991).

36. David Perkins, *Is Literary History Possible?* (Baltimore: The Johns Hopkins University, 1992), 33, 17, 185.

37. Christopher Clark, *The Roots of Rural Capitalism: Western Massachusetts, 1780–1860* (Ithaca, N.Y.: Cornell University Press, 1990); John Brooke, *The Heart of the Commonwealth: Society and Political Culture in Worcester County, Massachusetts, 1713–1861* (New York: Cambridge University Press, 1989); and William J. Gilmore, *Reading Becomes a Necessity of Life: Material and Cultural Life in Rural New England, 1780–1835* (Knoxville: University of Tennessee Press, 1989).

38. Richard D. Brown: *Knowledge Is Power: The Diffusion of Information in Early America, 1700–1865* (New York: Oxford University Press, 1989); and, *The Strength of a People: The Idea of an Informed Citizenry in America, 1650–1870* (Chapel Hill: University of North Carolina Press, 1996).

39. Nathaniel Hawthorne, "The Old Manse," in *Nathaniel Hawthorne: Tales and Sketches* (New York: Viking Press 1982), 1135–1138.

40. Henry David Thoreau, *A Week on the Concord and Merrimack Rivers* (1849; reprint, Princeton, N.J.: Princeton University Press, 1980), 155.

7
LITERACY AND EDUCATION
IN EIGHTEENTH-CENTURY NORTH AMERICA

Gerald F. Moran and Maris A. Vinovskis

D ESPITE THE INCREASED INTEREST and work in educational history since the mid-1960's, there have been surprisingly few comprehensive and in-depth analyses of eighteenth-century literacy and schooling in North America. Most educational historians have focused on the rise of the public common schools in the nineteenth century without paying much attention to colonial schooling. With a few notable exceptions, colonial historians have neglected to examine systematically the extent and nature of eighteenth-century education. Recently there have been, however, some useful and imaginative essays and books which have examined colonial literacy and schooling. Most of these are detailed case studies of literacy published in relatively specialized journals or narrowly-focused monographs. Their fragmented findings have not been thoroughly synthesized or incorporated fully into broader discussions of eighteenth-century culture and society.

In this essay we will investigate the trends in adult literacy in colonial America and place them within the context of comparable changes in western Europe. As we shall see, there is considerable debate among scholars on the nature and extent of eighteenth-century literacy – especially for North American women. We will analyze the alternative explanations for the changes in colonial literacy with particular attention to the ethnic, socioeconomic and regional variations. Finally, we will illustrate the need for investigating more carefully the impact of these changes by briefly examining how colonial religious and political developments may have been affected by shifts in literacy and education. Our goal is not only to synthesize much of the growing, but scattered literature on literacy and schooling, but also to pose some broad research questions which may stimulate further studies of eighteenth-century education.

Trends in Adult Literacy

The recent efforts to measure adult literacy quantitatively using a variety of different measures and sources constitute a major advance in the systematic study of education in the past. Most of the these studies have employed evidence of the ability to sign one's name (mark signature) as a crude approximation of literacy – in large part because signatures are one of the few indices of literacy widely available for individuals before the nineteenth century.

The use of the ability to sign one's name as an overall measure of literacy is limited, of course, by several considerations. More people could read than could write because reading was taught usually before someone learned to write; many people learned to read without ever having been taught how to write. Some groups, especially Protestants, emphasized the importance of reading the Bible rather than of learning to write – thus making any simple, general inferences about the ratio of readers to those signing their names problematic. Significant gender differences in the relative ability to read and write existed as women often were expected to be able to read, but not to write. Questions have even been raised about the extent to which one could write fluently compared to the more limited ability of just signing one's name. Moreover, doubts about the usefulness of ability to sign one's name later in life as an index of previous literacy have been raised due to possible physical infirmities associated with aging or to forgetfulness caused by the lack of writing experiences during adulthood. Finally, the actual usefulness of literacy to an individual depends to some degree upon the contexts in which it is being used so that someone judged literate in one setting or time might not be literate in another. As a result, scholars now tend to view literacy as a continuum of activities ranging from rudimentary reading to fluent writing with some analysts even adding the ability to calculate and manipulate simple numbers as an additional and necessary component of literacy.[1]

If the measures of adult literacy are varied and complex, so too are the sources of information. Many of the studies of adult literacy rely upon documents such as wills, deeds, or lists of church members, which are not representative of the population as a whole in regard to gender, wealth, or occupation. Therefore, great care must be taken in making inferences from the limited sources of information about literacy before the nineteenth century.[2]

Despite the limitations in our measures of literacy or in our sources of information about literacy, historians have made important strides in studying trends in adult literacy in the past. Careful and judicious studies of adult literacy have been made and we will report on the results from some of these investigations. Nevertheless, the reader should always bear in mind the tentativeness and fragility of the findings given the limited nature of the available evidence.

Analyses of adult literacy in Western Europe point to major overall improvements between 1500 and 1800 – though wide geographic, demographic and social variations in literacy were evident throughout this period. In 1500 a few adults, usually wealthier males living in urban communities, could read and write; by 1800 the ability to read and write had spread to other segments of the population including the middle class, women, and even portions of the working classes such as artisans. While high rates of illiteracy continued in areas such as southern France and Italy in 1800, there was nearly universal male literacy in other parts of Western Europe such as Scotland and Sweden.[3]

Throughout the three centuries, there were important differentials in literacy by location and group. Literacy was usually higher in urban areas than in the countryside; wealthier individuals and those engaged in commercial activities were more literate than the poor or common laborers. While the situation of women improved over time, their literacy continued to lag behind their male counterparts. Moreover, although the relationship between religion and literacy was rather complex; in general Protestants had a higher level of literacy than Catholics. And while there was a general, overall increase in literacy from 1500–1800, those changes tended to be gradual and uneven rather than sudden and always irreversible.[4]

England, the largest single source of settlers to North America, experienced major improvements in literacy in the sixteenth and seventeenth centuries.[5] But as David Cressy and others have shown, the improvements in literacy varied considerably by location and the characteristics of the population. Moreover, though there was an overall increase in literacy during these two centuries, there were temporary reversals in the early seventeenth century for groups such as the tradesmen and husbandmen in East Anglia.[6] Similarly, while literacy appears to have grown from 1660 to 1680, there was an apparent decrease from 1690 to 1710.[7]

Most of the eighteenth century only saw a very gradual and erratic increase in British literacy, but the last decades witnessed renewed growth in both literacy and schooling. Using signatures from a random sample of 274 British marriage registers, Roger Schofield has estimated that about 60 percent of males and 40 percent of females could sign their names in the mid-eighteenth century and that those figures improved only slightly for women and remained rather stable for men until 1800. While nearly all of the clergy and professional men were literate, more than half of the husbandmen and laborers still were unable to sign their names in the period 1785–1814.[8] At the same time, the increased access of the people in the middle class to print and art has led one scholar to label the eighteenth century a "cultural revolution."[9]

The situation in the English colonies in North America was somewhat different than in Britain. Rates of adult literacy tended to be higher, but again there were considerable variations by colony and social group. Part of the explanation for the higher rates of literacy in British North America was that the colonial settlers who came here from Britain or other parts of Western Europe usually were better educated than their counterparts who remained behind.[10] Indeed, sometimes there was a brief decrease in literacy rates in the New World, the so-called "creolean degeneracy" period, as the newly settled frontier areas were unable to maintain the same high level of literacy that was found among the immigrants.[11]

The now classic analysis of literacy in colonial America is by Kenneth Lockridge who studied the use of mark-signatures in New England wills in the seventeenth and eighteenth centuries. According to Lockridge, adult white male literacy in New England rose from about 60 percent in the mid-seventeenth century to nearly 90 percent by 1800 while white adult female literacy rose from about one-third to about 45 percent during the most of the eighteenth century. He also found sizable occupational and wealth differences in literacy as well as a large rural-urban split. Thus, according to Lockridge, the eighteenth century saw sizable increases in adult literacy for men, but a much more stagnant picture for women in New England. Moreover, while there was almost universal white male literacy by the end of the eighteenth century, a majority of white women, especially those in rural areas, still could not sign their names in New England.[12]

While applauding Lockridge's pioneering efforts, much of the recent scholarship on New England has challenged his findings – especially those in regard to the low level of literacy among New England women in the eighteenth century. Some scholars pointed out the small number of women in his sample and questioned the reliability of the findings. Since much of Lockridge's late eighteenth century came from a sample of wills in two Massachusetts counties (Suffolk and Middlesex) from 1787 to 1795, Joel Perlmann and Dennis Shirley expanded his Suffolk samples for women and found a higher rate of female literacy in both Boston (78 percent vs. 60 percent) and the rural areas (53 percent vs. 42 percent).[13]

Others have questioned the wisdom of using wills rather than deeds to study female literacy since so few women compared to men ever left a will.[14] Moreover, women who did write a will often did so at an advanced age when their writing may have been physically impaired or particularly hindered compared to men by their relative lack of writing during adulthood.[15]

Using deeds rather than wills, several scholars have argued that Lockridge has underestimated considerably the extent of female literacy in the eighteenth century.[16] But there still is considerable variation in the levels of female literacy according to these new studies. At one extreme, Linda Auwers's analysis of signatures on deeds in rural Windsor, Connecticut found nearly three fourths to universal literacy among successive cohorts of women born in the eighteenth century.[17] Ross Beales, on the other hand, found that 47 percent of women could sign deeds in rural Grafton, Massachusetts in 1747.[18] In between these two estimates, Gloria Main's study of rural Suffolk County (Massachusetts) and William Gilmore's analysis of rural Windsor District (Vermont) in the 1760s discovered that about 60 percent of women could sign deeds. By 1800 over 80 percent of women in the Windsor District were signing deeds.[19]

Several scholars had contrasted the relatively low rates of female literacy in New England at the end of the eighteenth century reported by Lockridge with the nearly universal rates of literacy among older New England women reported in the U.S. Census of 1850.[20] Perlmann and Dennis, in an interesting essay, looked at the literacy rates of a sample of elder New England women from the manuscript U.S. Census of 1850 and found nearly universal literacy for those born after 1765. While they acknowledge the problems of selectivity in using an elderly cohort of women and the ambiguities of the census question about literacy, they contend that their findings basically are consistent with the recent upward revisions of Lockridge's estimates of eighteenth-century female literacy in New England.[21]

Much of the debate about New England literacy has also centered on the issue of reading versus writing. Lockridge assumed that someone able to sign their name could read fluently, but he did not differentiate between males and females in this regard. Other scholars have argued that since the Puritans emphasized the importance of reading for everyone, but only writing for males, it is likely that the ratio of readers to signers was higher for females than for males. Moreover, since Puritan culture placed such a great emphasis on reading the Bible, the high rates of female illiteracy according to mark signatures probably seriously underestimates the proportion of New England women who could read throughout the colonial period.[22]

Compared to the studies of literacy in New England, the other regions of eighteenth-century America have not received much attention. For the middle colonies, the literacy of the residents of Pennsylvania have received the most attention. Using signatures on Philadelphia wills, Lawrence Cremin found that approximately 80 percent of males could sign their names throughout the eighteenth century while the percentage of literate women rose from approximately 60 percent to 80 percent just before the American Revolution.[23]

In rural Pennsylvania, however, the rates of literacy were not as high. Alan Tully's study of mark signatures on wills in two counties from 1729 to 1774 found that approximately 72 percent of males in Chester County and 63 percent in Lancaster County could sign their names – with no major trends over time. The literacy of women in Chester County fluctuated from about 19 percent to 46 percent while those in Lancaster County increased from virtually nothing to about 38 percent by 1765–74.[24] Thus, while the rates of male and female literacy in Philadelphia approached those of New England in the late eighteenth century, rates in the rural areas lagged somewhat behind.

Rates of literacy in the South appear to have been rather similar to those in rural Pennsylvania. In rural Virginia, Lockridge found that almost seven out of ten white males could sign their names on wills in the eighteenth century. He also discovered strong occupational and wealth differences – while most wealthy Virginian white males could sign their names, perhaps as many as half of the middle and lower class white males could not sign their names.[25]

An analysis of the literacy of free persons in seventeenth- and eighteenth-century Perquimans County, North Carolina, however, found somewhat higher literacy than other studies of the colonial South. Robert Gallman, using signatures from deeds, estimated that the proportion of males able to sign their names increased from 67 percent in 1661–95 to 79 percent in 1748–76 and that comparable figures for females rose slightly from 30 percent to 35 percent. The somewhat higher rates of male literacy in Perquimans County than elsewhere in the rural South perhaps may be explained in part by the fact that a large number of Quakers lived there and the area was wealthier.[26]

So far we have considered the literacy of white adults in British North America. But a sizable proportion of the eighteenth-century population were Africans brought to the New World as slaves. While many studies of antebellum slavery have made it clear that some African-Americans could read, we have very little information about the actual levels of literacy of eighteenth-century slaves or ex-slaves.[27]

The African cultures from which the slaves to the New World were based upon oral traditions. But in the British American colonies, some masters, mainly as part of their religious training of their chattel, taught slaves how to read the Bible. At the same time, other whites often periodically opposed teaching slaves either to read or write for fear that this might encourage disobedience and even led to slave insurrections. Earlier scholars have speculated that approximately 5–10 percent of the slave population on the eve of the Civil War were literate, but the evidence upon which this is based is rather limited.[28] More recent scholarship tends to accept the higher estimate and one study of advertisements for Kentucky slave runaways found that about one-fifth were described as being able to read and one-tenth as being able to write.[29]

Everyone agrees that freed African-Americans had a higher rate of literacy, but again there is little direct evidence for the eighteenth century. The U.S. Census of 1850, however, did inquire about the ability of free African-American adults to read and write. According to that census, 60 percent of free black males and 57 percent of free black females were literate. There were significant regional differences with about 85 percent of free blacks in New England literate compared to about half of those in the South Atlantic region.[30] Again, we do not have any specific estimates of the literacy of free African-Americans in the eighteenth century.

The British colonists sporadically devoted considerable efforts to trying to educate and "civilize" the native Americans they encountered. Native Americans, like the Africans, did not have a written language.[31] The British settlers and missionaries, anxious to proselytize the indigent inhabitants as well as to pacify them, embarked on a variety of often ambitious and lofty plans to educate native Americans, but in the end they failed to have much of an impact on the local population.

While the native Americans often were impressed by the technological achievements of the Europeans, they were less awed by their self-proclaimed cultural superiority. As the white settlers usually insisted that native Americans must abandon and renounce their own cultures as part of becoming Christians who would be able to read the Bible, most Indians showed little interest in acquiring literacy. Moreover, as the British missionaries often insisted that the children of the native Americans be separated from their parents and sent to a boarding school, most Indians refused to participate.[32]

Various schemes for educating the Indians were proposed and tried.[33] In Virginia, repeated efforts were made to set up special schools for native Americans, but these institutions floundered in the face of indifference from the indigent population and white hostility after any armed clashes with the Indians.[34] Massachusetts tried to gather Indians in areas designated as "praying towns" and even made efforts in the second half of the seventeenth century to translate and transliterate the Bible and other religious writings into the language of the native American population.[35] Unfortunately, from the perspective of the British settlers, almost all of these efforts failed to have much of a lasting impact.

One interesting exception to the repeated failures of the British settlers to convert and educate native Americans is the experience of the natives of Martha's Vineyard in the seventeenth and eighteenth centuries. Introduced to Christianity and literacy in the mid-seventeenth century, most of the Indians on Martha's Vineyard converted and displayed a genuine eagerness to learn to read the Bible, which was translated into their language. While very few of the Indians learned to write, a sizable proportion did learn to read. Jennifer Monaghan has estimated that by the early eighteenth century, approximately two-thirds of the adult devout Indians on Martha's Vineyard were able to read.[36]

Most studies of literacy in colonial America have focused almost exclusively on British colonies with very little, if any attention to comparable developments in either New France or New Spain. When comparisons are made to other countries, the examples are usually drawn from Western Europe rather than other regions of the New World. Since New France and New Spain were settled by Catholics rather than Protestants and had different strategies for settlement, they provide interesting and useful comparisons for developments in literacy in British North America.

Fortunately, there is growing interest in the study of education and literacy in New France and the initial results seem to be particularly intriguing.[37] Most of the French immigrants were dispersed throughout the countryside with very few of them living even in small villages. Few schools were maintained in the rural areas and literacy was not regarded as an essential occupational requirement for most inhabitants. The two urban areas, Montreal and Quebec, supported a series of schools and literacy was seen as useful for certain occupations. Although the Catholic Church was entrusted with providing schooling, it never placed the same emphasis on education that its Protestant counterparts did in British North America.[38]

Given the dispersed nature of settlement as well as the relatively low regard for schooling, it is not surprising that the rates of literacy for the French settlers were quite low. Based upon data from marriage registers for 1680–99, 56 percent of grooms and 44 percent of brides in

Quebec and Montreal signed their names compared to 34 percent of grooms and 23 percent of brides in rural parishes.[39]

Rather than seeing an increase in eighteenth-century literacy as in many other countries, the French inhabitants appear to have experienced a significant decline – especially in the rural districts. Only 45 percent of grooms and 37 percent of brides in Quebec and Montreal signed the marriage registers in 1750–59. And the proportion able to sign in the countryside dropped to 12 percent for grooms and 10 percent for brides.[40]

One is struck by the unusually low rate of literacy for the French living in the rural parishes in 1750–59. This is among the lowest rates of literacy for any population in Western Europe in the eighteenth century. Moreover, almost all of the other studies have shown male literacy to be significantly higher than female literacy – including studies of literacy in rural eighteenth-century France.[41] However, there was almost no difference in literacy by gender among the French inhabitants of mid-eighteenth-century Canada. Thus, the unexpected low patterns of literacy among the French in rural Canada as well as the lack of a significant gender gap raise important new comparative questions about the nature of education and literacy in the New World.

Like their British counterparts, the French missionaries tried to convert and educate the local Indians. Throughout most of the seventeenth and eighteenth centuries, the Jesuits took the lead in trying to educate the Indians. They translated the Bible into the native languages and set up special seminaries for Indian pupils. Nevertheless, while the French were more successful in working with many of the Indians as allies rather than as enemies than the British, they did not succeed in getting many native Americans either to adopt the French language or to learn to read and write. While the Indians freely borrowed and used the guns and tools of the French, they saw no reason to accept their culture as well.[42]

Causes of Levels and Changes in Literacy

Since the advent of quantitative studies of historical literacy in the 1960s, historians have vigorously debated the causes of levels and changes in literacy in early modern England and colonial America.

Broadly speaking, the debate has centered on the relative importance of different "push-and-pull" factors in providing formal or informal sources of literacy. Some studies have emphasized the role of religion or the state in pushing people to literacy, while others have stressed the agency of the people in acquiring the skill to meet the changing demands for a more literate work force. Even where consensus has existed on the specific path people took to literacy, historians have disputed the factors influencing either the supply of or the demand for educational resources among different social groups situated within different ideological or economic environments.

The first quantitative studies of English literacy isolated religion as the most powerful stimulus to elementary education in the seventeenth century. In a major study of literacy in early modern England, Lawrence Stone argued that the significant factor in determining the high literacy rates of some seventeenth-century parishes "was the presence or absence of dedicated resident clergymen-schoolmasters determined to instruct their flock to read the word as recorded in the Bible."[43] While acknowledging that the evidence was not conclusive, he noted that the hypothesis correlating literacy with Puritanism was plausible given the movement's stress on the necessity of Bible-reading for salvation.[44]

Although some historians have continued to examine the relationship of Puritanism to literacy,[45] David Cressy and others have recently found that the connection was weaker than was previously thought. Even though the Puritans pushed hard for universal literacy, their campaign was largely ineffective, primarily because it lacked the support of the state. As Cressy found in analyzing data for Essex County (England) the presence of a Puritan minister failed, alone, to account for high local literacy rates. The more significant association was that between literacy and formal schooling – the provision for which was linked to a complex mix of factors, including "cultural, ideological, economic and perhaps even accidental elements which fashioned the literacy of each community at a particular time."[46] Schooling in literacy was largely a function of demand, Cressy concluded, and until the state began to push it at the end of the eighteenth century, it remained associated with status, prosperity, and occupational requirements.[47]

Questioning the causal reliance of Cressy and others on formal schooling, English scholars have recently turned to informal educational processes to explain literacy differentials. R. A. Houston, in a major study of literacy in England and Scotland, has argued that "we need to know why schools were provided, but we must also understand why people wanted to be educated."[48] As Houston noted, the example of Sweden, where near universal reading literacy was achieved without formal education, warns against any effort to link literacy simply to schooling. In Scotland, the state, by providing the core of the educational system, contributed significantly to the country's advances in literacy, but it could not have done it alone, given the fact that education was neither free, compulsory, nor universal until the late nineteenth century.

Much Scottish education, in fact, occurred in private adventure schools that were not controlled by the church or state and were not privately endowed. In addition, literacy in Scotland, as in England, did not penetrate the population evenly – suggesting the presence of social-economic conditions, such as poverty, geographical mobility, child labor, or middle-class dominance of resources, that restricted access to formal education. In the absence of schools, people who desired literacy used informal methods to acquire it, including self-help, home learning, apprenticeship, and service. Service was particularly effective in providing literacy for people aged 15–24 in the north of England, and may have been responsible for the relatively high literacy rates in that region (which maintained its lead over the south and east until the advent of mass, compulsory education in the late nineteenth century). At the same time, while demand for literacy was stratified, it nevertheless existed at all levels of society, and was influenced by people's involvement in those everyday activities, such as court proceedings, that required literacy and were brought about by the state's increasing intrusion into local life as well as by local cultural biases. As Houston concluded, "the demand for schooling needs to exist before (schools) can have any effect in a society without compulsory education."[49]

As to England's North American colonies, schooling has traditionally played a key role in scholarly interpretations of the educational history of that region of the British empire. Even after the rise of the new educational history in the early 1960s, historians stressing

the role of informal, cultural processes in promoting learning still saw
schooling as a key source of educational improvement. Thus Bernard
Bailyn, in his seminal study *Education in the Forming of American Society*,
argued that the New England Puritans "not only endowed schools
with a new importance but expanded their purpose beyond pragmatic
vocationalism toward vaguer but more basic cultural goals." Where
Bailyn departed from former interpretations was the argument that
the Puritans' zeal for education derived from changes in environment
and family structure; frontier dislocations forced the Puritans to abandon the customary educational reliance on the extended family.
Nevertheless, Bailyn insisted that, "In the context of the age the
stress placed by the Puritans on formal schooling is astonishing."[50]
Feeling that in the New World they lacked stable families and
communities, the Puritans deliberately transferred education from informal to formal institutions, turning New England into a land
uniquely reliant on schooling for education.

Lockridge's pioneering study of literacy in early America
challenged the "environmentalist" interpretation of the new educational history, but repeated the traditional stress on schooling as the
primary source of colonial learning. Drawing heavily upon Stone's
analysis of religion and literacy in early modern England, Lockridge
contended that Puritanism, not frontier dislocations, was the primary
source of New England's desire for literacy. Yet despite the Puritans'
educational push, literacy initially failed to spread rapidly, displaying
for a long time "a traditional European causal structure." As late as
1710, the rank-order of local literacy matched the rank-order of the
founders, a correlation suggesting that education may well have occurred less at school than at home. Only after half a century did
literacy begin to rise "at the expected rate" and erase the "old causal
structure."[51]

To explain the delay, Lockridge tipped the environmentalist's
interpretation on its head, arguing that frontier conditions, by dis-
persing population, actually frustrated efforts to implement the school
laws. To explain the rise, Lockridge invoked the demography of the
new social history; Puritan educational ideology was able to effect a
surge in literacy once population had become more concentrated and
schooling more affordable. Lacking data on local educational practices
and processes, Lockridge nevertheless conceptually linked the rise of

literacy directly, even mechanistically to the rise of formal schooling. As schooling rose, so did literacy, spreading, without apparent resistance, through those segments of the population that had lacked opportunities for formal education, including farmers, artisans, and laborers. Despite evidence on Puritan declension and socioeconomic demand for literacy, Lockridge nevertheless insisted that "the Protestant impulse was the sole force powerful enough to work a transformation in the level of literacy."[52]

Lockridge found, however, that Puritan education was not an unmitigated success story, for it failed to dissolve traditional educational biases against women. Although literacy rates for men rose over the course of the eighteenth century, rates for women stagnated. By the time of the American Revolution, the gender gap in literacy was wider than at any other time in New England history. Why? Lockridge linked the gap to the rise of formal schooling, arguing that rural schools, which were the primary agents of male educational progress, consciously discriminated against women, denying them the means by which men achieved near universal literacy rates by the end of the eighteenth century.[53]

Since Lockridge's study appeared two decades ago, scholars have expanded and revised his findings on several important fronts, pursuing new lines of inquiry that echo English and European literacy histories, and reflect recent interest in the socioeconomic engendered contexts of demand and the informal sources of education. Several scholars have begun to explore such issues for the middle Atlantic and southern colonies, regions Lockridge largely ignored. In an analysis of servant contracts in late eighteenth-century Pennsylvania, Farley Grubb found that service was the locus of literacy there, particularly for German immigrant children. Acting upon their strong interest in education, German immigrants negotiated literacy education into their children's contracts with employers, stipulating the type and amount of education, and the length of additional service needed to finance it. Before the Revolution, informal employer instruction represented the great majority of educational stipulations, especially in the rural areas of Pennsylvania, where "informal instruction must have had a relative cost advantage" over formal instruction. The significance of this pattern, Grubb noted, was that "high levels of colonial literacy could have been achieved without extensive reliance on organized schools." After the Revolution, however, servant investment in formal over informal education increased markedly, perhaps in response to an expansion in rural schooling brought on by social concentration and an accompanying reduction in the cost advantage of informal education. By the 1790s, organized schools were used as much by rural as by urban areas, and "may have been important for the final surge to universal literacy."[54]

The South may also have used informal sources of education to achieve higher literacy levels, as Robert Gallman demonstrated in his literacy history of colonial Perquimans County, North Carolina. In the absence of a strong public school tradition, Perquimans turned to other institutions to educate its children – especially service, family, private tutoring, and the Quaker church. In explaining the rise in literacy after the 1710s, Gallman noted that the same causal structure (population density was strongly associated with literacy) may have prevailed in Perquimans as in New England because nonschool educational processes were as sensitive to demographic change as formal schools. In one sense, though, Perquimans was different from the Puritan north; immigration continued to effect literacy there well into the eighteenth century. "In this respect," Gallman concluded, "Perquimans may be representative of the South."[55]

Not only have historians begun to consider the regional configurations of colonial literacy, but as we discussed in the previous section, they have also started to study issues of gender and education arising out of Lockridge's analysis of female literacy in eighteenth-century New England. As early as 1980, Linda Auwers questioned Lockridge's contention that women showed no educational improvement before the Revolution. Working with deeds from colonial Windsor, Connecticut, Auwers made an important discovery. Female literacy rates, rather than stagnating, rose steadily during the eighteenth century, increasing from 27 percent for those women born in the 1650s and 1660s to 90 percent for those born in the 1740s. Simultaneously, the social determinants of female literacy diminished in significance, as did location – especially as increasing population density made schooling more accessible for everyone.

At the same time, two factors, both related to the role of fathers in the education of daughters, rose in importance: paternal aunts' signatures and paternal wealth suggest that fathers became more supportive of female education. Why the change in attitude? Auwers speculated that the feminization of church membership weakened traditional biases against female literacy. It encouraged the local minister to work on improving educational opportunities for daughters with local authorities, who had just gained control over schools from the town. Auwers maintained, "The overall impetus may have been religious, as was stated time and time again in school laws, but the action operated on a societal rather than an individual level."[56] Since no correlation existed between parents' church membership and daughters' literacy, however, it may be assumed that religious push played a larger role in women's educational progress than Auwers was willing to admit.

Since Auwers, surprisingly few historians have reconstituted the local sources of female literacy. Instead, scholars have relied on collecting data from larger geographic areas to test Lockridge. Gloria Main, for example, has recently deployed data from Suffolk County, Massachusetts, to argue that women's literacy rates, both rural and urban, actually rose during the middle eighteenth century. Since urban rates increased more rapidly than rural rates, Main speculated that commercial activity contributed to the rise. But how did the women overcome the traditional bias against female literacy? Main did not say. But she discovered that some women actually learned how to write on their own, and decided that they did so because they needed the skill to use the market. Given the evidence already existing on the development of female agency in other areas of late-colonial New England life, including spousal choice and divorce litigation, Main felt it reasonable to conclude that even before the Revolution women "were moving beyond dependency and beyond the emulation of traditional female virtues like silence and obedience."[57]

Historians will surely continue to gather data on this critical topic of women's rise to universal literacy, and as they do we hope that they will intensify the search for its sources. Joel Perlmann and Dennis Shirley have called for such inquiry, and so have William Gilmore and Jennifer Monaghan.[58] In a recent study of female education in eighteenth-century Massachusetts towns, Katherine Sklar has provided one promising approach to the topic of sources. Rather than study female literacy *per se*, Sklar analyzed local education for girls, introducing a new, political-economic approach to the old topic of schooling. Using public support of summer schools (which were limited to older girls and young children from both sexes) as a proxy for public support of female education, Sklar discovered that Massachusetts towns varied greatly in their political-economic support for female education. On one end of the spectrum was Northampton, which was the community most hostile to using public money for educating girls. Not until the early 1800s did Northampton open its public schools on a regular basis to girls, but not for want of money. One of the most wealthiest towns in the state, Northampton was dominated by a powerful elite, which monopolized public funds to run a grammar school to prepare their sons for college, allowing advanced education to be funded at the expense of more rudimentary learning. During the 1780s they established private coeducational schools, but confined them to the descendants of the original proprietors. What finally broke the elite's hegemony over schooling, Sklar showed, was a successful suit against the town by a baker with a large family of girls.[59]

On the other end of the spectrum was Sutton. As early as 1767, the town provided public funds for "school dames in the summer season," and by the late 1770s was allocating money for summer schools equal to that provided for winter schools. What made Sutton so different from Northampton? As Sklar argued, Sutton was newer and poorer than Northampton, lacked an elite, and had many families with school-age children who needed rudimentary reading and writing skills. For over thirty years after its founding in 1704, Sutton had neither primary nor grammar schools but only dame schools to teach its children literacy. Families with school-age children controlled decisions involving schooling because, in contrast to Northampton, they alone, not every householder, paid school taxes, and did so according to the number of children sent. As Sklar argued, such families of middling wealth may have allocated public funding for daughters because they recognized the need to strengthen literacy for "all young persons" who were entering the new world of commerce and consumption, but facing the prospect of downward social mobility arising from overpopulation. Ecclesiastical changes also helped to improve the educational environment for girls. The rise of religious pluralism in Sutton, by forcing churches to compete for women's allegiance, enabled them to influence local educational decision making.

As Sklar concluded, the competing stories of local girls' schooling suggested "a paradigm for the processes shaping female access to town schools." Gender inequities in education

> diminished faster and easier when male elites were relatively weak, when most of the town's wealth resided in the middle levels of wealth distribution, and when religious authority was decentralized. They endured longer and proved more difficult to erode when male elites dominated local political institutions, when most of the town's wealth was concentrated among the wealthiest fifth of the population, and when religious authority was centralized.[60]

In such cases, the education of women remained a hotly contested domain well into the nineteenth century. As we continue to investigate the topic of women's rise to literacy, we need to combine Sklar's political-economic model of local schooling with the demographic, quantitative approach to literacy; by failing to link schooling to hard data on literacy and its sources, Sklar could not address such critical issues as the intergenerational transmission of literacy, and the informal role of the family in girls' education. So numerous and rich are the records of Puritan towns, that historians have little excuse to ignore the local history of literacy and education in colonial and revolutionary New England.

A final development in colonial literacy history needs mentioning. Although the history of European literacy and the "other" is in its infancy, recent studies of the subject provide gist for much future research. One promising line of inquiry treats European literacy as a variable of empire,[61] a second as a domain of cultural assimilation, synchronization, and interaction, one in which old world tongues shaped and were shaped by native languages.[62] A third line of research focuses exclusively on the African-American community. As recent work has revealed, black literacy displays the same regional biases as white literacy, in part because of variations in black population density, both free and slave.

In New England, where the percentage of blacks was lowest, African-Americans had the greatest access to literacy education. Puritan colonies passed no statutory prohibitions against it, nor did Puritan churches attempt to restrict it. If the New England colonies failed to push it either, religious movements spawned, in part, by the

Great Awakening, nevertheless campaigned for black literacy. Yet, as recent studies have demonstrated, such efforts were limited by the contexts of black life, especially slavery and racial prejudice. Where local restrictions against black literacy were instituted, some blacks, especially freedmen, acquired it on their own, or from each other. Once slavery was abolished after the revolution, freedmen, now deeming education less a privilege than a right, established their own primary schools.[63]

Like New England, the mid-Atlantic colonies did not push black literacy, but unlike that region passed laws against it, perhaps because of the threat to white hegemony posed by the larger black population. Yet religious pluralism may have provided a counterweight to the laws. Although no data exist on the Quaker or Anglican campaigns for black literacy, we do know that New York and New Jersey were well ahead of other states in providing public schooling for blacks once the Revolution commenced. As in New England, slaves and freedmen needed no prodding to pursue their "natural right" to English literacy; indeed, as Gary Nash has demonstrated for Philadelphia, that the new freedmen valued education so highly suggests the presence of such values under slavery.[64]

Before Virginia became a slave society, literacy adhered to a traditional causal structure in this third region of the colonies. Class dictated educational levels for both blacks and whites, and freed blacks may have acquired literacy as readily as their white counterparts. After 1700, race appeared alongside class as a determinant of literacy. Even as mark-signature rates remained skewed along class lines, the Virginia Assembly moved against black literacy, passing laws prohibiting slave education. Did Virginia's shift toward slavery and racism effect lower-class literacy? Given what we know about planter behavior under slavery, this question seems worth considering. If planters, while nourishing racism to control the larger slave population, elevated the political and economic status of lower class whites, then it may be that they also tried to raise their educational levels, even though elites had always perceived lower-class literacy as threatening to their hegemony.[65] Yet we know too little at present about education in Virginia to make an accurate judgement about the relative impact of slavery on white and black literacy, and on elite attitudes towards it. With respect to blacks, they may have had less incentive to acquire literacy,

since the rise of isolated, densely-populated slave communities reduced the frequency of black-white interaction, and thus the
usefulness of English to slaves.[66] Yet important literacy differentials
may have existed in the black community, just as they existed in the
white, since those planters who wished to expand the occupational
range of their plantations encouraged some slaves to acquire literacy in
the process of becoming artisans. Overall, however, planters' fear of
slave literacy and white illiteracy may have intensified by the time of
the Revolution. No American was more effusive on the benefits of
yeoman literacy than the famous Virginian planter and revolutionary
leader, Thomas Jefferson. Nor was any American less benign about
black intellectual inferiority than he. In Jefferson we see the matura-
tion of a paradox that requires further exploration: the simultaneous
rise, in Virginia, of white literacy and black illiteracy.[67]

The one challenge to black illiteracy came from outside Virginia,
and was initiated by preachers primarily from New England, who in
the period of the Great Awakening campaigned for slave education in
those areas, located especially in the piedmont, that were least
subject to elite dominion. New side Presbyterians came first, then
New Light Baptists and Methodists, targeting the slave frontier as
fertile ground for the education and Christianization of unconverted
blacks. Since few quantifiable records on the movement exist, their
rate of success is difficult to measure, but examples of preacher ef-
fectiveness abound. Samuel Davies, for example, reported that "the
poor slaves are now commonly engaged in learning to read; some of
them can read the Bible, others can spell; and some are just learning
their letters," while John Todd noted that "hundreds of Negroes
beside white people, can read and spell, who a few years since did not
know one letter."[68]

Given historians' emphasis on the orality of the Awakening, it is
interesting to observe the bookish nature of the slave revivals.[69] Over
the long run, however, the movement for slave education may not
have effected a permanent improvement in black literacy, since
revivalism died out, revival churches that were once integrated became divided along racial lines, and the revivalists themselves became
more respectable and less tolerant of black education. Increasingly
confined to their own churches, black Christians would have to
achieve literacy on their own.[70]

In the lower-South, which had more slaves per capita than any other region, blacks faced the earliest and harshest laws against literacy, and had the least access to the English language. Still, even where blacks encountered few whites, they seemed to have valued literacy and to have had opportunities to learn how to read and write the language. In one of the first studies of slave literacy, Janet Cornelius argued that lower-South slaves, despite the lack of formal educational incentives, had many motives to learn to read and write, including the desire to preach, to gain freedom through forging passes, to survive in a hostile environment, and to engage in acts of resistance.

Comparing southern slaves to English workers, Cornelius noted remarkable similarities with respect to the effort expended by both groups on developing skills that were seldom in demand or were in fact discouraged. That many blacks along with English workers actually acquired literacy is testimony to the powerful role played by push forces in the history of literacy. As in the upper-South, lower-South slaves, if domestics, had more chances to learn to read and write than field hands. More often than not, agricultural slaves taught each other literacy skills, or learned them in Sunday schools operated by blacks as well as whites. That slaves were often forced to acquire literacy in secret, however, means that the history will remain illusive, and the extent of literacy resistant to measurement.[71]

The Consequences of Literacy

Scholars have made many, sometimes extravagant claims about the impact of literacy on individuals, communities, and states. Students of developing nations in particular have placed mass education and literacy at the center of the modernization process, arguing that literacy effected a profound transformation in the cognitive map of onetime illiterate peasants. Scholars studying the rise of modern man have also placed a heavy, interpretive burden upon literacy, claiming that it helped to produce people whose values and behavior differed markedly from those of pre-modern folk. As Daniel Lerner argued in his influential but very controversial study, "Literacy is the basic personal skill that underlies the whole modernizing sequence." More recently, Emmanuel Todd has claimed that "Literacy – associated with the rise in age at marriage – may be considered the central element in any region's or any nation's attainment of modernity."[72]

Taking a cue from earlier modernization theorists, historians of American education have advanced similar interpretive claims for colonial literacy. Thus Bernard Bailyn has claimed that colonial education served as "an agency of rapid social change, a powerful internal accelerator," by which students acquired "typical American individualism, optimism, and enterprise" and achieved economic mobility. Similarly, Lawrence Cremin has argued that the spread of literacy, particularly through the schools, and within "a relatively inclusive politics," had a liberating effect on early Americans, who turned their literacy skills "to liberal ends almost entirely on their own, limited only by financial wherewithal, the availability of materials, and his particular horizons."[73]

Scholarly reaction to such claims have proceeded on two fronts, one conceptual, the other methodological. Some have questioned the notion that literacy and orality are strictly dichotomous variables, and that the former's effects upon the latter are always linear; others have raised doubts about approaches to historical literacy that ignore context and fail to provide statistical measures for determining the consequences that are claimed to take place. As David Vincent has said, "What is required is a way of understanding the power of literacy in its specific historical context which will permit a cautious appraisal of the body of claims and counterclaims which now surround the issue."[74]

Lockridge's seminal study of colonial literacy was revisionist both conceptually and methodologically. Lockridge argued that literacy did not modernize New England, and provided a statistical test to prove it – though his particular index of modernization has been questioned by other scholars. Using data on bequests from wills as a measure of modernity, he found that literate and illiterate testators alike left gifts for traditional purposes, primarily to further religion and alleviate the suffering of the poor, and increasingly confined their gift giving to family members. Only rarely did will makers evince "modern" attitudes and behavior through bequests to rehabilitate the poor or "to turn religion to constructive secular needs." Most testators, even at the time of the Revolution, failed to exhibit modern, liberated attitudes or a wider, "liberal" consciousness, although their wealth should have disposed them to modernity. Instead, they limited their giftgiving to local and familial needs.[75]

Since Lockridge, surprisingly few historians of colonial literacy have undertaken similar, statistical studies of the effects of literacy on early Americans. Although recent work on the subject tends to reject older versions of modernization theory, and to acknowledge the importance of context in determining literacy outcomes, it never-the-less lacks clarity both in conceptualization and methodology. There has been little attempt, for example, to link data on literacy to key transformations in American life that historians have already quantified, such as fertility and commercialization. By focusing on several key areas of colonial literacy, particularly religion, politics, economics, and fertility, we can better understand the direction of recent literacy history and the needs and opportunities for future research.

From the work of David Hall on New England Puritanism comes the most influential recent interpretation of the impact of literacy on religion. Discounting evidence on mark-signatures as unreflective of the range and cultural meaning of literacy, Hall argues that most New Englanders, while they could not write, could read at least printed matter, albeit within meaningful but limited contexts (particularly the church). To American Puritans, reading and religion were inseparable, and reciprocal, for the way they used their remarkable literacy was "deeply consequential for popular religion," especially regarding the relationship between elite and lay religiosity. Until the sixteenth century, Latin literacy had served as an instrument of clerical domination, but the reformation, the revolution in print, and the spread of literacy gave the laity weapons for subverting sacerdotal structures. Although Puritan preachers presented sermons as truth, as truthful as the Word itself, literacy gave parishioners opportunities for learning the truth on their own, a situation that made clerical authority vulnerable to challenges from below. The rise of a marketplace for books had a similar effect on the relationship between preachers and people, especially those "steady sellers" that in the minds of readers symbolized the central myth of the culture: "freedom from the tyranny of priests." Yet the potential for such challenges to clerical rule rarely materialized, in part because of the pervasiveness of oral, verbal, and visual symbols that were drawn from a common source, Scripture. As Hall concludes, "Always there was freedom of interpretation, though a freedom held in check by catechisms and the 'learned' presence of the ministers."[76]

Despite his revisionary and stimulating work on literacy and popular religion, Hall's interpretation of New England society remains surprisingly conventional in many respects; the notion that Puritan pastors were at odds with their flocks was a mainstay of progressive history, while the idea that New England was otherwise a homogeneous region was central to Perry Miller's interpretation of Puritanism. In addition, Hall either ignores or dismisses work on literacy, gender, wealth, and race that undermines the picture of a homogeneous New England society, and reveals divisions that separated the laity as much from each other as from their ministers. To be sure, Hall's work on literacy has considerably advanced our understanding of the religious ramifications of popular reading and consumption of print. But in the future we need to focus more on examining how different sorts of New Englanders both understood and used writing (as opposed to reading), and study how it shaped their lives in ways historians can measure. Otherwise, our understanding of the relationship between literacy and areas of life as vital to the Puritans as religion will remain vague and incomplete.

Richard D. Brown's analysis of early American communications offers a recent, partial corrective to Hall's notions of lay uniformity in literacy and religion. Brown's findings on the shifting contexts of knowledge in colonial Massachusetts also gives temporal perspective to Hall's static picture of print and reading cultures. Although Brown does not examine literacy *per se*, his evidence on information and authority in early Massachusetts sheds light on the class contexts of Puritan literacy. During the seventeenth century, even Boston was highly stratified with respect to the dissemination of and access to knowledge, despite the rise of a book market after the 1650s. Information flowed within boundaries marked by class and hierarchic social structure. Magistrates, clerics, and merchants rarely shared casual information with non-elites; what they did pass on to their inferiors was mostly formal information designed for religious and civic edification and transmitted during ceremonial occasions that were under their strict control. Such information was diffused hierarchically, "within the elite first and, after verification and screening, outward to a broader spectrum of society." Brown's New England, where elites served as informational gatekeepers, conforms more to what we know about the engendered, class structures of seventeenth-century literacy than Hall's, where the common folk had easy access to elite information, and could use it to challenge elite hegemony.[77]

This closed, corporate way of information diffusion underwent gradual change over the course of the eighteenth century. According to Brown, the introduction of the print market and the newspaper had only a marginal effect on the communication environment. More important to the rise of new communication patterns was the increase in the number of newspapers after 1710, which together with the growth of competitive politics helped to break the elite's monopoly over print, and raised the potential for both intra- and inter-elite conflict. Although Brown does not say, the transformation in communication had implications for the popular, religious uses of literacy, and may have introduced into the eighteenth century the kind of world Hall envisioned for the seventeenth. If, as Hall argued, print shaped popular piety, then it should follow that those changes in print described by Brown would have had a profound effect on the religious uses of literacy, increasing, in part, the likelihood of lay access to and subversion of clerical culture and elite authority. As Brown says, the changes were gradual, and they may have accreted on to changes unexamined by Brown, especially the consumer and commercial revolutions, transformations that helped to democratize elite culture. Although such conclusions are speculative at best, they do comport with what we know about the spread of literacy during the eighteenth century.

With respect to such long-range changes in the religious uses of literacy, the role of the Great Awakening remains a mystery. Neither Hall nor Brown mentions it; nor does Lockridge, for that matter. Aside from brief speculations on the relation of literacy to the Great Awakening advanced by Gilmore, Beales, and Main, among others, the only serious discussion of the topic emerges from Harry Stout's work on the revival and communication.[78] Undertaken nearly twenty years ago, Stout's analysis suffers from outmoded conceptualization, in which oral and literate cultures are held to be dichotomous, and from neglect of data on literacy. Indeed, although Lockridge's data were available to him at the time, Stout chose to ignore them completely. Yet, at a time when historians are choosing to neglect the Great Awakening – even doubt its existence – some discussion of Stout's highly provocative analysis may serve as a prod for future, sorely needed research.

To Stout, the Great Awakening was a watershed in the history of colonial literacy and communication. Before the revival, the religious contexts of communication, both North and South, were highly structured; "speaker and audience were steadily reminded of their personal place in the community," while "no public gatherings took place outside of traditional associations based upon personal acquaintance and social rank." At the same time, the spread of printing, which placed increased importance on writing, reenforced the social divisions of American society. Colonial elites used a new, more uniform style of writing and a more learned, rational discourse to communicate with their peers and by so doing drove a wedge between themselves and the common folk. "Power became so closely tied to print that advanced literacy and a classical education were virtually prerequisite to authority, and a college education guaranteed rapid advance in the social hierarchy."[79]

The Great Awakening, by introducing new contexts of communication and forms of rhetoric, challenged "elitist typographic culture." As Stout contends, revivalists developed a new technique of mass address to a voluntary audience that ignored social place and local context. Attacking habits of deference to print and writing, and reviving the rhetoric of the gospels, revivalists also mobilized orality against the standing typographic order, utilizing "the only form of address that could be sure to impress all hearers: the spoken word proclaimed extemporaneously in everyday language."[80] Over the long term, the Great Awakening deeply divided American society, pitting an oral, egalitarian culture against an elitist, print-oriented one.

Despite our objections to Stout's dichotomization of orality and literacy, we suspect that his general contention that the Great Awakening was a watershed in the history of communication and literacy warrants further investigation. For purposes of stimulating research in this surprisingly neglected area, one might hypothesize that the revival did introduce new religious contexts and uses of writing, but not those identified by Stout. Given the data on the rapid spread of popular literacy during the era of the Great Awakening, it makes sense to speculate on the possible connections between that development and the growth of revivalism. In addition to using new techniques of mass persuasion to produce revivals, New Light itinerants, though lacking elite credentials, yet employed writing and print both to spread the word and to attack the standing order. Just as Whitefield had used an established, trans-Atlantic epistolary network to promote the new evangelism, so his less learned followers employed the same technique to create new regional and transregional networks both to reproduce the original revivals and to sustain the piety produced by them over time.[81] Although little is known about the forms of communication among New Lights, historians who are aware of the vast letter-writing activities of individual itinerants such as Eleazar Wheelock might speculate with us on the importance of epistolary networks to New Light evangelism. Even unlettered New Lights could deploy literacy to advance the cause, in ways that cast doubt on arguments regarding the inherent incompatibility of literacy and orality. Thus Richard Woodbury, an illiterate lay exhorter from Massachusetts, had Nicholas Gilman, a Harvard graduate, help him write letters to ministers notifying them of his plans to itinerate in their parishes.[82] New Lights, both preachers and common folk, also used literacy in conflicts with the tanding order, affixing signatures to petitions and covenants that were designed to legitimate resistance.[83] If linked to church and parish records, such petitions and covenants could produce the hard data that are currently missing in scholarship on the Great Awakening and literacy. Given this and other evidence on the relation of revivalism to communication, historians of colonial literacy need to place this topic on the top of their research agenda.

Stout's work on revivalism and communication must also be considered in our discussion of the second key area of colonial literacy, politics. Linking the Great Awakening directly to the Revolution, Stout contended that the rise of mass revivalism and egalitarian rhetoric helped to mobilize the American people against both British and colonial elites in the period after 1763. Questioning Bailyn's reliance on printed evidence to trace the rise of a revolutionary mentality, Stout argued that "no ideology that is pieced together solely from the literate world of print can fully comprehend the radical dynamic of the Revolution." A more important source of that dynamic was "the oral explosion and egalitarian style" of the Awakening. As Stout concluded, "the ethos and ideological fervor of republicanism" derived "from the translation of the evangelical experience into a secular theoretical vocabulary that more adequately embodied, for some, the revolutionary thrust first widely experienced in the revivals."[84]

Unlike his analysis of the Great Awakening, Stout's interpretation of the impact of revivalism and oral communication on the rise of revolutionary politics has provoked considerable, often negative comment. Included among Stout's recent critics is Michael Warner, whose important work on early American print and politics warrants discussion. Drawing upon recent social-scientific studies of communication, Warner contends that Stout's study "displays an unabashed and uncritical sentimentality, assuming that print was 'elitist and hierarchical' and that any form of speech, such as evangelical oratory, must be egalitarian 'opposition to the established order'."[85] Far from being unlettered, New Englanders used literacy "with an intensity equaled by few other cultures in the world at the time," a conclusion that iterates Lockridge's and Hall's findings on the subject. Orality never played an isolated role in revolutionary politics because it never occupied a distinct niche. The world of communication was linked to revolution through literacy itself, particularly through transformations in the way people valued and used reading. Contrary to what recent historians of the book have argued, new print technologies, according to Warner, had little to do with revolution. What mattered most was the rise of a new, "bourgeois public sphere," oriented around reading, that was so distinct from state and private life that it could produce a new printed discourse capable of criticizing both. Once the ideology of republicanism had heightened the value of print, "print discourse made it possible to imagine a people that could act as a people and in distinction from the state." Republican print in turn helped to broaden and solidify the public sphere, largely because it rested on a new set of assumptions that held print to be impersonal, meaning that readers identified with "indefinite others" who, while unknown to themselves, nevertheless shared a common language and were engaged in similar acts of interpretation. "For that reason," Warner argues, "it becomes possible to imagine oneself, in the act of reading, becoming part of an arena of the national people that cannot be realized except through such mediating imaginings."[86]

Conclusion

Recent analyses of literacy in Western Europe and North America have provided important new insights about the cultural and social developments of the eighteenth century. Despite the still limited number of studies, rates of adult literacy in British North America appear to have been higher than in most of Western Europe; but there is still disagreement among analysts on the exact meaning or level of illiteracy as evidenced by mark-signatures. Moreover, there were considerable variations in literacy by colony and social group. The New England colonies had higher rates of literacy than either the middle Atlantic or southern colonies and residents of urban areas were generally more literate than their rural counterparts. Much attention has been focused on gender differences with males being more literate than females. Fragmentary evidence also points to much higher rates of illiteracy among African-Americans and Native Americans than among the white population.

Most scholars agree that there was an increase in literacy in British North America in the eighteenth century, but disagree on the extent or nature of those changes. Initial work by scholars such as Lockridge had pointed to sizable increases in literacy for men, but much less improvement for women. More recent revisions, however, argue for higher rates of literacy among women than Lockridge envisioned, but still disagree on whether most of those changes occurred in the early or late eighteenth century.

Perhaps one of the most unexpected findings of this review was the extremely low level of literacy in French Canada. Most of the earlier analyses had compared literacy rates in British North America to Western Europe with almost no attention to developments in French Canada. Fortunately, studies of literacy in French Canada are now available and reveal among the lowest rates of literacy for any Western European population in the eighteenth century. In the rural areas of New France, literacy rates were not only unexpectedly low, they were also surprisingly undifferentiated by gender. These new findings will provide an interesting and useful new site for comparing and contextualizing British North American literacy levels and trends developments.

As debates over the levels and trends in eighteenth-century literacy are starting to be narrowed and resolved somewhat, those over the sources of these changes are increasing. Schooling has been cited traditionally as the cause of the rapid rise of literacy in the English colonies, but little empirical evidence is available so far to substantiate this hypothesis. Indeed, the few detailed studies of literacy at the local level suggest that much of it may have occurred initially in informal settings such as the home rather than in formal schools. The initial reliance on informal opportunities for learning to read appears to have been particularly important for women and African-Americans. By the end of the eighteenth-century in some areas, however, there was a significant increase in community-supported schools open to both boys and girls so that children now increasingly were likely to learn to read and write in a more formal context outside of their homes.

Scholars continue to disgree on the relative importance of religion and economic considerations in stimulating the rise in eighteenth-century literacy. Systematic studies of this important question simply do not exist for any area of British North America – though this has not deterred scholars from advancing strong views on this matter. While both factors are acknowledged as important contributing factors, the weight of recent speculations appear to be shifting toward economic explanations – as the demands for literacy in an increasingly commercial society rose, parents may have been willing to invest more in the education of their children.

Scholars frequently have made extravagant statements about the role of literacy in colonial society, but little effort has been made to explore or document that impact. Early crude theories of modernization, which mechanistically equated literacy and education with economic development and progress are giving way to more sophisticated discussions that see a more limited and subtle role for literacy in eighteenth-century North America. Our brief discussion of how literacy may have affected religious and political changes illustrates the need for further analyses of the consequences of changes in educational levels and experiences. Similar efforts should be made to explore the impact of literacy on other important facets of colonial society such as the growing commercialization of the eighteenth-century economy as well as the beginnings of a sustained decline in marital fertility in some areas. Thus, while considerable work on literacy has been completed recently, even more remains to be done.

Notes

1. There has been extensive discussion of the problems involved in trying to measure literacy on the basis of mark signatures. For useful introductions to this vast literature, see Suzanne de Castell, Allan Luke, and David Mac-Lennan, "On Defining Literacy," in *Literacy, Society, and Schooling: A Reader*, eds., Suzanne de Castell, Allan Luke, and Kieran Egan (Cambridge, Eng.: Cambridge University Press, 1986), 3–14; Harvey J. Graff, *The Legacies of Literacy: Continuities and Contradictions in Western Culture and Society* (Bloomington: Indiana University Press, 1987); R. A. Houston, *Literacy in Early Modern Europe: Culture and Education, 1500–1800* (London: Longman, 1988); Kenneth A. Lockridge, *Literacy in Colonial New England: An Enquiry into the Social Context of Literacy in the Early Modern West* (New York: W. W. Norton, 1974); David Vincent, *Literacy and Popular Culture: England, 1750–1914* (Cambridge, Eng.: Cambridge University Press, 1989), 16–20.

2. On the different sources for the study of literacy, see Graff, *Legacies of Literacy*; Harvey J. Graff, ed., *Literacy and Social Development in the West: A Reader* (Cambridge, Eng.: Cambridge University Press, 1981).

3. For summaries and discussions of trends in adult literacy in Western Europe, see Houston, *Literacy in Early Modern Europe*; Graff, *Legacies of Literacy*; Graff, *Literacy and Social Development in the West*.

4. Houston, *Literacy in Early Modern Europe*; Graff, *Legacies of Literacy*.

5. On English literacy and education in the fifteenth and sixteenth centuries, see Michael Van Cleave Alexander, *The Growth of English Education, 1348–1648* (University Park: Pennsylvania State University Press, 1990); David Cressy, *Literacy and the Social Order: Reading and Writing in Tudor and Stuart England* (Cambridge, Eng.: Cambridge University Press, 1980); John Lawson and Harold Silver, *A Social History of Education in England* (London: Methuen, 1973); John Morgan, *Godly Learning: Puritan Attitudes towards Reason, Learning and Education, 1560–1640* (Cambridge, Eng.: Cambridge University Press, 1986); Rosemary O'Day, *Education and Society, 1500–1800: The Social Foundations of Education in Early Modern Britain* (London: Longman, 1982); Margaret Spufford, *Small Books and Pleasant Histories: Popular Fiction and its Readership in Seventeenth-Century England* (Cambridge, Eng.: Cambridge University Press, 1981); Lawrence Stone, "Literacy and Education in England, 1640–1900," *Past and Present* 28 (1964): 41–80; Lawrence Stone, "Literacy in Seventeenth Century England," *Journal of Interdisciplinary History* 8 (1978): 799–800.

6. David Cressy, "Levels of Illiteracy in England, 1530–1730," *Historical Journal* 20 (1977): 1–23.

7. Graff, *Legacies of Literacy*, 231.

8. Roger S. Schofield, "Dimensions of Illiteracy, 1750–1850," *Explorations in Economic History* 10 (1973): 437–54.

9. J. H. Plumb, "The Public, Literature, and the Arts in the Eighteenth Century," in *The Triumph of Culture*, eds., Paul Fritz and David Williams (Toronto: A. M Hakkert, 1972), 27–48.

10. On the higher rates of literacy among those who left compared to those who stayed behind in Britain and elsewhere, see Farley Grubb, "Colonial Immigrant Literacy: An Economic Analysis of Pennsylvania Evidence, 1727–1775," *Explorations in Economic History* 24 (1987): 63–76; Farley Grubb, "Educational Choice in the Era Before Free Public Schooling: Evidence from German Immigrant Children in Pennsylvania, 1771–1817," *Journal of Economic History* 52 (992): 363–75; David W. Galenson, "Literacy and the Social Origins of Some Early Americans," *Historical Journal* 22 (1979): 75–91.

11. The idea of a "creolean degeneracy" in colonial education initially was analyzed by Bernard Bailyn, *Education in the Forming of American Society* (Chapel Hill: University of North Carolina Press, 1960). For a more recent update, see Farley W. Grubb, "Growth of Literacy in Colonial America: Longitudinal Patterns, Economic Models, and the Direction of Future Research," *Social Science History* 14 (1990): 451–82.

12. Lockridge, *Literacy in Colonial New England*.

13. It should be pointed out that in the rural area, Lockridge used data from both Middlesex and Suffolk Counties while Joel Perlmann and DennisShirley only had data for rural Suffolk County. However, Perlmann and Shirley cite an unpublished study of Middlesex County a decade later which found a female literacy rate of 56 percent – again considerably higher than the average reported by Lockridge for the two counties earlier. JoelPerlmann and Dennis Shirley, "When Did New England Women Acquire Literacy?" *William and Mary Quarterly* 48 (1991): 50–67; Joel Perlmann, Silvana R. Siddall, and Keith Whitescarver, "Literacy, Schooling, and Teaching among New England Women, 1730–1820," *History of Education Quarterly* 37 (1997): 117–39.

14. Linda Auwers, "Reading the Marks of the Past," *Historical Methods* 13 (1980): 204–14; Ross W. Beales, Jr., "Studying Literacy at the Community Level: A Research Note," *Journal of Interdisciplinary History* 9 (1978): 93–102; William J. Gilmore, "Elementary Literacy on the Eve of the Industrial Revolution: Trends in Rural New England, 1760–1830," *Proceedings of the American Antiquarian Society* 92, pt. 1 (1982): 87–177.

15. Gloria Main also argues that since colonial women lived longer than men, the wills of women testators overall will be older than those of men. While this is an intriguing possibility, it needs to be tested empirically since the life expectancy of adult men and women in colonial America was not as

dramatically different as it is. Gloria L. Main, "An Inquiry into When and Why Women Learned to Write in Colonial New England," *Journal of Social History* 24 (1991): 579–89. On estimates of eighteenth-century New England mortality, see Maris A. Vinovskis, *Fertility in Massachusetts from the Revolution to the Civil War* (New York: Academic Press, 1981).

16. These studies found that both male and female literacy was higher based upon information from deeds rather than wills. But since Lockridge had already found nearly universal white male literacy by the end of the eighteenth century, much of the focus of most of these new essays tends to be on white female literacy. For example, using information from deeds and probate records in mid-eighteenth century Grafton, Massachusetts, Beales found that 98 percent of males could sign their names while Lockridge's estimate of literacy for rural New England males in 1758–62 was about 80 percent. Beales, "Studying Literacy"; Lockridge, *Literacy in Colonial New England*.

17. Auwers, "Reading the Marks of the Past."

18. Beales, "Studying Literacy."

19. Main, "Inquiry into When and Why Women Learned to Write"; Gilmore, "Elementary Literacy on the Eve of the Industrial Revolution."

20. Maris A. Vinovskis and Richard M. Bernard, "Beyond Catherine Beecher: Female Education in the Antebellum Period," *Journal of Women in Culture and Society* 3 (1978): 856–69; Lee Soltow and Edward Stevens, *The Rise of Literacy and the Common School in the United States: A Socioeconomic Analysis to 1870* (Chicago: University of Chicago Press, 1981).

21. Perlmann and Shirley, "When Did New England Women Acquire Literacy?"

22. David D. Hall, *Worlds of Wonder, Days of Judgment: Popular Religious Belief in Early New England* (New York: Alfred A. Knopf, 1989); E. Jennifer Monaghan, "Literacy Instruction and Gender in Colonial New England," *American Quarterly* 40 (1988): 18–41; Gerald F. Moran and Maris A. Vinovskis, *Religion, Family, and the Life Course: Explorations in the Social History of Early America* (Ann Arbor: University of Michigan Press, 1992).

23. Lawrence A. Cremin, *American Education: The Colonial Experience, 1607–1783* (New York: Harper & Row, 1970), 540. Given the small sample size for women in the years 1699–1706 (n=10) and 1773–75 (n=38), the results presented may not be very reliable. Cremin also found that the rates of literacy for both males and females was slightly higher for those dying in the city proper rather than in the areas just north of Philadelphia.

24. Alan Tully, "Literacy Levels and Educational Development in Rural Pennsylvania, 1729–1775," *Pennsylvania History* 39 (1972): 301–12. Again, the sample size for the literacy of women is so small that one should be cautious about placing too much faith in those exact numbers.

25. Lockridge, *Literacy in Colonial New England*, 72–101.

26. Robert E. Gallman, "Changes in the Level of Literacy in a New Community of Early America," *Journal of Economic History* 48 (1988): 567–82. It is important to bear in mind that male and female literacy in Perquimans County, as in many other frontier areas, declined initially and then rose again later.

27. For a discussion of the education and literacy of antebellum slaves and exslaves, see Janet D. Cornelius, *When I Can Read My Title Clear: Literacy, Slavery, and Religion in the Antebellum South* (Columbia: University of South Carolina Press, 1991); William D. Pierson, *Black Yankees: The Development of an Afro-American Subculture in Eighteenth-Century New En.gland* (Amherst: University of Massachusetts Press, 1988); Thomas L. Webber, *Deep Like the Rivers: Education in the Slave Quarter Community, 1831–1865* (New York: W. W. Norton, 1978).

28. W. E. B. DuBois, *Black Reconstruction* (New York: Harcourt, Brace & Co., 1935); Carter G. Woodson, *Education of the Negro Prior to 1861: A History of the Education of the Colored People of the United States from the Beginning of Slavery to the Civil War*, 2nd ed., New York: Arno Press, 1968).

29. On the runaways in Kentucky, see Ivan McDougle, "Slavery in Kentucky," *Journal of Negro History* 3 (1983): 186. For more recent assessments of the extent of antebellum literacy, see Cornelius, *When I Can Read My Title Clear*; Weber, *Deep Like the Rivers*.

30. Vinovskis and Bernard, "Beyond Catherine Beecher."

31. On the culture of Indians before the coming of the British settlers, see Howard S. Russell, *Indian New England before the Mayflower* (Hanover, N.H.: University Press of New England, 1980); Helen C. Rountree, *Pocahontas's People: the Powhatan Indians of Virginia through Four Centuries* (Norman: University of Oklahoma Press, 1990).

32. James Axtell, *The European and the Indian: Essays in the Ethnohistory of Colonial North America* (New York: Oxford University Press, 1981); James Axtell, *The Invasion Within: The Contest of Cultures in Colonial North America* (New York: Oxford University Press, 1985).

33. For an overview of efforts of the British settlers to educate Indians, see Margaret C. Szasz, *Indian Education in the American Colonies, 1607–1783* (Albuquerque: University of New Mexico Press, 1988).

34. W. Stitt Robinson, Jr., "Indian Education and Missions in Colonial Virginia," *Journal of Southern History* 18 (1952): 152–68.

35. James Axtell, *The School upon a Hill: Education and Society in Colonial New England* (New Haven, Conn.: Yale University Press, 1974); Norman E. Tanis, "Education in John Ellot's Indian Utopias, 1646–1675," *History of Education Quarterly* 10 (1970): 308–23.

36. E. Jennifer Monaghan, "'She Loved to Read in Good Books': Literacy and the Indians of Martha's Vineyard, 1643–1725," *History of Education Quarterly* 30 (1990): 493–521. See also James P. Ronda, "Generations of Faith: The

Christian Indians of Martha's Vineyard," *William and Mary Quarterly* 38 (1981): 369–94.

37. For a discussion of recent work on French literacy, see Bruce Curtis, "Some Recent Work on the History of Literacy in Canada," *History of Education Quarterly* 30 (1990): 613–24.

38. Roger Magnuson, *Education in New France* (Montreal: McGill-Queen's University Press, 1992).

39. Ibid.,90. An interesting new study found significantly higher rates of French male and female literacy in eighteenth-century Michigan than in French Canada. Andris A. Vinovskis, "Literacy in Eighteenth-Century Michigan: The Marriage Register at Fort Michilimackinac," *Journal of the Midwest History of Education Society* (forthcoming).

40. Ibid., 90–91. Since Magnuson included data from Trois Rivieres (a town of 800 inhabitants) in his urban totals for 1750–59, it was necessary to recalculate his numbers for Quebec and Montreal by themselves. Moreover, whereas his rural data for 1680–99 was based upon five parishes, the rural information for 1750–59 came from twenty-two parishes. As there was considerable variation among the rural districts and as it was impossible to recalculate a separate literacy rate for the original five parishes at that later date, one must be careful in interpreting the apparent changes over time as an accurate indication of a decline in literacy in the same geographic areas.

41. François Furet and Jacques Ozouf, *Reading and Writing: Literacy in France from Calvin to Jules Ferry* (Cambridge, Eng.: Cambridge University Press, 1982).

42. David W. Adams, "Before Canada: Towards an Ethnohistory of Indian Education," *History of Education Quarterly* 28 (Spring 1988): 95–105; Magnuson, *Education in New France*.

43. Stone, "Literacy and Education in England,"101.

44. Ibid.

45. See especially Morgan, *Godly Learning*.

46. Cressy, *Literacy and the Social Order*, 96.

47. Ibid., 188.

48. R. A. Houston, *Scottish Literacy and the Scottish Identity; Illiteracy and Society in Scotland and Northern England, 1600–1800* (Cambridge, Eng.: Cambridge University Press, 1985), 110.

49. Ibid., 160.

50. Bailyn, *Education in the Forming of American Society*, 27.

51. Lockridge, *Literary in Colonial New England*, 44.

52. Ibid., 45.

53. Ibid., 57.

54. Grubb, "Educational Choice in the Era before Free Public Schooling," 368– 69.

55. Gallman, "Changes in the Level of Literacy in a New Community of Early America," 582.

56. Auwers, "Reading the Marks of the Past," 213.

57. Main, "Inquiry into When and Why Women Learned to Write," 584; Carol L. Winkelmann, "A Case Study of Women's Literacy in the Early Seventeenth Century: The Oxinden Family Letters," *Women and Language* 19 (1996): 14–20. For the view that the material culture of the "consumer revolution" provided outlets for expressions of expanding female literacy, see Laurel Thatcher Ulrich, "Hannah Barnard's Cupboard: Female Property and Identity in Eighteenth-Century New England," in *Through a Glass Darkly: Reflections on Personal Identity in Early America*, eds., Ronald Hoffman, Mechal Sobel, and Fredrika J. Teute (Chapel Hill: University of North Carolina Press, 1997), 238–73. For a provocative analysis of the uses of expanding seventeenth-century literacy in such female-dominated areas as childbirth, see David Cressy, *Birth, Marriage and Death: Ritual, Religion, and the Life-Cycle in Tudor and Stuart England* (New York: Oxford University Press, 1997), ch. 2.

58. William J. Gilmore, *Reading Becomes a Necessity of Life: Material and Cultural Life in Rural New England, 1780–1835* (Knoxville: University of Tennessee Press, 1989); Perlmann and Shirley, "When Did New England Women Acquire Literacy?"; Monaghan, "Literacy Instruction and Gender in Colonial New England"; Perlmann, Siddall, and Whitescarver, "Literacy, Schooling, and Teaching among New England Women, 1730–1820."

59. Katherine Kish Sklar, "The Schooling of Girls and Changing Community Values in Massachusetts Towns, 1750–1820," *History of Education Quarterly* 33 (1993): 522–23.

60. Ibid., 537.

61. See, for example, Tzvetan Todorov, *The Conquest of America: The Question of the Other* (New York: Harper & Row, 1984); Patricia Seed, "Taking Possession and Reading Texts: Establishing the Authority of Overseas Empires," *William and Mary Quarterly* 49 (1992): 184–209; and Walter Mignolo, *The Darker Side of the Renaissance: Literacy, Territoriality, and Colonization* (Ann Arbor: University of Michigan Press, 1995).

62. See in particular James H. Merrell, "'The Customes of Our Countrey': Indians and Colonists in Early America," in *Strangers Within the Realm: Cultural Margins of the First British Empire*, eds., Bernard Bailyn and Philip D. (Chapel Hill: University of North Carolina Press, 1991), 117–56.

63. See especially Pierson, *Black Yankees*.

64. Gary B. Nash, "Forging Freedom: The Emancipation Experience in the Northern Seaport Cities, 1775–1820," in *Slavery and Freedom in the Age of the American Revolution*, eds., Ira Berlin and Ronald Hoffman (Charlottesville: University Press of Virginia, 1986), 3–48.

65. On the development of racism in eighteenth-century Virginia, see Edmund S. Morgan, *American Slavery, American Freedom: The Ordeal of Colonial*

Virginia (New York: W. W. Norton, 1975), ch. 16; on negative elite attitudes toward non-elite learning, see, in addition to Morgan, David Hackett Fischer, *Albion's Seed: Four British Folkways in America* (New York: Oxford University Press, 1989), 347.

66. Alan Kulikoff, *Tobacco and Slaves: The Development of Southern Cultures in the Chesapeake, 1680–1800* (Chapel Hill: University of North Carolina Press, 1986), pt. 3.

67. For a recent analysis of Jefferson's attitudes toward slave education, see Lucia Stanton "'Those Who Labor For My Happiness': Thomas Jefferson and His Slaves," in *Jeffersonian Legacies*, ed., Peter S. Onuf (Charlottesville: University Press of Virginia, 1993), 167–69. See also John Hardin Best, "Education in the Forming of the American South," *History of Education Quarterly* 36 (1996): 39–65; Keith Whitescarver, "Political Economy, Schooling, and Literacy in the South: A Comparison of Plantation and Yeoman Communities in North Carolina, 1840–1860," Harvard School of Education qualifying paper, 1994.

68. Mechal Sobel, *The World They Made Together: Black and White Values in Eighteenth-Century Virginia* (Princeton, N.J.: Princeton University Press, 1987), 184.

69. Philip D. Morgan, "Slave Life in Piedmont Virginia, 1720–1800," in *Colonial Chesapeake Society*, eds., Lois Green Carr, Philip D. Morgan, and Jean B. Russo(Chapel Hill: University of North Carolina Press, 1988), 473.

70. Sobel, *World They Made Together*, ch. 15.

71. Cornelius, *When I Can Read My Title Clear*, 67–84.

72. Daniel Lerner, *The Passing of Traditional Society: Modernizing the Middle East* (Glencoe Illinois: Free Press, 1958), 64; Emmanuel Todd, *The Causes of Progress* (Oxford, Eng.: B. Blackwell, 1987), 131.

73. Bailyn, *Education in the Forming of American Society*, 48–49; Cremin, *American Education*, 549.

74. Vincent, *Literacy and Popular Culture*, 9.

75. Lockridge, *Literacy in Colonial New England*, 35.

76. Hall, *Worlds of Wonder*, 52, 70.

77. Richard D. Brown, *Knowledge is Power: The Diffusion of Information in Early America, 1700–1865* (New York: Oxford University Press, 1989), 36.

78. Harry S. Stout, "Religion, Communications, and the Ideological Origins of the American Revolution,." *William and Mary Quarterly* 34 (1977): 520–41.

79. Ibid., 526, 532.

80. Ibid., 527.

81. Susan O. Brien, "The Great Awakening and the First Evangelical Network, 1735–1755," *American Historical Review* 91 (1986): 811–32; Frank Lambert, "The Great Awakening as Artifact: George Whitefield and the Construction of Intercolonial Revival, 1739–1745," *Church History* 69 (1991): 223–46.

82. Richard Woodbury to William Parsons, letter of 23 May 1744, ms. in Nicholas Gilman Papers, Massachusetts Historical Society. We thank Eric Seeman for referring us to this piece of evidence.

83. For one such petition, containing the marks or signatures of over three hundred New Haven, Connecticut, men and women who signed for or against retaining the local minister, an Old Light, see New Haven, Connecticut, First Ecclesiastical Society Records 1715–1892, 7 vols., Connecticut State Library, ms. 1, 75–84.

84. Stout, "Religion, Communications, and the Ideological Origins of the American Revolution," 538–41.

85. Michael Warner, *The Letters of the Republic: Publication and the Public Sphere in Eighteenth-Century America* (Cambridge, Mass.: Harvard University Press, 1990), 182, n. 40. For the view that "early New England conceived of speech and script as independent, overlapping, actually contiguous," see Jane Kamensky, *Governing the Tongue: the Politics of Speech in Early New England* (New York: Oxford University Press, 1997), 14; Deborah Keller-Cohen, "Rethinking Literacy: Comparing Colonial and Contemporary America," *Anthropology and Education Quarterly* 24 (1993): 288–307. And for a discussion of the varieties of insurgent literacy among ordinary people, see Steven Justice, *Writing and Rebellion: England in 1381* (Berkeley: University of California Press, 1994), esp. ch. 1.

86. Warner, *Letters of the Republic*, xiii.

8

"NARCISSISM OF THE MINOR DIFFERENCES": WHAT IS AT ISSUE AND WHAT IS AT STAKE IN THE CIVIC HUMANISM QUESTION

Asher Horowitz and Richard K. Matthews

OVER THE PAST TWENTY YEARS the thesis advanced by Bernard Bailyn and Gordon Wood and then expanded by J. G. A. Pocock, that the revolutionary and nation-building American political culture of the eighteenth century must not be understood as an expression of liberalism but as a transformation of the civic republican tradition in political thought, has not only moved to center stage in historiographical effort and debate; it seems, rather, to have now become something of an orthodoxy along the lines of what it sought to challenge. Perhaps nothing indicates this more than the entrance of increasing numbers of legal scholars into the historiographic debate.[1] The liberal consensus analyzed and traced by writers such as Carl Becker, Richard Hofstadter, Daniel Boorstin and Louis Hartz seems to have shattered into a kaleidoscopic mosaic of concepts and themes that are intelligible not against the background of Locke's debate with Filmer, but in the terms that the British Court party inherited from Harrington, Machiavelli, Guicciardini, Polybius and Aristotle. It is perhaps no accident that at the same time the contemporary philosophical liberalisms of John Rawls, Ronald Dworkin and Robert Nozick should have received a powerful challenge from a diverse group of thinkers who, though politically and philosophically quite distinct, are nonetheless commonly labeled "communitarians" and sometimes recognized as being, in one way or another, "neo-Aristotelian": Michael Sandel, Michael Walzer, Alasdair MacIntyre and Charles Taylor. On another level, and somewhat closer to the arena of public rather than academic debate, the authors of *Habits of the Heart* have put civic republicanism forward as an antidote, if not a cure, for

224

NARCISSISM OF THE MINOR DIFFERENCES

the materialism, individualism and alienation that plague the American political community.[2] Clearly something more is in the air than a narrow and technical historiographical debate about the intellectual resources available to the politically articulate strata of late- and post-Colonial America. Indeed, these debates continue to be charged politically.[3]

Where an earlier generation of in some sense republican critics of American liberalism such as Hannah Arendt and Leo Strauss went directly to ancient and Renaissance philosophical sources for the tools to diagnose the modern malaise they associated with it, the current generation of philosophical critics apparently has available, but has hardly yet begun to call upon, the memory of a native tradition anterior and apparently antithetical to liberalism, a tradition that has been waiting quietly for revival as liberalism wanes under the weight of the unintended consequences of its own century and a half of virtually unchallenged success. In a sense these writers argue that this philosophical current, something akin to the pre-modern communitarianism Louis Hartz thought was never present in post-Revolutionary America, though somehow overlooked, was once a massive presence, and, if we follow the authors of *Habits*, remains present in America after all: a political ideology hostile to liberalism, with roots deep enough in language and expression to offer a challenge now. Indeed, the mere entrance of civic humanism, with its own language, history and *ethos*, has opened up the discussion of American history so that what America has *not* become can more clearly be articulated. This alternative, however, was not quite the feudalism with which liberalism struggled for two centuries in Europe. And no one, save Michael Sandel, seems to contend that the victory of liberalism was, relative to Europe, anything but swift and thorough. Even Pocock, whose one explicit revision of Gordon Wood was to argue that republicanism lived on past the constitutional period, employs little argument to give it weight past Tocqueville's time, except as a nostalgic antimodernism in figures as wildly different otherwise as Dwight Eisenhower and Herbert Marcuse.[4] Sandel is another story. He has recently put forward the claim that "As a reigning public philosophy, the version of liberalism that informs our present debates is a recent arrival, a development of the last forty or fifty years. Its distinctive character can best be seen by contrast with a rival public philosophy

that it gradually displaced." This rival, a version of republican political theory, "predominated earlier in American history, liberalism
later."[5]

The discussions among historians of political thought and culture
had gone through several distinct phases. The first can be termed a
phase of either/or interpretations, where advocates argued *either* liberalism *or* civic humanism explained the American experience; the
second phase could be labelled both/and, where scholars claim *both*
liberalism *and* civic humanism were present; and finally, with the
discovery of additional political discourses, pluralism appears to be the
diplomatic, pragmatic and "natural" conclusion. The debate now
seems to revolve around one central issue. The question is no longer
whether civic republicanism must be recognized as a major paradigm
informing the politics of the revolution and the constitutional debates. On the contrary, with a few notable exceptions, no one seems
to believe the idea of a hegemonic liberal consensus in American politics could have been taken seriously.[6]

The civic humanists' claim, as analyzed by one of its most spirited
critics, Isaac Kramnick, is twofold. Not only is Anglo-American political thought in the early eighteenth century suffused by the concepts
and problems of the classical republican tradition, constituting a debate between virtue and corruption, the dominance of the debate
between court and country extends through the rest of the century on
both sides of the Atlantic as well.[7]

Revisionism of course, has not gone without its critics. And these
have managed to throw something of a cold bath over what are seen as
overextensions of the revisionist thesis. Thus Kramnick, for example,
has demonstrated quite handily that for a number of significant
English radicals of the latter part of the eighteenth century, the
concept of virtue had acquired the new meaning of industry and the
country reform tradition "had been turned into a wholehearted ideology of the market" by the end of the century.[8] In almost direct response to Bailyn, who overturned the study of the American Revolution by making ideology the central focus of political study, Joyce
Appleby reemphasized the "material underpinnings" of Jeffersonian
democracy, uncovering "how the market economy influenced the way
people thought about politics and the human potential for purpose-
fully reworking social institutions." Indeed, Appleby persuasively

argues that what was genuinely revolutionary was "the replacement of the economy for the polity as the fundamental social system."[9] John Diggins, in recognition of the continued viability of Tocqueville's analysis of the U.S. as dominated by the spirit of individualism and egoism, has argued for the predominance of liberal individualism as the ideology of the Revolution and liberal pluralism as the ideal. informing the Constitution. The uniqueness of American liberalism comes from its debt to Hume's legitimation of factions and from its continued reliance upon Calvinist Christianity for the voice of its conscience.[10] Thomas Pangle has gone to some lengths to point out some of the crucial differences between the republicanism of the ancients, which required a divinely ordered cosmos, a view of reason as a pure transcendence of the passions capable of ruling them, a civil religion, and perhaps more important, a frankly aristocratic and hierarchical form of rule – all of which were absent from or straightforwardly denied by modern, including American, republicanism. In spite of the fact that, as a conservative critic of liberalism himself, Pangle seems to envision some sort of mutual accommodation of liberal human rights with classical republicanism, it is still quite clear that these two forms of republicanism are not two species of one genus. "The two types of republicanism dispute the basic principles of republicanism."[11] And this is so because "America's republicanism departs from previous forms of republicanism by taking as its chief goal the protection and fostering of individual or private rights and liberties."[12] Pangle, in spite of his hostility to Hartz, is quite clear that the heart of American republicanism is liberal.[13] Thus where Wood and Pocock see an antiliberal republicanism being more or less quickly abandoned, Pangle, as a result of his allegiance to the hierarchical and philosophical spirit of the ancients, is able to detect that

> during the Founding period, Americans tended to try to imitate or evoke the classical virtues, if only in diluted versions, while condemning or drastically subordinating the classical principles and practices that produced or attempted to produce those virtues.[14]

What we have were liberals speaking a language to some degree alien to their own experience and deepest conviction, yet serviceable nonetheless.

This impression has recently been given further substantiation by Jack Greene who, noting that historians have neglected the culture of virtue before the mid-1760s, warns against uncritical acceptance of Pocock's analysis of the country tradition in Britain as having been transferred over the Atlantic completely intact. In a preliminary examination of the pamphlet and sermon literature between 1720 and 1765, Greene has noted that, as one might expect given the radically different socioeconomic conditions, virtue in the colonies "seems to have been thought to be a function more of individual moral exertion than of the possession of landed property."[15] All, even landless laborers, were thought to be equally capable of virtue. Public spiritedness was urged not as a defense against a conniving court but against a spirit of rampant "individualism" and was articulated in largely Protestant terms. He concludes that "the significance of the concept of civic virtue in early America may have been considerably inflated."[16]

Critics such as these have done a good deal at least to modify the monism of Pocock, to question his notion that the country ideology was the only game in town. Yet what is at issue seems to be mainly the relative extent, or weight of civic republicanism in the period in question along with the related problems of the timing and strength of its eclipse. Civic Republicanism seems, the harder one looks for it, less and less like the predominant language of eighteenth-century American political discourse. Yet, for all of these metarevisions, the hermeneutic shift initiated by Bailyn and Wood and pursued with a vengeance by Pocock, seems to still predominate, if only by setting the terms of the debate. Everyone who does not subscribe to it must now laboriously attempt to make room for what was once virtually taken for granted. This is best seen in the efforts of some critics to find a place for republicanism alongside other, but still apparently quite distinct and competing idioms or paradigms. Kramnick, in a recent article, finds a total of four: republicanism, Lockean liberalism, work-ethic Protestantism, and "state-centered theories of sovereignty and power."[17] James T. Kloppenburg also finds four, but a rather different set: Protestantism, classical republicanism, and two varieties of liberalism, which he makes an effort to sharply distinguish, one based upon the values of autonomy and responsibility, the other on cupidity. What is particularly striking about these latter two approaches to the problem is how much they concede to the republican hypothesis, at the moment they intend to put it in its place, by recourse to that most American of all strategies of consensus – pluralism. And, what is equally striking is how the discussion gets moved to a radically different theoretical plane. Kramnick puts it best when he singles out for criticism not the abstractness of Pocock's methodological reliance on linguistic paradigms, but simply "the assumption that there is one language – one exclusive or even hegemonic paradigm."[18] As a result, the picture that emerges from Kramnick is characterized by "a full-blown confusion of idioms, the overlapping of political languages...."[19] Any given speaker could make use of more than one of these languages, and not necessarily at different times. This "profusion and confusion of political tongues" is only offensive to the latter day analyst, however; at the time it was so natural as to go unnoticed.

Paradigmatic pluralism of the kind pursued by Kramnick and Kloppenburg thus refrains from any methodological challenge to what has come to be known as the "ideology school," a trend in American historical studies away from what Forrest McDonald calls "social, political and economic reality" to an almost exclusive study of language.[20] It is Pocock who makes the striking claim that because humans can only think "about what they have the means of verbalizing" the historical study of thought should focus exclusively on "modes of discourse," languages and their idioms.[21]

Two things are conceded that perhaps need not be by Kramnick and Kloppenburg in their recourse to paradigmatic pluralism. One is that linguistic paradigms function more or less as Pocock takes them to, except they may be plural. Second is that civic republicanism in the American context must necessarily have the meaning given to it by Pocock. Left to stand in this form the recourse to paradigmatic pluralism may be anything but the "way out of our historiographical inferno" that Kloppenburg takes it to be.[22] If anything, it begins to resemble a decline from the highly theoretical approaches of *both* Hartz and Pocock (neither of whom are exclusively historians) toward a sort of empiricism without a hypothesis, or in this case an interpretation to test or refine. We seem to have moved from one orthodox monism – i.e., liberal consensus – through another – i.e. civic republicanism – to a pluralism so vague and undefined that the same speaker can now apparently be two or three different things at different times, or at the same time. This, of course, does not address the additional problem of the multiplex ways any speaker's words may be interpreted by a listener. The difficulty is not just that this is "untidy . . . to professors of history or political philosophy."[23] It is rather that the sort of attempt made by both Hartz and Pocock to analyze and criticize the development of American political thought and culture becomes impossible, or worse – moot and forgotten. What we have left is the task of tracing the minutiae of possible paradigm shifts as though these happen by themselves; or else perhaps we have a renewed effort to redescribe well-known thinkers in terms of the particular acts of *bricolage* according to which they meld and shave and refit the fluid elements of different paradigms (as though they were pieces of a child's "lego").

Pocock's analysis at least had the virtue of aiming at being a critical instrument. Had Hartz been familiar with it, one could have imagined him happily engaging another somewhat kindred spirit, since he was acutely critical of the progressive historians for having produced not "a study of American political thought . . . [but] a replica of it."[24] Paradigmatic pluralism tends in the same direction. Diggins has attempted to identify the problem with the exclusively linguistic approach differently than Kramnick, not as an erroneous monism clouding the objective reality of a plurality of paradigms, but as an overestimation of the power of ideas as opposed to interests. Thus Diggins will argue forcefully that scholars ought to "consider the possibility that what goes unsaid in overt political discourse may reveal even more than the content of public utterances."[25] But like the progressive historians who inform his approach, Diggins is compelled to conceive of ideas and interests as two separate sorts of entities, whose causal properties can somehow be weighed and measured when they could perhaps be more fruitfully understood as different logical types offering varying and related but irreducible descriptions of a process.[26] This does allow Diggins a certain critical distance from the plurality of paradigms he, too, is working with. But the great virtue of the linguistic approach is that at least it recognizes that an interest is barely worth historical notice unless it can somehow be articulated and conceptualized in an interpretation of the world. Yet the linguistic approach utterly collapses interests into the linguistic paradigms within which they are articulated. It thus also tends to miss the opportunity to really produce what Hartz meant by a "study" rather than a "replication."

A "study," in these terms, would at least involve keeping open the possibility that some paradigms are more appropriate, more complete, more open to all dimensions of experience, "truer" if you will, than others. Actually, Pocock recognizes this, if only implicitly, since his treatment of Civic Republicanism in the U.S. is critical, by his explicit comparison of it to two things: the development of civic republicanism in Scotland and Europe ending with Rousseau; and the very hypermodernity of American society since the eighteenth century. Yet this critical dimension, although it is possibly the most interesting thing about Pocock's treatment of the republican tradition, does not find a place in his official statements regarding methodology. One gets the impression that it is added on, but gratuitously in terms of his own methodology. Ironically, the revisers of revisionism turn out, with paradigmatic pluralism, to be truer to its own methodology. Does this mean they have beaten republicanism at its own language game? What game is being played out now? How, if all of these paradigms were present, could one begin to weigh them against each other and for what interpretive/theoretical ends? Is a larger interpretation still possible, especially one that recognizes and accommodates the mutual dependence and tension of interests with ideas? Who uses which ideas and how were they used? Do the words and idioms of agents constitute the only possible and fully adequate description of their actions? Do agents never conceal intentions in a language which provides legitimation?[27] To paraphrase Hegel, if you look at the world ideologically, it will look ideologically back.[28]

In Pocock's hands, however, the examination of the development of the civic humanist tradition from the fifteenth to the eighteenth centuries led to a partial critique of American political culture. The upshot, although largely implicit, is that to the degree American political thought is relatively *underdeveloped* – relative to American history itself and relative to the continental discovery of historicity in the nineteenth and twentieth centuries. It is backward not because, as Hartz thought, it was monistically liberal, but because the persistence of civic humanism held back the modernism latent in its developing liberalism. Here is a blatant irony which has barely been noticed by those engaged in this debate. Pocock's analysis of American political thought is actually an inversion rather than a simple rejection of Hartz: the trouble with American political thought is not that it is liberal only, but that it has not been liberal enough. Underdevelopment is due to a peculiar turn within the civic humanist tradition that takes place exclusively in the United States.[29] We would like to come back to this later, when looking at how far Pocock (and Wood) may have in fact escaped from the Hartz hypothesis. Both Pocock's and Hartz's interpretations are only possible, however, if we grant them the use of the comparative context and implicit standards they employ to project a grasp of American political culture as a unique whole.

The comparative context that might in turn help generate a standard (itself however heuristic) of what might constitute better and worse paradigms or paradigmatic developments are precisely what is missing in the further shift from monistic republicanism to paradigmatic pluralism. Once a plurality of paradigms is recognized one can argue for, or in terms of, reaching back to one or the other as a source of present criticism and renewal. Thus some proponents of civic humanism welcome its discovery by historians in America's own past (*Habits*; even Pangle ambiguously); others think that there are deeper and better sources to mine such as Calvinist Christianity. Still others who are civic humanists philosophically see little chance for its revival and hope at best to preserve something of its spirit through the coming dark age of hypermodernity.[30] Regardless of inclination, all concerned with American political development might well be pleased by the sudden explosion of terms, ideas and concepts to describe and explain a political culture in other than exclusively modern liberal language.

There is some question, however, of the philosophical value of recovering historical antecedents.[31] The fact that a set of ideas once existed and may have been extremely influential is not in itself, even for a traditionalist, a very powerful argument for their present truth or viability. Why argue different ideals by looking for historical antecedents? If they are true or valuable they speak to present and/or permanent needs, or else they have a transtemporal authority that does not depend upon their once having held sway. Political theory is not, after all, a courtroom run in the common law tradition.

Paradigmatic pluralism, then, at least insofar as it is premised upon Pocock's linguistic methodology, far from being a way out of either a philosophical or historiographical "inferno," may actually lead to less interesting, less fruitful interpretive efforts, especially for any interpretation that wishes to establish a critical perspective on that which is being interpreted. The results of paradigmatic pluralism so far leave completely open the crying question of how these apparently distinct and even antithetical paradigms were combined and what the meaning of the various combinations were. Do the combinations add up to or lead to a meaning different than each might have had by itself? Was one predominant for one phase, one region, one class? How is the meaning of a particular combination to be understood? What is to be done?

Perhaps the only way to advance interpretation beyond documenting the presence of "different" paradigms and tracing their separate and combined vicissitudes would be in an interpretation of how the paradigms were in fact used and by whom. This should not be entirely alien to the linguistic approach, which itself owes a good deal to Wittgenstein's understanding that meaning is a function of use in a language-game. But there is more to a language-game than a set of concepts. There is also the social action that language both makes possible and limits. Some of this action is strategic. It is consciously designed to affect the behavior (including the interpretive behavior) of other players. Insofar as it may be strategic, it opens up the possibility of the speaker having some autonomy from the paradigm(s) that map his/her interpretive stance. Pocock's dictum that "one cannot get out of a language that which was never in it," cannot be taken to mean that the interpreter knows in advance of understanding the situation of the speaker as a whole, the positive limits within which that speaker's thought must move.[32] One cannot restrict the meanings in a language only to what was in it before a speaker made use of it. Pocock's paradigms are themselves not intended to be pure and static. They are themselves fluid traditions available to speakers rather than dominating them. If they were to dominate speakers, then the tradition itself could not evolve in response to differing contexts and unforeseen events.

Paradigms, then, must be seen as open to even radical revision, to the incorporation of new conceptual content within old terminology and to mutation in the context of new and different experiences. New meanings may arise in a surprising ways and this may be to some degree either intentional or unintentional. Pocock himself recognizes quite clearly that political language especially is not free from ambiguity, but exhibits it to a high degree.[33] The greater the ambiguity, the more powerful the ideology: humans can use it as they wish. And to the degree that ambiguity has become present within a paradigm or has arisen as a result of distinct paradigms sharing the same or similar terms, new meanings may suddenly emerge in barely recognizable form specifically because the old terminology need not be entirely replaced. The shift in meaning may only become gradually and progressively more clear, in retrospect. The historian may be able to better understand his/her subjects' actions and even their intentions than they understood them themselves because he/she is in a position to see what became of their efforts.

Anthony Giddens, summarizing a great deal of argument within the philosophy of the human sciences, has pointed out that knowledge of social reality is always doubly hermeneutic: it always involves an interpretation of an intepretation. The interpreted situation that others communicate is only available to us insofar as we are already interpreting it.[34] If, then, we are going to ask how elements from different paradigms may have been combined and used, we must recognize that this can only be done within the framework of our own always tentative and always evolving interpretation. If the tradition of philosophical hermeneutics that Kloppenburg appeals to has emphasized anything, it is that there is no pure recovery of an objective past by an observing subject purified of preconceptions and preinterpretations. We do not face past linguistic paradigms as though they were simply out there to be discovered. Their recovery must always be due in large part to our interpretive construction, just as the possibility of understanding them is due to their survival, i.e. is due to the fact that we already share many of the same meanings – what the hermeneuticists call the "effective history" of ideas.[35]

Diggins has pointed out quite acutely that the extent to which eighteenth century theorists used and changed the terms and concepts of civic humanism has not yet been explored.[36] In one sense this is both true and apposite. (Even Kramnick, who shows how civic humanist and liberal languages were used by both Federalists and

Anti-Federalists, does not conceive himself as doing what Diggins requires.) But in another sense this is not quite the case, because this task was actually begun by Pocock himself. A large part of Pocock's account of the republican tradition in eighteenth-century America is devoted to showing how civic humanist rhetoric came to be used to pursue other goals, how it was modified to fit new assumptions. It is, in fact, central to Pocock's claim of civic humanism being able to outlive its usefulness in the U.S., that at one crucial moment it could be used to describe and legitimate a set of purposes and institutions that were not properly and classicly republican. Unfortunately Pocock simply reports these changes; he does not interpret them as a (partially) conscious modification of the paradigm to fit new assumptions and interpretations of experience that themselves undermined the possibility and legitimacy of republicanism in anything like its traditional meaning. Interestingly enough, one of the reasons Pocock does not see this is because he assumes, in his own Aristotelian moment, that deference and equality are, in fact, compatible – a view which found a home in later liberal thought largely through the efforts of John Stuart Mill.

It may be that scholars have not tended to look closely at the structure of Pocock's argument concerning what was taking place in the American eighteenth century. As a result, the fore-conception that guides it has not been subject to the same critical scrutiny as the claims that seem capable of "empirical testing" – the sorts of investigations that have led to the compromise of paradigmatic pluralism. Pocock's own claim, therefore, that his variation on Wood's account is radically at variance with the view of Louis Hartz, that "the interpretation put forward by Bailyn and Wood altogether replaces that of Boorstin and Hartz," has simply been taken for granted.[37] But if we pursue Pocock's own claim that, at one point at least, civic humanist rhetoric could be advanced to pursue other goals; that civic humanist rhetoric was open and amenable to modification to fit new assumptions and interpretations of experience, we may ironically find that his interpretation can be seen to confirm the notion of America as a "liberal civilization" at least as much as to reject it.

Hartz's argument remains far more complex than the thesis of liberal "uniformity" to which it has often been reduced. His theory of the *underdevelopment* of American political thought and culture comprises but a part of a larger, even more illuminating theory of political-cultural development applicable to all of the "new societies" that evolved in the course of the European colonization of the Americas and the South Pacific: Australia, New Zealand, Canada, the United States and the republics of Latin America.[38] Hartz argues that wherever a portion of European society, at a specific stage of its own more complex and dialectical development, detaches itself from Europe and establishes itself in a new setting, it may simultaneously lose some of the most important stimuli for development that the whole spectrum of political ideologies and forms of social experience provides. The complete European ideological spectrum consists of four broadly defined groups, which "range – in chronological order, and from right to left – from feudal or tory through liberal whig to liberal democrat to socialist."[39] In the United States, three of the four groupings are – for all practical purposes – missing, due to the accidents of the original migrations that established the Colonies as a "fragment" of British society. In the United States a situation exists in which the Lockean liberalism, which must wage a much longer and more difficult struggle to emerge and triumph in Britain, may flourish without the dynamic ideological counter-pressures it encounters in the mother country. In Europe, including Great Britain, the existence of feudalism provides the context that allows/forces liberalism to develop in direct response to, and with real understanding of, the ideological forces that lie on its right and its left.

In the North American context, French Canada comprises a "feudal fragment," founded by bearers of tory values with its point of departure prior to the liberal revolution. The United states, in contrast, begins as a "liberal fragment" established by liberal individualists who leave the tory end of the spectrum behind. Consequently, American history becomes the response of a fragment removed from European social and ideological developments. "Now there is nothing mysterious about this mechanism of fragmentation," Hartz writes. "A part detaches itself from the whole, the whole fails to renew itself, and the part develops without inhibition."[40] In order to understand a fragment's development it is crucial to note what was not present as much as what was. The crucial ideological distinction continues to be that between toryism and liberalism. In the American bourgeois fragment, with its rationalist-egalitarian-individualist ethos, the corporate-organic-collectivist element is missing: toryism has been left behind. Lacking a feudal past the United States lacks an important, if not essential, precondition for socialism. "In the United States," explains Hartz, "Marx dies because there is no sense of class, no spirit of revolution, no yearning for the corporate past."[41]

By the early nineteenth century, liberalism constitutes the alpha and omega of America's unfolding. As Gordon Wood describes the situation: "Americans had become, almost overnight, the most liberal, the most democratic, the most commercially minded, and the modern people in the world."[42] Escaping its past the United States also ironically forecloses options for the future. It forecloses until, that is, the future returns at the point where technological innovation and world hegemonic ambitions brings Europe and the rest of the world and the complete ideological spectrum back into immediate contact with the fragment.[43] With this occurrence, Americans return to a position where they become able to knowingly will their political destiny. Of course, there is nothing on the present horizon to suggest that they will consciously elect to do so, especially since so much of the world seems anxious to become a fragment of McWorld.[44]

To say that America was instinctively Lockean, as Hartz maintained, was not to say that people necessarily used Locke's language to the exclusion of other languages, although sometimes Locke's language might figure prominently.[45] What Hartz means is that the interpretive framework that Locke supplied fit the social experience and self-interpretation of the American colonists. Both projected a fundamentally similar implicit interpretation of the social universe. The relation of individual to society and the nature of individuals were understood by both in a way that was fundamentally different from the interpretations that served feudal or organic and hierarchical societies. When Hartz refers to liberalism, then, he is not referring by any necessary means to later doctrines within it that promoted unrestrained capitalist economic growth or to the pure politics of short-run self-interest. What Hartz has in mind is a sort of model of society that people accepted and used as a set of background assumptions describing what they felt themselves to be and what their relations with each other necessarily ought to be like.

In this liberal model of society the individual is taken to be prior to society. The individual is an atom, whose nature is given once and for all without reference to the structure or history of social relationships or institutions. To know what the individual is essentially, it is not necessary to examine the society of which that individual is a part, because the essential humanity of that individual is contained within him as a rational creature. To say that the individual is rational is to say that by his own lights he can discover and learn the fundamental principles that govern the material and moral universe (whether these are conceived of as basically one or radically distinct) and become, as an adult, self-directed. Reason liberates individuals from any unquestioned authoritative traditions; it liberates them from being identified with only a specific, narrow and compulsory social role, and it liberates them from any natural social hierarchy. Reason belongs to the free subject. It enables that subject to determine and pursue his own ends, independent of the authority and will of others. This instrumental (but not necessarily amoral) reason, which is given with the individual to be a servant to his wants and needs, because it makes each individual free, makes all individuals equal. They are equal in a fundamental sense, and not in a substantive sense. There may be a thousand differences between them, each of which can be ranged along a continuum of superiority and inferiority, but none of these differences touch the freedom of the rational creature to be his own master, and in this sense to be the equal of all other rational creatures. Society is understood to be nothing but that set of arrangements and relationships freely entered into by this individual to further his own ends. In society freedom is negative and essentially means the relative absence of external impediments to rationally willed activity. A society of rational, fundamentally equal and free individuals will necessarily be plural and competitive, because individuals are not restrained by the nature of their inescapable social roles and are, at bottom, each their own judge of the good life. Since competitive equal individuals must see in each other's freedom and equality not only the essential dignity of all individuals, but a potential threat to their own freedom, government is a necessity and its essential function is to protect the freedom of individuals in their competitive relations with their equals. Yet government is essentially itself an instrument rather than even a part of the ends of human life, and it is an instrument which, since it must be more powerful than what it controls, is necessarily an object of suspicion. It must be controlled by those whom it is to control in turn, otherwise it defeats its purpose.

This is more or less, in very brief form, what for Hartz was contained in the epithet "liberal." It can be summarized in the following table:

priority of the individual
reason
freedom (as negative)
equality (as fundamental)
competition (sometimes as friendly)
government as necessary, but necessarily evil

Liberalism in this sense can be expressed in purely Lockean terms, but obviously need not be. It could also be expressed in Kantian, Benthamite, Millian and Madisonian terms, to name a few.[46] And it is especially to be understood by contrast to the model of a feudal society.

By the term feudal Hartz did not primarily mean the sort of political arrangements of fealty between lord and vassal that grew up in medieval Europe, or even the existence of an hereditary aristocracy. In many, if not most ways a feudal society meant the inverse of the principal characteristics of a liberal model of society. Whereas the priority of the individual is fundamental to the liberal schema, feudalism meant the priority of the community. Individuality itself is here understood as being an expression of a particular form of society; it is tacitly accepted and felt that the individual is a dependent part of a whole. His purposes and abilities are only to be actualized within a set of social relationships, traditions and institutions that do not themselves depend on his separate, "natural" will. The best, most complete individuals are those who most adequately fulfill the highest functions in the organic social whole. In the Aristotelian and Platonic versions of such a society the fulfillment of the highest social functions is also (but with some ambiguity that does not concern us here) the attainment of that measure of possible freedom allotted to human beings. It is the freedom to engage in activities that are not governed by external need and blind necessity.

Since the community is prior, the source of individual obligation is not to be found in the reason that can be exercised by separate subjects. Divine or divinely inspired traditions supply the authoritative codes of behavior that organize and guarantee all of the tasks, functions, roles and relationships that characterize such societies in their specificity. Since the community is taken absolutely to precede the individual, it makes little or no sense (before the advent of the socialist idea, itself dependent upon the development of liberalism) to think of individuals as fundamentally equal. Since individuals do not exist apart from highly specific and interrelated social roles, they are relatively subordinate or superordinate by nature, to the degree that certain functions of the whole social organism are conceived to be necessarily hierarchically coordinated. Tradition and authority take the place of subjective rationality and negative freedom. Competition between individuals is understood as the primary source of disorder and equality is understood to mean nothing else than chaos and a reversal and degradation of the natural order of things. Here government is necessarily not an evil, but both a burden and dignity assigned to those parts of the community divinely appointed and/or best suited to carrying out the requisite tasks.

This is more or less what was for Hartz to be understood by the term feudal or "tory," and it can be summarized as follows:

> priority of the community
> tradition
> authority
> hierarchy
> cooperation (as organic)
> government as a burden of aristocratic dignity

"Feudal" in this sense can also be expressed and theoretically defended in a number of distinct languages, from that of Plato to those of Filmer and de Maistre.[47]

How could a civilization be "naturally Lockean," as Hartz maintains, yet frame its political life to some significant degree in the terms supplied by the civic humanist tradition, with its obvious kinship to the tory model outlined above? If we think, as Pocock does some of the time, that a linguistic paradigm is like a box in which only so many things of so many definite types can be put or removed, then liberalism and civic humanism will necessarily be seen as antithetical. Paradigmatic change will mean the abandonment of one and the adoption of the other. But if we think, even *à la* Pocock at other times, of language (especially the language appropriated for political purposes) as charged with ambiguity through and through, then it becomes possible to conceive of change, even qualitative change, as a discovery of a heretofore unnoticed potential that now appears to have been latent or implicit in what we have already been doing and using. In other words, the problems that preoccupy along with the conceptual resources supplied by, as well as the theoretical limitations, of the civic humanist tradition can be subordinated to the problems of a liberal civilization.

That is, in a sense, precisely what Americans throughout the eighteenth century may be seen to have been doing: arriving at a (never uncontested) theory of the liberal republic. What divides them among each other are, for example, problems for both liberals and republicans. The questions that divided Federalists and Anti-Federalists over centralization and participation and the meaning of popular sovereignty are problems for liberals that can be discussed and solved in (sometimes ambiguously) republican terms. Here, however we can not do all of the work Diggins asks for in determining how various writers used the languages at their disposal. Instead, all we have done is indicate what that task might look like and some of the possible reasons for undertaking it.

Let us look back, however, at some of the specifics of Pocock's argument that have been largely ignored in order to see how distant his description of the course of civic humanism in eighteenth-century America is from Hartz's liberal civilization properly understood. The tale Pocock weaves of the vicissitudes undergone by republican thought in the U.S. is based to some extent on Bailyn, but mostly on Wood's *Creation of the American Republic*.[48] According to Pocock, the revolutionary agitation was not expressed in liberal terms, but articulated as a civic humanist reaction to the threat of corruption emanating from efforts to integrate the colonies more thoroughly into the colonial system after the wars of 1757–63. Wood certainly recognizes this, but is quite clear in his account that Americans were resisting the threat corruption posed to liberty, not simply to virtue. The opposite of liberty is oppression. The threat of corruption was simultaneously a threat to liberty, the threat of oppression. Americans were struggling to protect the negative freedoms they already enjoyed as Englishmen, something that Edmund Burke understood, and not aiming to achieve the positive freedom of the Aristotelian citizen even in its Machiavellian moment.[49] Virtue was certainly a quality necessary to the preservation of liberty; but it was felt to be grounded not in the gentlemanly independence of court influence granted by the possession of landed property but in the relative equality of circumstance found in the colonies and in the virtually universal assumption of fundamental equality among adult white males. The fear of a new American aristocracy that so pervaded American politics was a fear not that a loss of liberty might lead to corruption, but that corruption might lead to the disappearance of that fundamental equality that was more than even the cornerstone of individual self-determination; they were in fact, in Lockean terms, two sides of the same coin. The republican concern over corruption that was the stock in trade of the country party could do admirable service in the defense of the liberal ideas of negative liberty and fundamental equality. Wood is full of this story, without laying it out simply in these terms.

For Pocock, the fact that there was no other language available than that of the civic humanism of Renaissance and of English writers such as Harrington, Bolingbroke, and Trenchard and Gordon meant that in the U.S. that tradition could and did become a restricting and compulsive force. Great Britain enjoyed, on the other hand a certain symbiosis of court and country that helped avert such a development there. Yet it is not at all clear why one cannot interpret especially the early agitation as an appeal in Whig terms to Whig values, as a search for allies in the metropolis. Wood, after all, does understand the dominant language of the revolutionary agitation to have been that of radical whiggery. For Pocock it was the fact that the Americans spoke the language of the country party in the absence of a court that led to the total suspicion of government. Yet, it is not at all clear why one cannot recognize here that basic suspicion of government that lies so close to the heart of the liberal conception of freedom as the absence of constraint. Did Americans come to suspect government because only the country language was spoken, or was the country language spoken because it could express the quite liberal fear of a distant, external and irresponsible power? If the American political culture started out so exclusively civic humanist as Pocock maintains, why then was the thrust of reform increasingly in the direction of autonomy and separation from Great Britain as opposed to integration with the opposition in the mother country? Certainly that separation could be accounted for and was in fact based upon an assertion of the limits of obligation and belonging that followed from liberal and not civic humanist assumptions.

Pocock not only bases his account mostly on Wood, he also overstates the importance of civic humanism to Wood's account. But perhaps more interesting for our purposes are Pocock's attempts to take issue with Wood explicitly, that is his complaint concerning Wood's "overstatement of the end of the classical paradigm."[50] According to Pocock, civic humanism was kept alive in the U.S. through the rhetoric of separation and balance embalmed in the Constitution. And it was able thus to outlive its appropriateness because for the Americans, "the confrontation of virtue and commerce was not absolute."[51] In Europe, on the other hand, in the writings of men such as Adam Ferguson in Scotland, but especially of Jean-Jacques Rousseau, the civic humanist tension between "commerce" and "virtue" gave rise to a critique of modern, liberal, market civilization that was to become a large part of the basis for the grand historical syntheses of Hegel and Marx. In the U.S., this theoretical moment was missed, *we* could say, because a liberal civilization would necessarily need to attempt to square virtue and commerce over and over again. Whatever tension was felt to exist between them, the absence (Marx) or victory (Hegel) of either could not be imagined. For Pocock what the accommodation of virtue to commerce meant was that, during the founding and for a long time afterward, if not even now, the extent to which virtue was being abandoned could be masked. What could easily and obviously be read as liberalism with a civic humanist face becomes, in the linguisticist account, a "partial abandonment of virtue."[52] Instead of the U.S. going on to feel and explore, like most other modern nations, the dialectic of virtue and commerce, development takes place spatially in the conquest of a continent on behalf of the idea of the freehold republic, but also in an escape from the inevitability of historical impermanence and the rise of a myth of permanent regeneration. For Pocock, there was clearly a positive issue for the civic humanist tradition in the quite modernist doctrines of nineteenth-century Europe that brought with them a realistic understanding of historical forces and realities.[53] This was quite distinct from the outcome in the U.S. where, because virtue and commerce were strange bedfellows from the start, political thinking was held back by veneration of premodern and antimodernist traditions.

Thus for Pocock, the persistence of civic humanism led to a backwardness in American political thought and culture; the only partial victory of liberalism led to a distortion relative to Europe. For Hartz, of course, it was the idea that liberalism already enjoyed a complete victory in America, that it did not need to conquer, that led to the underdevelopment not only of American liberalism, of its insular and antiphilosophical character, but of its political culture as a whole. One thing that Pocock interestingly assumes here is that the quarrel between commerce and virtue that can and does take place within liberalism is not and cannot be "absolute"; and that only an absolute confrontation between the two was able to lead beyond the civic humanist tradition into that "historicism" whose strength was the sense of the secular creativity of history. Thus, it is not liberalism that leads to the kind of historicism Pocock praises, but the critical confrontation of liberalism by writers who can draw upon the civic humanist tradition (among others) in its confrontation of virtue with commerce. Pocock does not venture to explain why, in Europe, conditions allowed for a transcendence of the civic humanist tradition in the doctrines of Rousseau, Hegel and Marx. For Hartz one essential condition would have been evident: nowhere and at no time was there in Europe a "liberal civilization." There, one of the main dilemmas of civic humanism, the contradiction between virtue and commerce, could be appropriated as the germ of various attempts to transcend both liberalism and civic humanism. In a liberal civilization, assuming such a thing exists, civic humanism could only be put to use to articulate or legitimate liberalism, or perhaps to oppose it ineffectually.[54] By saying that in America, the confrontation of virtue and commerce was not absolute, Pocock is virtually admitting, that for anyone but the most strictly mechanical linguisticist, it was already a liberal civilization partially understanding itself in preliberal terms. Of course, one should not forget that some confrontation between virtue and commerce is a theme that is quite at home in much of liberalism at least since John Stuart Mill if not Adam Smith. One could say that it animates the liberalism of Kant and certainly lies behind the efforts of John Rawls, probably the most important liberal thinker of the twentieth century. Pocock's incisive and quite valuable observation is that when that confrontation becomes absolute, liberalism is no longer possible. The inverse of this would be that as long as that tension cannot, under modern conditions, become absolute, liberalism is absolutely predominant.

If this is not enough to cast serious doubt on the view that the general and constant use of civic humanist language negates the existence of a liberal civilization, it is worth having a look at Pocock's understanding (still based on Wood) of what gave the constitutional crisis its specific shape. The reversion to the Harringtonian tradition that Pocock sees in the agitation of the 1760s and 1770s meant that, in accord with civic humanist theory, the people should have divided into a natural few and many performing complementary functions and possessing complementary virtues. The function of the few was to supply leadership while the function, and virtue, of the many was to exhibit deference to their natural leaders. And Pocock makes an absolutely crucial connection between virtue and the deference of the many that gives a stronger indication than anything else of the organic and hierarchical provenance of civic humanism. That Pocock himself does not see deference toward natural leaders as a hierarchical institution but as a "republican characteristic" means only that he has been persuaded by Guicciardini's argument. Liberalism, however, is less comfortable with, and in its more radical forms, strongly opposed to the identification of virtue and deference. Nor is it persuaded all that easily that in the deference of a natural aristocracy to the judgement of the many what takes place is a transcendence of hierarchy.

By Pocock's criteria, Aristotle's polity could not be called a hierarchical society. But what is primarily at issue here is not Pocock's strange defense of republican "equality." According to Pocock the natural differentiation demanded by and absolutely central to civic humanist theory failed to appear in America and this meant more than a threat to the status and power of patrician elites, but a "threat to virtue itself."[55] It had to be seen as a threat to republican virtue because, for Pocock, the essence of that virtue was the deference of the many to the few. The sacrifice of private for public good was in that "language" completely identified with the deference of the many to the few. Following Wood, Pocock understands the Federalist response to the "crisis" of the 1780s as being "predicated upon an abandonment of the closely related paradigms of deference and virtue."[56]

The question that Pocock fails to raise in all this is, of course, why the people failed to differentiate itself into a naturally deferential few and many, in spite of the wishes of some of the patrician elite. And the answer that naturally suggests itself is that in a liberal civilization this would be exactly what the people could not do. The many could not put up with it, because it went against the grain, not simply of interest group politics, but against the assumption – the lived presumption – of fundamental equality. And fundamental equality in America, where equality of circumstance was so much more of a reality than in Britain, would naturally mean that much less deference toward individuals who might be only one or two generations away from very humble origins. And many of the potential few themselves could not see it as legitimate. What is crucial here is not whether Pocock might have overestimated the speed at which deference declined, but a cluster of somewhat different questions: what was the meaning of deference? was it always identified with virtue by everyone who spoke that language? was the deference shown by the many the same as the deference expected by the few? were deference and virtue, even when partially identified, also at odds which each other? It should also be born in mind that the meaning and significance of whatever deference existed can best (perhaps only) be understood in comparative terms: did deference decline much more rapidly and easily in America than it did in Great Britain, France and Germany?

If, then, according to Pocock, the Federalists partially abandoned republicanism for liberalism and democracy – but only partially – it was because in America – but contrary to the republican tradition – virtue could not be seen as the absolute opposite of commerce and because virtue could not be equated with deference. But, to say this is to identify two of the most central objections liberalism has to civic humanism. To then turn around and say that America could not have been a liberal civilization because it spoke the language of civic humanism is truly a *coup de force*, when one could as easily have said that in America the language of civic humanism inevitably got increasingly molded to liberal realities and opinions. When the central crisis arrived, and the decision had to be faced as to whether the national political constitution would recognize an organically conceived polity naturally differentiated by political function into leadership and deference or whether it would express the essential liberal notion of fundamental equality, the answer was a foregone conclusion despite all of the not unimportant wrangling between Federalists and Anti-Federalists about the nature and degree of representation. Where else but in a liberal civilization would this have been possible? In France it took at least another hundred years for the liberal-democratic republic to find shaky but viable foundations after a series of bloody civil wars, and in Great Britain a more gradualist and less violent solution took at least as long.

If, then, we are again to raise the question of the meaning of the classicist episode in American political thought, the language of civic humanism need not be seen as the predominant language which in the constitutional crisis suddenly fades into disuse (Wood) or lingers on like a bad hangover (Pocock) or as a paradigm essentially separate from other competing paradigms (Kramnick, Appleby, Kloppenburg, Diggins). Instead it can be seen – in its peculiarly American form where commerce and virtue try to find room for each other and where deference for natural leaders cannot be presumed – as one expression of the self-interpretation of a civilization which is already fundamentally liberal. That civic humanism retires relatively quickly from the scene to make way for other languages then becomes something less than mysterious since it was never fully adequate to the task of expressing and articulating the basic thrust of American social development. Hartz might have said that both the use of civic humanist language and its being jettisoned with relative ease, are signs of the pervasive pragmatism which an ideologically unified liberal civilization has the luxury of enjoying. In the end, there is not nearly so much distance between the revisionist interpretation and the Hartzian as the revisionists might imagine. Pocock criticizes American political thought for its underdevelopment of liberal modernism and attributes this to the persistence of civic humanist language. But civic humanist language, according to him, could only persist because it could be used to mask and express liberal ideas of individualism, self-interest and interest-group politics.[57] He also criticizes the underdevelopment of civic humanist thought in the U.S. It never led, as it did in the Scottish Enlightenment and in Rousseau, to the historicist theories that seem for him to be the legitimate modern heirs of that tradition. And this too should be seen to be a consequence of the fact that civic humanism in the U.S. could not achieve sufficient differentiation from liberalism, as it could in Europe where it could be used to express new organicist conceptions of society and history on both the right and the left of liberalism. Pocock is looking for encumbrances to the development of modernist historicism and finds them, in the U.S., essentially in the relative *weakness* of civic humanism, of the Tory(ish) challenge to liberalism. How different is this in the end from Hartz, and behind him Tocqueville, who also found the key to the development of American civilization in the overwhelmingly natural character of its liberalism? Perhaps the principal difference is that Hartz was a postliberal critic of liberalism while Pocock, at least in *The Machiavellian Moment* is a modernist (and perhaps liberal) critic of civic humanism. Different theoretical projects and outlooks inform the hermeneutic efforts of both thinkers, yet despite the grand dismissal of the notion of a liberal civilization, Pocock simply registers that idea by different and far more circuitous means.

At stake today in all this is something more than the question of defining the research agenda of a politically detached segment of academia. By looking at civic humanist rhetoric as though it were an indigenous tradition formed in and out of long-standing social experience it might be only too possible to miss other and different sources of potential reform and the real obstacles to it. It also becomes too easy and too convenient to gloss over the substantial connection between the tradition of civic humanism before Rousseau and Jefferson and its commitment to hierarchy.[58] All of the efforts to revive civic humanism tend to ignore or eclipse the problem of the clash between the idea of a democratic community of individuals, which Hartz saw as the positive legacy of American liberalism with capitalist development. Along with this eclipse comes the danger of believing, whether one is liberal or communitarian, that an integral and virtuous community can only be based upon authority and uniformity – and a nebulous conception of deference to social superiors. We would, then, tend to agree, with both Hartz *and* Pocock insofar as both imply that reform in the United States is better off not orienting itself exclusively in terms of whatever civic republican sources might have existed here. It must make its way through – and perhaps break out of – the liberal tradition.

Notes

1. See Bruce Ackerman, *We The People* (Cambridge, Mass.: Belknap Press of Harvard University, 1991), 41, where he discusses the "Bicentennial Myth" and casually points out that "The problem is this: the stories lawyers tell" have important political consequences. The stories from historians and political scientists, from Ackerman's legal perspective, are somewhat insignificant until law-yers start to pay attention and begin to create their own tales. For a few examples see James Gray Pope, "Republican Moments: The Role of Direct Popular Power in the American Constitutional Order," *University of Pennsylvania Law Review* 139 (1990): 287–368; Mark Tushnet, *Red, White, and Blue: A Critical Analysis of Constitutional Law* (Cambridge, Eng.: Cambridge University Press, 1988); Cass R. Sunstein, "Interest Groups in American Public Law," *Stanford Law Review* 38 (1985): 29–87; Suzanna Sherry, "Civic Virtue and the Feminine Voice in Constitutional Adjudication," *Virginia Law Review* 72 (1986): 543–616; and Richard H. Fallon, Jr., "What is Republicanism and Is It Worth Reviving?" *Harvard Law Review* 102 (1989): 1695–735.

2. Robert Bellah et. al., *Habits of the Heart*, (New York: Harper & Row, 1986). In chapter 2 the authors identify three major strands of culture in the United States: these are the "biblical," the "republican" and the individualist; the latter is further subdivided into a utilitarian and an expressive strain. A good deal of the book laments the progressive weakening of the older "cultures" and their replacement by one or other or both strains of individualism. Again and again the authors call for a rehabilitation of "biblical and republican thought," almost as though these form a solid alliance, if not a unity; see, for example, 48, 50, 143, 144, 150, 155, 253–54, 281, 285, 292, 295–96. At one point they go so far as to assert that there are two languages spoken in the U.S., the first and primary language being one of "unencumbered" individualism, and the second a more submerged language of traditions and commitments (154). A little later on it becomes apparent that this second language, which they believe ought again to become the first, is the language of the "civic republican tradition" (251).

3. Gordon Wood, "The Fundamentalists and the Constitution," *New York Review of Books*, vol. 35, no. 2, 18 Feb. 1988, 35; Peter S. Onuf, "Reflections on the Founding," *William and Mary Quarterly* 46 (1989): 341–75; Colin Gordon,

"Crafting a Usable Past: Consensus, Ideology and Historians of the American Revolution," *William and Mary Quarterly* 46 (1989): 671–96; Richard K. Matthews, "Liberalism, Civic Humanism, and the American Political Tradition: Understanding Genesis," *Journal of Politics* 49 (1987): 1127–53; Thomas Pangle, *The Spirit of Modern Republicanism* (Chicago: University of Chicago Press, 1988).

4. J. G. A. Pocock, *The Machiavellian Moment: Florentine Political Thouht and the Atlantic Republican Tradition* (Princeton, N.J.: Princeton University Press, 1975), 543–45, 548

5.Michael Sandel, *Democracy's Discontent: America in Search of a Public Philosophy* (Cambridge, Mass.: Harvard University Press, 1996), 5–6 The closest Sandel comes to giving a precise time frame for the transition from republicanism to liberalism appears to be the late nineteenth, early twentieth century: "With the acceptance of wage labor as a permanent condition came a shift in American legal and political discourse from the civic to the voluntarist conception of freedom. . . . It thus marked a decisive moment in America's transition. . . . As the twentieth century began, however, the procedural [liberal] republic was still in formation; the political economy of citizenship had not wholly given way. . . (200)." To support the case for the presence of civic humanism in New England, Sandel relies on Tocqueville's description in his 1835 *Democracy in America*; a contrasting view of Tocqueville's America based on his 1831 "Fort-night in the Wilderness," where liberalism is everywhere and civic humanism is nowhere to be found, is presented in Richard K. Matthews, "Paradise Lost or Paradise Found? Virtue, Corruption, and Self-Interest in Tocqueville's Frontier," in *Virtue, Corruption and Self-Interest: Political Values in the Eighteenth Century*, ed., Richard K. Matthews (Bethlehem, Pa.: Lehigh University Press, 1994), 297–313.

6. It rarely is a matter of questioning the political character of civic republicanism, of criticizing or defending it as political theory, past or present. Some notable exceptions are Thomas Pangle, *Spirit of Modern Republicanism*; John P. Diggins, *The Lost Soul of American Politics: Virtue, Self-Interest, and the Foundations of Liberalism* (Chicago: Basic Books, 1984); and "Comrades and Citizens: New Mythologies in American Historiography," *American Historical Review* 90 (1985): 614–38; as well Joyce Appleby, "Republicanism in Old and New Contexts," *William and Mary Quarterly* 43 (1986): 20–34. See also the essays collected in the special issue "Joyce Appleby, ed., "Republicanism in the History and Historiography of the United States, *American Quarterly* 37 (1985): 461–598, and her "What Is Still American in the Political Philosophy of Thomas Jefferson?" *William and Mary Quarterly* 39 (1982): 287–304; and "Commercial Farming and the 'Agrarian Myth' in the Early Republic," *Journal of American History* 68 (1982): 833–49; and *Capitalism and a New Social Order: The Republican Vision of the 1790's* (New York: New York University Press, 1984).

7. Isaac Kramnick, "Republican Revisionism Revisited," *American Historical Review*, 87 (1982), 629–30.

8. Ibid., 661.

9. Appleby, *Capitalism*, ix; and "Republicanism in the History."

10. Diggins, *Lost Soul*, is as a result friendlier to the Hartzian interpretation of American political thought than most revisionists or antirevisionists, see, e.g., 103–04

11. Thomas Pangle, "The Classical Challenge to the American Constitution," *Chicago-Kent Law Review*, 24 (1990) 158.

12. Ibid., 172.

13. Pangle, *Spirit*, 25–27.

14. Pangle, "Classical Challenge," 173.

15. Jack Greene, "The Concept of Virtue in Late Colonial British America," in *Virtue, Corruption, and Self-Interest*, ed., Richard K. Matthews, 38.

16. Ibid., 48.

17. Isaac Kramnick, "The 'Great National Discussion': The Discourse of Politics in 1787, *William and Mary Quarterly* 45 (1988): 4.

18. Ibid., 4.

19. Ibid., 12.

20. Forrest McDonald, *Novus Ordo Seclorum* (Lawrence: University Press of Kansas, 1985): viii.

21. J. G. A. Pocock, *Virtue, Commerce, and History: Essays on Political Thought and History, Chiefly in the Eighteenth Century*, (Cambridge, Eng.: Cambridge University Press, 1985), 8–10, 13, 58; see his earlier, even more questionable assertion: "Men cannot do what they have no means of saying they have done; and what they do must in part be what they can say and conceive that it is, in "Virtue and Commerce in the Eighteenth Century, *Journal of Interdisciplin"ary History* 3 (1972): 122.

22. James T. Kloppenburg, "The Virtues of Liberalism: Christianity, Republicanism and Ethics in Early American Political Discourse," *The Journal of American History* 74 (1987): 9–33.

23. Kramnick, "Discourse of Politics," 32.

24. Louis Hartz, *The Liberal Tradition in America*, 2nd ed. (New York: Harcourt, Brace, Jovanovich, 1991), 101.

25. Diggins, *Lost Soul*, 105. See his "methodological appendix" for a more detailed critique of the ideology school.

26. For a characterization of "logical types" and the explanatory and logical conundra that result from their conflation, see Gregory Bateson, *Mind and Nature: A Necessary Unity* (New York: Dutton, 1979), esp. 122–35.

27. See H. Mark Roelofs, "The American Polity: A Systematic Ambiguity," *Review of Politics* 48 (1986) 344–45 where he points out that "Pocock's focus, like that of his authorities, Chiefly Bailyn . . . and Wood . . . is on the rhetoric of pamphleteers, and not on the detailed provisions of the federal constitu-

tion of 1787 or the practical political processes which emanated from its inauguration."

28. See Pocock, "Virtue and Commerce," 134 , where in a most revealing comment he states: "To a newcomer [himself] during the 1960's, the American psyche, if not the governing structure, suggested less a nation of pragmatic Lockeans than one of tormented saints. The clamor of jeremiads, sick jokes, and enquiries as to what became of the dream at times became deafening and obsessive. And it seemed evident that the eighteenth-century quarrel between virtue and commerce, citizen and government, republic and empire was still going on in the twentieth century, and that historiography and political philosophy were still much involved in it."

29. Alasdair MacIntyre, *After Virtue* (South Bend, Ind.: Notre Dame University Press, 1984), esp. 262–63.

30. See, e.g., Don Herzog, "Some Questions for Republicans," *Political Theory* 14 (1986): 473–93.

31. J. G. A. Pocock, *Virtue, Commerce and History*, 7–8.

32. J. G. A. Pocock, *Politics, Language, Time: Essays on Political Thought and History* (New York: Atheneum, 1971), 23 ff.

33. Ibid.

34. Anthony Giddens, *New Rules of Sociological Method* (London: Hutchinson, 1976), 158.

35. On the historicality of understanding, there is a good brief discussion in Richard E. Palmer, *Hermeneutics: Interpretation Theory in Schleiermacher, Dilthey, Heidegger and Gadamer* (Evanston, Ill.: Northwestern University Press, 1969), 176 ff; for a recent overview of developments and debates within philosophical hermeneutics, see Brice R. Wachterhauser, ed., *Hermeneutics and Modern Philosophy* (Albany: State University of New York Press, 1986).

36. Diggins, *Lost Soul*, 10.

37. See Daniel T. Rodgers, "Republicanism: The Career of a Concept," *The Journal of American History* 79 (1992): 16, where he suggests that *The Machiavellian Moment's* difficulty "was so notorious that few actually scaled it. . . . Most American historians . . . confined themselves to the book's last chapter, and still more . . . stuck with Pocock's earlier essay 'Virtue and Commerce.'" Rodgers distinguishes between the "Harvard Republicanism" of Bailyn and Wood and the "St. Louis Republicanism" of Pocock, Murrin, Banning and McCoy. Finally, he states, "Pocock, whose American chapter was second-order reinterpretation of others' research, had scarcely read any primary sources in American history at all," 24. Pocock, of course, modifies Wood's position, seeing the Constitution not as a movement toward liberalism but rather as a continuation of the civic humanist tradition where the framers attempted to save the republic from decay and corruption by means of a carefully crafted constitution and widespread civic virtue, *Machiavellian Moment*, 546).

38. Louis Hartz, *The Founding of New Societies* (New York: Harcourt, Brace, and World, 1964).

39. Gad Horowitz, *Canadian Labour in Politics* (Toronto: University of Toronto Press, 1968), 4.

40. Louis Hartz, *New Societies*, 3, 9. Building on de Tocqueville's astute observation in *Democracy in America* that "born equal" America did not have "to endure a democratic revolution," Hartz insists that his theory of American political-cultural development is a dual-factor analysis of social dynamics: "the absence of feudalism and the presence of the liberal idea." See Hartz, *Liberal Tradition*, 20.

41. Hartz, *New Societies*, 7. Hartz's theory can account for the presence of a viable socialist movement in Canada and the absence of a similar one in the United States. See Gad Horowitz, "Notes on Conservatism, Liberalism and Socialism in Canada," *Canadian Journal of Political Science* 11 (1978), and his *Canadian Labour*.

42. Gordon S. Wood, *The Radicalism of the American Revolution* (New York: Alfred A. Knopf, 1992), 6.

43. Hartz, *New Societies*, 44.

44. See Benjamin R. Barber, *Jihad versus McWorld* (New York: Time Books, 1995).

45. Diggins, *Lost Soul*, 5.

46. See Richard K. Matthews, *If Men Were Angles: James Madison and the Heartless Empire of Reason* (Lawrence: University Press of Kansas, 1995), 238.

47. For a fuller exploration of these models as well as others in the history of modern political theory, see Asher Horowitz and Gad Horowitz, *"Everywhere They are in Chains": Political Theory from Rousseau to Marx* (Toronto: University of Toronto Press, 1988). Perhaps Sandel, *Democracy's Discontent*, could now be added to the list; see 5–6.

48. Gordon Wood, *The Creation of the American Republic, 1776–1787* (Chapel Hill: University of North Carolina Press, 1969).

49. See, e.g., Pocock, *Politics*, 86.

50. Pocock, *Machiavellian Moment*, 526.

51. Ibid., 525.

52. Ibid., 526.

53. One thinks here of John Adams's platonism, as well as the current followers of Leo Strauss.

54. Pocock, *Machiavellian Moment*, 516.

55. Ibid., 523.

56. Ibid.

57. Ibid., 524–25.

58. See A. Horowitz, *Rousseau, Nature, and History* (Toronto: University of Toronto Press, 1987).

9

"WHAT AN ALARMING CRISIS IS THIS?":
EARLY AMERICAN WOMEN AND THEIR HISTORIES

Carol R. Berkin

A RICH, REMARKABLE, AND CHALLENGING literature in American women's history has developed over the past twenty-five years. Many of us can remember a time when no such history existed at all. American history was the history of dead, white, middle-aged, middle-class men, and it was written primarily by living, white, middle-aged, middle-class men. Suddenly, however – sometime around the mid-1960s – women (primarily white and middle class, we must confess) began to appear on the historical scene, causing both excitement and consternation within the profession. To some, the flow of the narrative saga of presidents, reformers, generals and "action heroes" was disturbing.

This new attention to women's history, like other areas of social history, began in that rare moment of confluence between politics writ large – the civil rights movement, the antiwar movement, the rise of the New Left, and the rebirth of the feminist movement – and the small politics of the academy, where the expansion of higher education led to new faces in our graduate schools, including working class and minority men and women. These new students looked into the past and sought their own image there; and because many were activists or intellectually committed radicals, the questions they asked were most often about power, social status, and the divisions of labor among the classes and between the genders and the races. In seeking answers to such questions, these scholars proved highly resourceful, adapting tools from other disciplines such as anthropology, linguistics, sociology, and archeology. They also learned to apply quantitative methods and models to the indirect sources through which the voices of the "inarticulate," could be heard, sources such as court records, wills, census data, and plantation ledgers. Many of these scholars conceptualized their work in Marxist, neo-Marxist, or structuralist terms, or found concepts such as "agency" and "cultural hegemony" to be valuable keys to understanding the relationships between the powerful social groups and their own subjects of study. The legacy of these decades of experimentation and exploration are fields familiar to us all: African American and women's history, gay and lesbian studies, and the study of the working classes and their cultures.

Women's history, like its companion fields in social history, has survived the shifts in political winds since the 1960s. The depth and breadth of our field can be measured by familiar academic yardsticks: library shelves groaning under the weight of monographs, collections of essays, reprints of articles, syntheses and the records of heated interpretive debates; conference programs devoted to various specialized aspects of women's history; advanced degrees in women's history, prestigious fellowships, endowed chairs occupied by scholars who specialize in a field once considered a quixotic enterprise. In fact, women's history has endured long enough to have its own history – and those of us inclined to look back see patterns of interpretation, modes of argument, favored methodologies, and misguided enterprises and missed opportunities.[1] This essay will focus on three main symptoms of what I call the "alarming crisis" in early American women's history: the first is an obsession with a myth; the second is a fear of illegitimacy; and the third is a fatal attraction to gender.

In the earliest years in the evolution of women's history little was written about seventeenth- and eighteenth-century American women. Scholars seemed content to accept the arguments of Elizabeth Dexter, Richard Morris, and Mary Beard that the colonial era was a "golden age" for white women, (centuries when demography and necessity combined to produce a paradise of opportunity for women of every region and social class.[2] With more men than women among the immigrants, marriage-minded females, especially in the southern colonies, had their choice of husbands. With a Puritan religion that endorsed companionship as the strongest matrimonial bond, New England women enjoyed satisfying lives as matrons. And, with labor shortages and pioneer conditions, older more rigid sexual divisions of labor broke down, giving women the chance to become printers and shopkeepers, blacksmiths and tavernkeepers in communities that

welcomed their expertise or talents. Most importantly, farm wives in
every colony provided visible, tangible contributions to the survival
and prosperity of the family business. These contributions earned
them the respect and appreciation of their husbands. In the spartan
world of agricultural America, where women's work was as back-
breaking as men's, a rough equality between the sexes was believed to
have emerged. This edenic existence came to an end only when
industrializing America separated home and work, productive labor
and reproductive labor, and created a dependent and socially inferior
condition for women of the modern era. It was this process of declension, or fall from grace, that captured the imagination of the earliest
generation of women's historians who were, after all, interested in
how the inequalities of their own lifetimes had come to be. It was
useful for them to believe – and to argue – that the economic, political
and social inequities legitimated as "natural" in the twentieth century had historical origins, and that before industrialization, a different
and more desirable set of gender relations had been a reality. Colonial
women's experience was critically important – but only as an untested
myth.

Although the main focus in women's history was the analysis of
mid-nineteenth-century circumstances, there were some who had
trained in early American history and wanted to turn their attention to
colonial women. Not surprisingly, it was comforting to enter the
archives with a preformulated question as a guide. Thus "was there a
golden age?" was an appealing place to begin. However, this serviceable starting point proved to be tenuous. The "golden girl" of the
colonial era was nothing more than a straw woman that was to be
rescued and given a real life. The result was that a poorly framed
question rode us rather that we it. It galloped away with us, leading us
down paths that seemed promising but have ultimately proven to be
dead ends. In fact, long after nineteenth-century historians abandoned the golden age model and the simplistic, mechanistic model of
the "transition to capitalism" as well, we continue to be seduced by
both.[3]

Much of the work that clusters around the conundrum of the
golden age is excellent and inventive; in fact, all of it is revelatory and
informative to some measure. Even casual readers of women's history
are probably familiar with Lois Carr and Lorena Walsh's "The Planters

Wife," Mary Beth Norton's *Liberty's Daughters*, Joan Wilson's "Illusion of Change," and the elegantly written works of Laurel Ulrich.[4] What has emerged, however, is an intracolonialist battle between supporters of the notion of advantaged colonial women and their critics who stand the argument on its head, claiming a greater oppression of women in the seventeenth and eighteenth centuries than in industrialized America. Either way, this question of the relative position of colonial and modern women reappears, causing us to repeatedly select and organize our evidence in such a way as to continue the "golden age" debate.

Yet when we step back from this debate, we must be struck by its many methodological problems. It seems fundamental to ask: what conditions or circumstances are being compared? What variables are being measured, and how? By what standards do we determine, for example, if legal rights are more significant than psychological self-esteem? Are we measuring values? Norms? Affective responses? Material realities? Have we established a scale of measurement for "better" and "worse?" Who are the women we are comparing across the centuries? From what social class, region, age group, or race do they come?

Even if we were to identify, carefully separate out, and comparatively analyze the strands we wish to consider (for example, looking at legal proscriptions or ideological prescriptions, comparing the variety of economic participation or the degrees of economic authority and autonomy), there would still remain a deep fallacy in such a procedure for historians. For, as historians, we know that none of these strands can be isolated in the reconstruction and interpretation of human experience. We know that it is the interrelationships among them in a given time and place that gives them meaning. Long before deconstructionists made such a discovery, historians recognized that context is all. The obsession with the golden age negates, or at the very least, obscures, the contextualization of women's experiences in both the colonial eras and in the centuries that followed.

Unfortunately, women's historians are no longer content to compare the nineteenth century with the eighteenth. We have made the debate an intramural sport, with the colonial Chesapeake and New England vying for the golden crown. Thus, a sizable segment of our scholarship since the 1980s asks: were seventeenth century

Chesapeake women better off than New England women?[5] In the issues this literature raises, we can see how heavily its authors must rely on a subjective value system to determine "better" and "worse."

Consider, for example, the critically important choice of a marriage partner. In the early Chesapeake, as Walsh and Carr and Darrett and Anita Rutman have shown us, single women had great discretion in selecting a husband, because there were neither parents nor family members to consult or obey. In New England a young women's living parents were participants in this selection process. How shall we measure the relative advantage of either circumstance? Not by the longevity of the marriage, for neither society had liberal divorce laws. Mortality figures were skewed between the regions so that "till death us do part" meant only seven years in the South, but perhaps forty years in the northern colonies. Nor can we rely on some qualitative evidence of marital happiness in a society that defined marriage in economic and reproductive terms rather than romantic ones. A moment's reflection on this literature will show that the value given to "free choice" or to "a little help from your family and friends" is doubly subjective, since the yardstick by which we measure the results are likely to be the presentist values of individualism and self-fulfillment, which are inappropriate to these seventeenth-century brides.[6]

In another, example, Southern scholars interpret the fact that Chesapeake husbands left their widows greater control over their estates as an indictor of higher esteem for women of this region than women in New England. But, perhaps, as Laurel Ulrich argued in *Good Wives* and Lisa Wilson restates in her study of Pennsylvania widows, *Life after Death*, the assumption of male duties in widowhood were seen as a burden rather than as an opportunity to exercise independent judgment or bask in higher esteem. Despite the most meticulous mustering of evidence on each side, interpretations continue to be shaped by the historian's subjective hierarchy of values.[7]

It is my hope that this debate, in all its forms, will disappear. "Better or worse" is at best a primitive tool of the historian's craft. Its opportunity costs are high; such comparison obscures the more important need to explore difference, variation, and shared experience in particular circumstances of time and space. Rather, historians should work to delineate the different configurations of women's lives within colonial society – configurations formed by the intersection of race, region, age, ethnicity, the dominant modes of production, and social class. Such work is underway, but we are a long way from the crucial recovery of this complexity of lives. History tells us nothing more, and sometimes frustratingly less, than what we choose to ask of it. If we focus on the task of recovery and reconstruction of the process by which sexual and racial divisions of labor, religious ideology and church structure, demographic realities and material exigencies, legal prescriptions and legal praxis, accidents and intentional events shape the experiences of the women we study, we will at least be asking the type of questions historians need to ask.

Another characteristic these efforts to develop women's history have is the search for legitimacy. Central to this second topic is the debate over the impact of the American Revolution on women's lives and of republican ideology on American gender ideals. The debate has two parts, a descriptive and an analytical one, although the lines often blur. Let me dispose of the simpler, descriptive one first, if for no other reason than it provides a few humorous moments in a scholarly discussion.

We could begin with Elizabeth Ellet's three volumes on *The Women of the American Revolution*, published before the Civil War, a collection that combined innocent hagiography with a genteel exhortation to remember the influence good mothers have upon great sons. Almost a century later, in 1947, Elizabeth Cometti published a more scholarly article describing the activities of women during the war years – activities ranging from the organization of boycotts and spinning bees before the war and fundraising drives and knitting sessions after it began, to operating farms and businesses in the absence of husbands and fathers, serving as spies and couriers, campfollowers (both the honorable and the dishonorable sort), and even as soldiers on the battlefield.[8] Both of these works were largely forgotten – if they were ever widely read by the new generation of women's historians – and their subjects consigned to the historical wastelands until the approach of the bicentennial generated a virtual cottage industry on the heroines of the Revolution, and tales from the distaff side. Bookshelves filled with volumes that strung together first person accounts of life in a home-front revolution and minibiographies of women of daring-do. There was even speculation by one author that patriot women had larger breasts than those unfortunate female Loyalists. Generally the tone of these books was amazement that, in the midst of a long home-front struggle, women had not been comatose or analytically passive, but had registered that "something was going on" and thus joined History – for a moment at least. When the smoke cleared and the celebration of the bicentennial had ended, colonial women's historians could see that these books and articles had made a contribution after all: we knew, in excruciating detail, what women had done during the war.

The second, and decidedly more important analytic literature, focused upon a new gender ideology for women termed Republican Motherhood. It began with the publication in 1974 of Linda Kerber's "Daughters of Columbia: Educating Women of the Republic, 1787–1805." It reached its peak in 1980 with the simultaneous publications of Kerber's *Women of the Republic* and Mary Beth Norton's *Liberty's Daughters*, and Nancy Cott's *The Bonds of Womanhood* the following year. It took on new life – and a surprising interpretive twist – in 1987 with the publication of Jan Lewis's article on "The Republic Wife." This scholarship argued that a sea change in gender ideals had occurred between 1750 and 1815. It was not a change in what roles women performed, but a shift in the importance attached to them. Thus motherhood and the socialization of the next generation into the virtues of republican life came to be valorized, while housewifery – the repertoire of productive household skills – lost its primacy in the hierarchy of womanly duties and responsibilities.[9]

What had caused this change? Norton and Kerber both implicated the Revolution. Norton argued that the legacy of women's participation in the war was a changed consciousness for women, a politicization that outlived the war itself and, in the years of the early republic, was harnessed to serve the interests of the new nation. Republican motherhood, endorsed by educators and nationalist opinion makers of both sexes, offered women less than full political equality, but increased political recognition. As the educators of citizens, women were encouraged to see themselves as political actors in the new nation, patriots without portfolios. Norton acknowledged that republican motherhood fell far short of political equality. Yet she saw, particularly in the rise of educational opportunities for women, a trajectory toward nineteenth-century feminism and the campaign for suffrage.

Kerber argued also for the impact of revolutionary participation in politicizing women. She was less sanguine than Norton about the net gains made in the aftermath of the revolution, noting the failure of legal reform and the price women paid for their enthronement as "patriot mothers." While men were testing the potential benefits of bourgeois individualism, Kerber observed, their wives were being asked to sacrifice self on the alter of family and state. Lewis's Hitch-cockian twist – that the new ideology did not emphasize mothering, but the wifely mission to insure a husband's continuing public and private virtue – did not alter the central point of this literature: that the Revolution had decisively revised gender ideals. The literature carried a warning as well. No account of the Revolution could be considered complete unless the role of women in the war and the impact of the war on the role of women was considered.

To a great degree, however, the scholarship on women, revolution, and republicanism illustrates a problem common to the writing on most marginalized historical subjects. It is the problem of legitimacy; of establishing a subject's claim to the attention of the discipline. One strategy, conscious or unconscious, is to join your subject to a major mainstream historiographical issue, to argue that your subject, too, played a critical role in an event or movement generally acknowledged as important, or to insist that the full effects of that event or movement cannot be measured without reference to its impact on your own subject. What better choice of such an aegis in early American history than the American Revolution? The lustre of the Revolution, it was clearly hoped, would rub off on these marginal women, much as the sign "George Washington Slept Here" is assumed to make a country inn or small town lodging house worthy of a reservation.

I do not mean to argue that this is a base or ignoble motivation, nor do I want to argue that the choice of the role of women in the Revolution or the impact of republican ideology on women's lives is an artificially generated interest. Many of us – Norton, Kerber, myself, for instance – were trained in and wrote our early books on the Revolution and the early republic. We come to this topic honestly. Nor do I mean to argue that there is no legitimacy to the study of the relationship of women to so cataclysmic a pair of events as the Revolution and the creation of an independent nation. But the quest for legitimacy has blinded these women's historians to critical, still unanswered, questions.

First, have we firmly established the causal relationship between the revolution, its republican ideology, and several significant changes in women's roles, status, and gender proscriptions? Or have we over-valued the role of the revolution, overemphasized the changes we described, or failed to assess the role of other factors in prompting these and other changes? How have we measured the impact of the Revolution? Where have we found evidence of it in the material circumstances of women's lives? For whom was republican motherhood a reality as much as a prescription? Michael Foucault argues that the defining issue for historians is "how things happen." In our desire to make our study of the women of the eighteenth century significant, my generation of scholars may have compromised our duty to pursue this question wherever it may lead us.

Fortunately, this does not seem to be the case with younger historians of the eighteenth century. For example, in 1994 a Cornell graduate student challenged the intimate relationship between the Revolution and the women of the new Republic.[10] Her research into the lives of a group of elite New York women suggests that they framed the moral instruction of their daughters in traditional, pre-revolutionary religious terms rather than in the language of republicanism. In addition, they had almost no role in the education and socialization of their sons, and little role in providing more formal education to children of either sex. Her tentative conclusions are that the Revolution was – in and of itself – not so absolute a break with older traditions and self-perceptions. She argues that these older traditions proved adaptable and persistent and that we must look to other social and material forces and factors, not simply ideological ones, to understand women's lives after the revolution.

The changes in gender prescriptions we observe owe much to the development of a bourgeois social class in America, an uneven process spanning many decades before and after the revolution, and that the impact of the war lay in its politicizing many aspects of class relations and gender relations that might otherwise have remained private or broadly cultural. But the current crisis in eighteenth-century women's history is not a competition of interpretations, but rather a need to let go of the Revolution as our route to legitimacy, and pursue women's experiences – their context and causes – wherever we find them. The demographic expert, Robert Wells, once had the temerity to say that the revolution had little impact on the great social changes that marked the transition from premodern to modern American society. We could not hear him then, but we must certainly consider propositions like his now.

The final aspect of today's "alarming crisis" in early American women's history I want to discuss is our fatal attraction to gender. I am not challenging the importance of gender as a critical variable in understanding the experiences and actions of women or men in the past. Nor am I challenging the importance of studying women as the primary focus of our scholarly research, reconstructing their lives and the world as they perceived it and shaped it. But I do reject the notion that we can understand these women, or reconstruct their lives, if we view them through the prism of gender alone. No more than class or race, gender cannot stand majestically alone as the critical variable in a human life, nor can we place it always at the pinnacle of some pyramid of variables. Earlier I dealt with context and the contextualization of our historical subjects in terms of space and time. Yet the same principle surely holds true when we think about that constellation of variables – most particularly race, class, region, age – that create the context in which gender acquires its many meanings. The costs are high if we continue to isolate gender, and women, from the society around them and to deny them the complexity that arises from the process of overdetermination.

Difficult as it may be, we must resist that causal hierarchy that makes gender the necessary and sufficient variable in explaining women's lives. Elizabeth Fox-Genovese's *Within the Plantation Household* offered a good example of the benefits gained when a scholar refuses to privilege gender, or isolate it from, race and class. Fox-Genovese insisted that gender is *situational*; that it is formed and reformed in a context, and thus the women she studied were never just women. They were slave women, old women, young women, white plantation mistresses, or members of the yeoman class. And, when Sarah Hughes addressed the overdetermination in women's lives in her excellent article, "Slaves for Hire: The Allocation of Black Labor in Elizabeth

City County Virginia," she was able to show us one of its exquisite ironies: by hiring out a slave woman, and thus separating her from her family and friends, a white widow was often able to hold her own family together. Here, race cuts across, or rather enfolds, gender, and permits one set of women to conform to gender roles and forces another to adapt to their denial.[11]

If we insist on privileging gender, we run many risks, among them the risk of essentialism. And even in some of our best works, the dangers of the effort to find fundamental, universally shared attributes and experiences that weave all women into a pattern so general that the critical differences in their experience were lost. All colonial white women did, it is true, do domestic work. But we must consider what is lost as much as what is gained by linking the gentility – defining needlework of the urban bourgeois class with the productive labors of housewifery in a yeoman household. The risk also appears in the temptation to allow a small group of women to speak for others, to elevate the voices we have found into the representative female voice of the era. A scholar like Laurel Ulrich performed herculean efforts when she searched the written records, read the traces of female life in material culture, and clues to a woman's life in the memories and memorabilia of her husband or father or son. But the excitement of finding similar remnants in the lives of a few women does not justify the construction of a universal colonial New England woman, held together with a gender glue that strains out social class and race. We cannot know the meaning of these similarities if we have no clear sense of the differences that cut across them. Jean Soderland addressed such a risk in "Women in Eighteenth-Century Pennsylvania: Toward a Model of Diversity," a provocative essay that challenged the carved-in-marble models of the colonial New England woman or her Chesapeake counterpart.[12] The problem with these models is not simply their validity, but that they bring false closure to our inquiries rather than spurring us to find greater complexities.

Historians of women are correct to demand that students of class and of race consider the gendered meanings of both. But it is also essential that we reciprocate. Our literature is depressingly bereft of works that examine closely how class and race and even region shape gender ideals and women's personal identities. As a result, our portraits are often one-dimensional, our narratives capture only partial stories, and our analyses are incomplete. The subject we are exploring is complex; the artificial isolation of gender only deludes us into thinking otherwise.

Notes

1. Many historians have explored the roots and the historiographical development of modern scholarship in American women's history. See, for example, Gerda Lerner, "Placing Women in History: Definitions and Challenges," *Feminist Studies* 3 (1975): 5–14, which was reprinted in Gerda Lerner, *The Majority Finds Its Past: Placing Women in History* (New York: Oxford University Press, 1979); Elizabeth Fox-Genovese, "Placing Women's History in History," *New Left Review* 13 (1982) 5–29; Nancy Hewett, "Beyond the Search for Sisterhood: American Women's History in the 1980's," *Social History* 10 (1985): 299–321; Myra Jehlen, "Patrolling the Borders: Feminist Historiography and the New Historicism," *Radical History Review* 43 (1989): 31–37; Linda Kerber, "Separate Spheres, Female Worlds, Woman's Place: The Rhetoric of Women's History," *Journal of American History* 75 (1988): 9–39; Carroll Smith-Rosenberg, "The New Woman and the New History," *Feminist Studies* 3 (1975): 185–98; Carol Berkin, "Clio in Search of Her Daughters/Women in Search of Their Past," *Liberal Education* (1985): 205–15.

2. Elizabeth Anthony Dexter, *Colonial Women of Affairs* (Boston: Houghton Mifflin, 1931) and *Career Women of America 1776–1840* (Francestown, N.H.: M. Jones & Co.,1950); Richard B. Morris, *Studies in the History of American Law* (Philadelphia: J. M. Mitchell Co., 1959): 126–200; Mary Beard, *Woman as Force in History: A Study in Traditions and Realities* (New York: Macmillan Co., 1946).

3. For the best discussion of this "myth of the golden age," see Mary Beth Norton, "The Myth of the Golden Age," in *Women of America: A History*, eds., Carol Berkin and Mary Beth Norton (Boston: Houghton and Mifflin, 1979): 37–47.

4. Lois Green Carr and Lorena Walsh, "The Planter's Wife: The Experience of White Women in Seventeenth Century Maryland," *William and Mary Quarterly* 34 (1977): 542–71; Mary Beth Norton, *Liberty's Daughters: The Revolutionary Experience of American Women, 1750–1800* (Boston: Little Brown, 1980); Joan Hoff Wilson, "The Illusion of Change: Women and the American Revolution," in *The American Revolution: Explorations in the History of American Radicalism*, ed., Alfred Young (DeKalb: Northern Illinois University, 1976); Laurel Thatcher Ulrich, *Good Wives: Image and Reality in the Lives of Women in Northern New England, 1650–1750* (New York: Alfred A. Knopf, 1982); and *A*

Midwife's Tale: The Life of Martha Ballard, Based on Her Diary, 1785–1812 (New York: Alfred A. Knopf, 1991). See also, Lyle Koehler, *A Search for Power: The Weaker Sex in Seventeenth Century New England* (Urbana: University of Illinois Press, 1980) and Mary Beth Norton, *Founding Mothers and Fathers: Gendered Power and the Forming of American Society* (New York: Alfred A. Knopf, 1996).

5. For a discussion of the historiography of the relative advantages and disadvantages of New England and Chesapeake Bay area women, see Mary Beth Norton, "The Evolution of White Women's Experience in Early America," *American Historical Review* 89 (1984): 593–619.

6. Carr and Walsh, "The Planter's Wife"; Lorena Walsh, "'Til Death Us Do Part': Marriage and the Family in 17th Century Maryland" in *The Chesapeake in the Seventeenth Century: Essays on Anglo-American Society*, eds., Thad Tate and David Ammerman (Chapel Hill: University of North Carolina Press, 1980); Darrett and Anita Ruttman, "'Now – Wives and Sons-in-Law': Parental Death in a 17th Century Virginia County," in *Seventeenth Century*, eds., Tate and Ammerman, 153–82.

7. Ulrich, *Good Wives*; Lisa Wilson, *Life After Death: Widows in Pennsylvania, 1750–1850* (Philadelphia, Pa.: Temple University Press, 1992).

8. Elizabeth Ellet, *The Women of the American Revolution*, 3 vols. (New York: Baker and Scribner, 1848–50); Elizabeth Cometti, "Women in the American Revolution," *New England Quarterly* 20 (1947) 329–46. For the discussion of female anatomy and political loyalties, see Philip Young, *Revolutionary Ladies* (New York: Alfred A. Knopf, 1977). For other representative work on women's participation in the American Revolution, see Elizabeth Evans, *Weathering the Storm: Women of the American Revolution* (New York: Scribner, 1975); Sally S. Booth, *The Women of '76* (New York: Hastings House, 1973); Paul Engle, *Women in the American Revolution* (Chicago: Follett, 1976). For an earlier discussion of these popular works, see Carol Berkin, "Remembering the Ladies," in *The American Revolution: Changing Perspectives*, eds., William Fowler, Jr. and Wallace Coyle (Boston, Mass.: Northeastern University Press, 1979).

9. Linda Kerber, "Daughters of Columbia: Educating Women for the Republic, 1787–1805," in *The Hofstadter Aegis: A Memorial*, eds., Stanley Elkins and Eric McKitrick (New York: Alfred A. Knopf, 1974); Kerber, "The Republican Mother: Women and the Enlightenment – An American Perspective," *American Quarterly* 28 (1976): 187–205; Kerber, *Woman of the Republic: Intellect and Ideology in Revolutionary America* (Chapel Hill: University of North Carolina Press, 1980); Kerber, *Toward an Intellectual History of Women* (Chapel Hill: University of North Carolina Press, 1997); Mary Beth Norton, *Liberty's Daughters*; Nancy Cott, *The Bonds of Womanhood: 'Woman's Sphere' in New England, 1780– 1835* (New Haven, Conn.: Yale University Press, 1977); Jan Lewis, "The Republican Wife: Virtue and Seduction in the Early Republic," *William and Mary Quarterly* 44 (1987): 687–721. See also Mary Beth Norton, "Eighteenth Century American Women in Peace and War: The Case of the

Loyalists," *William and Mary Quarterly* 33 (1976): 386–409, and Ruth Bloch, "The Gendered Meanings of Virtue in Revolutionary America," *Signs* 13 (1987): 37–59. For an earlier discussion of literature on gender roles and the Revolution, see Carol Berkin, "Remembering the Ladies."

10. Leslie Horowitz, "Reappraising Republican Motherhood: Protestant Values in Children's Literature in the 18th Century," essay presented at the annual meeting of the Organization of American Historians, 1994.

11. Elizabeth Fox-Genovese, *Within the Plantation Household: Black and White Women of the Old South* (Chapel Hill: University of North Carolina Press, 1988); Sara Hughes, "'Slaves for Hire': The Allocation of Black Labor in Elizabeth City Country, Virginia," *William and Mary Quarterly*, 35 (1978): 260–86.

12. Jean Soderlund, "Women in Eighteenth-Century Pennsylvania: Toward a Model of Diversity," *Pennsylvania Magazine of History and Biography* 115 (1991): 163–83. See also Carol Berkin, *First Generations: Women in Colonial America* (New York: Hill and Wang, 1996).

10

NATIVE AMERICAN HISTORY:
PERSPECTIVES ON THE EIGHTEENTH CENTURY

Daniel K. Richter

THE PAST TWENTY YEARS have produced a revolution in professional historical scholarship on interactions between the Native communities of eastern North America and colonizers from Europe. Indian peoples once seen merely as part of a wilderness environment that White pioneers had to subdue or as archetypes for James Fenimore Cooper-like tales of the forest have come alive in a flourishing interdisciplinary literature. But an almost equally flourishing literature laments that these findings have made little impact on broader circles of professional scholarship – much less on historical understanding in the culture as a whole. Although in recent years history textbooks have been revised to give Native Americans – along with other traditionally silenced groups – a more prominent place, the basic story remains little changed: America's drama began with Columbus, and Indians played roles as, at best, victims in a European morality play. As a result, the "master narrative" of colonial America that most people carry in their heads either maintains a Eurocentric orientation or develops romanticized visions of a native Arcadia destroyed by evil Europeans sweeping westward.[1]

As James Hijiya, William Cronon, and other scholars have suggested, perhaps the problems lie deeper than questions about what we include in our story of the past, about the way we tell that story, or about whose voices we listen to in the telling. Instead, they argue, the master narrative itself needs to be recast in a way that allows Indians to be something more than adjuncts, foils, or critics of an essentially Euro-American tale. One fruitful approach suggested by several recent efforts to imagine such a narrative is to begin with a basic set of questions regarding what, or who, "American" history is about. If, as traditionally has seemed the case, "American History" is a teleological tale of the rise of a nation-state from European roots, then Native Americans really are *not* part of the narrative except as outsiders. If, however, we conceive of North America as a *place* where diverse peoples have lived and struggled rather than a nation-state in the process of being born, a very different tale becomes possible.[2]

Even from such a shifted perspective, however, the eighteenth century seems problematic ground for an inclusive narrative. After 1700, North America can no longer be described as a place of "encounters" between New Worlds and Old; it had long ceased to be a "new world" for anybody. Patterns appear to us to be set, as a dreary tale of European advance and Indian retreat plods steadily ahead. How then, do we tell a Native *American* story for the eighteenth century?

We might begin by briefly surveying other available narratives about the eighteenth century. For our culture as a whole, the master narrative apparently remains one in which the eighteenth century – or at least the first two thirds of it – hardly exists: English colonists jumped off the boat in 1607 or 1620, killed a few Indians and invited some others to Thanksgiving Dinner, hanged some pesky witches, and then waited around for Independence to happen. Even more serious popular treatments of the colonial period tend to give the first two thirds of the eighteenth century short shrift – if for no other reason than its apparently appalling boringness in contrast to the dramas of the 1620s and 1770s. Tourists, after all, flock to Colonial Williamsburg in search of George Washington and Patrick Henry, not Alexander Spotswood and William Byrd II.[3]

All that said, professional historians – who have never been noted for their fear of boring topics – *have* polished a coherent narrative of the development of eighteenth-century British America. The story turns out to be anything but boring. According to what I understand to be the current scholarly narrative, the eighteenth century opened, not in 1701, but in 1689, with the American counterparts to the Glorious Revolution and the beginning of the first of two imperial wars in which great powers struggled for control of the lands, trade, and riches of eastern North America. By the time those wars came to an end with the Treaty of Utrecht in 1713, a generation of conflict had established a balance of diplomatic, political, and economic forces that made possible the thirty-odd years of the "Long Peace," the apparently uneventful "provincial" period that so readily escapes popular notice.[4]

In this historians' narrative of eighteenth-century North America, the Long Peace is characterized by three broad themes. The first is economic prosperity – uneven, cyclical, and unequally distributed, but prosperity nonetheless, and prosperity that was largely a function of the multitude of ways that the eighteenth-century North American provinces became integrated into transatlantic trading networks. The eighteenth-century British empire was, observes T. H. Breen, "An Empire of Goods," and its North American subjects experienced their prosperity in the form of a "consumer revolution."[5]

If the first theme of British North American history during the Long Peace is that consumer revolution, the second is the political stability of the eighteenth-century provinces, as marked by their elaborated governmental institutions and self-assured political elites. "By the middle of the century," Jack Greene concludes, "there existed in virtually every colony authoritative ruling groups with great social and economic power, extensive political experience, confidence in their capacity to govern, and broad public support."[6]

The third theme centers on a growing, mobile, and ethnically and religiously diverse population. From midcentury, a quickened pace of immigration – particularly by people from the German principalities and the borderlands of North Britain and Ireland – accentuated that theme.[7] So too did the successive waves of religious enthusiasm (deeply rooted in the German and Scotch-Irish communities) later called the "Great Awakening."[8] These trends placed increasing strains upon the stability characteristic of the Long Peace, at just the historical point when the underpinnings of that stability were irrevocably disrupted by the all-too-thorough British victory in the Seven Years' War. The result was that colossal historical accident we call the American Revolution, which involved not just a "war for independence" but a period of profound social and cultural change historians encapsulate by the much overused term "republicanism."[9]

This, then, summarizes a (although certainly not the) current scholarly narrative of British North America in the eighteenth century: an initial cycle of international warfare that set the terms for a period of stability marked by a consumer revolution, political equilibrium, and an ethnically and religiously diversifying population; a collapse of that stability during a renewed midcentury round of imperial warfare that led unpredictably into a revolutionary period of social and cultural change. The remainder of this essay suggests that the Native experience in eastern North America was profoundly a part of this same narrative – or, rather, that the British and Indian tales were parallel chapters in a single eighteenth-century *American* story.

The centrality of Native Americans to turn of the eighteenth-century military conflicts should be self-evident; these have not traditionally been called the "French and Indian wars" for nothing. Yet, as we shift our perspective to tell a story about a continent and its peoples rather than about a single nation-state and its evolution, three points come into focus. The first reveals why many historians no longer use the term "French and Indian wars" and why that phrase should be banished from our historiographical vocabulary. Once we adopt a continental perspective, the literal inaccuracy (not to mention the Anglo-centricity) of the phrase becomes clear: far from pitting the English against the French and the Indians, these wars involved grand alliances of the several English colonies with their diverse Indian allies against the French of both New France and Louisiana with *their* various Indian allies, and the Spanish of Florida and *their* assorted Indian allies.[10]

This complex continental picture becomes even more complicated as a second aspect of the turn of the eighteenth-century wars comes into focus: these conflicts were an integral part of the struggle among three European powers for control, not just of North America, but of the transatlantic world. The English colonists themselves recognized the external nature of the imperial dimension of these conflicts when they used terms like "King William's" and "Queen Anne's" wars to describe them. Similarly, some historians have taken to using the European names for these conflicts (the War of the League of Augsburg and the War of the Spanish Succession, respectively) to place them in a broader imperial framework.[11]

But those terms won't do either, because of a third aspect of the turn of the century wars that comes into view once we adopt a North American continental perspective. As we examine the reasons for Native American involvement as allies on all sides in imperial struggles

for control of the continent, the *European* nature of the wars themselves shrinks in significance. These were, after all, North *American*
wars that grew from longstanding inter-Indian and Indian-colonial
rivalries and conflicts; they were every bit as much a matter of Native
Americans involving European allies in Indian conflicts as they were of
Europeans involving Native Americans in theirs. From this perspective, then, in the Great Lakes region, the War of the League of
Augsburg might well be seen as the climactic episode in an ongoing
struggle between the Five Nations Iroquois and their Algonquian-
speaking rivals to the north and west; the English were pulled into
that conflict as allies of the former, the French as allies of the latter.[12]
The struggle came to an effective end not with the Peace of Ryswick
in 1697, but with the so-called "Grand Settlement" treaties at Albany
and Montreal in 1701. This French-brokered peace among the Native
peoples of the Great Lakes region made the War of the Spanish Succession (like, for that matter, the War of the Austrian Succession in
the 1740s) a virtual nonevent in that theater.[13]

It was quite a different story in Northern New England, where
the imperial wars of the 1690s through 1710s might better be seen as
a continuation of struggles stretching back at least to Metacom's
("King Philip's") War of the 1670s. Western and Eastern Abenaki
refugees from that conflict resettled in Roman Catholic mission villages in the St. Lawrence River valley and used the War of the League
of Augsburg to pull both French and Native allies into an ongoing
quarrel with the New Englanders that would continue well beyond
the War of the Spanish Succession into the conflict variously known as
"Dummer's" or "Rale's" war of the mid-1720s. Less than two decades
later, the violence would begin anew in what Europeans called "the
War of the Austrian Succession."[14]

In the southeastern portion of the continent, a shifted perspective
on the wars of the 1690s through 1710s reveals a similar story of
European imperial powers being pulled into complex rivalries among
various Indian groups and English, Spanish, and French colonists.
There again war and peace refused to conform to European calendars
and diplomatic arrangements. As the War of the Spanish Succession
was winding down in Europe, in the Carolinas, conflicts among Indian
groups and their English, Spanish, and French allies came to a head in
the Tuscarora War of 1711–13 and the Yamasee War of 1715–16. When

those bloody struggles were over, the map of the Southeast, and the diplomatic and economic connections among its surviving Indian and Euro-American peoples, had been massively rearranged. So, for that matter, had the map of Indian North America from the Appalachians to the Mississippi and the Great Lakes to the Ohio.[15]

If, then, our narrative of the eighteenth century opens with a cycle of warfare from the 1690s through the mid-1710s, the significance of those wars to the narrative becomes more, not less, important as we shift our perspective to the continental rather than the teleological. But the nature of the narrative also begins to mutate as we look at events in this way; the difficulties we have in even figuring out what to call the conflicts are perhaps the best indicators of that. "French and Indian Wars," "Imperial Wars," "Intercolonial Wars," "Wars of Obscure European Leagues and Successions," or "Wars Belonging to English Monarchs" all fail to capture the texture of what was happening on the dynamic ground of North America as the complicated rivalries between and among dozens of Native peoples and nearly a score of European colonies intersected with the rivalries of European monarchs, merchants, and armies. Similarly, skipping ahead to a later chapter in our narrative, the label for a later installment favored by Lawrence Henry Gipson, "the Great War for the Empire," similarly fails us. So, too, does something as seemingly neutral as "Seven Years' War," when we speak of an event that, in North America, lasted *nine* years before the Peace of Paris and then, hardly skipping a beat, continued in the decentralized events we usually call "Pontiac's War." That episode in turn might be seen as the first of a series of "Indian wars for independence" that would not be over until the 1810s.[16]

Whatever we call these wars, however, they remain an important part of our narrative of the eighteenth century. Equally important is the long hiatus in those wars between the late 1710s and the mid-1750s. In the vast swathe of Indian North America from the Great Lakes to the Gulf of Mexico, small-scale skirmishing persisted and the occasional more major flare-up occurred, but the same Long Peace that figures so prominently in our narrative of eighteenth-century British North America prevailed in the continental interior as well. And, during that Long Peace, if we shift our perspective just a bit, we can find very similar economic, political, and demographic trends occurring on both sides of a frontier that might not seem quite so impermeable as we once thought.

"The Original great tye between the Indians and Europeans was Mutual conveniency," British Indian Agent John Stuart wrote to the Board of Trade in 1761. "This alone could at first have induced the Indians to receive white people differing so much from themselves into their country." But, Stuart continued, "a modern Indian cannot subsist without Europeans; And would handle a Flint Ax or any other rude utinsil used by his ancestors very awkwardly; So that what was only Conveniency at first in now become Necessity and the Original tye Strengthened."[17] The list of necessities and conveniences that tied Native Americans into the eighteenth-century trans-Atlantic commercial world was extensive indeed. As Swedish naturalist Peter Kalm observed on his travels through Indian country at mid- century, Indians relied on trade with Europe and Europeans for items as diverse as weapons and ammunition; woollen textiles used for men's cloaks and women's skirts; linen shirts for men and shifts for women; strips of wool to be used as leggings; vermilion and verdigris for body and face painting; knives, hatchets, needles, scissors, and flint; brass kettles; earrings; mirrors and burning glasses; glass beads; brass wire and steel; liquor; tobacco; wampum (which in the eighteenth century was mostly turned out in Albany workshops).[18] In short, apart from food and shelter, virtually every aspect of Indian material life in eastern North America seems to have been dependent upon economic ties with Europe. When one considers the role that European tools and weapons also played in agriculture, hunting, and building construction, Stuart's conclusion that "a modern Indian cannot subsist without Europeans" seems all the more apt. Eighteenth-century Indians, then, were just as much a part of the "Empire of Goods" as were eighteenth-century Euro-Americans; indeed, as James Axtell notes, Native Americans experienced the full effects of a consumer revolution before most British Americans did.[19]

As consumers, however, "modern Indians" very much remained "Indians," who used imported goods in ways deeply rooted in their own, rather than European cultures; they were no more "decultur- ated" or turned into Europeans by the process than are twentieth- century North Americans made Japanese by their purchase of Sony televisions. In fact, it is more accurate – and more revealing of the complex interconnections among eighteenth-century Native and Euro-American histories – to describe the imports, not as *European* goods, but as "Indian goods" made in Europe to suit Native tastes. The highly specialized commodities designed specifically for Indian markets included the varieties of heavy woolen cloth known as "duffels," made in present-day Belgium, and "strouds" or "strowd-waters," manufactured in Gloucestershire. Inexperienced Euro-American traders soon learned that, if duffels or strouds were not cut to precisely the right size and died in the appropriate shades of deep blue, dark red, or steel gray, the items were virtually unsalable. Similarly precise specifications applied to glass beads (for which fashions in size, shape, and color changed so precisely with the times that archaeologists find them the most reliable date markers for Native American sites); to the wampum cranked out in eighteenth-century Albany workshops; to brass kettles and iron axes (each of which was made to lighter and simpler specifications for Indian customers); and to muskets, which at Indian insistence were to be extremely light-weight and equipped with advanced flintlock mechanisms.[20]

If the specifications of such artifacts – along with the cumulative effect seen in any number of surviving portraits and engravings depicting eighteenth-century Native people wearing and using them – reveal the complex ways in which Indians integrated themselves into the transatlantic "Empire of Goods" without losing their distinct cultural identity, so too does the way the acquisition and use of those goods fit into traditional patterns of reciprocity and exchange. The limited degree to which capitalist assumptions about property and accumulation had penetrated early eighteenth-century Native societies is illustrated by the comments of a group of Iroquois head-men on their way to the markets of Philadelphia in 1736. According to Pennsylvania interpreter Conrad Weiser, the Native leaders were worried that their people would simply walk off with the unattended possessions of merchants in the big city. "Those that have been in Philadelphia tell us [that] your goods lie alone . . . upon the Street about the Shops . . . ," the Iroquois said. "We desire that it may be Kept in house while we are There [so that] it may be Seen for all when the shop is open. We will be very Careful." After the Iroquois reached the banks of the Schuylkill they explained "that amongst them there is never any Victuals sold, the Indians give to each other freely what they can spare." When Philadelphians charged them for food, therefore, the Iroquois were deeply offended that hosts "should take Money of this Score."[21]

Such traditional economic patterns came under tremendous stress, of course, in the mid- to late eighteenth century. There is considerable evidence that, in many parts of eighteenth-century Indian North America, distinct class lines were beginning to emerge between those with greater access to consumer goods (many of whom tended to be *métis*, or "mixed-bloods") and those without. These and other troubling cultural implications of Native dependence on European trade provide a crucial backdrop for the preaching of such charismatic religious figures as the "Delaware prophet" Neolin in the 1760s, the Seneca visionary Handsome Lake at the turn of the nineteenth century, and the Muskogee (Creek) "Red Stick" leader Hillis Hadjo (Josiah Francis) in the 1810s. In various ways, each preached a ceremonial and symbolic purgation of European material goods that had corrupted Native life, and did so through a vision of pan-Indian political unity and independence.[22] For all their cultural distinctiveness, however, such developments only entrench Native people more firmly in a broader narrative of eighteenth-century North American history in which British Americans were plagued by increasing disparities of wealth, poverty, and class, troubled by the apparent contradictions between republican virtue and capitalist acquisition, and prone to use agreements not to import British goods as assertions of moral worth and mechanisms of intercolonial unity.[23]

In the transatlantic economy, Indians were producers as well as consumers. What we often call the "fur trade" was a complex system in which Native peoples functioned as a labor force producing a variety of commodities for European markets. Just *how* complex and historically dynamic the Indian side of the trade could be is illustrated by Kathryn Holland Braund's recent study of the way in which the Muskogees shrewdly exploited the changing demands of eighteenth-century European markets. In the mid-1680s, they provided their new South Carolina trading partners with horses stolen from Spanish Florida and slaves captured from the Muskogees' Native enemies. Then, just as the chaos of the Yamasee War (1715–16) threw connections with Carolina into disarray, a series of bovine epidemics struck continental Europe, creating a huge market among English leather workers for North American deerskins. The Muskogees – controlling territories that, largely due to their own slave-raiding expeditions, were largely depopulated of humans but now thronged with white-tailed deer – were ideally placed to profit from that de-mand. And so were the South Carolina merchants who, in the mid- 1730s, made the new town of Augusta, Georgia, "the heart of a vast trading system that stretched from the manufacturing and commercial centers of the British Isles to Charleston, South Carolina, and, via Augusta, to" the Muskogee country and beyond. By midcentury, per-haps a million deerskins a year – half of them harvested by Musko-gees – moved through the system.[24]

Whether Native peoples produced deerskins, beaver furs, or slaves for European markets, the changing role of Indian producers in the eighteenth-century empire of goods is perhaps more important than their role as consumers in helping us to appreciate the dilemmas of their Indian economic dependence. Furs and hides were, of course, raw materials; their processing into more valuable finished products such as felt hats or leather goods took place in Europe. There, and in the counting houses of a string of merchant middlemen, profits and capital accumulated, while Indians merely consumed and produced. The resulting lopsided character of the economic relationship was captured well by an Iroquois spokesman in 1740. The New York trad-ing post at Oswego "is a vast advantage . . . , because we can get there what we want or desire," he told provincial Governor George Clarke. "But we think Brother, that your people who trade there have the most advantage by it, and that it is as good for them as a Silver mine."[25]

Silver mine or no, however, posts such as Oswego or Augusta – and the intercultural trade that they represented and that was so vital to Native Americans – were of steadily declining economic significance to Euro-Americans in the mid-eighteenth century. In the 1730s, while the deerskin trade boomed, prices of beaver and other furs plum-meted on oversupplied European markets, with devastating impacts on the northern Native peoples who relied on the trade. More important, even after the market for furs revived in the 1740s, the Indian trade was becoming less important for the increasingly diversified economies of the British North American colonies as each year went by. Studies of the New York and Pennsylvania economies, for instance, estimate that, while absolute exports of furs and hides fluctuated around a steady average, their relative significance declined steadily from the 1720s to the 1740s, when exports of the two commodities began a rapid absolute decline. In deliveries to London markets alone, New York's furs and hides slipped from approximately 40 percent of the total in the 1720s to less than 25 percent in the 1740s; Pennsylvania's declined over the same period from 50 to 44 percent. Both statistics are highly misleading, for they do not take into account the massive exports of grain to the West Indies and elsewhere that were becoming the economic mainstays of the two provinces. New France defied the pattern; its fur exports grew in relative importance as those of the British provinces declined, but only because diplomatic and strategic, rather than economic, considerations primarily motivated its largely government-controlled Indian trade. Thus, there too, Native peoples were losing the political clout that comes from economic power.[26]

The struggle to maintain some of that political clout brings us at last to the second theme in our narrative of eighteenth-century North America during the Long Peace: the stabilization of political systems. In a world of increasing economic dependence and declining economic fortunes, Native communities depended on sophisticated leadership able to secure maneuvering room for their people. Politically as well as culturally, eighteenth-century Native America was a very diverse place, but within that diversity – at least for the area east of the Mississippi River and west of the Appalachian Mountains – three structural elements maintained stability during the Long Peace.

The first and most fundamental was recognized in the 1750s by New York Indian affairs secretary Peter Wraxall: "To preserve the Ballance between us and the French," he observed, "is the great ruling Principle of the Modern Indian Politics."[27] The great swath of territory between the Great Lakes and the Gulf of Mexico was dominated by seven regional population clusters that acted more or less as coherent political units. Each was geographically well positioned for, and politically well adept at, some form of "the Modern Indian politics" of balancing ties to one European colony off against another. South of Lake Ontario, the Six Nations of the Iroquois

League counterbalanced their primary economic and diplomatic ties
to British New York with well-cultivated connections to Pennsylvania
and – most threatening to Wraxall and other New York leaders – New
France. To the west of Iroquoia, among the loose grouping of Wyan-
dots, Ottawas, Miamis and others whose intermingled villages com-
prised the territory known as the *pays d'en haut*, the equation was
reversed, with primary ties to New France counterbalanced by trade
with New York through Oswego.[28] In the "Ohio Country," multiethnic
villages of Shawnees, Delawares, and emigrants from Iroquoia were
strategically placed to trade with New France and Virginia, as well as
with their main suppliers from Pennsylvania.[29] Similarly, in the Southeast, Cherokees and Catawbas independently dealt with both Virginia
and South Carolina; Muskogees balanced their primary ties to English
Carolina with connections to French Louisiana and the potential of
closer relations to Spanish Florida; and Choctaws, Chickasaws, Louis-
ianians, and Carolinians engaged in an intricate four-way balancing
act.[30]

In every case, the "modern Indian politics" eluded the worst consequences of economic dependence on Europeans by maintaining ties
with bitter colonial rivals who dared not let trading partners who were
also potential military allies go over entirely to the other side. Yet the
extent to which balance-of-power diplomacy was a coherent strategy
pursued by far-seeing Native leaders should not be overstated. In the
previous paragraph, the awkward phrase describing "seven regional
population clusters that acted more or less as coherent political units"
was chosen carefully, for the second structural element in the mature
eighteenth-century politics of Indian eastern North America was an
extraordinarily complicated pattern of factionalism, localism, and decentralized leadership. Muskogees were divided between Upper and
Lower Towns, "Mixed Bloods" and "Full Bloods"; Ohio Country and
Great Lakes Indians by a host of conflicting ethnic and village
loyalties; Iroquois by rivalries among anglophiles, francophiles, and
neutralists that cut across lines of clan, village, and nation. In a
paradoxical way, it was precisely this *lack* of centralized political unity
that made the "modern Indian politics" work: *factional* leaders
independently cultivated ties to particular European colonies; the
cumulative results were the multiple connections that warded off

political as well as economic dependence on powerful European neighbors.[31]

A third structural characteristic of eighteenth-century Indian politics kept factionalism and localism from spinning out of control, while providing a general cross-cultural framework within which the intricate balances of power in eastern North America could be mediated. This was the nearly universal system of diplomatic procedures that anthropologist William Fenton has labeled "Forest Diplomacy." Throughout eastern North America in the eighteenth century, the grand public spectacles that were Indian treaty conferences conformed to a set of procedural rules that – while bi- or multi-cultural in origin – were fundamentally rooted in Indian political patterns that stressed ceremonial consensus, ritualized oratory, broadly based participation, and reciprocal exchanges of goods – not least among the latter the wampum belts that circulated ubiquitously in that diplomatic world.[32] This pan-Indian culture of diplomacy provides a structural parallel to the influences of English common law, parliamentary procedures, and Royal government that, on a deep level, were drawing the eighteenth-century British colonies into a shared, Anglicized imperial universe. And the culture of intercultural diplomacy provided – especially through the royal governors who participated in both systems – an overarching political framework for all eastern North Americans in the early eighteenth century.[33]

The pan-Indian dimension of the culture of intercultural diplomacy points to a final theme in our narrative of North America during the Long Peace: ethnic diversity. Much of what I have already said about the seven population clusters that dominated the map of eighteenth-century Indian eastern North America suggests the ethnic and linguistic complexity of those configurations. It needs further to be stressed, however, that *all* of the eighteenth-century groups we neatly tag with labels such as "Creek," or "Cherokee," or "Mohawk" were relatively new social forms that were the product of as much as two centuries of depopulation by European diseases, of warfare (whether with Europeans or, more often, among Native American rivals), and of migrations and resettlements. During the seventeenth century, for example, the Five Nations Iroquois adopted thousands of Indian war captives to replenish their losses from disease; in the process, they depopulated much of the region surrounding their homeland and became a biological minority within their own villages, where adoptees substantially outnumbered the native-born in the 1660s. The eighteenth-century Iroquois League was a melting pot of people whose ancestors came from throughout the Northeast.[34] Similarly – in ways archaeologists are still attempting to sort out – Cherokees, Muskogees, Chickasaws, and Choctaws were reconfigurations of remnant populations from the great Mississippian chiefdoms whose cities and temple mounds had dominated the region in the sixteenth century.[35] And the Ohio Country and *pays d'en haut* were populated almost entirely by refugee groups whose original homes were elsewhere; the latter region was, in historian Richard White's phrase, "a world made of fragments."[36] And so, too, was all of Indian eastern North America in the eighteenth century, for east of the Appalachians as well – in the Catawba country of the Carolina Piedmont, on small reservations in Virginia, in the surviving "praying towns" of New England, or in the Roman Catholic *reserves* of the St. Lawrence Valley – people of diverse inheritance (including African and European) mingled in what James Merrell aptly calls "the Indians' New World."[37]

Thus, eighteenth-century Indians – perhaps even *more* than eighteenth-century Euro-Americans – were an ethnically diverse and geographically mobile lot. Moreover, those communities of Indians were caught up in something much like the successive waves of religious fervor known in British America as "The Great Awakening." In some cases, the link with the world of George Whitefield and Jonathan Edwards was direct – Congregationalist mission villages such as Stockbridge in Massachusetts and later New York, and the Moravian settlements that originated near Bethlehem, Pennsylvania, and ultimately relocated to present-day Ohio and then Ontario embraced pietistic Protestantism as part of the new identity their mixed populations were in the process of creating.[38] In others cases, religious enthusiasm involved more the kind of interesting parallel – or rather participation in the same broad process – we have seen with British America in politics and economics. As Gregory Dowd has shown, from Neolin, the "Delaware prophet" of the period of "Pontiac's War," through Tenskwatawa, the "Shawnee prophet" of the early nineteenth century, the ethnically mixed communities of the Ohio Country and Great Lakes region were repeatedly swept by religious revivals of profound political significance. Joel Martin's work on the Red Stick movement among early nineteenth-century Muskogees finds a similar process at work in the Southeast.[39]

The prophetic message in all these cases was not just spiritual renewal but pan-Indianism, an effort to unite diverse Native peoples in the period of what was, after all, a series of wars for *Indian* independence that – not entirely coincidentally – happened to coincide with a Euro-American War for Independence that also sought to unite formerly fractious groups. For both wars of independence, the Seven Years' War (or whatever we choose to call it) was the crucial opening act, because it profoundly disrupted the diplomatic, political, and economic arrangements that had undergirded the stability of the eighteenth-century's Long Peace. With Great Britain as the sole imperial power, the modern Indian politics of balance became as obsolete as did Salutary Neglect in the British Empire.[40]

Finally, if the Seven Years' War sent Euro-Americans spinning off not just into a war for independence but into an unprecedented period of social and cultural change, so it did too for Native North Americans. That Indians lost *their* wars for independence – and that the social and cultural equivalents of republicanism evident in such phenomena as the evolution of the Cherokee nation in the early nineteenth century culminated in the forced removal of most of the Native population to west of the Mississippi – does not make the Native experience any less a central part of the narrative we historians spin about the long eighteenth century.[41] If anything, the tragic outcome only brings the Indian story more clearly into focus as the *American* story it is.

Notes

1. Frederick E. Hoxie, *The Indians Versus the Textbooks: Is There Any Way Out?* D'Arcy McNickle Center for the History of the American Indian Occasional Papers in Curriculum Series, no. 1 (Chicago: Newberry Library, 1984); James Axtell, "Europeans, Indians, and the Age of Discovery in American History Textbooks," *American Historical Review* 17 (1987): 621–32; David E. Stannard, "The Invisible People of Early American History," *American Quarterly* 39 (1987), 649–55; James H. Merrell, "Some Thoughts on Colonial Historians and American Indians," *William and Mary Quarterly* 3d ser., 46 (1989): 96;

Daniel K. Richter, "Whose Indian History?" *William and Mary Quarterly* 50 (1993): 379–93. The term "master narrative" is borrowed from Nathan Irvin Huggins, "The Deforming Mirror of Truth," in *Black Odyssey: The African-American Ordeal in Slavery*, reissued ed. (New York: Vintage Books, 1990), xi–lvii, quotation from xiii.

2. James Axtell, "A North American Perspective for Colonial History," *History Teacher* 12 (1979): 549–62; T. H. Breen, "Creative Adaptations: Peoples and Cultures," in *Colonial British America: Essays in the New History of the Early Modern Era*, eds., Jack P. Greene and J. R. Pole (Baltimore: The Johns Hopkins University Press, 1984), 195–232; William Cronon, "A Place for Stories: Nature, History, and Narrative," *Journal of American History* 78 (1991–92): 1347–76; James A. Hijiya, "Why the West Is Lost," *William and Mary Quarterly* 51 (1992): 276–92.

3. Notably, even in so ambitious an attempt to revision the American historical narrative as Ronald Takaki, *A Different Mirror: A History of Multi-cultural America* (Boston: Little Brown & Co., 1993), Native Americans almost completely disappear for the century and a half between the Pequot War and the era of Thomas Jefferson.

4. For varying perspectives on the significance of political and military developments at the turn of the eighteenth century, see, among many other works, David S. Lovejoy, *The Glorious Revolution in America* (New York: Harper & Row, 1972); T. H. Breen, "A Changing Labor Force and Race Relations in Virginia, 1660–1710," *Journal of Social History* 7 (1973–74): 3–25; Richard R. Johnson, *Adjustment to Empire: The New England Colonies, 1675–1715* (New Brunswick, N.J.: Rutgers University Press, 1981); J. M. Sosin, *English America and the Revolution of 1688: Rural Administration and the Structure of Provincial Government* (Lincoln: University of Nebraska Press, 1982); and Jack P. Greene, *Peripheries and Center: Constitutional Development in the Extended Polities of the British Empire and the United States, 1607–1788* (Athens: University of Georgia Press, 1986), 7–76.

5. T. H. Breen, "An Empire of Goods: The Anglicization of Colonial America, 1690–1776," *Journal of British Studies* 25 (1986): 467–99; John J. McCusker and Russell R. Menard, *The Economy of British America, 1607–1789* (Chapel Hill: University of North Carolina Press, 1985), esp. 277–94; Jack P. Greene, *Pursuits of Happiness: the Social Development of Early Modern British Colonies and the Formation of American Culture* (Chapel Hill: University of North Carolina Press, 1988), 170–206; Carole Shammas, *The PreIndustrial Consumer in England and America* (Oxford, Eng.: Clarendon Press, 1990).

6. Jack P. Greene, "An Uneasy Connection: An Analysis of the Preconditions of the American Revolution," in *Essays on the American Revolution*, eds., Stephen G. Kurtz and James H. Hutson (Chapel Hill: University of North Carolina Press, 1973), 32–80, quotation from p. 36; John M. Murrin,

"Political Development," in *Colonial British America*, eds., Greene and Pole, 408–56.

7. Bernard Bailyn, *The Peopling of British North America: An Introduction* (New York: Alfred A. Knopf, 1986); David Hackett Fischer, *Albion's Seed: Four British Folkways in America* (New York: Oxford University Press, 1989), 605–32; A. G. Roeber, "'The Origin of Whatever Is Not English among Us': The Dutch-Speaking and the German-Speaking Peoples of Colonial British America," in *Strangers within the Realm*, eds. Bernard Bailyn and Philip D. Morgan (Chapel Hill: University of North Carolina Press, 1991), 220–83; Maldwyn A. Jones, "The Scotch-Irish in British America," in *Strangers within the Realm*, eds. Baylin and Morgan, 284–313.

8. Alan Heimert, *Religion and the American Mind from the Great Awakening to the Revolution* (Cambridge, Mass.: Harvard University Press, 1966); Ruth Bloch, *Visionary Republic: Millennial Themes in American Thought, 1756–1800* (Cambridge, Eng.: Cambridge University Press, 1985); Patricia U. Bonomi, *Under the Cope of Heaven: Religion, Society, and Politics in Colonial America* (New York: Oxford University Press, 1986), 131–216; Sally Schwartz, *"A Mixed Multitude": The Struggle for Toleration in Colonial Pennsylvania* (New York: New York University Press, 1987), 120–58; Marilyn J. Westerkamp, *The Triumph of the Laity: Scots-Irish Piety and the Great Awakening, 1625–1760* (New York: Oxford University Press, 1988).

9. Among the countless works on these subjects, imaginative efforts to connect the Revolution to the economic, political, demographic, and religious themes stressed here include Gary B. Nash, *The Urban Crucible: Social Change, Political Consciousness, and the Origins of the American Revolution* (Cambridge, Mass.: Harvard University Press, 1979); Rhys Isaac, *The Transformation of Virginia, 1740–1790* (Chapel Hill: University of North Carolina Press, 1982); Fred Anderson, *A People's Army: Massachusetts Soldiers and Society in the Seven Year's War* (Chapel Hill: University of North Carolina Press, 1984); and Gordon S. Wood, *The Radicalism of the American Revolution* (New York: Alfred A. Knopf, 1992).

10. James Axtell, *After Columbus: Essays in the Ethnohistory of Colonial North America* (New York: Oxford University Press, 1988), 43.

11. W. A. Speck, "The International and Imperial Context," in *Colonial British America*, eds. Greene and Pole, 384–407, esp. 399–401; Francis Jennings, *The Ambiguous Iroquois Empire: The Covenant Chain Confederation of Indian Tribes with English Colonies from Its Beginnings to the Lancaster Treaty of 1744* (New York: W. W. Norton, 1984). Though now in many ways conceptually dated, the best general introduction to the eighteenth-century imperial conflicts remains Howard H. Peckham, *The Colonial Wars, 1689–1762* (Chicago: University of Chicago Press, 1964).

12. Allen Forbes, Jr., "Two and a Half Centuries of Conflict: The Iroquois and the Laurentian Wars," *Pennsylvania Archaeologist* 40 (1970): 1– 20; Daniel

K. Richter, *The Ordeal of the Longhouse: The Peoples of the Iroquois League in the Era of European Colonization* (Chapel Hill: University of North Carolina Press, 1992), 133–89.

13. Anthony F. C. Wallace, "Origins of Iroquois Neutrality: The Grand Settlement of 1701," *Pennsylvania History* 24 (1957): 223–35; Yves Zoltvany, "New France and the West, 1701–1713," *Canadian Historical Review* 46 (1965): 301–22; Richter, *Ordeal of the Longhouse*, 190–235.

14. Kenneth M. Morrison, *The Embattled Northeast: The Elusive Ideal of Alliance in Abenaki-Euramerican Relations* (Berkeley: University of California Press, 1984); Colin G. Calloway, *The Western Abenakis of Vermont, 1600–1800: War, Migration, and the Survival of an Indian People* (Norman: University of Oklahoma, 1990); Evan Haefell and Kevin Sweeney, "Revisiting *The Redeemed Captive*: New Perspectives on the 1704 Attack on Deerfield," *William and Mary Quarterly* 52 (1995): 3–46.

15. Peter H. Wood, "The Changing Population of the Colonial South: An Overview by Race and Region, 1685–1790," in *Powhatan's Mantle: Indians in the Colonial Southeast*, eds. Wood, Gregory A. Waselkov, and M. Thomas Harley (Lincoln: University of Nebraska, 1989), 34–103; James H. Merrell, *The Indians' New World: Catawbas and Their Neighbors from European Contact through the Era of Removal* (Chapel Hill: University of North Carolina Press, 1989), 92–133; Kathryn E. Holland Braund, *Deerskins and Duffels: Creek Indian Trade with Anglo-America, 1685–1815* (Lincoln: University of Nebraska Press, 1993), 26–39.

16. Francis Jennings, "The Indians' Revolution," in *The American Revolution: Explorations in the History of American Radicalism*, ed. Alfred F. Young (DeKalb: Northern Illinois University Press, 1976), 319–48; *Empire of Fortune: Crowns, Colonies, and Tribes in the Seven Years War in America* (New York: New York University Press, 1988); James H. Merrell, "Declarations of Independence: Indian-White Relations in the New Nation," in *The American Revolution: Its Character and Limits*, ed. Jack P. Greene (New York: New York University Press, 1987), 197–223; Gregory Evans Dowd, *A Spirited Resistance: The North American Indian Struggle for Unity, 1745–1815* (Baltimore: The Johns Hopkins University Press, 1992).

17. Quoted in Braund, *Deerskins and Duffels*, 26, 30.

18. Adolph B. Benson, ed., *The America of 1750: Peter Kalm's Travels in North America* (New York: Wilson Erickson, Inc., 1937), 2, 518–21. On wampum production see E. S. Peña, "Wampum Production in New Netherland and Colonial New York: the Historical and Archaeological Context" (Ph.D. diss., Boston University, 1990).

19. James Axtell, *Beyond 1492: Encounters in Colonial North America* (New York: Oxford University Press, 1992), 125–51.

20. George I. Quimby, *Indian Culture and European Trade Goods: The Archaeology of the Historic Period in the Western Great Lakes Region* (Madison:

University of Wisconsin Press, 1966), 63–80; Francis Jennings, *The Invasion of America: Indians, Colonialism, and the Cant of Conquest* (Chapel Hill: University of North Carolina Press, 1975), 97–104; Arthur J. Ray, "Indians as Consumers in the Eighteenth Century," in *Old Trails and New Directions: Papers of the Third North American Fur Trade Conference*, eds., Carol Judd and Arthur J. Ray (Toronto: University of Toronto Press, 1980), 255–71; James H. Merrell, "'Our Bond of Peace': Patterns of Intercultural Exchange in the Carolina Piedmont," in *Powhatan's Mantel*, eds.,Wood, Waselkov, and Harley, 196–222. It needs to be stressed in this context that, when "trade axes" broke the first time they were used or "trade muskets" blew up in their native owners' faces, the problem was not necessarily or even primarily that unscrupulous traders were pawning off cheap junk on unsuspecting Indians. In both cases, the customers' demand for inexpensive, lightweight, easily portable items stretched the technological capabilities of European manufacturers to their limits. There was a good reason why, to be reliable, the thick-barreled standard issue British army "Brown Bess" musket had to weight more than twice as much as a remarkably thin-barreled trade musket.

21. Conrad Weiser to James Logan, 16 Sept. 1736, LP, X, 62 (1st quotation, spelling modernized); *A Treaty of Friendship Held with the Chiefs of the Six Nations, at Philadelphia in September and October, 1736* (Philadelphia: B. Franklin, 1737), 13 (2d quotation).

22. J. Leitch Wright, *The Only Land They Knew: The Tragic Story of the American Indians in the Old South* (New York: Free Press, 1981), 172–73, 234–37; David B. Guldenzopf, "The Colonial Transformation of Mohawk Iroquois Society" (Ph.D. diss., State University of New York at Albany, 1986); Joel W. Martin, *Sacred Revolt: the Muskogees' Struggle for a New World* (Boston: Beacon Press, 1991); Dowd, *Spirited Resistance*.

23. Axtell, *Beyond 1492*, 150–51; T. H. Breen, "Narratives of Commercial Life: Consumption, Ideology, and Community on the Eve of the American Revolution," *William and Mary Quarterly* 50 (1993): 471–501.

24. Braund, *Deerskins and Duffels*, 26–80, quotation from 43.

25. E. B. O'Callaghan and B. Fernow, eds., *Documents Relative to the Colonial History of the State of New York* (Albany: Fernow, Weed, Parsons & Co., 1853–87), vi, 177.

26. Albright G. Zimmerman, "The Indian Trade of Colonial Pennsylvania" (Ph.D. diss., University of Delaware, 1966), 463–64; Thomas Elliot Norton, *The Fur Trade in Colonial New York, 1686–1776* (Madison: University of Wisconsin Press 1974), 92–94, 101–2, 148–49, 221–23; Stephen H. Cutcliffe, "Colonial Indian Policy as a Measure of Rising Imperialism: New York and Pennsylvania, 1700–1755," *Western Pennsylvania Historical Magazine* 44 (1981): 240–44; W. J. Eccles, "The Fur Trade and Eighteenth-Century Imperialism," *William and Mary Quarterly* 40 (1983): 341–62; Richter, *Ordeal of the Longhouse*, 268–70, 384–85.

27. Peter Wraxall, *An Abridgment of the Indian Affairs Contained in Four Folio Volumes, Transacted in the Colony of New York, from the Year 1678 to the Year 1751*, ed. Charles Howard McIlwain (Cambridge, Mass.: Harvard University Press, 1915), 219n.

28. Richter, *Ordeal of the Longhouse*, 214–54; Richard White, *The Middle Ground: Indians, Empires, and Republics in the Great Lakes Region, 1650–1815* (Cambridge, Eng.: Cambridge University Press, 1991), 104–28.

29. Michael N. McConnell, *A Country Between: The Upper Ohio Valley and Its Peoples, 1724–1774* (Lincoln: University of Nebraska Press, 1992), esp. 35–60.

30. Merrell, *Indians' New World*, 134–66; Braund, *Deerskins and Duffels*, 35–39; Daniel H. Usner, Jr., *Indians, Settlers, and Slaves in a Frontier Exchange Economy: The Lower Mississippi Valley before 1783* (Chapel Hill: University of North Carolina Press, 1992), 77–104.

31. Robert F. Berkhofer, Jr., "The Political Context of a New Indian History," *Pacific Historical Review* 40 (1971): 357–82; Richard L. Haan, "Covenant and Consensus: Iroquois and English, 1676–1760," in *Beyond the Covenant Chain: The Iroquois and Their Neighbors in Indian North America, 1600–1800*, eds., Daniel K. Richter and James H. Merrell (Syracuse, N.Y.: Syracuse University Press, 1987), 41–57; Daniel K. Richter, "Cultural Brokers and Intercultural Politics: New York-Iroquois Relations, 1664–1701," *Journal of American History* 75 (1988): 40–67; Martin, *Sacred Revolt*, 81–84.

32. The best introduction to the culture of "forest diplomacy" is Francis Jennings, et al., eds., *The History and Culture of Iroquois Diplomacy: An Interdisciplinary Guide to the Treaties of the Six Nations and Their League* (Syracuse, N.Y.: Syracuse University Press, 1985), 3–124. For suggestive comments on the spread of intercultural diplomatic patterns from their northern origins southward, see Theda Perdue, "Cherokee Relations with the Iroquois in the Eighteenth Century," in *Beyond the Covenant Chain*, eds., Richter and Merrell, 135–49.

33. Dorothy B. Jones, *License for Empire: Colonialism by Treaty in Early America* (Chicago: University of Chicago Press, 1982), 1–92; Ian K. Steele, *The English Atlantic, 1675–1740: An Exploration of Communication and Community* (New York: Oxford University Press, 1986), 259.

34. Laurence M. Hauptman, "Refugee Havens: The Iroquois Villages of the Eighteenth Century," in *American Indian Environments: Ecological Issues in Native American History*, eds., Christopher Vecsey and Robert W. Venables (Syracuse, N.Y.: Syracuse University Press, 1980), 128–39; Richter, *Ordeal of the Longhouse*, 65–74.

35. Marvin T. Smith, "Aboriginal Population Movements in the Early Historic Period Interior Southeast," in *Powhatan's Mantel*, eds., Wood, Waselkov, and Harley, 21–34.

36. McConnell, *Country Between*, 5–20; White, *Middle Ground*, 1–49.

37. James H. Merrell, "The Indians' New World: The Catawba Experience," *William and Mary Quarterly* 41 (1984): 537–65; Frank W. Porter, ed., *Strategies for Survival: American Indians in the Eastern United States* (Westport, Conn.: Greenwood Press, 1986); James P. Ronda, "Generations of Faith: the Christian Indians of Martha's Vineyard," *William and Mary Quarterly* 38 (1981): 369–94; Axtell, *After Columbus*, 47–57; Gordon Day, *The Identity of the Saint Francis Indians*, National Museum of Man, Mercury Series, Canadian Ethnology Service Paper no. 71 (Ottawa: National Museums of Canada, 1981).

38. William Simmons, "The Great Awakening and Indian Conversion in Southern New England," in *Papers of the Tenth Algonquian Conference*, ed., William Cowan (Ottawa: Carleton University Press, 1979), 25–36; Patrick Fraser, *The Mohicans of Stockbridge* (Lincoln: University of Nebraska Press, 1992), 39–68; Harry L. Williams, "A Brief Survey of the Moravian Mission to the North American Indians," *Unitax Fratrum*, nos. 21–22 (1987): 29–35; David A Schattschnelder, "Moravians Approach the Indians: Theories an Realities," *Unitax Fratrum*, nos. 21–22 (1987): 37–45.

39. Dowd, *Spirited Resistance*; Martin, *Sacred Revolt*.

40. Barbara Graymont, *The Iroquois in the American Revolution* (Syracuse, N.Y.: Syracuse University Press, 1972); Colin G. Calloway, *Crown and Calumet: British-Indian Relations, 1783–1815* (Norman: University of Oklahoma Press, 1987); White, *Middle Ground*, 269–468.

41. Mary Young, "The Cherokee Nation: Mirror of the Republic," *American Quarterly* 33 (1981): 502–25.

11

SPAIN'S CONQUEST BY CONTRACT: PACIFICATION AND THE MISSION SYSTEM IN EASTERN NORTH AMERICA

Amy Turner Bushnell

PACIFICATION, Spain's policy for basing title to the Indies upon the consent of American Indians, represented an effort to break the universal bond between the extension of empire and acts of violence and coercion. In frontier areas, it led to the mission system, supported through a combination of royal subsidies and Indian labor. Underlying and giving structure to both policy and system was a kind of expanding covenant which can be called the "conquest by contract."[1] Together, they offer early modern historians of North America a Spanish model of Indian-European relations to add to the better known French and English ones.[2]

Those whose knowledge of Spain in America is limited to the period of discovery may find it hard to reconcile the looting, slave-hunting mentality of early sixteenth-century conquistadores with this relatively enlightened policy of the late sixteenth century, yet the two were closely related,[3] as Silvio Zavala, Joseph Höffner, and Lewis Hanke argued fifty years ago and as was thereafter shown in monographs about northern New Spain and Chile.[4] Pacification was forged in the crucible of the high conquest. In the words of James Muldoon,

> The Spanish, and only the Spanish, reflected at length on the morality or legality of what they were doing as they encountered the New World and its inhabitants. . . . The great official concern about the legitimacy of the conquest of the Americas and about the rights of the Indians who lived there provided a dominant theme for Spanish intellectual life in the sixteenth century.[5]

If Spain was precociously self-critical, it is equally true that, as Anthony Pagden has pointed out, "only Spain" was "able to carry out sustained and well-publicized conquests," only Spain established "an empire based upon people, defeated subjects who could be transformed into a pliant labour force," and, thanks to the discovery of huge deposits of gold and silver in Mexico and Peru and the importation of American specie, only Spain had the resources to finance at once European wars and American pacifications.[6]

The debate about the ethics of American conquest and conversion, sometimes referred to as "the rights of barbarians," progressed by stages which can be correlated to the three kinds of barbarians adventuring Spaniards encountered. The first were the island peoples of the Antilles, in the "great Gulf of the Ocean Sea" now called the Caribbean.[7] Next were the imperial peoples of the Mexican and Peruvian highlands. Last were the wild peoples found on the edges of the empire. Jurists and theologians in Spain and the Indies responded to news of discovery, chronicles of conquest, and reports of rapine by fashioning a series of rationales designed to reconcile at once their monarch's claim to hold *dominium* over most of America, their Church's claim to represent the one true faith, and their own growing sense of the rights of all men.

Their intellectual exertions produced four separate modes of legalizing title to the Indies: (1) Right of first claim, based upon discovery and sanctioned, in advance or afterward, by the pope. (2) Right of conquest, based upon the winning of a just war on pagan or schismatic enemies of Christ. (3) Right of guardianship, based upon the supposed incapacity or immaturity of the Indians themselves. (4) Right of lordship, based upon the consent of Indian leaders to become vassals of the king and permit conversions. This last, neofeudal mode came to be known as "pacification."

Meanwhile, four separate models of Indian-Spanish relations evolved in the Americas, each pursuing the logic of one or more of the modes of legalizing title. All but one of these was an adaptation of an earlier model of conquest and conversion derived either from the Christian kingdoms' expansion in Iberia at the expense of Muslim states or from Portuguese and Castilian ventures in West and North Africa and the Atlantic isles. Spain's conquest of the Guanche people of the Canary Islands provided a particularly fresh precedent.[8]

(1) The *Encomienda*, a system of settler wardship perfected in the Canaries, was imposed in the Antilles and extended to the imperial peoples of the American mainland. (2) Enslavement, a system for moving native labor by force from "wild" to settled areas, was likewise carried to the Antilles in the form practiced on the Guanches. (3) Indirect Rule, also known as the system of two republics, one of Spaniards and the other of Indians, had its origins in the *al dhimma*, a Muslim system for governing a tributary agricultural population through its own leaders and laws; Christian Spaniards adopted it during the Reconquest and applied it to subject populations in the Americas.[9] (4) The Mission, whose antecedents can be found in the twelfth- and thirteenth-century expansion of Latin Christendom into eastern Europe, used the Indians themselves to hold Spanish America's settler-poor frontiers.[10]

During the more than seventy years that it took for settlement to reach the relatively lightly populated regions north of New Spain, these four modes of legalizing title and four models of Indian-Spanish relations had ample time to develop and be tested. Although they appeared sequentially, they were not stages through which each Spanish American frontier could expect to pass. Which system or systems the Spanish would try in any particular place depended upon their assessment of the Indians to be found there, for what worked with one group did not necessarily work with another. As we shall see, in the captaincy general of Florida, a maritime periphery with little Spanish settlement and a hinterland of mission provinces, they tried them all.

Concepts of contract permeated all four modes by which Spain established title to the Indies and all four models of Indian-Spanish relations. During the period of exploration, European powers often took possession of *terra nullius*, or lands unclaimed by any Christian monarch. Planting a wooden cross, erecting a stone pillar, or incising a tree trunk, they paid as little attention to the native inhabitants as to forest creatures. In this discourse the intended recipients of the signs were not the watching Indians, but Europeans off the scene to whom the acts would be reported.[11] Christopher Columbus's recorded acts of possession-taking laid claim to islands that he represented as places without civilized habitation. Uninhabited, the islands were not. The manioc-producing Tainos of Hispaniola lived in large villages organized into paramount chiefdoms; their numbers had almost reached the Malthusian limits of their environment.[12]

Isabella welcomed the island peoples as new subjects, placing them on a par, not with Castilians, but with her Jewish and Muslim subjects who paid a personal headtax modeled on the Islamic *jizya*.[13] She commended them in groups to Castilian settlers called *encomenderos* for protection, religious instruction, and training in "good habits." More fitted to be wolves than shepherds, the encomenderos forced their charges to leave their plantings and pan for alluvial gold. The death rate that followed was shocking even by early modern standards. In 1511, the Dominican preacher Antonio de Montesinos condemned the settlers in two fiery sermons which stopped just short of challenging Spain's presence altogether.[14]

The Queen's ready acceptance of submissive Indians as tributary subjects had left her Castilian subjects without a source of slaves. This omission, she corrected in 1503 by authorizing the enslavement of Carib Indians, said to be "cannibals."[15] Ferdinand, ruling as regent after Isabella's death, called a council of canon and civil lawyers in the city of Burgos in 1512 to examine the legal issues involved in the American conquests. The council broke no new ground, but it did offer a loophole to those who hoped to solve their labor deficit with Indians who were less bellicose than the Caribs. A legal conquest, the lawyers informed the regent, was the result of a just war against pagan or schismatic enemies of the faith. Captives taken in a just war were a legitimate source of civil slaves. If the slavehunters confined their raids to regions as yet unclaimed and unsettled, they would not be preying upon the subjects of the Crown.

European Christians did not object to slavery on moral grounds. Many still believed that it was meaningless to speak of rights outside the congregation of the faithful, St. Augustine's City of God. The enslavement of Muslims and Slavs had been a feature of Iberian society for centuries. In the fourteenth and fifteenth centuries, Portugal's trading posts in Africa had introduced a new source of slaves who were either Muslims or animist pagans, and Spanish Christians purchased them without a qualm.[16] But how could people who had never heard, much less rejected, the preaching of the gospel be considered enemies of the faith? The jurist Juan López Palacios Rubios stepped forward with the *requerimiento*, or requirement, a protocol requiring those who heard it to accept the Castilian monarch as their sovereign, on the authority of the pope.[17] Rejecting these peace terms would shift the hearers out of the category of blameless barbarians into the category of bona fide enemies of Christ: persons who had heard the Word and rejected it. On them, it was argued, a Christian could wage a just, slave-taking war. Written in 1513, the requerimiento became law in 1526.[18]

The solution only raised new problems. In the words of Patricia Seed, the "core of the Requirement was an Islamic-inspired summons to submit to a superior religion" or "face a military attack." It was incompatible with the Christian tradition of just war.[19] Long experience with Jews and Muslims had shown that forcing persons to profess Christianity did not produce Christians. In 1535 and 1536, Alvar Núñez Cabeza de Vaca, with three other survivors of Pánfilo de Narváez's failed 1528 expedition to Florida, walked from Texas to the west coast and from there down to Mexico City. With his own eyes he saw the depopulation caused by Nuño de Guzmán's slave-hunting parties in the "conquest" of New Galicia. In Culiacán, where he witnessed a reading of the requerimiento, Cabeza de Vaca pleaded with the natives to return to their homes and successfully resettled those who promised to receive and befriend Christians. This early experiment in pacification he reported to the emperor in person and made available as a model with the publication of his *Relación* in 1542.[20]

A second problem with the requerimiento was that it was incompatible with early modern ideas of *monarchia*. By basing title to the Indies upon a papal donation, it lent support to the position that the pope possessed temporal authority over pagans who were not and never had been subject to any Christian prince. Iberian monarchs might turn to the pope to sanction their treaties, but they did not want their titles to rest on papal approval, nor did they wish to base them on the personal merits of the sovereign, for that way lay insurrection.[21] The works of the Scottish theologian John Mair, living in Paris, offered a way out of the dilemma of how Christians could rule over pagans: Aristotle's theory of natural slavery. Some men, low on the scale of humanity, required a master for their own good. Spain's title to the Indies could rest, not on the juridical rights of conquerors, but on the defective nature of the Indians themselves.[22]

What shook the foundations of Mair's argument were the conquests of Mexico and Peru. No Spaniard who had seen the shining cities of Tenochtitlán or Tihuantinsuyu could regard the Aztecs or Incas as rude inferiors. These barbarians, like the ones in Asia, possessed all the signs of human reason and *civilitas*: cities, magistrates, rulers, laws, patriarchal families, industry, commerce and diplomacy, religious cults with priests and temples, and a leisure class to enjoy the life of the mind. The justification for conquering the imperial peoples was not their *sub*humanity but their *in*humanity: their tyrannies over other nations and their crimes against nature.[23]

During the conquest of central Mexico from 1519 to 1521, Hernán Cortés assumed the role of deliverer. City by city, he cast down idols, ended human sacrifices, and established Christianity as the state religion.[24] The youthful emperor Charles V, donning the mantle of a vicar king, appointed viceroys to represent him in his American kingdoms of New Spain and Peru and sent out Franciscan Apostles to instruct and baptize his millions of new subjects. The New Laws of 1542 proclaimed their personal liberty. Indians were not to be held as slaves or forced into service; they could live and work wherever they chose.[25] The New Laws outraged the conquerors of Peru to the point of civil war: was this the way for a king to reward those who won him kingdoms? Unable to enforce his will, the emperor had to be satisfied with phasing out the privately held encomienda.

For the vanishing island peoples of the Caribbean and for the civilized imperial peoples, conquest was a fait accompli. But a hundred other nations of barbarians lived beyond the borders of the king's new realms. Were these wild peoples truly natural slaves, fit only for bondage? Was it morally justifiable to impose Roman Catholic Christianity and Spanish fealty on them by force? Pope Paul III had declared in 1537 that Indians "should neither be enslaved nor be deprived of their property." They were "rational beings, capable of becoming Christians."[26] The unarticulated assumption in the pope's declaration was that a rational being would, given the opportunity, accept Christianity and Spanish overlordship. Cabeza de Vaca's experience and relation showed only that a rational being would choose the lesser of two evils.

In the opinion of the Dominican scholar Francisco de Vitoria, Professor of Theology at the University of Salamanca, giving a public lecture on "the Affair of the Indies" in 1532, no human being should be forced to make this choice.[27] Indians did not give valid cause for war by being uncivilized, nor by rejecting Christianity and living in mortal sin. Vitoria was an exponent of Thomas of Aquinas's theory of natural law, which opposed St. Augustine's faith-centered categorical distinctions. By Thomist reasoning, the illumination which God granted to all men made all governments legitimate and entitled all subjects to the undisturbed possession of their property. The rights of barbarians were natural, human rights.[28]

Should, then, a Christian ever wage war on barbarous Indians? Vitoria identified three circumstances under which a Christian emperor might. (1) If the Indians were guilty of impeding the free commerce of nations. (2) If they prevented the preaching of the gospel, interfering with the free adoption of Christianity. (3) If their laws and leaders permitted "tyrannies" against the innocent. Barbarians, he argued, were characterized by mistakes of reasoning, a failure to distinguish between the clean and the unclean, what was fitting and what was not. This defect led them into such category errors as cannibalism, sodomy, and human sacrifice. Spain's title to the Indies, said Vitoria, rested on the natives' need to be protected and kept in tutelage until they achieved Christian maturity. They were not natural slaves, but natural children.[29]

By the mid-sixteenth century, epidemic disease had decimated the sedentary native populations, producing severe labor shortages and various forms of labor rationing. Francisco de Toledo, Viceroy of Peru, imposed a general resettlement of the indigenous population in the kingdom of Peru.[30] His system for the congregating of survivors into new towns was imitated in the kingdom of New Spain. In Michoacán, the humanist Vasco de Quiroga established communities modeled on Sir Thomas More's Utopia.[31] The missionary orders assumed the role of guardians, segregating their converts from lay Spaniards and giving religious endorsement to a society of castes in the Republic of Spaniards and the Republic of Indians. As Seed points out, this system for allowing a defeated sedentary agricultural people "to keep their own lands, to retain indigenous forms of government, and to transmit property according to their own rules," was of Arabic origin. Christians adopted it after the conquest of Toledo in 1085 left them with large numbers of subject Muslims, and the Catholic Kings

Ferdinand and Isabella altered it by ceasing to guarantee freedom of religion to non-Christians.[32]

A gowned professor was one kind of Spaniard; a conquistador was another. *Entradas*, or forays into new territory by companies of adventurers in search of booty, persisted. It was a violent age, and in the lands of constant war, conquest was personal violence carried to a higher power. On the northern and southern extremes of empire – the Chichimeca frontier above New Spain and the Araucanian frontier below Chile – captains of conquest prolonged the wars in order to take and sell captives.[33] The peoples of these and other wild frontiers on the "rim of Christendom" seemed to have none of Aristotle's characteristics of human reason.[34] They were the New World's savages.[35] "Near men" roaming about "like wild beasts" must be "reduced" to civility, their mobility restricted until they could be taught human ways.[36] But a forced reduction was tantamount to war, and the kind of war being waged against Araucanians and Chichimecas was the "*guerra a fuego y a sangre*," a war without quarter. The lives of the captured were forfeit; their captors could dispatch them, hold them for ransom, or sell them as slaves.

In 1550, Prince Philip, acting as regent, called a special court in Valladolid to reexamine the rights of barbarians.[37] Arguing that it was lawful to subdue the Indians of America by force because they were "barbarous and inhuman peoples abhorring all civil life, customs, and virtues" was Charles V's chaplain and chronicler, Juan Ginés de Sepúlveda, whose inflammatory manuscript on the subject had been denied publication. Leading the opposition was the seventy-five-year-old defender of the Indians and Bishop of Chiapas, the Dominican Bartolomé de Las Casas, who was largely responsible for the Council of the Indies' having advised the emperor to suspend all expeditions and conquests until questions about their legality could be resolved.[38]

Despite its broad implications, the Valladolid debate was a minor moment in the intellectual life of mid-sixteenth-century Europe, preoccupied with religious rebellions and the doctrinal deliberations of the Council of Trent. The judges were slow to submit their opinions; it was not until late in 1554 that the Council of the Indies took note of their pragmatic conclusions. The Crown's American titles were valid, they held, but conquest, the means by which the new territories had been added, was to cease.[39] Sepúlveda's treatise remained in manu-script and Las Casas's long countertreatise, *The Apologetic History of the Indies*, a major work of comparative ethnology, was published. In it, he demonstrated that by Aristotle's own standards American Indians were true men, with communities, laws, social classes, religion, and marriage. Differences between them and Europeans were not innate but cultural: American civilizations were in their infancy.[40]

Meanwhile, yet another Dominican, Alonso de la Vera Cruz, a member of the Salamanca School that had formed around Vitoria, startled his students at the new University of Mexico in 1553 with a series of lectures on the natural rights of Indians – in particular, on their right not to be visited with violence in the name of Christianity. Natives who had enjoyed freedom, owned property, and governed themselves did not, he contended, lose those rights when Spaniards landed on their shores. To say this in Salamanca or Valladolid was one thing; to say it in Mexico City was another. This voice of one crying in the wilderness provoked so loud a roar of protest that, for his own safety, metropolitan officials recalled Vera Cruz to Spain.[41]

By the time Spain came under pressure to settle the east coast of North America and the Philippines, the official position on conquest and conversion had thus shifted several times. With the 1573 Ordinances of Pacification[42] and Ordinances for the Laying out of Towns, Philip II institutionalized the conquest, giving notice that the Crown would no longer countenance old-style entradas, unprovoked wars, or unsupervised distributions of Indians. Even the word "conquest" was to be dropped, transmuted in official discourse to "pacification."[43] Captains of conquest would give way to bureaucrats, the pursuit of booty to the receipt of wages, the impromptu campsite to the well-planned town, and conquest by the sword to conquest by the gospel. The royal standard was passed to the missionary orders, who would go forth armed with the gospel and reduce the wild people to settlements. Conversion would be voluntary. Spaniards might not even enter Indian territory until a natural lord of the land had made a certified request for friars. In the new order of things, the military's mandate was not to advance the frontier, but to defend the advancing missionary.

Charles V had initiated the royal underwriting of missions in the 1520s; his son institutionalized the process, soothing the apprehensions of mendicant Franciscans that royal support would compromise their strict vow of poverty.[44] Among the "king's alms" laid upon the royal treasury were the costs of transporting a missionary from mother house to assigned post, a journey that could take up to two years; military-style rations of wheat flour, olive oil, wine, and vinegar; a clothing allowance for "habit and sandals"; an "altar allowance" of wax, wheat, and wine to each priest of the mass; books; and, for each new "fixed" as opposed to "flying" mission, a 1,000-peso endowment of bells, vestments, sacred vessels, and church ornaments.[45] These costs, too, were part of the price of pacification.

Equally resolved to establish control over the powerful preaching orders that had accomplished the spiritual conquests of Mexico and Peru – the "regular," or Rule-governed, clergy who posed as great a challenge to his royal authority as the encomenderos of an earlier generation had to his father's – Philip II completed his lawgiving with the 1574 Ordinance of Patronage.[46] A move toward secularization, it transformed the Franciscans, Dominicans, and Augustinians who ministered to Indian parishes from members of international religious orders answering to their leaders and the pope into civil servants of the Crown answering to a royally appointed bishop.[47] Only in places too thinly settled to support an ecclesiastical hierarchy could the orders maintain a measure of autonomy. To these frontiers many members of the orders headed, increasing missionary manpower and heralding a "Golden Age" of missions in North America.[48]

The Church in the Indies supported the king's new pacification policy. The Third Mexican Provincial Council of Bishops, meeting in 1585, condemned the war of "fire and blood" against the Chichimecas. For forty years these wild people had preyed on the supply trains passing through their territory en route to the silver mines of Zaca-tecas, and for forty years Spanish captains had raided their hideouts and come back with slaves. The bishops denied that the Chichimeca War was a just war or the captives lawfully taken. In a statement that rang with authority, they declared that the rudest of barbarians had a right to live unmolested.[49]

Surrendering the road to the silver mines was out of the question. Two succeeding viceroys of New Spain, the Marqués de Villaman-rique and his successor, Luis de Velasco II, brought the war to a close by a policy of pacification by gifts, attracting the Chichimecas to "reductions" where they could be taught and tamed. By 1600 the northern frontier had done an about face. At government expense and under the eye of Franciscan observers, captains of war, relabeled "captains of peace," distributed food, clothing, iron tools, oxen, and, in a touch of whimsy, reading primers and games. The success of this reverse tribute, dubbed by historian Philip Wayne Powell "peace by purchase," discredited the military solution and virtually guaranteed that material goods and fixed missions would act in tandem to advance Spain's North American frontier.[50] In time, the drawbacks of the policy of reducing the Indians to missions by means of gifts would be exposed. Where Indians rejected the sedentary life that Catholic Christianity required, the frontier could not advance, and when Indians received the gospel invitation sweetened by gifts, they expected the regaling to continue. The Spanish in North America would come to regret the link they had forged between heavenly and earthly goods.

Jesuit historian José de Acosta summarized Spain's first century of experience in America in his *Natural and Moral History of the Indies*, published in 1590. In it, he identified four types of barbarians, complete with four levels of social organization, religious observance, and linguistic development. The Chinese, Japanese, and some peoples of India would, he predicted, become Christians once they were reasoned with and shown the superiority of European technology. The other three types of barbarians he situated in America. The "higher" ones were those who possessed ordered societies and religious cults based on idol worship – the imperial peoples. Below these were the tribes who had settlements and chieftains and who worshiped animals – the island peoples. The lowest type of barbarians were the true savages: naked, cultureless, virtually speechless, living outside of human community, without family structure or civil organization, eating unclean things, and worshiping stones, streams, and mountains – the wild peoples. In this category Acosta placed the Caribs, some of the Amazonian tribes, all the peoples of Brazil (the Atlantic coast of South America), and all the inhabitants of Florida (the Atlantic and Gulf coasts of North America). The miserable bands along the Texas seashore with their stomach-centered seasons of prickly pears, pecans, acorns, and blackberries and their delicacy, pine nuts pounded with dirt, which the castaway Cabeza de Vaca so feelingly described, were, Acosta imagined, typical. All of these legions of wild men and women must be driven out of the jungles and deserts and reduced to "*pueblos en forma*" (that is, to proper settlements under hierarchical forms of government) and be instructed in the ways of "true men" before they could hope to live a Christian life. Yet however uncouth their customs, savages were not subhuman; with proper handling, the meanest nomad could be civilized.[51]

Acosta was wrong about the universal appeal of Western ways. At least three categories of wild peoples resisted pacification, refusing to be conquered by the sword, the gospel, or the gift. In one category were the seasonal nomads who, defying the imperatives of Roman Catholic ritual which demanded that Christians stay within reach of the sacraments, refused to settle down in agrarian villages. Inasmuch as the transindividual values of Catholicism ruled out baptizing persons who were likely to fall into apostasy, Indians who persisted in a nomadic life were effectively excluded from the king's realms.[52] In a second category were the decentralized nations whose leaders could not command obedience. A nation ruled by consensus instead of coercion – or, as the Spanish put it, one in which the Indians obeyed their chiefs poorly – was too inconstant to be accepted into the ecumene. The third category was that of natives who could not be quarantined from contact with Spain's rivals. The trade goods of northern Europeans were increasingly tempting and plentiful, and they were less likely to come with strings attached.

To hold the line on the embattled frontiers, the king resorted to the presidial system perfected in North Africa. Garrisons were posted to presidios on the edges of empire, each outpost or fortified port being subsidized out of the defense fund of the nearest royal treasury. The soldiers were regular troops on wages, expressly forbidden to support themselves in the manner of conquistadores from booty and captives, or in the manner of encomenderos from the tribute or services of Indians. Governors and treasury officials stationed in a "land of constant war" were supported by the same defense fund, as were the chiefs who consented to be their allies. This too was part of the price of pacification.

For all of the royal fifths of American silver deposited in them, the king's coffers were unequal to the task of pacifying every New World Indian nation.[53] Spain had to confine its attention to those wild peoples occupying or threatening strategic areas such as mining regions or the contested coasts beside important seaways. Founded in 1565 to stand guard over the Gulf Stream, the captaincy general of Florida was integral to Spain's naval defenses. Easternmost in the tier of Spain's colonies in North America, which historians of the United States group together under the label of "Spanish Borderlands," Florida had more in common with the maritime peripheries of Chile and the Philippines than with New Mexico, and its missions came and went before the California missions were founded. As Spain's nor-thern-most outpost on the Atlantic, St. Augustine was closer in travel time to Madrid than to Mexico City, and after the foundings of Carolina and Georgia, it was nearer to Charleston and Savannah than to any Spanish port. During the long conquest of Florida, Spaniards exercised every mode of legitimating title, pressed into service every model of Indian-Spanish relations, and did their best to sound like ad-vocates of pacification.

When Pedro Menéndez de Avilés stepped ashore on the east coast of Florida in 1565, he took possession of the mainland as *terra nullius*, beyond the jurisdiction of any Christian prince – he would shortly seek out and remove evidence to the contrary, in the form of a stone pillar left by the Frenchman Jean Ribault. Menéndez's properly certified and recorded act, in the words of Eugene Lyon, "validated the Spanish king's continental title," tacitly granted by Pope Alexander VI, and "constituted the lands of North America as *tierras de realengo*, which the Crown could either retain or alienate to third parties. It was "the semifeudal basis for the power of treaty making with the native peoples." The legal basis for Menéndez's action was his renewable three-year contract with Philip II, naming him *adelantado*, governor, and captain general of Florida, with lands fit for a nobleman and privileges of lordship, patronage, and trade.[54]

One of the contract's clauses enlisted the adelantado as a royal champion to enforce Spain's claim to a stretch of the Atlantic coast which France had lately challenged by building a fort. Menéndez was a man of means and connections, but his resources were unequal to financing an armada. As military intelligence supplied details about the strength of French forces, the king himself became a partner in the enterprise, adding some 200,000 ducats to his champion's 75,000. The venture was successful. "King Philip II ordered him to evict the

French corsair Juan Rimbao [sic] from the coast of Florida which he had seized with many people and ships," recalled an heir, which mandate "he complied with at the total risk of his person, his people being greatly outnumbered," and "he cut the throats of . . . the majority of the enemy's people, whereby His Majesty obtained his object and the coast was cleaned of them."[55]

Menéndez had wiped out a fortified settlement of Huguenots, assuring his king that Spain and not France would be the power to establish itself in eastern North America. He further fulfilled his contract by founding three settlements of Spaniards. But, despite concluding limited military and trading alliances with several chiefdoms, sealed by the exchange of gifts and hostages, he did not conquer the land. The Jesuits he introduced, again in fulfillment of contract, distributing them among the garrisons stationed at every deepwater port around the peninsula, soon recognized that their efforts to convert the natives would be fruitless as long as food shortages compelled Spanish soldiers to raid native storehouses. Unwilling to give up their missionary calling to serve as military chaplains, some of the Jesuits left to found a mission in Virginia, where members of the Powhatan confederacy quickly killed them. The other Jesuits withdrew.[56]

Written treaties of the kind the adelantado sought served three modest purposes: they attested to amicable relations with a defined group of natives; they obligated the leaders of that group to offer assistance when needed; and they provided Spaniards with a written claim to present to foreign rivals. In his 1977 presidential address to the American Historical Association, Charles Gibson questioned whether the Spanish ever actually *treated* with Indians as did other Europeans. The network of agreements whereby Spaniards legitimated hegemony over foreign populations was not, he argued, one of formal agreements between equally sovereign entities, the only parties by definition capable of treaty making; it was, instead, one of "*capitulaciones*," which he identified as a contract between unequals.[57] Whether the Portuguese, English, French, Dutch, or Russians ever treated Indians as equals is debatable, but Spanish efforts to "*tratar y contratar*," or "treat and contract," had distinctly feudal overtones.[58] They were the familiar, frankly unequal arrangements of a patrimonial, hierarchical society that bound lord to vassal, patron to client, and God to man.

The Indians along the seaways of south Florida and up the Atlantic coast saw no reason to harbor hungry strangers. They had been dealing with Europeans of varying nationality, bartering salvaged cargoes and castaways for items of foreign manufacture, at least since 1503, when the peninsula first appeared on the Cantino map. After the adelantado himself suffered shipwreck below St. Augustine and had his life threatened by the natives of that area, he petitioned the Crown to let him recoup his losses with a war of "fire and blood" on the coastal Indians, punishing their "treacheries," mistreatment of castaways, and practice of sacrificing Christians to idols. His plan was to sell them to the islands as slaves.[59] This request to declare a total war on persistently hostile Indians the Crown denied. In 1574, Menéndez died in the shipyards of Santander, where the king had called him to build another armada. His three small settlements – St. Augustine, San Mateo, at the mouth of the St. Johns River, and Santa Elena, on Parris Island in present South Carolina – were plagued by famine, mutinies, and Indian hostility, as lieutenant governors attempted to progress from gifts and trade to tribute and services. Two of the three fell by the way. First, the French corsair Dominique de Gourgues destroyed the fort at San Mateo with the help of eastern Timucuans. Then, after Sir Francis Drake assaulted the fort at St. Augustine and the Indians of the vicinity, another group of eastern Timucuans, sacked the settlement, the Spanish abandoned, not St. Augustine, but Santa Elena, to concentrate their efforts farther south.

Philip II's institutionalizing of the conquest in the 1570s had a positive effect on Florida, which changed from a proprietary colony to a royal colony with a *situado*, or treasury subvention. Missions of Franciscans traveled from Spain to reopen conversions. Budgetarily, they were interchangeable with the soldiers of the three hundred-man garrison, although out of respect for a Franciscan's vow of poverty, his stipend of 115 ducats a year was issued in kind. The regular delivery of supplies introduced new problems. French corsairs harassed the small colony, seizing the supply ships en route from Havana. They continued their trade with the coastal Indians for salvage and, increasingly, the "fruits of the land": ambergris found on the beaches of Ais below St. Augustine and medicinal herbs from the sea islands of Guale in present-day Georgia.[60] It was inevitable that in Ais and Guale the interests of European rivals would collide. In 1596, Florida governor

Domingo Martínez de Avendaño took defensive action by compact, turning both places into provinces. The chiefs of Ais and Guale promised, respectively, to accept missionaries, send laborers to St. Augustine, and report any foreigners in their waters. In Spanish eyes, the chiefs ratified the compacts when they accepted gifts, the currency of diplomacy.[61]

The compacts of 1596 contained all three of the elements basic to the conquest by contract: a promise of mutual defense and exclusive trade, producing a Spanish sphere of influence; a promise of obedience to the distant king of Spain in the person of his appointed governor, extending the king's realms and bringing a particular region into the ecumene of the captaincy general; and a promise to receive missionaries, undergo indoctrination, and form a mission province. Together, these promises instituted the expanding covenant of pacification.

Solemn ceremonies sealed the compacts and contractualized the covenant. The native calumet ceremony, smoking the feathered "peace pipe" to make fictive kinsmen of one's trading partners, followed by an exchange of gifts and hostages, cemented the alliances for defense and trade. The act of homage, in which a chief kissed the king's hand in the person of the governor's, ritually expressed the oath of fealty, renewed yearly. The act of raising a cross on a town plaza symbolized the town's readiness to receive friars and tolerate their irksome interventions. The act of baptism announced an individual's preparedness to accept the law of God and the demands of decent worship. Calumet ceremony, homage, cross raising, baptism – all were acts in evidence of contract, the signatures of a preliterate society.

By taking the oath of fealty and performing the act of homage the *cacique* proclaimed himself a vassal of the king of Spain and his vassals Spanish subjects. This was not enough. It was necessary for the Spanish to represent all new subjects as under indoctrination, for Pope Alexander VI's bulls of donation had been a charter to evangelize, and many specialists in international law remained persuaded that Spain's title to the Indies depended on fulfilling it. Therefore, the chief was pressured to acquiesce to Christianity and register a formal request for friars. The chief's promise of obedience to God not only committed him to become a Christian, but, under the principle of *cujus regio, ejus religio,* obligated his vassals to attend *doctrina,* learn the prayers and catechism, and be subject to the law of God. The process of indoctrination, once begun, would carry its own momentum.

In the remotest of frontiers, royal officials pursued their paperwork.[62] But the governmental notary was not in attendance to validate a contract; his function was to witness the acts of the participants and prepare a document attesting that the proper ceremony had been performed and the contract validated in his presence. The agreements of peace, friendship, and trade that survive in the Florida archives; the acts of homage, records of mission foundings, declarations of just war, and lists of chiefs appearing before the governor to receive presents – all are the carefully preserved evidences of contracts that officials in the captaincy general for reasons of their own called into existence, documented, and were prepared to enforce. Early modern historians whose research takes them to official archives learn to recognize the formulaic source for what it was: a paper trail designed to provide an official with a sure defense should higher authorities ever question his actions in office. After an Indian rebellion, charges flew left and right. It was wise to be forearmed.

The covenant lasted no longer than the contracts composing it were honored. One year after the annexations of Ais and Guale, uprisings broke out in both new provinces. First the Indians of Ais refused to let Spaniards come ashore in their territory, then those of Guale killed five Franciscans and enslaved another, to be tormented by small boys. Governor Gonzalo Méndez Canzo quickly defeated the Ais rebels and distributed them to his men as slaves. The rebellion in Guale lasted longer. For six years French ships came and went in Georgia harbors, some of them leaving factors to accumulate cargoes for their return. Only when the governor was able to divide the Guales, setting one faction against another, did the rebellion end.[63] For Méndez Canzo and his men the rewards of conquest were fleeting. By royal command, all the Florida Indians he had condemned to terms of slavery were set free.[64] The market for medicinal herbs collapsed soon after 1600, but the value of ambergris remained steady. Cuban fishermen competed for it with soldiers and officers from St. Augustine, detached to patrol the coast. Dutch corsairs returning from the Indies took on wood and water at Cape Canaveral, where the Gulf Stream swings out of sight of land. Local Indians bearing ambergris welcomed the landing parties, and no treaty of exclusive trade with Spaniards would stop them.

Franciscans on "flying missions" to the towns along the St. Johns River raised crosses and promised to return, as soon as their numbers permitted, to begin the process of conversion. Dividing the eastern Timucuans into "freshwater" and "tidewater" provinces, they established, in the towns of paramount chiefs, *doctrinas* consisting of a church and a convent, from which they serviced strings of *visitas* in the subject towns. The doctrinas doubled as boarding schools; the friars took in foundlings, orphans, and the sons of chiefs and raised their own sacristans, musicians, interpreters, catechists, and overseers. After the preparatory stage of conversion, each doctrina received from the king a gift of religious essentials: vestments, linens, images, sacred vessels, baptismal registers, large bells, and an altarstone containing a holy relic. From the governor's hand, the chiefs received European clothing for themselves and cloth, blankets, knives, tools, and beads to distribute to their vassals.

As far as the settlers were concerned, there was much to be said for mission provinces. (1) The Christian towns provided an early warning system and a buffer zone against invasion. They were St. Augustine's first line of defense. (2) The Indians included Spanish authorities, civil and religious, in the native system for public finance, the *sabana* system. Each planting season, the commoners of the town planted sabanas of maize for them along with the usual fields for the chiefs and headmen and community. (3) The chiefs provided labor to the presidio. This practice began during the sixteenthth century, when caciques and cacicas offered their vassals to the Spanish as scouts, burdeners, couriers, canoemen, and archers. The colony became increasingly dependent on this labor distribution.

Because a vow obtained by coercion was invalid, the Spanish showed a decent respect for free will, or the forms thereof. In theory, every adult accepted Christianity of his own volition and every vassal declared himself a vassal by choice – legal precautions that Gibson termed "theoretical voluntarism."[65] Commoners undergoing indoctrination were no longer free to do as they pleased. With the consent of their natural lord or lady they had made solemn promises, and the Spanish stood ready to see that they fulfilled them. Properly executed, these promises were binding obligations, like a marriage vow or an army induction. They were not to be entered into lightly.[66] The doctrineros withheld baptism from common Indians until Christian habits and attitudes had become second nature, for the soul of an apostate stood in more peril than that of a heathen. Exceptions to the rule of delayed baptism were made for the caciques and cacicas, who with their families bowed their necks to the "yoke of the gospel" as an example to their vassals. Governors stood godfather to these births in Christ, bestowing rich baptismal gifts and, frequently, their own surnames upon the noble converts.

For the first twenty years of the seventeenth century, the documentary record for Florida is sparse. Only the service records of soldiers reveal when and with whom the captaincy general was at war. In a 1613 petition, Juan Rodríguez de Cartaya, a captain of the launches, informed the Crown that in his twenty-five years of service he had been present "in the war with the strangers who take themselves to those coasts, and in the war with the natives of the land, and in the peace and pacification of the said natives, behaving always as an honorable soldier." Each governor in turn had made use of him, "sending him by land and sea among the natives on embassies of peace and of war, assisting allied chiefs, ransoming the Spaniards in enemy hands, bringing provisions to the presidio, escorting the *situado* ships, and patrolling the coasts." He had capped his career with "the pacification of" the "chiefs of the coast from Carlos to Apalache," reducing them "to the obedience of Governor Juan Fernández de Olivera in the name of Your Majesty, in everything respecting the religious on the frontier." Understanding as he did "the nature of Indians," he was able "to subject that coast to peace for the first time, when it had formerly attracted many ships of enemies who did great damage to those of friends passing through the Gulf."[67] Even the cacique of Carlos sent word that "he wanted no more war with Christians." Compacts of peace were ratified by the exchange of presents, and other chiefs arrived for other gifts.[68] With the corsairs in retreat and the Gulf coast conquered, pacification could begin in earnest.

"The hour of God has come," wrote the Franciscans to the Crown in 1612.

> We who have been here twenty years taming and mastering Indians are overwhelmed. . . . The governor is affable, benign, pious, and

generous. . . . Chiefs come from more than 100 leagues to render obedience to Your Majesty and ask to be baptized. The governor receives them kindly, regaling, feeding, and clothing them and giving them the kind of things they value, sending them to their lands again content.

"The governor has nothing to give them but what Your Majesty orders," the friars continued.

Whatever they receive in peace to please them and reduce them to the service of God and Your Majesty is as nothing compared to the cost of making war on them, for the matchcord alone would cost more. Besides, a war has no effect on them, because they have no properties . . . to lose. . . . But with the word of the gospel and by clothing the naked, they come to us offering their lands, their wills, and their bit of food.[69]

In the early 1630s Spanish Florida extended its boundaries to the Gulf coast with new provinces in western Timucua and in fertile Apalache, near present Tallahassee. This second impulse for expansion came from within the colony: it was not a royal initiative. Spain, deeply involved in European wars and peninsular rebellions, could scarcely maintain the centers, much less the peripheries. During the middle fifty years of the seventeenth century, Florida's annual situado for soldiers, friars, and caciques was stolen by privateers, sequestered by the Crown, lost at sea, swamped in red tape, and delayed for years together. Although most of the missing funds were in time replaced, their delivery was so unpredictable that people learned to rely less on royal support and more on their own devices.

The populous western provinces replenished the number of peasant farmers and laborers in the colony, while the new ports offered outlets for a flourishing coastal trade with Havana in deerskins, maize and beans, chickens, hogs, and ranch products – a trade that soon drew Caribbean buccaneers into Gulf waters. That the Gulf trade with Cuba paid no duties and was therefore illegal did not disturb the self-reliant provincials. Even the friars participated in it, selling the surpluses of convent sabanas to adorn their churches and support their dependents. Under the guise of controlling contraband and despite strong Franciscan opposition, the governors stationed detachments of soldiers in the main town of each province. These secondary garrisons functioned as covert trading posts, and the lieutenants and soldiers who manned them, as agents for the governors' private enterprises.

During this period of reduced and irregular royal support, Spanish demands on Christian Indians rose. When the situado failed to arrive and the chiefs did not receive the customary gifts for themselves and their vassals, the Spanish pressed them all the more urgently to sell their towns' stored provisions to the presidio on credit. The new secondary garrisons meant that the Indians now had local soldiers and their families, as well as friars, to feed. Communities of Spanish traders and ranchers grew up around the garrisons and these provincial settlers expected their own share of "service Indians."

Sooner or later, most advances into new territory were followed by an uprising, as natives under indoctrination began to have second thoughts about the disruptive new order. From their point of view, by far the worst abuse was burdening. Because the journey by sea from St. Augustine to the west coast called for sailing against the strong current of the Gulf Stream, and because the narrow waters were increasingly pirate infested, most traffic went by land on Indian backs. The yearly ration for every Franciscan weighed no less than 1,800 pounds. As the number of doctrinas increased and the supply lines lengthened, more and more burdener-days were required to take the friars their rations, and the burdeners were loaded going and coming. Both of the major mid-seventeenth century west coast rebellions were related to burdening.

The chief who rose in rebellion was guilty of a breach of contract. If subdued, he could be sent into exile, deposed from office, or stripped of his inherited privileges over lands and people. To be restored, he must undergo ritual humiliation. Performing the act of submission, duly witnessed and notarized, a repentant cacique threw himself at the governor's feet to beg for mercy. This act, too, marked a change of legal status. Those who had followed his lead forfeited the status of Christians conquered by the gospel and entered the ranks of nations conquered by the sword, liable to forced labor. Whole towns could be relocated to serve this open-ended sentence.[70]

Contrary to the impression left by the reams of paperwork produced after every rebellion, as officials scrambled to escape blame, communal rejections of the covenant were relatively rare. More often, commoners simply withdrew from the king's realms. They were as guilty of repudiating the covenant as those who rose up in arms, for the conquest by contract was irrevocable. Once yielded, obedience could not be withdrawn. A convert could not unbaptize himself by striking his forehead and declaring, "Water begone! I am no Christian," any more than a married man could divorce himself by abandoning his family.[71] Soldiers were sent after these fugitives to return them to their duties as subjects, Christians, and spouses. Although sometimes the Franciscans sided with the rebels, going over the governor's head to present their grievances to the Crown, and although the governor readily returned the favor when converts fled from the doctrinas, the Spanish system included no provision for secession. From a safe distance, the Crown invariably advised that the Indians concerned be treated, not as rebels deserved, but with "sweetness," attracted back to their obligations with pardons and kind words.

The captaincy general of Florida in the mid-seventeenth century offers a frontier version of the system of two republics.[72] The Republic of Indians, 26,000 Christian Indians in three provinces with close to forty doctrinas, coexisted with the Republic of Spaniards, a population of 1,500 non-Indians, all officially residents of one city, St. Augustine, and members of one parish. But Florida's elite was a mixed one. Friars, settlers, officers, and Hispanized chiefs were all busy ranching, trading with Indian nations to the north, and conducting a coastal trade from Apalache to Havana, where there was a growing market for ranch products, deerskins, and naval stores and provisions.[73]

The Florida mission model differs markedly from the isolated reductions of South America and the mission-presidios of the North American southwest. Florida missionaries were never wholly able to segregate or control their converts. They raised their crosses on the plazas of established towns and built their churches and convents by sufferance of native leaders. In Florida, Christian chiefs functioned as brokers, delivering in lieu of tribute the native labor and agricultural produce necessary to support the soldiers and friars, distributing payment in the form of trade goods charged against the "gasto de indios," or Indian fund in the situado, and commanding, as well as one could command, the native auxiliaries. If Florida had no recognized encomienda, it was not because it had no privileged order of guardians, but because the chiefs filled the role of encomenderos. They made the arrangements, and the commoners did the work.[74]

The heyday of the mission provinces in Florida was brief. The first indication of danger came with the English capture of Jamaica in 1655. If the English had not shared in the initial orgy of looting in America, known to all Europe via the translated works of Las Casas, neither had they taken part in the subsequent debate about the rights of Indians. Juan de Solórzano Pereira's *De Indiarum Jure* (1629, 1639), which examined the legality of ten of the basic arguments used over the years to justify the conquest of the New World, could have been written only by a Spaniard.[75] Unable to picture Indians as wards of any Crown, much less a Spanish one, Englishmen regarded all Indians under Spanish rule as living in slavery. Robert Searles, an English corsair out of Jamaica who sacked St. Augustine in 1668, said as much to Father Francisco de Sotolongo, the parish priest negotiating ransoms. Searles's patent from the governor of Jamaica, he said, licensed him to carry off anyone who was not "a Spaniard," meaning anyone who wasn't white. The presumption was that any black, Indian, or mixed-race person in Spanish hands was a slave already.[76]

Reacting to Searles's attack, Queen Regent Mariana ordered the viceroy of New Spain to catch up Florida's overdue situados, support more soldiers, and send the Florida treasury 10,000 pesos extra per year with which to build a stone fort. The founding of Charleston in 1670 underscored the urgency of this project. All told, the building of the Castillo de San Marcos took twenty-four years and cost the Crown over 138,000 pesos, most of which went for labor. Twice as many native workmen came to the capital as formerly; many brought their families and stayed. The influx of money and people caused prices to rise, stimulating ranching and agriculture.

In the late seventeenth century, a time of retrenchment throughout the Spanish empire,[77] the captaincy general of Florida reverted to its sixteenth-century reputation as a "land of constant war."[77] Seeking to tie French Canada and the Illinois country to the Lower Mississippi and the Gulf, the French moved southward, increasing English fears of encirclement. Creek Indians, armed with English firearms in the Southeastern version of the proxy war, began to raid the missions in search of slaves for English buyers. But Florida's defense funds were consumed by the castillo, leaving none for the protection of Indian towns. When the viceroy sent an extra 6,000 pesos with which to build a stone tower on Cumberland Island for the few remaining Guales, the governor used it to build a seawall in St. Augustine.

North of Apalache, men from Charleston were taking over the trade with the Apalachicola Indians, who had been part of the Spanish sphere of influence since the 1640s. Florida governors countered the English advance with extra gifts, warnings, and buffer zones of hastily founded "live missions." But the force field of the firearms revolution could attract as well as repulse. Between 1684 and 1706 a majority of the Christian Indians of Florida deserted their doctrinas for a life of liberty without friars, soldiers, or chiefs. First the Guales defected, then the Apalaches, then the Timucuans. When, during Queen Anne's War, Colonel James Moore of Carolina invaded the province of Apalache, burning churches and taking captives with the military objective of weakening a French ally, he was surprised at the number of mission Indians who left their homes to join him.[78] The commoners were in rebellion.

In the early eighteenth century, when the mission provinces were but a memory, only a handful of Indian "Old Christians" remained around St. Augustine, in refugee pueblos under the guns of the fort, where, according to the displeased Franciscans, they lived "by their wits" and were "worse than the gypsies of Spain." The women went shamelessly from tavern to tavern, while the men argued that "if it were a bad thing to get drunk the king would not give them *aguardiente*."[79] Coastal Indians who had long kept their distance from Spaniards appeared in St. Augustine seeking sanctuary from the slavehunters. To keep them from going over to the British, officials accepted them as "vassals of His Majesty" and assigned them living space and missionaries. The experience was frustrating all around. Unable to communicate with the wild people or persuade them to stay in one place, the friars described them in phrases reminiscent of Sepúlveda: "indomitable," "unreasonable," "vile by nature," "an utterly useless nation."[80]

Diplomats from the Creek confederacy, playing one set of white people against another, visited the Spanish capital for talks but demanded gifts of British manufacture: coats trimmed in gold braid, kerchiefs in bright red or blue with white borders, rifles and ammunition, vermilion, beads, and copper cauldrons. To satisfy these exacting consumers, the Spanish governor was forced to go clandestinely to British merchants, lest the Indians should "return to the English or the French of Mobile, who are always giving them presents."[81] The Franciscan Antonio de Florencia, from an old Florida family, which had made its money in intercolonial commerce, explained the secret of English and French success in a letter of advice to the Crown. When the French first made their entrance in a new place, he wrote, they announced,

> We are Europeans who are habitants of Canada and we come to drink tobacco with you from the pipes of peace . . . and introduce commerce, to bring you merchandise from Europe in exchange for beaver pelts. . . . We will give you better prices than the Dutch, and all we ask from you is your safe conduct.

The Spanish should do the same. The "road to conquest," said Father Florencia, was trade.[82]

From a Spanish point of view, the English were curiously detached from questions of moral responsibility. The kings of England called no councils of theologians to discuss Indian rights; they maintained no mission provinces. English settlers made little effort to assimilate the natives and dispossessed them with equanimity once their lands became more valuable than their trade. Carolina Governor John Colleton's response to Florida Governor Diego de Quiroga y Losada's inquiry about some fugitive vassals was representative. Wrote Colleton,

> As for the Yamases Indians, they have nothing to do with our government nor do we trouble ourselves about them, . . . showing no profit but of a few deerskins for which we sell them powder, guns and shot as we do to all Indians indifferently.[83]

In the sixteenth century and well into the seventeenth, pacification was both an enlightened policy and a successful design for the mastery of North America. For years after the English planted colonies on the Atlantic seaboard, the outcome of imperial rivalry remained unclear. What won the race for English-speaking settlers in the Southeast was a combination of population growth and commerce.

The Indians of Florida, caught in the crossfire of eighteenth-century empires, broke their covenant with Spain to join the side of more people and more guns.

The Spanish Crown had backed the conquest by contract with funds for peacekeeping garrisons, missionaries, civil officials, and, not least, allied chiefs. But the model of pacification posited an exclusive relationship that could not be sustained. It confined people who loved the seasonal round of food gathering to the small world of European peasants. And it suborned the native leadership, turning caciques and cacicas into agents of a foreign power. In the eighteenth century, a peaceful conquest was worse than an anachronism, it was an oxymoron, and in Florida, its internal contradictions were laid bare. In Spain's pacification model, the missionary had replaced the conqueror. In the British model, the trader, with his slave cords and his rum-laden packhorses, would replace the missionary. For good or for ill, Great Britain – aggressively secular, exclusionary, and commercial – would prevail.[84]

Notes

First delivered as the 1993 Lawrence Henry Gipson Lecture at Lehigh University, Bethlehem, Penn., this paper has also been presented at the University of Canterbury, Christchurch, New Zealand (1996), Michigan State University, East Lansing, Mich. (1997), and Central Michigan University, Mount Pleasant, Mich. (1997). Jack P. Greene, David J. Weber, Paul E. Hoffman, and Simon Dyke have generously read and critiqued it in various versions.

1. The term was introduced in Amy Turner Bushnell, *Situado and Sabana: Spain's Support System for the Presidio and Mission Provinces of Florida* Anthropological Papers, no. 74 (New York: American Museum of Natural History, 1994), 33–35.

2. Anthony Pagden examines the principal theories of empire of these three European powers in *Lords of All the World: Ideologies of Empire in Spain, Britain and France c. 1500–c. 1800* (New Haven: Yale University Press, 1995). For a review of the historiographical literature, see the "Introduction: Do the Americas Have a Comparable Colonial History?" in *Establishing Exceptionalism: Historiography and the Colonial Americas*, ed., Amy Turner Bushnell (Aldershot, Hampshire, U.K.: Variorum, 1995), xiii–xxv.

3. Pagden, *Lords of All the World*, 87; Richard L. Kagan, "Prescott's Paradigm: American Historical Scholarship and the Decline of Spain," *The American Historical Review* 101, no. 2 (April 1996): 423–46.

4. Silvio Zavala, *Servidumbre natural y libertad cristiana según los tratadistas españoles de los siglos XVI y XVII* (Buenos Aires: Peuser, S. A., 1944); Joseph Höffner, *Christentum und Menschenwürde. Das Anliegen der spanischen Kolonialethik im goldenen Zeitalter* (Trier, 1947), published in Spanish translation by Francisco de Asis Caballero as *La ética colonial española del siglo de oro. Cristianismo y dignidad humana* (Madrid, 1957); Lewis Hanke, *The Spanish Struggle for Justice in the Conquest of America* (Philadelphia: University of Pennsylvania Press, 1949); Philip Wayne Powell, *Soldiers, Indians, and Silver* (Berkeley: University of California Press, 1952); Eugene H. Korth, S.J., *Spanish Policy in Colonial Chile: The Struggle for Social Justice, 1535–1700* (Stanford, Calif.: Stanford University Press, 1968), esp. chap. 1: "Historical and Doctrinal Background," 1–21. For a succinct essay on the subject see J. H. Parry, "Rights and Duties," in *The Spanish Seaborne Empire* (London: Hutchinson, 1966), 137–51.

5. James Muldoon, *The Americas in the Spanish World Order: The Justification for Conquest in the Seventeenth Century* (Philadelphia: University of Pennsylvania Press, 1994), 4–5.

6. Pagden, *Lords of All the World*, 63–73.

7. Antonio Gaztambide-Géigel, "The Invention of the Caribbean in the 20th Century" (paper presented to the Association of Caribbean Historians, Barbados, April 1996).

8. Alfred W. Crosby, "The Fortunate Isles," in *Ecological Imperialism: The Biological Expansion of Europe, 900–1900* (Cambridge: Cambridge University Press, 1986), 70–103.

9. Patricia Seed, *Ceremonies of Possession in Europe's Conquest of the New World, 1492–1640* (Cambridge: Cambridge University Press, 1995), 84–88.

10. Robert Bartlett, *The Making of Europe: Conquest, Colonization and Cultural Change, 950–1350* (Princeton, N. J.: Princeton University Press, 1993), 255–60.

11. Manuel Servin, "Religious Aspects of Symbolic Acts of Sovereignty," *The Americas* 13, no. 3 (1957): 255–67. See also Seed, *Ceremonies of Possession*.

12. Peter Hulme, *Colonial Encounters: Europe and the Native Caribbean 1492–1797* (London: Methuen, 1986), 73–78; Angel Rosenblat, "The Population of Hispaniola at the Time of Columbus," in *The Native Population of the Americas in 1492*, 2nd ed., ed., William M. Denevan (Madison: University of Wisconsin, 1992), 43–66.

13. Seed, *Ceremonies of Possession*, 78–84.

14. Anthony Pagden, *The Fall of Natural Man: The American Indian and the Origins of Comparative Ethnology* (Cambridge, Eng.: Cambridge University Press, 1982), 30–35.

15. Philip P. Boucher, *Cannibal Encounters: Europeans and Island Caribs, 1492–1763* (Baltimore: The Johns Hopkins University Press, 1992), 16.

16. Robert A. Williams, Jr., *The American Indian in Western Legal Thought: the Discourses of Conquest* (New York: Oxford University Press, 1990), 67–74.

17. Lewis Hanke, "The Development of Regulations for Conquistadores," *Contribuciones para el estudio de la historia de América: Homenaje al Dr. Emilio Ravignani* (Buenos Aires: Peuser, S. A., 1941), 73–75.

18. For an English translation of the requerimiento see Marvin Lunenfeld, ed., *1492. Discovery, Invasion, Encounter: Sources and Interpretations* (Lexington, Mass.: D. C. Heath, 1991), 188–90.

19. Seed, *Ceremonies of Possession*, 88. On the just war, see Silvio Zavala, *New Viewpoints on the Spanish Colonization of America* (Philadelphia: University of Pennsylvania Press, 1943), 38–48, and Pagden, *Lords of All the World*, 94–100.

20. Enrique Pupo-Walker, ed., *Castaways: The Narrative of Alvar Núñez Cabeza de Vaca*, trans. by Frances M. López-Morillas (Berkeley: University of California Press, 1993); Rolena Adomo, "Peaceful Conquest and Law in the Relación (Account) of Alvar Nuñez Cabeza de Vaca," in *Coded Encounters: Writing, Gender, and Ethnicity in Colonial Latin America*, eds., Francisco Javier Cevallos-Candau et al. (Amherst: University of Massachusetts Press, 1994), 76–79; Rolena Adomo, "The Negotiation of Fear in Cabeza de Vaca's *Naufragios*," in *New World Encounters*, ed., Stephen Greenblatt (Berkeley: University of California Press, 1993),

21. Pagden, *Fall of Natural Man*, 37–38; James Muldoon, "John Wyclif and the Rights of the Infidels: The *Requerimiento* Reexamined," *The Americas* 36, no. 3 (January 1980): 301–16.

22. Pagden, *The Fall of Natural Man*, 38–50; Padgen, *Lords of All the World*, 20–21.

23. Pagden, *Fall of Natural Man*, 58–59.

24. Beatriz Pastor Bodmer, "Hernán Cortés and the Creation of the Model Conqueror," in *The Armature of Conquest: Spanish Accounts of the Discovery of America, 1492–1589*, trans. by Lydia Longstreth Hunt (Stanford, Calif.: Stanford University Press, 1992), 50–100.

25. Luciano Pereña, "Derechos y deberes entre Indios y Españoles. Declaración de Francisco de Vitoria," in *L'universalità dei diritti umani e il pensiero cristiano del '500*, ed., Salvino Biolo (Torino, 1995), 51–66.

26. Justus M. Van der Kroef, "Francisco de Vitoria and the Nature of Colonial Policy," *The Catholic Historical Review* 35, no. 2 (1949): 133, 140; Hector José Tanzi, "El derecho de guerra en la América Hispana," *Revista de Historia de América* (1973): 95–97; Tzvetan Todorov, *The Conquest of America: The Question of the Other*, trans. by Richard Howard (New York: Harper & Row, 1984), 149–50; Patricia Seed, "'Are These Not Also Men?': The Indians' Humanity and Capacity for Spanish Civilisation," *Journal of Latin American Studies* 25, no. 3 (October 1993): 629–52.

27. Francisco de Vitoria, *De Indis et De Jure Belli relectiones*, ed., Ernest Nys (Buffalo, N. Y.: William S. Hein, 1995). The points Vitoria made in *De Indis* are summarized in Lunenfeld, *1492*, 191– 198.

28. Pagden, *Fall of Natural Man*, 59–108.

29. Williams, *American Indian in Western Legal Thought*, 96–108.

30. D. A. Brading, *The First America: The Spanish Monarchy, Creole Patriots, and the Liberal State, 1492–1867* (Cambridge: Cambridge University Press, 1991), 128–38.

31. Todorov, *Conquest of America*, 194–95.

32. Seed, *Ceremonies of Possession*, 80–97.

33. Stafford Poole, "'War by Fire and Blood': The Church and the Chichimecas, 1585," *The Americas* 22, no. 2 (1965): 115–37; Korth, *Spanish Policy in Colonial Chile*, 78–95.

34. See Herbert E. Bolton, *Rim of Christendom: A Biography of Eusebio Francisco Kino, Pacific Coast Pioneer* (New York: Macmillan, 1936).

35. Pagden, *Fall of Natural Man*, 67–79, 164.

36. John Howland Rowe, "Ethnography and Ethnology in the Sixteenth Century," *Kroeber Anthropological Society Papers* 30 (1964): 18; Amy Tumer Bushnell, "The Sacramental Imperative: Catholic Ritual and Indian Sedentism in the Provinces of Florida," in *Columbian Consequences*, vol. 2: *Archaeological and Historical Perspectives on the Spanish Borderlands East*, ed., David Hurst Thomas (Washington, D.C.: Smithsonian Institution Press, 1990), 475–90.

37. On the Valladolid debate and its sixteenth-century setting, see Brading, *First America*, 58–101; Pagden, *Fall of Natural Man*, 109–45; Demetrio Ramos Perez et al., *La ética en la conquista de América: Francisco de Vitoria y la Escuela de Salamanca* (Madrid: Consejo Superior de Investigaciones Científicas, 1984).

38. Ralph H. Vigil, *Alonso de Zorita: Royal Judge and Christian Humanist, 1512–1585* (Norman: University of Oklahoma Press, 1987), 215–17.

39. Jaime González Rodríguez, "La junta de Valladolid convocada por el emperador," in *Francisco de Vitoria*, Ramos Perez et al., 199–227.

40. For Las Casas's tumultuous intellectual life and times, see Lewis Hanke, *Aristotle and the American Indians: A Study in Race Prejudice in the Modern World* (Chicago: H. Regnery Co., 1959).

41. Emest J. Burrus, "Alonso de la Vera Cruz (1584), Pioneer Defender of the American Indians," *The Catholic Historical Review* 70, no. 4 (1984): 535–39.

42. "Ordenanzas de Su Magestad para los nuevos descubrimientos, conquistas y pacificaciones. Julio de 1573," *Colección de documentos inéditos relatives al descubrimiento, conquista y organización de las antiguas posesiones españolas de América y Oceanía, sacados de los archivos del reino y muy especialmente del de Indias* (Madrid, 1864–84), 16: 142–87.

43. On the "discourse of seeming" in the Ordinances of Pacification, see Todorov, *Conquest of America*, 173–74.

44. Antonine Tibesar, O.F.M., *Franciscan Beginnings in Colonial Peru* (Washington, D.C.: Academy of American Franciscan History, 1953), 37–5 1.

45. Bushnell, *Situado and Sabana*, 49–59.

46. Peter Bakewell, "Conquest after the Conquest: the Rise of Spanish Domination in America," in *Spain, Europe and the Atlantic World: Essays in Honour of John H. Elliott*, eds., Richard L. Kagan and Geoffrey Parker (Cambridge: Cambridge University Press, 1995), 296–315, es. 301–3.

47. John Leddy Phelan, *The Millennial Kingdom of the Franciscans in the New World*, 2nd ed. (Berkeley: University of California Press, 1970), 54–55.

48. Charles W. Spellman, "The 'Golden Age' of the Florida Missions, 1632–1674," *The Catholic Historical Review* 51 (October 1965): 354–72; Michael V. Gannon, "The Golden Age of the Florida Missions 1606–1675," in *The Cross in the Sand: The Early Catholic Church in Florida 1513–1870* (Gainesville: University of Florida Press, 1965), 49–67.

49. Poole, "War by Fire and Blood."

50. Philip Wayne Powell, "Peacemaking on North America's First Frontier," *The Americas* 16, no. 3 (1960): 221–50.

51. Pagden, *Fall of Natural Man*, 146–97; Brading, *First America*, 184–95.

52. Bushnell, "Sacramental Imperative," 475–90.

53. For a study of royal finances on the frontier see Amy Turner Bushnell, *The King's Coffer: Proprietors of the Spanish Florida Treasury, 1565–1702* (Gainesville: University of Florida Press, 1981).

54. For an analysis of this contractual relationship, see Eugene Lyon, *The Enterprise of Florida: Pedro Menéndez de Avilés and the Spanish Conquest of 1565–1568* (Gainesville: University of Florida Press, 1976).

55. Martin Menéndez de Avilés, Petition, n.d. (seen in *Escribanía de Cámara* on 8 Jan. 1646), Archivo General de Indias, Gobiemo: Audiencia de Santo Domingo (hereafter SD), legajo 233.

56. See Bushnell, *Situado and Sabana*, 30–31, 104–24, 207–11.

57. Charles Gibson, "Conquest, Capitulation, and Indian Treaties," *The American Historical Review* 83, no. 1 (1978): 1–8.

58. In 1646, the government of Virginia made a treaty with Necotowance, "King of the Indians," whereby his people ceded a large part of their territory to the English king, received a portion back with title derived from the Crown, and agreed to pay tribute to the English for it. See Martha W. McCartney, "Cockacoeske, Queen of Pamunkey: Diplomat and Suzeraine," in *Powhatan's Mantle: Indians in the Colonial Southeast*, eds., Peter Wood, M. Thomas Hatley, and Gregory A. Waselkov (Lincoln: University of Nebraska Press, 1989), 174–75.

59. "Report of the Adelantado, Pedro Menéndez, on the Damage and Murders Caused by the Coast Indians of Florida, Madrid, 1573, 1574," in

Colonial Records of Spanish Florida, vol. 1: *Letters and Reports of Governors and Secular Persons, 1570–1577*, in trans. and ed., Jeannette Thurber Connor (Deland, Fla.: The Florida State Historical Society, 1925), 31–81.

60. P.F.X. de Charlevoix, S.J., *History and General Description of New France* [1744], trans. by John Gilmary Shea [1870] (New York: F. P. Harper, 1900), 140–43; Mary Ross, "The French on the Savannah, 1605," *The Georgia Historical Quarterly* 8, no. 3 (September 1924): 167–94, esp. 171–73.

61. Governor Gonzalo Méndez Canzo to the Crown, 22 May 1602, SD 224/ 40; Alonso Sánchez Sáez de Mercado to the Crown, 6 Jan. 1596, SD 231/72; Mary Ross, "The Restoration of the Spanish Missions in Georgia, 1598–1606," *The Georgia Historical Quarterly* 10, no. 3 (September 1926): 171–99, especially 178, 182; Charles W. Amade, *Florida on Trial, 1593–1602* (Coral Gables, Fla.: University of Miami Press, 1959), 26–43. See also Maynard Geiger, O.F.M., *The Franciscan Conquest of Florida (1573–1618)* (Washington, D.C.: Catholic University of America, 1937).

62. For the duties of royal officials, see Bushnell, *King's Coffer*.

63. Juan Menéndez Márquez to the Crown, 21 Apr. 1603, SD 232/27.

64. Robert Allen Matter, *Pre-Seminole Florida: Spanish Soldiers, Friars, and Indian Missions, 1513–1763* (New York: Garland Publishing, 1990), 44; Ross, "Restoration of the Spanish Missions in Georgia," 173–74.

65. Gibson, "Conquest, Capitulation, and Indian Treaties," 11–13.

66. Daniel D. McGarry, "Educational Methods of the Franciscans in Spanish California," *The Americas* 6, no. 3 (1950): 355.

67. Juan Rodríguez de Cartaya, Petition, 7 May 1613, *Indiferente General* 1863.

68. Governor Juan Femández de Olivera to the Crown, 13 Oct. 1612, SD 229/74.

69. Frailes Pedro Ruíz, Pedro Bennejo, Francisco Martínez, and Esteban de San Andrés to the Crown, 16 Oct. 1612, SD 232/61.

70. Tanzi, "El derecho de guerra," 118–20.

71. Francisco de San Buenaventura Martínez Tejada, Bishop of Tricale, to the Crown, 29 Apr. 1736, SD 863/119.

72. See Amy Turner Bushnell. "Patricio de Hinachuba: Defender of the Word of God, the Crown of the King, and the Little Children of Ivitachuco," *American Indian Culture and Research Journal* 3 (July 1979): 1-21; idem, "Ruling the Republic of Indians in Seventeenth-Century Florida," in *Powhatan's Mantle: Indians in the American Southeast*, eds., Peter H.Wood, Gregory A. Waselkov, and M. Thomas Hatley (Lincoln: University of Nebraska Press, 1989), 134-50; idem, "Republic of Spaniards, Republic of Indians," in *The New History of Florida*, ed., Michael Gannon (Gainsville, University of Florida Press, 1996).

73. See Amy Turner Bushnell, "How to Fight a Pirate: Provincials, Loyalists and the Defense of Minor Ports During the Age of Buccaneers," *Gulf Coast Historical Review* 5 (Spring 1990): 18–35.

74. Friars of Apalache to Governor Diego de Rebolledo, Apalache, 10/5/1657, enclosed with *Auto* on the abuses of Governor Diego de Rebolledo, 10/9/1657, SD 235.

75. Muldoon, *The Americas in the Spanish World Order*, 8–14.

76. Francisco de Sotolongo to the Crown, 4/7/1668, SD 235.

77. Pagden, *Lords of All the World*, 108

78. Ian K. Steele, *Warpaths: Invasions of North America* (New York: Oxford University Press, 1994), 153–55.

79. Declaration of Fray Manuel Beteta from Nombre de Dios de Macaris, 8/7/1738, in *Auto* on the *doctrinas*, ordered on 9/6/1738, SD 865; *Indios* and *principales* of St. Augustine to Antonio de Arredondo, 30/9/1636, SD 861/A16; Certification of Fray Pablo Rodríguez from Palica, 16/10/1736, SD 861/25.

80. Bushnell, "Sacramental Imperative," 480–83.

81. *Cédula* to Juan Esteban de Peña, *tesorero*, and Manuel Mozo, *contador*, 31/10/1722, SD 849/9.

82. Fray Antonio de Florencia to the Crown, n.d. [1724?], SD 864/72.

83. Letter from the Governor of Carolina [James Colleton] to Governor [Diego de] Quiroga y Losada, 1/4/1688, SD 839.

84. Anthony Pagden, *Spanish Imperialism and the Political Imagination: Studies in European and Spanish-American Social and Political Theory 1513–1830* (New Haven: Yale University Press, 1990), 7–9.

Epilogue

"*CAPITALISM AND SLAVERY*":
PERSONAL REFLECTIONS ON ERIC WILLIAMS
AND RECONSTRUCTION OF EARLY AMERICAN HISTORY

Russell R. Menard

T HIRTY YEARS AGO, early American history was a clearly articulated field of study. It was Colonial history, that is, the "prehistory of the United States." As such, it had a clear geographic boundary, a recognizable cast of characters, a definite chronology, and a well defined research agenda. Joyce Appleby has noted within this paradigm, that colonialists constructed a "patriotic narrative" that emphasized American exceptionalism and divinely appointed destiny that was used to deflect criticism of the nation's shortcomings:

> With roots reaching deep into the pasts of ancient Greece and medieval England, American institutions stood forth in this account, as both climax and new beginning. As the organic metaphor suggests seeds once planted – the they town meetings or the practice of religious toleration – require only a favorable setting to come to fruition. And for the many years historical scholarship on early America drew on this image of potent plantings in a uniquely favored environment to explain how a great nation emerged from a cluster British colonies on the Atlantic shelf of North America.[1]

Trapped in this narrative structure, historians bestowed the lion's share of their attention on origins – origins of the democratic practices, of religious liberty, of free enterprise, of the distinctive traits of an American character. This paradigm began to unravel in the early 1960s, and by the end of that decade it had come apart completely. What did it in was new research responding to two distinctive imperatives. On the one hand, some colonialists were attracted to the

321

social sciences by way of early modern European social history, especially as practiced in England by the Cambridge group for the study of the population and social structure and in France by the *Annales* school. On the other hand, responding to contemporary political movements, especially the civil rights and women's movements, colonialists began to explore the multicultural reality of early America.

I have no quarrel with the multicultural movement in American history. Multiculturalism isolates a fundamental truth about the past, that is, individuals have different histories. That is not simply a way of saying that everyone is unique, but that different aspects of the past require attention to understand the lives of different people. Women have a different history than men, workers than merchants, Europeans than Native peoples. It is not just that they experience the same stories differently, but rather that they have different histories, different critical events and central texts, different heroes and villains, different periodizations and appropriate analytical units. This does not lead to the anarchy of everyone her own historian. However, certain structural facts, particularly those of class, gender, region, race, and ethnicity, do lead to important commonalities. To teach American history without regard to cultural diversity would be like teaching biology while ignoring DNA, economics without supply and demand, or statistics with only measures of central tendency and none of dispersion.

This new research, which often emphasized the experience of particular groups and the history of small communities rather than the colonial experience as a whole, led to what Jack Greene calls the "deconstruction of Early America." The explosion of monographs and articles with new information led some quarters to a sense of crisis, to a fear that the "the new scholarship has destroyed any sense of coherence for the field as a whole;" what has been called, "a severe case of intellectual indigestion," or a sense that the field was in "disarray."[2] It seemed that the new information was appearing so fast that it was outrunning the ability to contain, organize, and synthesize it; that the field was out of control, without a sense of direction and purpose, and that a new paradigm was needed to take the place of the one undermined.[3] The recent appearance of major synthetic works in the field, by such distinguished colonialists as Jack Greene, Bernard Bailyn, and David Fischer, all of which fell short in their efforts to define the state of the art in the field, reinforced my inclination to take a backdoor approach to the problem.[4] Since Greene, Bailyn, and Fischer are eminent scholars, it is worth asking why they failed to construct a new paradigm and if one is possible or even desirable.

Some of the difficulties they faced are structural and likely to plague any effort to synthesize and bring order to an academic field. Organizing and disciplining academics, particularly those who have successfully cut a niche for themselves, is particularly difficult. The more interesting difficulties are particular to the current state of early American history. As I argued earlier, two lines of force destroyed the previously reigning paradigm. These lines have quite different implications for the future of the field. Melding them together into a unified synthesis is a daunting task. These recent efforts at synthesis dealt with the problem is largely by ignoring multiculturalism and by pulling together early American history as if early modern social history were the whole story. Much of the best recent work in the field, however has been done in response to a multicultural imperative, producing as a result, works that foster the illusion that early America was a "white man's country."

Bailyn, for example admits that his synthesis does "not involve to any significant extent . . . either of the two non-Caucasian peoples, Native Americans and Africans."[5] He then goes to explain away this extraordinary admission of his book's irrelevance to a major part of our enterprise, by claiming that "despite the mass of writing, much of it polemical, that is available on most of these groups, we know as yet relatively little about them."[6] The real explanation, I would submit, is that the organizing generalizations he wishes to impose on the field simply failed to illuminate their experiences. As Greene notes in a comprehensive review of recent synthetic works, "the failure of all the frameworks considered here to give much explicit attention to the processes of racial and ethnic interaction is lamentable."[7] It is more than that, however; it is a major failure of imagination.

In March 1947, when the "old" Colonial history paradigm still thoroughly dominated the field, ten prominent colonialists met at Princeton to consider the state of the field. It must have been a depressing meeting for they concluded that the field was in terrible shape, in sharp decline and in danger of dying out altogether.[8] The explanation these wise men offered for the crisis, that colonial history had "all been written," now seems absurd, given the volume and quality of scholarship produced since then.[9] From the perspective of the old paradigm, however, it was an accurate observation. By 1947, we probably knew all anyone wanted to know about the colonial origins of this or that distinctively American trait. What Bridenbaugh failed to note is that by 1947, historians had become bored with the field as it was then constituted. Woodrow Wilson captured a similar sentiment more than a half century earlier, when he complained of going into a colonial history exam "crammed with one or two thousand minute particulars about the quarrels of nobody knows who with an obscure Governor, for nobody knows what. Just think of all that energy is wasted! The only comfort is that this mass of information won't long burden me. I shall forget it with great ease."[10] This is the problem with dominant paradigms. While they can bring clarity, order and coherence to a field, they sometimes achieve this by killing off its creativity.

Early American history is a lively, intellectually exciting field, and the last thing it needs is the kind of discipline that professors Greene, Bailyn, and Fischer wish to impose upon it, especially since they propose to achieve coherence by throwing out a major part of the enterprise. I am not persuaded we either want or need a new paradigm. It is instructive to contrast Bridenbaugh's despairing assessment with the generally upbeat optimism that pervades the essays published in *William and Mary Quarterly*'s 1993 symposium "Early American History: Its Past and Future." Fred Anderson and Andrew Cayton captured the spirit of those essays, when they announced that "there has never been a better time than the present to be an early American historian."[11]

An additional reason for my skepticism is that we already have a successful synthetic work in Eric Williams's *Capitalism and Slavery*. Williams integrates both the concerns of the early modernists and the multiculturalists into a coherent and still compelling interpretation of early American history.[12] Because Williams was determined to place slavery and the African experience at the center of American and North Atlantic history, he avoids the stifling Eurocentrism that shapes and directs the efforts of Bailyn, Greene, and Fischer.

Capitalism and Slavery, like Williams's less-known general history, *From Columbus to Castro*, weaves together the great themes of early modern social history, multiculturalism, the origins of capitalism and the social transformations it wrought, and the resistence of ordinary peoples to the oppression those transformations brought, into a comprehensive account of early American history.[13] There has been considerable debate over Williams's work, and he has been proven wrong on many particulars, however his broad vision of the field still has considerable power. His particular arguments can, with only slight adjustment, be accommodated to his critics, while remaining consistent with his overall perspective.

Capitalism and Slavery shaped the debate on several of the central themes in the history of the North Atlantic world for half a century. As Barbara Solow and Stanley Engerman have pointed out, Williams's major contribution was in advancing four controversial arguments on the relationships between slavery, racism, abolition, the American colonies, and England's industrial revolution: 1) slavery was a way of exploiting workers and racism was thus "a consequence, not the cause slavery;" 2) profits earned in the slave trade and in the colonies helped finance British industrialization; 3) the profitability of slavery, the slave trade and the Caribbean colonies declined in the aftermath of the American Revolution and their importance to England's economy waned; and 4) "abolition of the slave trade and emancipation in the British West Indies were driven not by philanthropy or humanitarianism but by economic motives within England."[14] Each of these propositions is a "Williams's thesis." What I propose to examine is how Williams stands up after a half-century of criticism.

I'll begin with his first proposition that slavery was a way of exploiting workers and racism was thus, a consequence of rather than the cause of slavery.[15] The first part of this proposition is entirely consistent with current scholarship, especially given Williams's emphasis on supply to explain why African slaves eventually came to dominate the work force of the plantation districts of European America.[16] The second part of the proposition, that racism was a consequence of slavery has fared less well, especially in the literature on Virginia.[17] In contrast to Barbados and the Carolina low country, where the commitment to slavery came early and quickly, it took planters in Maryland and Virginia the better part of a century to commit their society to slavery, Africanize their work force, and articulate their own distinctive plantation regime. "Chesapeake gradualism" has provided the setting for a long and often acrimonious debate on the origins of slavery and racism and relationship between them in Maryland and Virginia.[18] Much of the literature on this issue has been beside the point, because of its failure to recognize something Williams makes so prominent a feature of his analysis – the Atlantic context in which Chesapeake slavery developed. Slavery did not have "origins" in the Chesapeake, nor did planters there decide to enslave Africans. Slavery was thoroughly entwined with Europe's Atlantic colonies by the time the English reached Jamestown; the identification of slaves as Africans was an American commonplace. If Chesapeake planters would have slaves, they would have Africans; if the region would have more than a handful of blacks, it would have slaves. Nevertheless, this literature has established that blacks were discriminated against in the early Chesapeake before slavery was their universal condition or of much importance to the regional economy, a powerful challenge to this particular Williams's thesis. However, if we follow recent scholarship and distinguish between attitudes and ideology, it appears that racism as a systematic body of thought, constructed to justify existing social arrangements and defend the interests of the planters, appeared relatively late in the region, well after planters had thoroughly committed to slavery.[19]

The best known, and most controversial of Williams' theses, however, is the proposition that profits earned in the slave trade and in the colonies, helped finance British industrialization. More fully, Williams argued that the large profits earned by Britons engaged in all colonial enterprises but especially in the plantation colonies, provided the capital that funded British economic development. The trade in slaves, Williams maintained, was central to colonial commerce.

"It was," in the words of one British mercantilist, "the spring and parent whence the others flow;" "the first principle and foundation of all the rest," echoed another; "the mainspring of the machine which sets every wheel in motion." The slave trade kept the wheels of metropolitan industry turning; it stimulated navigation and shipbuilding and employed seamen; it raised fishing villages into flourishing cities; it gave sustenance to new industries based on the processing of raw materials; it yielded large profits, which were ploughed back into metropolitan industry; and finally, it gave rise to an unprecedented commerce in the West Indies and made the Caribbean territories among the most valuable world has ever known.[20]

Critics of the Williams thesis disagree, and seem to have the better of the argument, at least if one insists on reading Williams narrowly. The notion that slave trade profits were a cheap source of capital accumulation in Great Britain, simply fails when tested against the evidence.[21] The slave trade was not unusually profitable, at least not for European traders, and the revenues it generated were not big enough to constitute a major factor in British capital formation. Some men grew rich in the slave trade and put there profits into factories, but they were at best of minor importance in financing the Industrial Revolution. While there may be problems with the particular terms of Williams's formulation, the case is not so easily decided. Certainly it would be premature to conclude that colonies were irrelevant to the performance of England's economy, or to accept Adam Smith's inversion of the Williams's thesis and argue that the colonies were a net loss, a drain on metropolitan resources.

While the specific argument that profits from the slave trade were crucial to financing British industrialization now finds few defenders, the more general idea that colonial products and markets were important to metropolitan growth has some persuasive advocates. "Development of underdevelopment" scholars such as Immanuel Wallerstein, Andre Gunder Frank, Samir Amin, and Walter Rodney, believe that the creation of a European "world system" in the centuries after 1450 and the subsequent unequal relationships between metropolitan or core regions and peripheral areas was essential to the economic development of western Europe.[22]

Patrick O'Brien, a harsh critic of the school, provides a concise summary of the argument:

> The relative backwardness of Asia, Africa, and Latin America, and Eastern Europe . . . originated in the mercantile era when Western Europe turned the terms and conditions of international trade heavily in its favor through the deployment of military power and superior forms of state organization, the Europeans either plundered and colonized territories in Asia, Africa, and the Americas or reduced weaker economies to conditions of dependency. They actively promoted or encouraged forms of labor control . . . which maintained the cost of producing exports for

Western Europe close to the level of subsistence wages. Patterns of
trade evolved in which the products of the periphery were exchanged for the manufactured goods and high quality farm
products of the core on highly unequal terms. Over time, such
patterns of specialization pushed the economics of western Europe
towards industrialization and higher standards of living and the
economies of the periphery toward primary production, mono-
culture, and far lower levels of per capita income.[23]

The grand sweep of that generalization is compelling, as is its promise
of an integrated history of the world economy since 1500. But when
statistics are brought to bear on the basic issues, the "development of
underdevelopment" tradition seems weak indeed, at least that part of
the analysis that seeks to explain growth in the core.

The profits earned in colonial trades were not unusually high, nor
were they sufficient to generate a significant source of capital, and
such profits were rarely invested directly in industry. Colonial products, although available to consumers in wide variety at low prices,
did not engender major processing industries in the metropolis, and
did little to stimulate the economy as a whole. Throughout the seventeenth and eighteenth centuries, colonial markets for British manufactures were generally small, seldom accounting for more than 20
percent of the output of any industry, and were greatly over shadowed
by the home market. Furthermore, those industries in Britain that
were directly tied to colonial trade, shipbuilding, for example, were
relatively minor. These points gain support from those who argue that
it was largely internal processes, especially productivity gains in agriculture, that fueled British industrialization. For the development of
the core, much recent scholarship suggests, "the periphery was
peripheral."[24]

Whatever the problems with such grand generalizations, Williams
is not so easily dismissed. As Jacob Price notes, there seems to have
been "a strategic importance to the external, particularly colonial
trades, which their mere quantitative dimensions do not convey."[25]
Three areas especially merit further investigation. First, processing
colonial products and manufacturing for colonial markets provided
jobs for British workers and used British resources that would have
been otherwise underemployed with some multiplier effects to the
core economy. Second, in some industries overseas demand put

pressure on scarce resources and perhaps provided a major spur toward innovation. For example, "with domestic demand more than fully utilizing available local supplies of iron and linen and cotton yarn, the extra or marginal demand coming from the overseas colonies particularly, should have been a marked upward pressure on prices and thus significantly increased the incentives to experiment with cost-reducing technologies. In this case, colonial demand *was* particularly strategic."[26] Third, Price suggests, colonial trades may have induced certain institutional changes that fostered the greater financial sophistication important to the mobilization of substantial sums of capital. Long-distance trade, because of the risks involved, the time required to turn a profit, and various scale economies, apparently demanded merchant firms significantly bigger than those that worked the home market. Bigger firms in turn required larger suppliers, more efficient credit arrangements, bigger insurers, and more capital. The foreign sector thus "may well have been the hothouse of the British economy, where progressive institutional innovations were forced, decades or generations ahead of the times they 'normally' appeared elsewhere in the economy."[27] The plantation trades, Williams argued, "provided one of the main streams of that accumulation of wealth in England which financed the Industrial Revolution."[28] Perhaps not directly, but the general notion that the colonies played a key role in British economic growth may have more merit than recent critics have allowed.

Since the publication of Seymour Drescher's *Econocide*, few historians defend Williams's argument that the British sugar islands were in severe economic decline when England abolished first the slave trade and then slavery. *Econocide* stood this particular proposition on its head, arguing fairly persuasively, that the islands were still profitable and expanding, when the British government did them in by acting against slavery.[29] While Drescher's case is well made, one could still argue that there had been a relative decline in the importance of the sugar-slave complex to Great Britain just prior to abolition, if only because manufacturing and the home market had grown so rapidly in the decades following the American Revolution. In the seventeenth and eighteenth centuries, colonial-connected enterprises had been the fastest-growing sector of an otherwise sluggish economy and as a consequence colonial interests were well-protected in Parliament. By the early nineteenth century, however, colonial enterprises were no longer the growth sector of the British economy, and as their importance fell, their vulnerability to political attack rose.

Finally, Williams's effort to explain the abolition movement in terms of economic interests, as Williams put it, "the capitalists had first encouraged slavery and then helped to destroy it," has been sharply criticized and sometimes dismissed as "reductionist."[30] Yet this Williams thesis seems entirely consistent with his critic, David Brion Davis's main themes, "that antislavery cannot be divorced from the economic changes that were intensifying social conflicts and heightening class consciousness; [and] that in Britain it was part of a larger ideology that helped to ensure stability while accommodating society in political and social change."[31] This view of abolitionism as an ideology is one that served to justify and legitimize the emerging capitalist elite, the new forms of exploitation of free labor in England's factories and gave England's ruling classes a chance to claim moral leadership by directing a reform movement that threatened none of their vital interests. "The antislavery movement," Davis explained, "like [Adam] Smith's political economy reflected the needs and values of the emerging capitalist order. Smith provided theoretical justification for the belief that all classes and segments of society share a natural identity of interests. The antislavery movement, while absorbing the ambivalent emotions of the age, was essentially devoted to a practical demonstration of the same reassuring message."[32] While Williams might be accused of reductionism, he at least addresses what ought to be the central problem in understanding abolitionism by trying to come to terms with what role the behavior and aspirations of slaves had in the process, a concern missing entirely from the much celebrated debate on the subject.[33] In fact, Williams intimates a distinction between the *abolition* of slavery, an abstract legal matter accomplished by politicians in the metropolitan capitols of the Atlantic economy, and *emancipation*, an intensely practical matter involving the work of particular slaves in the plantation districts. Legislatures might pass laws saying that slaves were now free, but not until the slaves themselves asserted that "Massa Day Done," would that freedom become a reality.[34] The distinction between abolition and emancipation is likely to dominate future efforts to understand the fall of American slave regimes.

Williams had little interest in gender as an analytic category, and practically nothing to say about women's history; nor did he describe at any length the efforts of ordinary people to construct lives of meaning and dignity as they lived out their lives within the severe constraints imposed upon them by the development of a world-capitalist economy, a topic at the center of modern social history. He does, however, provide a framework in which such issues can be related to the great themes of American and North Atlantic history and as such, *Capitalism and Slavery* seems much more current than the more recent efforts at synthesis by Bailyn, Greene, and Fischer.

Notes

An earlier version of this paper was presented to the Minnesota Colonial History Workshop. The author would like to thank workshop participants for helpful comments and Leon and Lindy Webster for careful editing.

1. Joyce Appleby, "A Different Kind of Independence: The Postwar Restructuring of the Historical Study of the United States," *William and Mary Quarterly* 50 (1993): 245–46.

2. Jack P. Greene, "Interpretive Frameworks: The Quest for Intellectual Order in Early American History," *William and Mary Quarterly* 48 (1991): 515; Jack P. Greene and J. R. Pole, "Reconstructing British-American Colonial History: An Introduction," in *Colonial British America: Essays in the New History of the Early Modern Era*, eds., Greene and Pole (Baltimore: The Johns Hopkins University Press, 1984), 7.

3. Bernard Bailyn, *The Peopling of British North America: An Introduction,* (New York: Knopf, 1986), 6–7; David Hackett Fischer, *Albion's Seed: Four British Folkways in America* (New York: Oxford University Press, 1989), vii–xi.

4. Jack P. Greene, *Pursuits of Happiness: The Social Development of Early Modern British Colonies and the Formation of American Culture* (Chapel Hill: University of North Carolina Press, 1988); Bailyn, *Peopling of British North America*; Fischer, *Albion's Seed,* 62.

5. Bailyn, *Peopling of British North America,* 20.

6. Ibid., 20.

7. Greene, "Interpretive Frameworks," 529.

8. Carl Bridenbaugh, "The Neglected First Half of American History," *American Historical Review* 53 (1947–48): 509; Greene and Pole, "Reconstructing British-American Colonial History," 1–9.

9. Bridenbaugh, "Neglected First Half of American History," 509.

10. Wilson to J. H. Kennard, Jr., 18 Nov., 1884, quoted in Bernard Bailyn, *The Origins of American Politics* (New York: Alfred A . Knopf. 1968), vii–viii.

11. Fred Anderson and Andrew R. L. Cayton, "The Problem of Fragmentation and the Prospects for Synthesis in Early American Social History," *William and Mary Quarterly* 50 (1993): 299.

12. Eric Eustace Williams, *Capitalism and Slavery* (Chapel Hill: University of North Carolina Press, 1944).

13. Eric Eustace Williams, *From Columbus to Castro: The History of the Caribbean, 1492–1969* (New York: Harper & Row, 1970).

14. Barbara L. Solow and Stanley Engerman, "British Capitalism and Caribbean Slavery: The Legacy of Eric Williams: An Introduction," in *British Capitalism and Caribbean Slavery: The Legacy of Eric Williams*, eds., Solow and Engerman (Cambridge, Eng.: Cambridge University Press, 1987), 1.

15. This aspect of Williams's argument is assessed in William A. Green, "Race and Slavery: Considerations on the Williams Theses," in *British Capitalism and Caribbean Slavery*, eds., Solow and Engerman, 25–50.

16. There is now a large literature advancing this argument. David Galenson, *White Servitude in Colonial America* (New York: Cambridge University Press, 1981), is an especially clear statement.

17. Green, "Race and Slavery," 25–50.

18. Alden T. Vaughan, "The Origins Debate: Slavery and Racism in Seventeenth-Century Virginia," *Virginia Magazine of History and Biography* 97 (1989): 279–310, provides a thoughtful summary of this debate.

19. This is my reading of Edmund S. Morgan's magnificent *American Slavery American Freedom: The Ordeal of Colonial Virginia* (New York: W. W. Norton, 1975), although his argument is much more subtle than so brief a summary suggests.

20. Williams, *From Columbus to Castro*, 149.

21. Stanley L. Engerman, "The Slave Trade and British Capital Formation in the Eighteenth Century: A Comment on the Williams Thesis," *Business History Review* 46 (1972): 430–43.

22. Immanuel Wallerstein, *The Modern World-System: Capitalist Agriculture and the Origins of the European World Economy in the Sixteenth Century* (New York: Academic Press, 1974); Andre Gunder Frank, *World Accumulation, 1492–1789* (New York: Monthly Review Press, 1978); Samir Amin, *Accumulation on a World Scale: A Critique of the Theory of Underdevelopment* (New York: Monthly Review Press, 1974); Walter Rodney, *How Europe Underdeveloped Africa* (Washington, D.C.: Howard University Press, 1982).

23. Patrick O'Brien, "European Economic Development: The Contribution of the Periphery," *Economic History Review* 35 (1982): 2.

24. Ibid., 18.

25. Jacob M. Price, "Colonial Trade and British Economic Development, 1660–1775," *Lex et Scientia: The International Journal of Law and Science* 14

(1978): 123. (This paper was presented at the Gipson Institute symposium in 1978 and published as part of the proceedings.)

26. Ibid., 122–23.

27. Ibid., 123.

28. Williams, *Capitalism and Slavery,* 52.

29. Seymour Drescher, *Econocide: British Slavery in the Era of Abolition* (Pittsburgh: University of Pittsburgh Press, 1977).

30. David Brion Davis, "Capitalism, Abolitionism, and Hegemony," in *British Capitalism and Caribbean Slavery,* eds., Solow and Engerman, 209–28.

31. Ibid., 218.

32. David Brion Davis, *The Problem of Slavery in the Age of Revolution* (Ithaca, N.Y.: Cornell University Press, 1975), 350.

33. Thomas Bender, ed., *The Antislavery Debate: Capitalism and Abolitionism as a Problem in Historical Interpretation* (Berkeley: University of California Press, 1992).

34. The quotation is the title of a lecture by Williams at the "University of Woodford Square," see Selwyn R. Cudjoe, ed., *Eric E. Williams Speaks: Essays on Colonialism and Independence* (Amherst: University of Massachusetts Press, 1993), 237.

Contributors

WILLIAM G. SHADE, Professor of History at Lehigh University, and author of *Banks or No Banks: The Money Issue in Western Politics, 1832–1865* (Wayne State University Press, 1972) and *Democratizing the Old Dominion: Virginia and the Second Party System, 1824–1861* (University of Virginia Press, 1996).

MICHAEL V. KENNEDY, Assistant Professor of History, University of Michigan-Flint, coeditor (with Christine Daniels) of *Over the Threshold: Intimate Violence in Early America* (Routledge Press, 1999).

CAROL R. BERKIN, Professor of History at the Graduate School and University Center of the City University of New York, and author of *First Generations: Women in Colonial America* (Hill and Wang, 1996) and (with Mary Beth Norton) *Women of America: A History* (Houghton-Mifflin, 1979).

RICHARD L. BUSHMAN, Professor of History, Columbia University, and author of *From Puritan to Yankee: Character and the Social Order in Connecticut, 1690–1765* (Harvard University Press, 1967), and *The Refinement of America: Persons, Houses, Cities* (Knopf, 1992).

AMY TURNER BUSHNELL, Professor of History, College of Charleston, and author of the *King's Coffer: Proprietors of the Spanish Florida Treasury, 1565–1702* (University Presses of Florida, 1981) and *Sistuado and Sabana: Spain's Support System for the Presideo and Mission Provinces* (University of Georgia Press, 1994).

CHRISTINE DANIELS, Associate Professor of History, Michigan State University, coauthor (with T. Stephen Whitman) of *Orphan Apprenticeship: Family, Labor, and Society in the Upper South* (University Press of Virginia, forthcoming 2002) and coeditor (with Michael V. Kennedy) of *Over the Threshold: Intimate Violence in Early America* (Routledge Press, 1999).

DAVID HACKETT FISCHER, Professor of History at Brandeis University, and author of *Albion's Seed: Four British Folkways in America* (Oxford University Press, 1989) and *The Great Wave: Price Revolutions and the Rhythm of History* (Oxford University Press, 1996.)

PHILIP F. GURA, Professor of English, University of North Carolina, and author of *A Glimpse of Sion's Glory: Puritan Radicalism in Seventeenth-Century New England* (Wesleyan University Press, 1984) and *The Crossroads of American History and Literature* (Penn State University Press, 1996).

DAVID D. HALL, Professor of Religious History, Harvard University Business School, and author of *Worlds of Wonder, Days of Judgment: Popular Religious Belief in Early New England* (Knopf, 1989) and *Cultures in Print: Essays in the History of the Book* (University of Massachusetts Press, 1996).

ASHER HOROWITZ, Professor of Politics, University of York, and author of *Rousseau, Nature and History* (University of Toronto Press), and coauthor (with Gad Horowitz) of *Everywhere They Are in Chains: Political Theory from Rousseau to Marx* (Nelson Canada, 1988).

RICHARD K. MATTHEWS, Professor of Politics, Lehigh University, and author of *If Men Were Angels: James Madison and the Heartless Empire of Reason* (University of Kansas Press, 1995) and coauthor (with David E. Ingersoll) of *The Philosophic Roots of Modern Ideology: Liberalism, Communism, Fascism* (Prentice-Hall, 1991).

JUDITH A. MCGAW, Professor of History, University of Pennsylvania, and author of *Most Wonderful Machine: Mechanization and Social Change in Berkshire Paper Making, 1801–1885* (Princeton University Press, 1987) and editor of *Early American Technology: Making and Doing Things from the Colonial Era to 1850* (University of North Carolina Press, 1994).

RUSSELL R. MENARD, Professor of History at the University of Minnesota, and author of *Economy and Society in Early Colonial Maryland* (Garland Press, 1985) and coauthor (with John J. McCusker) of *The Economy of British America, 1607–1789* (University of North Carolina Press, 1991).

GERALD F. MORAN, Professor of History, University of Michigan-Dearborn, coauthor (with Maris A. Vinovskis) of *Religion, Family and the Life Course: Exploration in the Social History of Early America* (University of Michigan Press, 1992).

DANIEL K. RICHTER, Professor of History, Dickinson College, and author of *The Ordeal of the Longhouse: The Peoples of the Iroquois League in the Era of European Colonization* (University of North Carolina Press, 1992) and coauthor (with James H. Merrill) of *Beyond the Covenant Chain: The Iroquois and Their Neighbors in Indian North America* (Syracuse University Press, 1987).

MARIS A. VINOVSKIS, Professor of History, University of Michigan, and author of *An "Epidemic" of Adolescent Pregnancy?: Some Historical and Policy Considerations* (Oxford University Press, 1988) and *Education, Society, and Economic Opportunity: A Historical Perspective on Persistent Issues* (Yale University Press, 1995).